FARM ESTATE

& Business Planning

By Neil E. Harl

D0815964

Preface

This book traces its origin to a series of articles that appeared in *Agri Finance* magazine. Widespread interest in estate planning and inter-generation property transfer provided the impetus for the series. The articles have been collected and edited for conformity with the state of the law as of Spring 1996. This edition includes the relevant provisions from early 1996 legislation and all prior legislation affecting estate and business planning. Further legal change is inevitable and must be taken into account as use is made of the materials herein.

The field of estate planning embodies several complex subject matter areas. Federal estate and state inheritance taxation, trusts, wills, insurance and business organization all involve a substantial body of knowledge. This small volume attempts not at all to provide a complete reference source for each of the areas. Rather the objective is to sketch a brief overview. The reader interested in more detailed information is referred to the standard works on estate and business planning including the author's multi-volume treatise, *Agricultural Law,* and the single-volume, *Agricultural Law Manual*, and to his or her professional advisers. Obviously, this publication is not intended to serve as legal counsel.

In the belief that estate planning decisions should properly follow a rather complete understanding of the estate planning tools available, this book emphasizes the basic alternatives available to the estate planner. The estate planner plays a key role as an educator as well as a legal analyst and draftsman.

In estate planning, the objectives of the farm family should govern in the choice of alternative devices and in evaluation of a completed plan. There is sufficient flexibility in the law to assure, with a high degree of probability, that identified objectives can be accomplished within the range of available estate planning alternatives. Identification and weighting of objectives continue to be major problems in estate and business planning.

– Neil E. Harl

Contents

1. An Introduction 1
What is estate planning?
Role of objectives
Family business plans
Three levels of concern
If there is no will
"Principles" of estate and business planning
Role of advisors
Importance of being knowledgeable
Role of agents
  General Rule
  "Section 1402" rule
  Passive loss rule

2. Effects of title ownership on estate planning 13
Sole ownership
Life estates and remainders
Co-ownership
  Disposition at death
  Creating and changing co-ownership
  Ease of access after death
  Gift tax problems
  Death tax implications
  Short form probate
  Discounts in valuation
Community property

3. Federal estate tax considerations 29
The gross estate
  Property valuation
  Special use valuation for land
    What interest rate to use?
    Source of cash rents
    What is comparable land?

I

Pre-death eligibility requirements
Property passing by inheritance
Qualified use test
"Present interest" test
Rules for timber
Situation for the farm residence
Agreement to be signed
Material participation
Active management
Income tax considerations
Recapture of benefits after death
Transfer outside the family
Change of use
Death of qualified heir
Qualified use test
Absence of material participation
Bankruptcy
Foreclosure
Amount recaptured
New basis on recapture
Special use value for partnerships, corporations and trusts
Material participation for lease arrangements
Special use value lien
Making the election
Gifts within three years of death
Life insurance
Joint tenancy
Transfers with retained powers
Powers of appointment
Allowable deductions
The marital deduction
Charitable deduction
Calculating the tax
Illustrative calculation
Making full use of the unified credit
Generation skipping transfer tax

II

4. Optimal tax saving **101**
Model I
Model II
Modified Model II
The three zones

5. Liquidity considerations **117**
Pre- and post-death funding
The liquidity plan
Pre-death funding choices
  Life insurance
  "Flower Bonds"
Post-death funding possibilities
Installment payment of federal estate tax over 15 years
  Basic rules of eligibility
  Benefits from installment payment
  Is interest deductible?
  What is a "business"?
    Partnerships and corporations
    Sole proprietorships
    Trusts
    Lease arrangements
    "Passive assets"
    Size of business relative to estate
  Dispositions that make tax due
  Making the election
  The lien to secure tax payment
  In summary
Installment payment of federal estate tax over 10 years
Extensions of time for payment of federal estate tax
Stock redemption after death

6. Gifts in estate planning **143**
Pros and cons of gifts
Gift taxes
  Annual exclusion

Marital deduction
Charitable deduction
Gift tax calculation
Gift tax return
Gifts of farmland
Gifts of life insurance
  Valuing the gift
  Beware of multiple owners
Unusual gift tax situations
  Bank account
  U.S. Government savings bonds
  Land in joint tenancy
    The general rule
    The third exception
Below market interest rates on installment sales
Transfer of property subject to valuation "freezes"
Gifts to minors

7. Income tax considerations **157**
Income tax basis
  Property acquired by gift
  Property acquired by purchase
  Property acquired by inheritance
Allocating basis on purchase
Carryover basis rules – repealed in 1980
Income in respect of decedent
  Share rents
  Series E bond interest
  Installment sales
  Income tax deduction
Transferring residences
  Sale after age 65
  Sale after age 55
  Sale of residence and reinvestment
Part gift-part sale
Effect on plans for property transfer

8. The installment contract..............................**175**
　Income tax angles
　　Calculation procedure
　　Reporting interest
　　Recapture of depreciation
　　Claiming depreciation
　Handling mortgages
　　Special situation
　　Seller's liabilities
　Escrow arrangements
　Disposing of installment obligations
　Death of the seller

9. Uses of the installment contract...................**187**
　Ways to use contracts
　Flexibility in drafting contracts
　　Payment plan
　　Pre-payment privilege
　　Risk of loss
　　When title to pass
　　Default by buyer

10. The private annuity......................................**193**
　Gift tax problems
　Estate tax aspects
　Income tax treatment for the annuitant
　Income tax treatment for the obligor
　Self-cancelling installment notes

11. Trusts and estate planning...........................**201**
　Nature of a trust
　　State law
　　Federal law
　How trusts are used
　Types of trusts
　　Living trusts
　　Revocable living trusts

Irrevocable living trusts
Testamentary trusts
Short-term trusts
Life insurance trusts
Generation skipping trusts
Family estate trusts
  Assignment of income
  Death tax liability
  Gift tax liability
  How the trust is taxed
  Title problems
  Expense involved

12. Life insurance in estate planning 225
Role of life insurance
Economic dependency
Liquidity for costs and taxes
Capital for inherited shares
Retirement funds of parents
Types of life insurance
  Term insurance
  Whole life insurance
Policy ownership and beneficiary designation
Other insurance aspects of estate planning

13. Charitable giving 233
Governing objectives
Outright transfers
Transfers with retained interests
Another variation – the "lead" trust
Federal estate tax savings

14. Retirement and estate planning 241
Security of income
Domicile
Insurance coverage

15. Organizing the farm business:
   parent-child arrangements.............................**249**
   Business continuity
   Three types of arrangements
      The "spin-off" model
      The "super firm"
      Landlord-tenant relationship
   Problems common to all three
      Income sharing
      Investment opportunities
      Involvement in management
   Strategies for shifting ownership
      Maximum risk for on-farm heir
      Minimum risk for on-farm heir
   Put it in writing

16. Structuring the farm business.............................**257**
   Reasons for multiple entities
   Personal holding company problems
   S corporation as landlord
   Installment payment of federal estate tax
   "Section 303" stock redemptions
   Special use valuation of land
   Why is the farm business being restructured?
   Government program limitations
   Passive losses
   Other considerations

17. Partnerships and estate planning.............................**275**
   Partnership – what it is
      Unlimited liability
      Partnership termination
      Income tax treatment
         Income tax return
         Method of accounting

VII

Taxable year
Formation of partnership
Family members as partners
Minors as partners
Limited partnerships
Partners as employees

18. Farm corporations and estate planning 287
Nature of the corporation
Corporate management
  Shareholders
  Board of directors
  Officers
State limits on farm incorporation
Future of large-scale farming
Economic pressures for incorporating family farms
  Business planning
  Dividing up farm income

19. The farm corporation and business continuation 303
Transfer of stock
Transfers to minors
Estate settlement simplified
Loss of capital by inheritance

20. Income tax implications of farm incorporation...........309
Depreciation or cost recovery
Methods of income taxation
  Regular method
  Tax-option method
   How it works
   Distribute income each year?
   Changing stock basis
   Employee benefits
   Requirements for the election
   Terminating the election

Corporate elections
  Method of accounting
  Taxable year

21. Farm corporations – employee status of the farmer ...329
  Social security tax
  Possibly higher social security benefits
  The retirement years
  Withholding
    Employee compensation
    Dividends and interest
  Workers' compensation
  Unemployment compensation
  Employee benefits
    Group term life insurance
    Retirement plans
    Health and accident plans
    "Cafeteria" plans
    Death benefit
  The corporation's house
  Using the corporation's auto

22. Disadvantages of the corporation.................................347
  Tax-option corporations
  The surviving spouse's plight
  Minority off-farm heirs
  Effects of shareholder death
  Cost, red tape
  Debtor relief
  Governmentally related loans
  Dissolution and liquidation
    Requirements for liquidation before 1989
    Tax on "built-in" gains
    Liquidation after 1988
  Reorganizations
  Other reorganization choices

23. Where does the corporation fit?......................359
   Why incorporate?
     Case I
     Case II

24. Steps in forming a farm corporation 365
   Making the decision
   Drafting articles of incorporation
   Determining the capitalization structure
     Stock
     Debt securities
   Other components of articles of incorporation
   Preparing the inventory
   Tax-free or taxable exchange
   Which assets to incorporate
   First board of directors' meeting
     Property transfer
     Other details
   Update estate plans

25. Limited liability companies 383
   Nature of entity
   Management
   Doing business in other states
   Dissolution
   Income tax treatment

26. The estate planning process: how to go about it..........393
   Establishing objectives
   Preparing an inventory
     Description
     Ownership
     Location
     Indebtedness
     Value
   Deciding on basic alternatives

X

Whether to "freeze" asset values
Implementing the plan
Wills
Changes in insurance
Gifts
Keeping the plan up-to-date

Appendixes...403-424
Appendix A
Federal unified estate and gift tax rate schedule 403

Appendix B
Credit for state death taxes paid 405

Appendix C
Checklist for farm incorporation 407

Appendix D
Tax-free incorporation of Willess Farm, Inc. 413

Appendix E
Annual determination of basis of stock in
S corporation 414

Appendix F
Deduction for income in respect of decedent.........................415

Appendix G
General checklist for estate settlement..................................417

Appendix H
Tax treatment of leased property 424

1
An Introduction

A great many people are optimists; they believe that estate planning is only for people over age 65, and even then only for those with large estates. However, the over-65 individual may be better able to afford an unplanned estate than the 40-year-old farmer with a spouse, four minor children, a $300,000 investment and $160,000 of debt.

Younger age persons – and those with smaller estates – may actually have a greater need for estate planning. A young couple with minor children is generally least able to afford a break-up of property interests among the heirs, the complications of property ownership by minors and erosion of family capital to pay death taxes and estate settlement costs.

It's important to note that there is no such thing as "no estate plan." While it's possible, of course, not to have a will, everyone has an estate plan. If an individual does not have a personal plan, the state where he or she lives has a plan of general applicability. It's basically the same set of legal rules for everyone – whether the individual is a farmer, a factory worker or a banker.

The basic question that one should ask is: "Could I improve on the state's plan?" If so, estate planning is advisable. In most cases, the objectives of the family can be met more completely and more precisely under a plan prepared for their particular needs.

What is estate planning?

Some people equate estate planning with the making of a will. But estate planning is much more than that. Besides will making, it includes:

• An examination of how property is held or owned (sole ownership, tenancy in common, joint tenancy and, in some states, tenancy by the entirety). In the eight community property states,

1

assets are held as community property or as separate property. Wisconsin has adopted similar rules by statute.

• A review of the family insurance program (including policy partnership and beneficiary designations).

• Consideration of the advisability of gifts during life to save income or death taxes and to benefit the recipients.

• Possible disposition of property by sale during life including sale for cash, installment sale, a private annuity or a part gift-part sale transaction.

Estate planning may also involve review of the organization of the family business.

Role of objectives

The first and probably most important step in estate planning is the articulation of the objectives to be met. The chances are quite good that if one can identify his or her objectives then the law, in its enormous flexibility, can be used to accomplish those aims. Some restrictions are imposed – for example, a spouse generally cannot be disinherited – but a great amount of latitude exists in formulating a plan. And even the restrictions have exceptions. Thus, in some states (but not all) a spouse can be disinherited, as discussed in Chapter 26, if the spouses had signed an antenuptial agreement before marriage.

For most farm families, the estate and business planning objectives held by various members of the family are strikingly diverse. In fact, some of the objectives may be competitive. One of the most difficult problems in the estate and business planning process is deciding which objectives can be accomplished fully, which ones can be met only in part and which ones not at all.

Some objectives are almost universal. Most parents want to assure themselves an adequate amount of income and security whether they live to be 85 or 115. Secondly, parents generally want the children to be treated equitably including those associated actively with the family business.

2

Some children may have been given additional help in obtaining an education or getting started in business and the parents may wish to take this into account. Therefore, an equitable sharing by the children may not necessarily be an equal sharing. Finally, nearly everyone desires to minimize death taxes and estate settlement costs.

Efforts to minimize death taxes and estate settlement costs depend somewhat upon whether the parents desire to – (1) minimize taxes and costs for *both* their deaths and pass the maximum amount of wealth on to the children or favored charities; or (2) minimize costs and taxes at the death of the *first* of the parents to die, leave the surviving parent with maximum wealth and control over the property and worry less about the plight of the children. This is an important decision and may influence property ownership patterns within the family as well as plans for disposition of the property at the death of the first of the spouses to die.

The parents, individually, may harbor concerns about property disposition. The father, for example, may be worried about rights of a successor spouse if he should die and his surviving spouse should remarry. And he rarely thinks in terms of a nice, clean-cut, upstanding successor who might make life livable once again for the survivor. He may be thinking of a villainous second spouse and he can scarcely abide the thought of establishing a plan that might benefit such a successor. The mother, on the other hand, may be concerned about the burden of property management if he dies first. She may be secretly wishing for management assistance.

The mother – and wives generally – seem to be increasingly concerned about their role in the operation. It may come down to two key issues – (1) the place of the wife in the organizational structure of the operation – partner in a partnership or officer, director or shareholder in a corporation, for example – and her entitlement to part of the income, and (2) the opportunity to build up a property interest in her own name or at least in tenancy in common with the husband. These concerns may stem from the wife's contributions to the farm business or from operation of the household as an activity warranting recognition in terms of sharing in income and accrued wealth. Plans to memorialize the wife's contribution to the farm business (or to the household) thus may involve creating a property ownership pattern for the land or organizational structure for the farm business that entitles the wife to a portion of the annual income directly and then giving careful attention to ownership of the accrued family wealth to build an estate for the wife.

For example, ownership of the farmland in tenancy in common with equal ownership interests would assure the wife half of a landlord's normal share of the income even if she's not heavily involved in the operation. But in some states, income from joint tenancy property is credited to whomever provided the funds for its acquisition – often the husband. Of course, if the wife is a partner in a legal partnership or an employee-shareholder of a family corporation, her right to some income is assured in a more formal manner. It's now possible to make gifts between spouses with no concern about federal gift tax. The unlimited federal gift tax marital deduction eases the task of balancing estates between husband and wife. In fewer than one-fourth of the states, state gift tax provisions should be taken into account in making transfers between spouses by gift.

Such individually held objectives are rarely discussed. Yet they may block effective estate planning unless the underlying concerns are resolved satisfactorily.

For those families that do not plan for continuation of the farm business beyond the retirement or death of the parent or parents, and that is the case for many farm businesses, these are usually the key objectives.

Family business plans

If a decision has been made for the family business to continue into the next generation, there may be additional objectives. The

4

parents may wish to recognize, accurately and promptly, the labor and capital contributions of the children who are actively associated with the firm.

If a son's payments on a livestock confinement facility built on the parents' farm go unrecognized, the resulting uncertainty of ownership may create problems within the family. The son who devotes his most productive years to the family business on the assurance that "you'll be taken care of when we die" faces substantial uncertainty as to his rights on death of the parents.

These problems can be avoided if careful attention is given to recognizing the labor, management and capital contributions of each individual to the family business.

It may also be desired for the family business to have sufficient stability at the death of the parent to withstand being broken up or its continuation placed in jeopardy. If heirs outside the firm receive a part of the family wealth at death, withdrawal of that capital may affect the family business adversely unless the transfer has been carefully planned.

The loss of equity capital at death in a farm business is particularly noticeable because of the relatively high rate of out-migration of farm- reared people. In the usual situation of four children in a family, with one desiring to farm, rights to 75 percent of the family wealth remaining after payment of death taxes and estate settlement costs may flow off the farm and outside agriculture at the deaths of the parents.

The objectives of the on-farm heirs and the off-farm heirs can become considerably more important if it's planned for the farm business to continue beyond the parents' lives. This planning problem is discussed in Chapter 15.

Three levels of concern

There are basically three levels of concern in family estate planning. Each level creates problems to be solved in the estate planning process.

The first level involves decisions as to disposition of property if one parent should die survived by the other parent and the children.

The second level requires solutions to the problem of the decease of both parents leaving children surviving. If the surviving children are minors, two additional problems are created: (1) what to do with the minors' property since minors are generally not competent under state law to manage their own property, and (2) what to do with the minors themselves in terms of custody. Solution to the first might involve a testamentary trust in the parents' wills to hold the property until the children each reach a designated age if both parents die. The second might involve nomination of a guardian for the children.

The third level of concern involves the passage of property if the entire immediate family should die – parents and children. Without planning at this stage, the order of death would determine who receives the property. Thus, if a family were to be involved in an automobile accident with the husband dying first, the children dying next and the wife dying last, in most states the property involved passes to her parents, if living, and if not, to other heirs on her side of the family. That's because, at the husband's death, his property generally passes in part to his wife and partly to the children. Later, at the deaths of the children, their property passes to their surviving parent, their mother. At her death, the total amount of property would pass to the wife's side of the family.

On the other hand, if the wife were to die first, the children next and the husband last, the property would pass to the husband's side of the family. The wife's property at her death, passes to her surviving husband and to the children. At the children's deaths, their property passes to their father, as the surviving parent. At his death, the property typically passes to his parents, if living, and if not to heirs on his side of the family. Survivorship by even a few minutes can favor one group of heirs over another.

If there is no will

Upon death intestate (without a will), state law takes over in disposing of the decedent's property. This is the generalized, uniformly applicable estate plan for those who do not choose to develop their own.

Joint tenancy property passes to the surviving joint tenant. And life insurance proceeds pass to the designated beneficiaries. Beyond that, the rules of inheritance specify who's in line to inherit. If no spouse or children survive, the decedent's property typically passes to the surviving parents, to their other descendants and to their ascendants and their heirs, in that order. If a spouse but no children survive, usually part of the estate (all in a few states) passes to the spouse and the rest to the decedent's side of the family. If a spouse and children survive, the spouse is generally entitled to a portion of the estate (as little as one-third) and the children share the rest.

A number of states stipulate that all of the property up to some specified level – typically $25,000 to $100,000 – passes to the surviving spouse even if children survive. In a few states, all property passes to the surviving spouse if the children are all descendants of the surviving spouse and the decedent. The theory seems to be to leave all of the property in estates of modest size to the surviving spouse under the assumption that he or she will care for the children and can do so more flexibly with outright ownership of the property. The rules of inheritance are detailed and highly specific for each state.

If one is not completely satisfied with the state's estate plan, an effort should be made to develop a plan that would accomplish the person's objectives.

"Principles" of estate and business planning

From years of watching farm and ranch families come to grips with estate and business planning decisions, it has been possible to identify several basic warnings in the nature of "principles" –

• Never give property away during life unless there is a willingness to lose the property. Unanticipated events such a dissolution of a child's marriage, death or actions of creditors can result in loss of the property.

• In general, structure the family business such that off-farm heirs can become owners or co-owners of the land but without becoming involved in ownership or management of the operating entity. If off-farm heirs become involved in ownership of the operating or production entity, collisions in expectations may occur as between on-farm heirs and off-farm heirs. That is less likely to occur if the off-farm heirs are limited to ownership interests in the land or land-owning entity.

• An increasing concern is how to assure the income desired by parents in retirement from the cash flow of the operation and still leave sufficient income for the others involved in the business and for modernization and expansion of the operation. Harmonization of objectives is highly important in successful two or three generation operations.

• Always test organizational options or choices against a worst case scenario as well as a best case or favorable scenario. Estate and business planning are typically done in relatively good times. But an important test for their success is how the plans fare in less favorable times.

• In general, estate planning and business planning should be carried on simultaneously or at least in the same general time frame in order to assure adequate integration of the two tasks. Moving ahead on one of the tasks – such as estate planning – without considering the implications for business planning may narrow options down the road when business planning is taken up. And the opposite is true as well.

• A major concern is how to assure a perception of fairness among the children and other interested heirs. While actual unfairness by parent is believed to be relatively rare, perceptions of unfairness are relatively common and often arise because of lack of communication by parents as to why certain decisions were made. Parents should be urged to initiate family discussions about estate and business planning decisions to the extent the parents feel comfortable with such discussions.

Role of advisors

What is the role of advisors in the estate planning process?

Although the primary responsibility for estate planning rests with the family's attorney, others including the lender, the insurance representative and the accountant may play an important part in the development and ultimate implementation of the plan.

Advisors in close contact with the individual may provide the spark that initiates the planning process. For example, with property transfer related to the acquisition of credit, and with the lender in possession of important facts regarding the financial position of the individual, the lender may be able to spot an estate planning problem at an early stage and encourage the individual to seek estate planning advice. Likewise, the attorney or accountant is often in a position to make initial estate planning suggestions.

Close teamwork between or among advisors is important. For example the banker may work closely with the family and the attorney as trustee, if a trust is to be used, or as the executor, if a corporate executor is desired.

Coordination of the insurance plan with the overall estate plan involves the insurance representative and the attorney.

The attorney is a key individual on the estate planning team and can draw together ideas from the accountant, lender, insurance representative, university extension representative and others into a well-integrated, well-orchestrated plan. The attorney carries the estate planning process through the implementation stage as wills, trusts and other documents are drafted and property transfers are made.

Advisors, in their frequent contacts with the individual, may be in a position to suggest that the plan be reviewed from time to time by the attorney. Such a reminder may be particularly important if the family's wealth position changes, the marital status of members changes, or deaths occur. Of course, changes in the law may necessitate modifications in the estate plan, also.

Importance of being knowledgeable

One should never sign a document – and that includes a will – until one is clear on what the document will do for – or to – the individual. That means a level of awareness of major features at the "black box" level. It's not necessary to acquire a detailed, technical understanding of what's being done. That's for the attorney to master.

But if a general understanding of the will and the rest of the estate plan resulting from weeks of planning effort is lacking, two major problems can arise – (1) the individual won't know when the plan needs changing, and (2) the individual may be unable to deal with suggestions from others as to what an estate plan should contain. The latter can lead to a crisis of confidence in the plan; the former can lead to continued reliance on an out-of-date plan.

Role of agents

Throughout estate and business planning, there are various tests that have to be met in order to be eligible for the tax provisions made available to those owning interests in farms or other small businesses. Some of the rules specify a required level of involvement in management under a variety of tests (material participation, active participation, meaningful participation). Other tests relate to required ownership of business assets, typically in relation to the overall size of the estate. Those provisions are discussed in later chapters of this book.

A highly important question is whether the tests can be met only by the decedent or whether the tests can be met by an agent or employee of the decedent. For example, can a farm manager meet the tests? Can a family member serving without pay meet the tests?

Actually, there are three different rules governing the relationship of agents or employees to the property owner. The question is whether the activities of the agent or employer are imputed to the property owner.

GENERAL RULE. Under the general rule, the activities of an agent are imputed to the property owner. The tests can be met by an agent or employee as well as by the property owner.

The general rule applies unless a statute or regulation specifies otherwise. In particular, the general rule applies to 15-year installment payment of federal estate tax, determining whether income received after death is "income in respect of decedent," the passive loss rule for S corporations and the rules imposing the personal holding company tax on C corporations.

"SECTION 1402" RULE. The second rule governs whenever the question of involvement is routed through section 1402 of the Internal Revenue Code. That code section was amended in 1974 to make it clear that activities of an agent or employee were irrelevant for all purposes governed by that code section. The section was amended because farm managers were losing retired clients who had too much earned income. The high level of activity of the farm manager was being imputed to retired landowners such that the "rents" were considered earned income.

This provision, however, only applies for purposes of liability for self-employment tax and eligibility for special use valuation of land.

PASSIVE LOSS RULE. The third rule, and the harshest of the three, resulted from the provisions enacted in 1986 involving limitations on using passive losses to offset active income. Under those regulations, the presence of a *paid* manager or agent destroys the property owner's own record of involvement.

The three rules are portrayed in Appendix H in a setting of various types of leases and the various tax provisions of possible interest in farm estate and business planning.

2
Effects of title ownership on estate planning

Individuals seldom focus their attention on estate planning until substantial amounts of property have already been acquired. Nonetheless, the method by which titles are held – to land, livestock, machinery and other property – can have important estate planning implications. And, making changes in titles late in life to accomplish estate planning objectives may create problems of a different sort, such as gift taxes (although gift tax liability is not likely to be encountered in conjunction with transfers between spouses). That's why it's suggested that young couples develop specific plans for property ownership before it's acquired, taking into account their estate planning objectives.

Generally, five major factors influence choice of ownership form:

1. Preferences as to sole ownership or co-ownership,
2. The desired disposition of property at death,
3. Estate and inheritance tax effects,
4. Gift tax implications, and
5. Differences in estate settlement costs.

Since the choice may be heavily influenced by size of estate and the family situation, the following ideas are general in nature; specifics should always be checked against applicable state law.

Sole ownership

Ownership of property in one name is normally the simplest during life and gives the holder the most complete ownership possible. Transfers require a minimum of red tape since the title holder has the right to dispose of the property (except that a spouse may have to consent to the transfer of real property to give up

13

any rights to the property at death).

At death, property solely owned passes under a will or according to state law if there is no will. Federal estate and state inheritance taxes generally reach the total value of the property when held in sole ownership, although property ownership must exceed some threshold in order for tax to be due.

Outright ownership of property is referred to as a *fee simple.* That's the nearest thing to absolute ownership. It's generally not possible to own assets absolutely – the state can restrict property use through the police power, as with zoning and pollution controls. And the government can take property for a public use, under the power of eminent domain, so long as just compensation is paid; also, taxes can be levied on property. Given these limitations on private ownership, the most complete ownership possible is known as the fee simple.

As noted in a later section, in the eight community property states and Wisconsin, property acquired during marriage is considered owned equally by the spouses. In general, the community property feature prevails over the way title to the property is actually held. Thus, even if a deed places title to land in sole ownership in the husband's name, the property may still be considered equally owned as community property.

Life estates and remainders

For added flexibility in estate planning, ownership of assets may be carved up into limited interests. Thus, a farm could be left by a husband in his will to his wife for her life with the property passing to children at her death. During her life, the wife is a *life tenant,* holding a *life estate.* At the same time, the children have a *remainder* interest in the property and are commonly known as remaindermen or remainder persons. Theirs is a future interest – so long as their mother lives and retains the life estate, the children have little more than a hope, an expectancy, that some day the property will be theirs.

The wife, as the life tenant, has certain rights and responsibilities. She generally has the right to possession of the property which includes the right to receive the income from the property. And she has responsibilities – to pay interest on any mortgage, pay property taxes, and keep the property in a reasonable state of maintenance; not let pigeons fly through broken window panes or the pipes freeze up on a cold winter morning.

Acting alone, the life tenant generally cannot sell or mortgage the property. But with specific approval of the remainder persons – assuming they're all adults and are mentally competent – the property could be sold or mortgaged.

Life estates and remainders are often held in a trust with management of the property, distribution of income and other tasks performed by the trustee. A life estate not held in trust is referred to as a *legal life estate*. Such life estates are generally created by deed or in a will.

Legal life estates in farm personal property – machinery, livestock and equipment – can create troublesome problems of a practical nature because of the limited life of the assets involved. It isn't completely clear, for example, what is involved with a life estate in a sow – and her pigs. Thus, if assets other than land are to be held in a life estate, a trust can ease the management problems.

Even with land, problems may arise with a legal life estate. In some states, farm leases between a life tenant (as landlord) and a farm tenant terminate at the death of the life tenant. The "doctrine of emblements" may give the farm tenant the right to harvest crops already planted but the lease is otherwise terminated. To avoid this problem, leases with life tenants should also be signed by the holders of the remainder interest unless state law (as in Iowa) provides clearly that the lease continues until the appointed time for termination of the lease despite death of the life tenant. Leases entered into with trustees of trusts usually do not encounter this problem. The trustee typically has the power to enter into a lease that is binding on the holders of the remainder interest as well as on the life tenant.

15

Problems may also arise with legal life estates over the question of how far the life tenant can go in demolishing or remodeling buildings, removing trees or minerals or taking steps to change the basic use of the property where an expenditure of funds would be needed to return the land to its previous condition. For these reasons and more – including ease of sale or mortgage of the property – a trust with carefully drafted powers for the trustee can provide a more flexible management structure. More on trusts in Chapter 11.

The life estate/remainder combination is often a part of efforts to reduce the federal estate tax burden. At the death of a surviving spouse as a life tenant, who never held more than a life estate interest in the property, no part of the value of the property is subject to the federal estate tax. However, as noted in Chapter 3, for a *retained* life estate – meaning that the holder of the life estate had previously owned perhaps a fee simple interest in the property – the full value of the property is included in the estate for federal estate tax purposes.

Thus, there is an enormous tax difference between a *granted* life estate (which is generally not subject to federal estate tax in the estate of the life tenant) and a *retained* life estate (which usually makes the entire value of the property taxable in the estate of the life tenant – who previously owned a greater interest but transferred away all but a life estate).

The granted life estate feature is used in "generation skipping" plans. A grandparent might leave a farm to a child for life with remainder interest to a grandchild. Even though the child would be entitled to its income, the property would not be taxed in the child's estate. Rather, the property would be taxed in the estate of the grandfather and not again until the death of the grandchild – for federal estate tax purposes.

Provisions in the Tax Reform Act of 1976 restricted this brand of tax treatment to transfers skipping children and placed a limit of $250,000 on the amount of property that could pass without a tax at the death of the "skipped" child. Above that level, and for all transfers skipping other than children, federal estate tax was imposed at the death of the "skipped" individual approximately equal to the tax that would have been due had the "skipped" person died owning the property outright. The Tax Reform Act of 1986 repealed the 1976 provision and instead subjects generation-skipping transfers to a flat rate federal tax at death equal to the maximum federal estate and gift tax rate (now 55 percent). However, an exemption of $1 million per transferor is provided and, until 1990, an exclusion of $2 million applied per grandchild of the transferor. The generation skipping transfer tax is discussed in greater detail in Chapter 3.

It should be noted that a granted life estate may be subject to state inheritance tax even though not subject to federal estate tax. If so, the value of the life estate for inheritance tax purposes depends upon the life expectancy of the life tenant.

Co-ownership

Joint tenancy and tenancy in common are the most widely used forms of co-ownership. Both involve undivided ownership of a specific item of property by two or more persons. In some states, tenancy by the entirety can be created between husband and wife with many of the features of joint tenancy. Unlike joint tenancies, tenancies by the entirety are generally not severable by action of one of the co-owners.

In the past, joint tenancy appears to have been a popular form of co-ownership, particularly for land. A 1964 study revealed that 84 percent of the real property acquired in co-ownership in five Iowa counties in that year was in joint tenancy. In one county, over 80 percent of all deeds were to joint tenants. Joint tenancy continues to be widely used but less so than in years past.

The vast popularity of joint tenancy may have been due to the belief that joint tenancy substitutes for a will, saves death taxes and reduces estate settlement costs. Whether all of these goals are accomplished is doubtful. It depends on the situation. In general, as estates grow larger, joint tenancy becomes less and less advisable because of the death tax "traps" of joint tenancy. These are discussed later in this chapter and in Chapter 3.

DISPOSITION AT DEATH. The major difference between joint tenancy and tenancy in common is in the disposition of the interest of a deceased co-owner. At the death of a tenant in common, that individual's undivided interest passes to that individual's heirs under state law or under the person's will.

Joint tenancy is characterized by a right of survivorship. When one joint tenant dies, the survivor immediately becomes the full owner. For joint tenancy property, a will does not operate to transfer the property at death of the first joint tenant.

The "right of survivorship" is characteristic only of joint tenancies and tenancies by the entirety and does not extend to tenancies in common. Therefore, joint tenancy, in effect, has a built-in will to transfer the property to the survivor.

Of course, at later death of the surviving joint tenant, a will may be needed to dispose of the property. Moreover, it would be rare for an individual to have all of his or her property in joint tenancy. It is often difficult to prove that livestock, stored grain and machinery, for example, were owned jointly. So, joint tenancy is rarely a complete substitute for a will.

Joint tenancy ownership of breeding stock can be particularly perplexing. If a herd of cows – and the bull – are held in joint tenancy, are the calves in joint tenancy also? The answer can be important to the surviving joint tenant. In one New York case, that question was raised after the husband's death. If the calves were in joint tenancy, the wife as the surviving joint tenant got them all. If not, the wife – as the surviving spouse – received only one-third since the husband died without a will. The New York court said in that case the calves were in joint tenancy. State law is an important factor in whether offspring from breeding stock in joint tenancy or crops on joint tenancy land would also be in joint tenancy.

The survivorship rule of joint tenancy may operate satisfacto-

18

rily for husband and wife as joint tenants. But the same rule applied to a father and son or unrelated persons as joint tenants may produce unexpected results.

In one case, a father and son had farmed together for 15 years with all of the farmland in joint tenancy under the assumption that upon death of the father, the son would become sole owner. But the unexpected happened: the son was killed in an automobile accident leaving a wife and five children. The son's family was almost totally "disinherited" because the joint tenancy property passed to the father as survivor.

Those considering joint tenancy should examine carefully all possible combinations of death and assure themselves that joint tenancy would be a satisfactory device regardless of who died first.

CREATING AND CHANGING CO-OWNERSHIP. State law controls how patterns of property ownership may be created or changed. For land, it's done by deed and it's a matter of how the names appear on the deed.

For tenancies in common, a transfer to "A and B" generally creates tenancy in common ownership. Because of presumptions against joint tenancies, some states require that language used to create one be highly specific. Typical wording on a deed to create joint tenancy would be "to (A party) and (B party) as joint tenants with right of survivorship and not as tenants in common." Doubtful cases may be treated as tenancies in common. This depends, of course, on state law.

Joint tenancy is a fragile device for property ownership. In many states, a sale, a contract to sell, or a transfer of one joint tenant's interest destroys the joint tenancy characteristic. And the owners then hold the property in tenancy in common.

If a co-owner becomes dissatisfied and is unable to arrange a mutually agreeable solution as a joint tenant or tenant in common to sever interests in the property, a court order may be sought to force a division or sale of the property. With such "partition and sale" actions, a co-owner is assured of receiving his or her share of the property or the proceeds from its sale. Co-owners are not locked into the relationship.

EASE OF ACCESS AFTER DEATH. One feature of joint tenancy that may be especially helpful for an automobile and a bank account is ease of access to the property after death of the first joint tenant to die. In most states (but not all), the surviving joint tenant can continue writing checks on a jointly owned bank account and can obtain control of motor vehicles in joint tenancy with a minimum of red tape, expense and delay.

An argument against joint tenancy ownership of an automobile involves liability for damages. Both joint tenants as owners of the vehicle can be held liable for damages from its negligent operation.

GIFT TAX PROBLEMS. When a joint tenancy or tenancy in common is created, a gift may result unless each owner contributes to the acquisition. There are exceptions, but in general the federal gift tax (and state gift taxes where applicable) would be imposed except for the allowable exclusions and deductions. See Chapter 6 for information on this.

DEATH TAX IMPLICATIONS. As noted in Chapter 3, joint tenancy and tenancy in common property are treated differently for death tax purposes at death of one of the co-owners. For tenancy in common ownership, only the portion owned by the deceased tenant in common is taxed in the estate. Typically, if husband and wife own property in tenancy in common, one-half of the value would be included in the estate of the first to die for death tax purposes. And that portion of the property's value would receive a new income tax basis at death.

Upon the death of a joint tenant, the rule under federal estate tax law (and state inheritance tax statutes in some states) has been that the full amount of the joint tenancy property is subjected to death tax (and possibly to estate settlement costs) except to the extent that the surviving joint tenant can prove that he or she provided part or all of the money when the property was acquired or the mortgage paid off. That was often difficult for a widow to do

20

unless evidence of outside income, inheritances or gifts had been preserved. It was a heavy burden for the wife, if she survived, to argue that part of the sole proprietorship income (and property) should be credited to her efforts. Of course, if she had been a partner in a partnership or an employee-shareholder of a family corporation, her chances would have been better. This is the "consideration furnished" rule.

It's generally not been enough to prove that the down payment and mortgage payment came from a joint account. The important question was who put money into the account. Generally, earnings of a family business operated as a sole proprietorship are assumed to belong to the husband, not the wife.

Therefore, with joint tenancy, the death taxes and estate settlement costs have often been higher upon the death of the first to die compared to a tenancy in common. The odds have favored taxation of the entire value of the property in joint tenancy at the husband's death and taxation again later at the death of the wife if that happened to be the order of death.

The Tax Reform Act of 1976 undertook to solve the joint tenancy problem for federal estate tax purposes. And it did – in part. But it was not a complete solution and it was not automatically implemented. Under the rules, property owned by husbands and wives in joint tenancy or tenancy by the entirety was considered half owned by each for federal estate tax purposes at the death of the first to die. This was the "fractional share" rule. But that rule *only applied to joint tenancies created after December 31, 1976.* It didn't reach those in existence prior to 1977 – unless they were brought under the new rule after 1976.

Moreover, the new "fractional share" treatment applied only if the transaction creating the joint tenancy or tenancy by the entirety was subject to federal gift tax. Many transactions involving creation of joint tenancies were subject to gift tax – if the contributions were unequal. But three weren't, as discussed in Chapter 6 – (1) joint tenancy bank accounts, (2) U.S. Government savings bonds in joint tenancy, and (3) real property or land acquired by a husband and wife in joint tenancy (or tenancy by the entirety) since December 31, 1954. The last exception – for land – was of major concern in agriculture.

It was possible to treat a joint tenancy land acquisition as a gift, on a gift tax return timely filed. Few had done so.

A 1978 federal amendment permitted joint tenancies created before 1977 to be treated as gifts (through 1979) on a timely filed federal gift tax return in order to bring the property under the "fractional share" rule. Such a move would have made it necessary to come to grips with any gift tax liability, of course.

A third rule for taxing joint tenancy property for federal estate tax purposes was added in 1978, also. It was the "credit for services" rule designed to credit the surviving spouse with part of the value of the property based on the number of years' service to the business. Effective for deaths after 1978 (and before 1982), the services of a spouse could be taken into account if the spouse *materially participated* in the management and operation of the business. It was a matter of election by the estate whether to take advantage of the new rule. The "credit for services" rule was repealed at the end of 1981.

Dissatisfaction with all three rules for joint tenancy taxation resulted, in 1981, in a major change in the federal estate taxation of property owned in joint tenancy or tenancy by the entirety. Commencing with deaths in 1982, one-half the value of property owned by husbands and wives in joint tenancy is taxed at the death of the first joint tenant (or tenant by the entirety). This is the "fractional share" rule. In general, one-half the value of joint tenancy (or tenancy by the entirety) property is taxed at the death of the first to die and one-half receives a new income tax basis at that time. The new income tax basis wipes out any potential gain (or loss) on that part of the property.

EXAMPLE: Husband and wife own a 160-acre farm acquired in 1960 with the husband's earnings before marriage. At his death in 1996, survived by his wife, one-half would be taxed in his estate for federal estate tax purposes.

A recent court case permitted the estate of a deceased farmer to apply the "consideration furnished" rule to land acquired before 1977 even though the death occurred after 1981. The full value of the property was included in the deceased's estate and the full value received a new income tax basis because the deceased had provided all of the funds when the land was acquired in 1955. Why did the estate argue for the right to use the consideration furnished rule? The entire amount of gain on the farm was eliminated as a result, which was important because the land was sold at a relatively high price soon after death.

Keep in mind that the 100 percent federal estate tax marital deduction covers the amount of any estate tax liability for deaths after 1981.

The 1981 rule is arbitrary and does not depend upon proof of who contributed toward purchase of the property. That is a major plus where proof of contribution would be difficult. Income tax considerations may also be an important factor. In that case, the consideration furnished rule may be helpful in husband-wife joint tenancies, particularly where the federal estate tax marital deduction is available to reduce the federal estate tax at the death of the first of the joint tenants to die. Congress may, however, act to deny use of the consideration furnished rule for husband-wife joint tenancies where the death occurs after 1981.

EXAMPLE: Husband and wife own a 320-acre farm acquired in 1960 with the husband's earnings before marriage. At his death in 1996, survived by his wife, under the fractional share rule one-half would be taxed in his estate for federal estate tax purposes and one-half would receive a new income tax basis. If instead the wife died in 1996 survived by her husband, one-half the value of the farm would be included in her estate for federal estate tax purposes and would receive a new income tax basis.

On the other hand, if the consideration furnished rule were applied, the entire value would be included in the husband's estate (if he died first) and the entire property would receive a new basis. In the event the wife were to die first, no part of the property would be included in her estate under the consideration furnished rule and no part of the property would receive a new income tax basis at the wife's death.

For joint tenants who are not husbands and wives, the "consideration furnished" rule continues to apply. The consideration furnished rule also applies to joint tenancies involving one or more co-owners who are not husbands and wives married to each other.

EXAMPLE: A quarter section of farmland is owned by mother, father and daughter in joint tenancy. At the death of any of the three co-owners, federal estate tax liability would be determined under the consideration furnished rule.

To sum up: even with the various rules for taxing joint tenancy property at death for federal estate tax purposes, property owned in joint tenancy may encounter tax traps in estates large enough to be subject to federal estate tax. Joint tenancy property is often taxed in the estate of the first joint tenant to die to the extent of 50 to 100 percent of its value. Because joint tenancy ownership leaves the property to the survivor *outright,* it may mean a heavy tax bite at the survivor's death. That's because joint tenancy ownership of property precludes use of any of the techniques to save death taxes at death of the surviving joint tenant – usually the surviving spouse. Tax saving efforts often involve a life estate created at the death of the first spouse to die. A major feature of joint tenancy is the way it leaves the property with the survivor *outright.* Finally, there may be a tax trap in joint tenancy ownership because of possible gift tax liability when the property is moved from ownership in joint tenancy to some other ownership pattern – such as tenancy in common. The potential gift tax problems of changing joint tenancy ownership patterns are discussed in Chapter 6.

Chapter 3 discusses how large an estate must be before death taxes are imposed.

Important point: joint tenancy must go if much headway is to be made in saving death taxes in the estates of both husband and wife for those with fairly large estates. That's a fairly typical conclusion for estates of $600,000 or more and for some smaller in size but growing.

For those with estates of $600,000 or less, and not expected to grow much larger, joint tenancy or tenancy by the entirety may be an acceptable pattern of co-ownership. For husband-wife joint tenancies, it leaves the property to the survivor outright and keeps property ownership out of the hands of minor children. And in all but about a half dozen states, joint tenancy permits ease of estate settlement at the death of the first joint tenant to die as discussed in the next section.

The $600,000 figure represents the threshold of federal estate tax liability for most couples as discussed in Chapter 3. A lower threshold for state death tax purposes could encourage a shift away from joint tenancy at lower levels of property ownership.

Legislation pending in Congress would raise the $600,000 figure to $750,000 over a period of a few years.

SHORT FORM PROBATE. Upon death of the first joint tenant, it may be possible in some states for the estate settlement process to be somewhat simplified, particularly in estates not subject to death taxes. It is necessary, of course, in all estates to satisfy state and federal death tax claims, if any. Once that is accomplished, a complete probate of the estate may not be required if the property of the decedent was all in joint tenancy with someone who survives.

An estate is probated for one or more of the following reasons: (1) to settle all disagreements over who is entitled to receive property; (2) to obtain good title to the property; and (3) to pay the necessary taxes.

The survivorship right precludes disagreements over who is entitled to the property held in joint tenancy. The property goes to the surviving joint tenant or tenants. That takes care of the first reason for probate.

In most states – all but about a half dozen – it is possible for a surviving joint tenant to obtain clear title to property without a complete probate process. Death of a joint tenant in those states

25

cuts off the claims of the deceased's creditors who do not have a commitment from the surviving joint tenant to shoulder the obligation.

The third reason for probating an estate – payment of taxes – cannot be avoided. If valuation of the property and payment of taxes (or obtaining tax clearances) is all that is necessary, "short-form" probate may be possible. Joint tenancy ownership of property permits such short-form probate in many states. Because of the death tax treatment of joint tenancy property, only estates of $600,000 or less may find joint tenancy generally useful, however. Moreover, it may be that not all of a person's property is owned in joint tenancy. Probate may be necessary to establish rights to property not held jointly.

In most states, by contrast, clear title cannot be obtained to property owned by a deceased tenant in common or sole owner without formal probate before a specified number of years (five in some states) has elapsed.

Discounts in valuation. Over the past dozen years, several court cases have allowed discounts in valuation of land owned in co-ownership. Discounts of 15 to 20 percent have been permitted for federal gift tax and federal estate tax purposes. The Internal Revenue Service has continued to maintain that the discount should be limited to the cost of partitioning the property under state law.

Community property

In eight states – Arizona, California, Idaho, Louisiana, Nevada, New Mexico, Texas and Washington – *community property* is an important co-ownership concept. By virtue of recent legislation, Wisconsin follows similar rules. Although the details vary from state to state, as a general rule all property acquired during marriage – except that acquired by gift or inheritance – becomes community property and is owned essentially half by each.

As a general rule, property acquired while domiciled in a *com-

mon law state – a state other than the community property states – retains its character and does not necessarily become community property even if a move occurs to a community property state. Likewise, community property, once acquired, retains that status even if a shift occurs to a common law state.

Although the rules differ among the community property states, the way title to community property is actually held generally does not affect its status as community property. Property actually held in separate ownership or in joint tenancy or tenancy in common is usually subject to the community property rules if acquired during marriage while residing permanently in a community property state.

In most of the community property states, it is possible to vary the community property rules by use of an *antenuptial* agreement. These agreements entered into before marriage specify the rights of the prospective spouses in their property.

If all of a couple's assets were acquired during marriage and the community property rules are applicable, the estates would be expected to be approximately equal in size. This is an important factor in selecting an appropriate property ownership pattern and will provision to minimize death taxes and estate settlement costs over both deaths as discussed in Chapter 4.

For federal estate tax purposes, generally all of a decedent's separate property and one-half of the community property owned by the decedent and spouse at death are subject to tax.

The entire amount of community property receives a new income tax basis at the first death.

Interests in land held as community property have been eligible for a discount for non-marketability of the decedent's interest.

IN CONCLUSION. The size of the estate may have a great deal to do with choice of co-ownership methods. For those with smaller estates (those not likely to be subject to death taxes) joint tenancy may be acceptable. As the estate increases in size, and becomes potentially subject to death taxes, joint tenancy may become less satisfactory as a means for holding title.

3
Federal estate tax considerations

Thirty years ago, relatively few farm estates were subject to the federal estate tax. However, rapid increases in value of farm assets (particularly farmland) in the 1970s assured that federal estate tax considerations were among the most important parts of estate planning. In the 1980s, land values in some areas dropped sharply – by more than 50 percent in some states – with the result that federal estate tax has become relatively less important. Moreover, sharp increases in the unified credit that were enacted in 1981 (phased in over a six year period) reduced the federal estate tax concerns for those with estates under $600,000. Those with estates of this size or smaller have no federal estate tax liability unless Congress acts to change the level of the unified credit. Legislation is pending in Congress to increase the $600,000 figure to $750,000 over a period of several years. Many estates have continued to increase in size and are above even the $750,000 level. For that group, planning to minimize federal estate tax liability is often one of the objectives guiding the planning process.

For many, therefore, careful planning during life can produce dramatic savings in the federal estate tax imposed at death. It's perfectly legal for individuals to take advantage of these planning opportunities.

The gross estate

Examination of the federal estate tax properly begins with a look at the gross estate, which includes the property subject to the tax. In general, all property owned by the decedent at the time of death – stocks, bonds, farmland, checking accounts and other property – is included in the gross estate.

PROPERTY VALUATION. Except for land, the property is valued at fair market value either as of the date of death or, at the election of the executor or administrator, as of the alternate valuation date. For most purposes, though not all, the alternate valuation date is six months after death. Assets disposed of during the six-month period are valued as of the date of disposition if the alternate valuation date is elected.

The alternate valuation option may be used if the value of property and the federal estate tax liability are reduced by making the election and the gross estate exceeds the value required for filing a federal estate tax return. That's $600,000 for deaths in 1996.

The alternate valuation rules, if elected, apply even though the assets may undergo a change in form. Thus, hay, grain or other feed on hand as of the date of death which is fed to livestock after death is subject to the alternate valuation rules with the time of disposition being the date the feed was fed. Therefore, records should be maintained of grain and feed on hand at the date of death, the amount on hand six months later and the time and circumstances of disposition for the amounts disposed of during the six month period after death. Crops that are not yet "growing crops" at the date of death aren't subject to the alternate valuation rules. The same treatment is accorded rents, dividends and interest earned or accrued after the decedent's death. Likewise, animals born after death aren't subject to the alternate valuation provisions.

On the other hand, crops planted and animals born before death are "included property" and may be valued six months after death unless sold earlier. In the event of sale, the valuation at the date of sale is used to set the federal estate tax value under the alternate valuation rules.

The alternate valuation date may be elected along with special use valuation of land. If that is done, the six month later date is used for purposes of determining eligibility for special use valuation and for determining the value.

SPECIAL USE VALUE FOR LAND. The Tax Reform Act of

1976 added a special procedure for valuing real property at death. It's referred to as special use or "use" value. And it applies to land devoted to farming or other business use.

Special use valuation was used by many farm estates in the late 1970s and early 1980s. Although still available, special use valuation was used less often in the mid to late 1980s but is being used more frequently in the 1990s. A major concern in recent years has been how to avoid recapture of special use valuation benefits in the 10 or 15 year period after death.

If eligible, farmland can be valued in either of two ways. The method most likely to be used involves capitalization of cash rent, which can only be used for valuing farmland.

It's done by dividing the average annual gross cash rental for comparable land in the locality (less property taxes on comparable land) by the average annual effective interest rate for all new Federal Land Bank loans. The calculations are to use interest rate, cash rent and property tax information for the five most recent calendar years ending before the decedent's death.

EXAMPLE: average cash rent of $100 per acre, property taxes of $10 per acre, leaving $90 to be capitalized. Assuming the average annual effective Federal Land Bank loan rate is 9 percent, the land value per acre would be –

$$\frac{100 - 10}{.09} = \frac{90}{.09} = \$1,000$$

The other method of valuation – which can be used to value farmland or land used in another business – involves a five factor formula. The factors include – (1) capitalization of income that the property can be expected to yield over a reasonable period under prudent management; (2) capitalization of the fair rental value; (3) assessed values for property tax purposes if the state bases assessments on current use; (4) comparable sales in the same geographical area but without significant influence from metropolitan or resort areas; and (5) any other factor that could

Table 1. Effective Federal Land Bank Interest Rates.

Average annual effective interest rates in percent
for special use valuation for death in

Bank District	1977	1978	1979	1980	1981	1982	1983	1984	1985	1986	1987	1988	1989	1990	1991	1992	1993	1994	1995	1996
Baltimore	8.65	8.86	9.04	9.24	9.66	10.48	11.82	12.07	12.60	12.82	12.60	11.94	11.44	11.13	10.68	10.15	9.75	9.34	8.93	–
Columbia	8.58	8.79	8.96	9.17	9.40	9.81	10.93	11.14	11.69	12.14	12.37	11.99	11.76	11.52	11.31	10.87	10.35	9.70	9.2	8.98
Jackson	8.26	8.48	8.72	8.96	9.33	9.88	11.13	11.37	11.94	12.30	12.54	11.95	11.60	–	–	–	–	–	–	–
Louisville	8.64	8.80	8.88	9.21	9.53	10.02	11.39	11.76	12.27	12.86	13.19	12.66	12.28	11.98	11.45	10.81	10.16	–	–	–
Omaha	8.70	8.92	9.05	9.25	9.59	10.17	11.52	11.86	12.45	12.99	13.22	12.56	12.07	11.59	10.87	10.10	9.54	9.15	8.63	8.38
Sacramento	8.67	8.82	9.04	9.35	9.63	10.12	11.35	11.43	11.92	12.31	12.50	12.19	12.03	11.87	11.65	11.50	11.03	10.46	9.87	9.28
St. Louis	8.50	8.71	8.93	9.20	9.77	10.37	11.71	11.93	12.44	12.65	12.69	11.91	11.50	11.18	10.73	10.18	–	–	–	–
St. Paul	8.21	8.47	8.69	8.95	9.30	9.84	11.17	11.43	11.98	12.46	12.70	12.15	11.87	11.60	11.14	10.54	10.28	9.64	9.03	8.73
Spokane	8.63	8.88	9.10	9.31	9.60	10.13	11.31	11.57	12.12	12.51	12.62	12.14	11.79	11.59	11.28	10.65	10.27	9.60	8.97	8.48
Springfield	8.42	8.55	8.65	8.81	9.10	9.52	10.71	11.03	11.73	12.20	12.44	11.94	11.66	11.34	11.01	10.44	10.10	9.51	8.90	8.59
Texas	8.29	8.48	8.60	8.76	9.09	9.74	10.88	10.92	11.41	11.71	11.85	11.50	11.09	11.22	10.55	10.21	10.05	9.79	9.28	8.86
Wichita	8.52	8.72	8.88	9.08	9.56	10.26	11.65	11.91	12.41	12.77	12.86	12.14	11.74	11.39	10.83	10.13	9.75	9.22	8.79	8.44

fairly value the real property. If the decision is made to use the five factors, all five of the factors must be used – it's not possible to pick one or two and base the value only on those factors. Actually, the five factor formula is rarely used for valuing either farmland or other land.

What Interest Rate to Use? Under the cash rent capitalization approach, the capitalization (interest) rate has a great impact on the resulting land values. Reducing the interest rate by half doubles the value of the farmland. The special use value law specifies that the interest rate is to be the annual *effective* interest rate for the last five full calendar years. That makes it possible to figure in the cost for owning Federal Land Bank stock. The average interest rate differs by Federal Land Bank District. The calculations are to use the district rate where the land is located. The rates by Federal Land Bank District are figured by the Internal Revenue Service. Table 1 shows the average annual effective interest rate for each Federal Land Bank District for deaths in 1977 through 1996.

Source of Cash Rents. Actual cash rent figures from comparable land in the locality are needed to make the special use valuation procedure operational. The U.S. Department of Agriculture in an annual publication, *Farm Real Estate Market Developments,* provides information from a survey conducted early each year on expected cash rents for the coming crop season by state. The data are also available by crop reporting district within each state. However, the data are only averages and, at best, would be expected to be of only limited usefulness in special use valuation calculations. In regulations, IRS has taken the position that such data may not be used to determine special use value. IRS also says that cash rental figures cannot be established by appraisal or expert testimony. The IRS position is that special use valuation requires actual cash rents on tracts of comparable land.

Regulations indicate that IRS may object to use of some cash rental figures. Only rentals from "arm's length" lease arrangements are eligible for consideration. Specifically, cash rent data

33

from leases between family members are not acceptable "which do not provide a return on the property commensurate with that received under leases between unrelated parties in the locality." Tracts under "material participation" leases, sufficient for special use valuation, may not be used as a source of rental information according to the regulations.

Information from crop share rents on comparable land can be used if cash rent information does not exist. Crop share calculations are to use "average net share rentals" from crop share leases. The term "net share rentals" means the landowner's portion of the crop share return from the land minus the "cash operating expenses which, under the lease, are paid by the lessor."

What Is Comparable Land? A major task in locating usable cash rented tracts is in determining what is "comparable land." The regulations identify 10 factors to be used in making that determination –

1. In some states, productivity indexes have been developed to take into account soil properties and weather conditions as the dominant factors affecting yield potential. Where available, these indexes may be used in determining what is comparable land. Typically, such indexes rate each parcel of land (usually by 40 acre tract) on a scale of one to 100 or five to 100, taking into account soil properties and weather conditions as factors affecting yield potential. The indexes are generally based on recently conducted soil surveys. Such indexes exist in a number of midwestern states.

The indexes do not take into account differences in land value based on differences in crop prices. In general, the greater the distance from a shipping terminal, the lower the crop price – by about the shipping cost. That difference is believed to influence land values. For that reason, comparisons of land tracts many miles apart should be handled with added care as indicated in the tenth factor below.

2. Whether soil depleting crops have been grown equally on the tracts being compared.

3. Soil conservation practices used on the tracts.

4. Flooding possibilities.

5. Slope of the land.

6. Carrying capacity for livestock, where appropriate.

7. Comparability of timber, if any.

8. Whether the tracts are unified or separate.

9. The number, type and condition of buildings as those factors affect "efficient management and use of property and value per se."

10. Availability and type of transportation facilities in terms of costs and proximity of the properties to local markets.

The rules do not make it clear whether the 10 factors are to be weighted equally or whether all need to be used in a particular instance. Presumably, only those applicable would be taken into account.

A key point: This special valuation provision cannot reduce the gross estate by more than $750,000.

Pre-death Eligibility Requirements. To qualify for special use valuation, several conditions must be met – (1) the value of the farm or other business real or personal property must be at least 50 percent of the adjusted value of the gross estate (gross estate less allowable unpaid indebtedness attributable to the property in question – using fair market value figures for this calculation) and that amount or more must pass to a qualified heir or heirs, (2) at least 25 percent of the adjusted value of the gross estate must be qualified farm or business real property, again using fair market value figures, (3) the decedent or a member of the decedent's family must have had an "equity interest" in the farm or ranch operation (the "qualified use" test) at the time of death and for five or more of the last eight years before death, (4) during five or more years in the eight-year period ending with the decedent's death, the real property must have been owned by the decedent or a member of the decedent's family and used as a farm or other business, (5) the decedent or a member of the family must have participated materially in the operation of the farm or other business for five or more of the last eight years before retirement, disability or death and (6) a qualified heir must receive a present interest in the land from the decedent. An amendment effective for decedents dying after 1981 eased the material participation requirement for landowners who are disabled or retired and receiving social security benefits. The material participation test need be met only for five or more of the last eight years before the date of disability or retirement. Thus, the material participation test must be met during periods totalling five or more of the eight years ending with the earlier of – (a) the date of death, (b) the date on which the decedent became disabled (if the condition lasted until the decedent's death) or (c) the date on which the individual began receiving social security retirement benefits (if that status continued until death).

The amendment also specifies that a surviving spouse of a decedent who had held qualified real property (and who received the property from the decedent) and who is involved in "active management" of the farm or other business meets the material participation test. The term "active management" is defined as "the making of the management decisions of a business (other than the daily operating decisions)." More on this point in a later paragraph.

For deaths after 1981, the "tacking on" of ownership, qualified use and material participation requirements is permitted in the case of replacement property acquired in conjunction with tax-free exchanges and "involuntary conversions" such as land taken by condemnation. The replacement property must be used in the same use as the property disposed of.

Member of Family. "Member of family" is important for five reasons – (1) qualified heirs inheriting special use value land must be members of the family, (2) material participation in the pre-death period must be by the decedent-to-be or a member of the family of the decedent-to-be, (3) the qualified use test must be met during the pre-death period by the decedent-to-be or a member of the family of the decedent-to-be, (4) material participation in the after-death period must be by the qualified heir or a member of the qualified heir's family and (5) eligible purchasers of land, in the after-death period must be a member of the qualified heir's family.

The term "member of family" should always be viewed in terms of a *base person* – the decedent-to-be in the pre-death period and the qualified heir in the after-death period.

For deaths *through* 1981, the term "member of family" is defined to include the spouse, ancestors, lineal descendants, lineal descendants of grandparents, and spouses of descendants. Thus, the term includes uncles, aunts, and first cousins as well as parents, grandparents, children and grandchildren and their spouses.

The term "member of family" was amended *effective for deaths after 1981.* For deaths after 1981, "member of family" has been narrowed to include only the ancestors of the individual, the person's spouse, lineal descendants of the individual, lineal descendants of the individual's spouse, lineal descendants of the *parents* of the individual and the spouse of any lineal descendant. The new definition narrows "member of the family" to exclude uncles and aunts and their descendants, for example, while including the lineal descendants of the individual's spouse (who were usually included under the old rule as the individual's descendants except for children born of another).

Legally adopted children are treated as a child of blood relationship. Apparently, adoption relates back to the date of birth of the individual.

Note that the more narrow definition of family member applies to deaths after 1981. Therefore, for all purposes (including recapture determinations) for deaths before 1982, the pre-1982 rules continue to apply. Uncles, aunts and first cousins are considered to be members of the family for that group.

Property Passing by Inheritance. The requirement that at least 50 percent of the adjusted value of the gross estate must pass from the decedent to a qualified heir or heirs merits special comment. It appears that farmland and other farm property passing

37

directly by inheritance to qualified heirs qualifies. However, property passing into the decedent's estate and then passing by *purchase* to the on-farm heirs, for example, did not meet the test until a 1981 amendment became effective.

The 1981 amendment, which was retroactive to January 1, 1977, solved part of the problem. This law permitted property to pass to qualified heirs by purchase without losing eligibility for special use valuation. Thus, it is possible for qualified heirs to – (1) purchase land from the estate that is valued under special use valuation, (2) purchase farm personal property from the estate needed to meet the requirement that at least 50 percent of the estate must be comprised of farm real and personal property and must pass to qualified heirs and (3) purchase corporate stock or partnership shares from the estate during estate settlement.

However, a related problem remains. If the real property is less than 50 percent of the estate and all farm personal property – machinery, livestock, equipment and stored grain – is sold outside the family before the estate is closed, the requirement would not be met that at least 50 percent of the estate must be farm real and personal property *and must pass to the qualified heirs.* Therefore, it may be necessary to delay sale of some farm personal property until after the estate is closed or to obtain a court order for a partial distribution of property from the estate to the qualified heirs if early sale is desired.

The importance of the 1981 legislation in this area is underscored by an IRS ruling (under the old law) holding that farmland was ineligible for special use valuation because the on-farm heirs contributed funds to pay the other heirs and costs of estate settlement. By the IRS view, the land did not pass by inheritance as is required. The result is different under the 1981 legislation. Purchases by qualified heirs are permitted and advancing funds to the estate should be permissible, also.

Note, however, that it's not merely the *land* that must pass to qualified heirs. At least 50 percent of the adjusted value of the gross estate must be made up of farm real and personal property and must pass to qualified heirs by inheritance or by purchase.

A potential trap: if qualified heirs do purchase special use value land from the estate, there's no new income tax basis for the property. The special use value as determined in the estate continues to be the income tax basis even in the hands of the purchaser. This problem is discussed in detail below under "Income Tax Considerations."

Qualified Use Test. The final IRS regulations, issued in 1980, contained a new test – the "qualified use" test. That test is based upon language in the special use value law that the land must be used as a "farm" for "farming purposes" or used in a trade or business other than farming. The emphasis on "business" in the law led IRS to impose a requirement that, to meet the qualified use test, the decedent must have had an "equity interest in the farm operation." The wording of the law was such that the qualified use test had to be met *by the decedent* – (1) at the time of death and (2) for five or more of the last eight years before death. In addition, each qualified heir was required to meet the test in the recapture period after death – the period when events could occur that could cause repayment of the federal estate tax benefit from special use valuation.

The requirement of an equity interest in the farm business by the decedent meant that cash rent leases would not be permissible. With cash rent leases, the land owner is not "at risk" with respect to production and so the land owner is not viewed as having an equity interest *in the farm business.* By the IRS interpretation, even a cash rent lease to a family member as farm tenant would disqualify the land for special use valuation.

The reaction to the IRS position was swift – and adverse. Accordingly, on April 27, 1981, IRS announced a change in interpretation for the qualified use test in the pre-death period. IRS indicated that regulations would be issued at a later date permitting the qualified use test to be met by the decedent *or a member of the decedent's family* in the period before death. The practical result of that announcement was to permit cash rent leases to family members as farm tenants in the period before death. Legislation enacted in 1981 adopted the same rule – the qualified use test could be met in the pre-death period by the decedent or a member of the decedent's family.

Participation in government farm programs involving the idling of land (such as under the 1983 payment-in-kind program or the 1985 Conservation Reserve Program) has led to concerns about whether the qualified use test is met on the idled land. Legislation was enacted in 1983 (but not made permanent) to permit participation in payment-in-kind programs without loss of special use valuation so long as the farmer receives agricultural commodities in exchange for idling land under the payment-in-kind program. An IRS announcement in early 1983 was broader in scope and indicated there was no problem of eligibility for special use valuation in idling land under any government land diversion program. Several IRS rulings in 1987 and 1988 cited the 1983 announcement as authority for participation in the Conservation Reserve Program without recapture of special use valuation benefits.

"Present Interest" Test. In the final regulations, published in 1980, IRS indicated that some qualified heir (or heirs) must have a present interest in the land for the land to be eligible for special use valuation. It was permissible for qualified heirs to hold a remainder interest, but the land would be eligible for special use valuation only if a qualified heir or heirs held a present interest in the property. In a letter ruling, IRS further noted that if land was left in trust and the trustee had *discretion* to distribute income or principal or both, the qualified heir holding the income interest did not have a *present interest.* Essentially, the IRS view was that the trustee could, with discretion in paying income and principal to trust beneficiaries, undercut the qualified heir's income interest.

As a practical matter, the IRS position meant that trustees could not have discretion in paying income or principal to beneficiaries.

Again, the outcry was swift – and adverse. And IRS announced a change of interpretation. On April 27, 1981, IRS indicated that regulations would be issued permitting trustees to have discretion in paying trust income or principal to beneficiaries *so long as all actual and potential beneficiaries were members of the decedent's family.* The 1981 amendments gave the IRS interpretation the force of law, retroactive to 1977.

The requirement of a present interest for some qualified heir could cause problems of eligibility for land owned by a corporation. Gifts of stock in a corporation with a history of no dividend declaration and highly limiting restrictions on stock transfer have been held to be future interests, not present interests, for federal gift tax purposes. The same outcome is entirely possible for purposes of special use valuation. For that reason, it is suggested that corporations owning farmland avoid building up a history of no dividends declared.

It is also necessary, for special use valuation eligibility, for qualified heirs to hold all interests in the property.

• If land is left by the decedent to a family member – such as a spouse – for life with a remainder interest to a charitable organization, special use valuation is not available.

• If land is left by the decedent to a non-family member – such as a trusted employee, an unadopted foster child or the surviving spouse's niece – special use valuation could not be used.

These rules call for special care in planning for the passage of property at death where contingencies are involved. This often involves provisions in the will disposing of the property if immediate family members do not survive or provisions disposing of property to individuals determined at some point after the decedent's death.

EXAMPLE: A dies, without lineal descendants surviving, leaving property in trust for those nieces and nephews surviving 21 years after the decedent's death. If no nieces or nephews survive, the property is to be divided into two equal portions, one portion passing to the Iowa State University Foundation "for the benefit of poor professors of economics at Iowa State University." The other portion is to pass to other heirs of the decedent according to state law. Farmland in neither portion would qualify for special use valuation.

EXAMPLE: B dies, leaving farmland in trust to such of her four children as survive to age 40. In the event a child does not reach age 40, that child's share is to pass to that child's heirs as though the child had died without a will. At B's death, the youngest child was 35 years of age, married with two children. Although it would indeed be unlikely that the interest of the child of B would pass to individuals who were not members of B's family (such an outcome would require death of the child's spouse, children, brothers and sisters, and their spouses), it could occur. Conceivably, special use value would not be available in B's estate *because of the contingency and the fact that the land could pass to non-family members.* In rulings, IRS confirmed that the mere chance that an interest in land valued under special use valuation could pass to non-family members – even a low probability chance – would bar special use valuation. In three 1986 Tax Court cases and in two Court of Appeal cases in 1989, however, highly remote chances that land could pass to non-family members were held not to bar special use valuation and IRS has now agreed in private letter rulings. Nonetheless, it is suggested that *all interests in special use valuation land vest in family members at the death of the landowner and that wills and trusts be specifically drafted to prevent passage of the property to non-family members.*

Rules for Timber. In 1980, IRS ruled that trees are not part of the land for purposes of special use valuation. Trees were to be treated and valued as a crop. The 1981 amendments made several changes affecting eligibility of timber and timber land for special use valuation. For "qualified woodlands," if the executor elects, growing trees are treated as part of the real estate and not as a crop. The term "qualified woodlands" is defined as land "used in timber operations, and … is an identifiable area of land … for which records are normally maintained in conducting tim-

42

ber operations."

If the executor elects to treat growing trees as part of the real estate, with the trees subject to special use valuation, any cutting of trees during the recapture period after death is a recapture event.

Situation for the Farm Residence. The farm residence is eligible real property for purposes of special use valuation if occupied on a regular basis by the owner, tenant or an employee of the owner or tenant for the purpose of "operating or maintaining such real property." Thus, when the parents retire and move off the farm, the way the residence is handled could affect eligibility of the land for special use valuation.

If the residence is occupied by a resident farm tenant, for example, the value of the residence counts as eligible real property for purposes of special use valuation. But if the land is rented to a neighbor and the residence is rented to someone working in town, the residence is no longer eligible real property for purposes of special use valuation.

Agreement to be Signed. To be eligible, the land must be designated in a written agreement signed by each person in being who has an interest in the property. Those persons must consent to payment of any additional tax if the land is disposed of after death or is managed in a way to trigger repayment of part or all of the benefits from special use valuation. The agreement must designate an agent who is to notify IRS of the name of the person (or persons) who will be providing material participation in the period after death if material participation is required in the post-death period. More on this "recapture" problem in a later paragraph.

Material Participation. The requirement that the deceased or member of the deceased's family must have participated materially is crucial for many. It's the major "fence" that determines whether non-farm investors can take advantage of the special use valuation rules. A key question is whether material participation can be achieved through an agent such as a farm manager. The Tax Reform Act of 1976 states that the matter of material participation is to be handled in a manner "similar" to the way it's defined for social security purposes. An amendment to the social security law in 1974 provided that rentals from real estate, including crop share rents, are not to be treated as earnings from self-employment and thus are not subject to social security tax and are not treated as earned income to reduce social security benefits after retirement if the material participation results from activities of an agent. Hence, it appears that material participation cannot be attained through an agent. More on material participation strategies in a later paragraph.

The importance of the material participation issue is underscored by the fact that if non-farmers in large numbers can qualify for special use valuation, and if there is sufficient tax saving advantage in special use valuation to attract those non-farm investors, land values would be expected to reflect that investment interest in the form of higher land values.

Land values could be strengthened because of special use valuation even if the "fence" holds and non-farmers are ineligible except for those in a position to participate materially in person or through a member of the family. As farmers grow older, the relative advantage of investment in land compared to investment in "non-land" resources – machinery, livestock and equipment – would be expected to shift investment behavior in favor of land because of the tax break. This could have a long-range effect of enabling farmers to bid land away from non-farmers as well.

Active Management. The 1981 legislation created a new concept, "active management," which replaces material participation in specified instances. A surviving spouse (of a decedent who had held qualified real property), who received the real property from the decedent and who is involved in "active management" of the farm or other business meets the material participation test. It is not necessary that the land have been subject to special use valuation in the decedent's estate. But a question exists whether the "active management" option can be used if the decedent died before 1977 when special use valuation went into effect. The "active management" concept also applies in specified instances in the recapture period after death as noted below.

The term "active management" is defined as "the making of the management decisions of a business (other than the daily operating decisions)." As stated in the Senate Finance Committee Report, "the determination of whether active management occurs is factual, and the requirement can be met even though no self-employment tax is payable ... by the spouse with respect to income derived from the farm or other trade or business operation. Among the farming activities, various combinations of which constitute active management, are inspecting growing crops, reviewing and approving annual crop plans in advance of planting, making a substantial number of the management decisions of the business operation, and approving expenditures for other than nominal operating expenses in advance of the time the amounts are expended. Examples of management decisions are decisions such as what crops to plant or how many cattle to raise, what fields to leave fallow, where and when to market crops and other business products, how to finance business operations, and what capital expenditures the trade or business should undertake."

Perhaps the most significant statement in the report (which, it should be noted, does not have the force of law) is that the active management test can be met without income under a lease being treated as self employment income subject to social security tax. This is especially important for surviving spouses leasing to farm tenants who are not members of the family. If the farm tenant is a member of the family, the material participation requirement can be met by the family member as farm tenant.

There has been a problem with the pre-death active management test for the surviving spouse.

EXAMPLE: Assume the husband owned the farmland and retired in 1981 after 40 years of farming. The husband took advantage of the rule requiring material participation only for five or more of the last eight years before retirement. The husband died in 1994, leaving the farmland to his wife. She utilized the active management option for meeting the material participation test and died in 1996. The problem: did the wife or a member of her family participate materially for five or more of the last eight years before her retirement, disability or death as is required? The answer, apparently was no if the land was not rented to a family member. Did the wife meet the active management test for five or more of the last eight years before her retirement, disability or death? Again, the answer would appear to be no. Even if she had begun active management in 1991, she did not become a "surviving spouse" until 1994 and that is a requirement in order to take advantage of the active management test. This is a loophole that has been corrected by legislation.

Under a late 1982 amendment, the husband's material participation before his retirement (in the example above) is treated as occurring immediately before his death. Thus, the wife as the surviving spouse could use his pre-retirement material participation to meet her own pre-death material participation requirement.

Remember, the material participation test can be met by material participation on the part of the decedent *or a member of the decedent's family or active management personally by the surviving spouse Active management by a family member does not count toward meeting the requirement.*

Income Tax Considerations. Where cash rent figures are available, special use valuation is likely to give the lowest land value. Although minimization of federal estate tax is often the objective, for some estates a higher land value may be desirable for reasons relating to obtaining a larger income tax basis for the property. Special use valuation also establishes the income tax basis for the property at death.

EXAMPLE 1: Farmland that would have sold for $3,000 per acre was valued at death in 1980 under the special use valuation rules for $1,400 per acre. The figure of $1,400 per acre was used in figuring federal estate liability and also became the income tax basis for purposes of computing depreciation and gain or loss on disposition after death. If the land had been sold by the heirs in

1996 for $3,000 per acre, the gain would have been $1,600 per acre assuming no improvements made after death and no depreciation claimed after death ($3,000 minus $1,400) if special use valuation had been utilized at death. The potential for substantial income tax liability is great.

EXAMPLE 2: Assume the same facts as in Example 1, except that the land was sold in 1996 for $1,500 per acre. The selling qualified heirs would have a gain of $100 per acre ($1,500 minus $1,400). Had special use valuation not been used, and the farmland had been valued at $3,000 per acre at death, that figure would have become the income tax basis. In that case, sale for $1,500 per acre would have produced $1,500 per acre loss.

The way the land is acquired from the estate can influence who bears the income tax liability on later sale.

EXAMPLE 3: Grandfather dies, owning 320 acres of farmland with a fair market value at death of $2,000 per acre. The special use valuation is $800 per acre. During estate settlement, a grandson purchases the 320 acres for $2,000 per acre and pays cash. The estate would have no gain on the $640,000 sale even though the income tax basis is only $256,000 or $800 per acre. The purchasing grandson would have an income tax basis in the property of only $256,000 for purposes of computing depreciation and for figuring gain or loss on sale. Thus, if the grandson were to sell the land for $640,000, the grandson would have gain of $384,000. *A purchaser of land from the estate does not receive an income tax basis equal to the purchase price as is usually the case.*

EXAMPLE 4: Assuming the same facts as in Example 3 except that grandfather's estate is closed, the land is distributed to the four children and the children sell the land to the grandson for $640,000. The selling heirs would have gain of $384,000 ($96,000 each) because their income tax basis was only $256,000. The purchasing grandson would have an income tax basis – for purposes of figuring gain or loss or calculating depreciation – equal to the purchase price of $640,000.

Thus, from the standpoint of overall family wealth it's usually better for the land to be purchased from the estate – rather than from the other heirs. The purchasing heir ends up with less depreciation claimable. But it's not necessary for anyone to pay income tax on the potential gain – until and unless the land is sold by the purchasing heir.

Another point: if the land increases in value between the date of death and the date of sale, the estate has gain for income tax purposes to that extent.

EXAMPLE 5: Returning to Example 3 above, assume the fair market value of the land at the time of sale has increased to $2,200 per acre. The estate would have a gain of $200 per acre and the purchasing heir would have an income tax basis of $1,000 per acre.

A final point: it can be costly for an estate to sell special use value land under an installment contract or contract for deed.

EXAMPLE 6: Returning to Example 3 above, assume the estate sells the land to the grandson for $640,000 under a 20 year installment contract. There would be no gain to the estate on sale (assuming the fair market value for the land at the time of sale does not exceed the fair market value at death). But what happens when the estate is closed and the contract is distributed to the heirs? Apparently, *all of the gain in the contract would be subject to income tax at that time.* Therefore, great care should be exercised in selling land from the estate under installment contract.

The income tax aspects of property disposition are discussed in greater detail in Chapter 7. It should be noted that the special use valuation procedures are not mandatory and real property can always be valued at its fair market value.

Recapture of Benefits After Death. If special use value is used, disposition of the real property may trigger repayment or "recapture" of the tax benefits involved. There's partial or total recapture if the property is disposed of within the recapture period after the death of the decedent to non-family members, the "qualified use" test is not met, material participation (or "active management") is not maintained or the land ceases to be used for

48

farming or other business purposes. For deaths before 1982, full recapture occurs within the first 10 years with a phase-out between 10 and 15 years.

For deaths after 1981, the recapture period has been reduced to 10 years after the decedent's death or 10 years after the commencement of "qualified use" under the two-year grace period discussed below. In effect, the 1981 amendment dropped the five year phase-out (between 10 and 15 years) applicable before 1982. Partial dispositions lead to partial recapture.

Transfer Outside the Family. Recapture occurs on transfer of the land outside the family. That is the case even though the transfer may be income-tax free – because it is a tax-free sale of the residence and reinvestment in another or sale of residence after reaching age 55 for example. However, if property transfer is because of condemnation or other "involuntary conversion" and the proceeds are invested fully in real property used for the same purpose, the recapture rules do not apply. For tax-free exchanges of land after 1981, recapture does not occur if qualified real property is exchanged for "qualified exchange property." Qualified exchange property is real property used for the same qualified use as the property transferred. The lien securing payment of the additional estate tax (that might be recaptured) would have to be transferred to the replacement property before the original qualified property is discharged from the lien.

For all transfers of special use value land after death, it is important to double check the definition of family member. Remember, in the recapture period after death the family member test is applied to the qualified heir as the "base person."

EXAMPLE: Two brothers, A and B, had been farming together for 35 years. Each owned 320 acres of land. B died, leaving his 320 acres to his wife, Z, who survived. After B's estate had been closed, Z sold the 320 acres to her late husband's brother, A. The special use valuation benefits would be recaptured if the sale occurred during the recapture period after death. *A is not a member of Z's family.* Ironically, A could have purchased the land directly from B's estate. At that point, the question is whether the purchaser is a member of the *decedent's* family. This illustrates why it is important to ascertain where ownership of the land will ultimately come to rest before the estate is closed and the land is distributed to the heirs.

Apparently, it was not intended for recapture to occur on tax-free transfer of real property to a partnership or corporation. That seems to be the result if – (1) the qualified heir retains the same interest in the partnership share or corporate stock as the individual held in the property given up, (2) the firm is a closely held business (20 percent or more of the partnership capital or corporation voting stock included in the estate or the firm must have 15 or fewer partners or shareholders, as the case may be) and (3) the partnership or corporation consents to personal liability for the recapture tax if it disposes of the real property or ceases to use the property for qualified purposes during the period in which recapture could occur.

Change of Use. In general, a change of use from farming to another use triggers recapture of special use valuation benefits. Moreover, a change in use that results in interruption of the surface use of the land for farming causes recapture of federal estate tax benefits. Mere execution of an oil and gas lease apparently does not trigger recapture. But commencement of drilling activity would lead to recapture to the extent of the interruption of the farming operation.

In one IRS ruling, the question was whether construction of a house on land under special use valuation would cause recapture. The ruling indicated that it would not, if the residence was occupied on a regular basis by someone involved in management of the farming operation.

Death of Qualified Heir. Recapture does not occur on death of the qualified heir. In fact, death of the qualified heir terminates the possibility of recapture of special use valuation benefits on the property involved. Some might be inclined to select qualified heirs in part on the basis of life expectancy – the shorter the better!

But death of a qualified heir immunizes only that qualified heir's interest from recapture – not the interests of others.

Qualified Use Test. The recapture rules are also activated on "cessation of qualified use." The qualified use test requires that *each qualified heir* must have an equity interest in the farm operation. That means that cash renting in the recapture period after death (except for a two-year grace period immediately after death and leases by some surviving spouses as explained below) triggers recapture of the federal estate tax benefit from special use valuation. Unlike the qualified use test in the pre-death period, where IRS has announced that the qualified use test could be met by the decedent *or member of the decedent's family,* no such interpretation applies for the period after death. The 1981 amendments that specifically authorized the qualified use test to be met in the pre-death period by the decedent *or a member of the decedent's family* and that created the two-year grace period after death did not specify how the qualified use test could be met in the period after death. The committee reports state, however, that "the bill does not change the present requirement that the qualified heir owning the real property after the decedent's death use it in the qualified use throughout the recapture period." Thus, except for the two-year grace period after death and leases by some surviving spouses, *qualified heirs should not be parties to cash rent leases.* Use of any part of the two-year grace period extends the recapture period for a like time for all types of events leading to recapture.

Retroactive to 1977, a 1988 amendment permits a surviving spouse who inherits qualified real property to lease the land on a "net cash basis" *to a member of the spouse's family* without causing recapture. Trusts may enter into cash rent leases to a member of the surviving spouse's family if the surviving spouse is the only beneficiary. Otherwise, the minimum "at risk" position that would meet the qualified use test would appear to be a non-material participation crop share lease for each qualified heir. This requirement would appear to be the most difficult to meet in

51

ranching businesses.

EXAMPLE: Mother dies, leaving 320 acres of farmland to her daughter Ellen and her son John. John continues farming the land after death of his mother and pays his sister a cash rent of $75 per acre. If the cash renting continues after the two-year grace period, the recapture rules would be activated as to Ellen and her one-half interest in the land.

As a practical matter, with the two exceptions noted above, all leases of special use value land after death must be crop share or livestock share or the arrangement must give each qualified heir an "equity interest" in the farm operation otherwise. In one IRS private letter ruling (the least authoritative of the rulings), a "bushel lease" met the qualified use test. In the facts of that ruling, the landowner would receive the first 40 bushels of corn or the first 13 bushels of soybeans. If actual production was less, the landowner agreed to accept the lesser figure. The presence of the latter clause in the lease was sufficient to meet the qualified use test requiring each landowner to be "at risk" in the farming operation.

A 1994 Eighth Circuit Court of Appeals case involved a family ownership arrangement where the three children (two daughters and a son) owned the land equally after their mother's death. The land was cash rented to a family corporation in which the son owned 88 percent of the stock and the daughters owned six percent each. The question was whether each of the daughters, owning one-third of the land but only six percent of the "tenant" was sufficiently "at risk" to meet the qualified use test. Over IRS objections, the court approved the arrangement and said the qualified use test was met. The case has been criticized. To be on the safe side, it is a good idea to be *fully* at risk. Without question, the qualified use test would have been met had the daughters each owned one-third of the stock in the family corporation as tenant.

Participation in payment-in-kind and other government acreage diversion programs raises the question of whether a qualified heir is "at risk" with respect to idled land. Legislation was enacted to eliminate the recapture concern as to the 1983 PIK program with legislation extending the solution to 1984 PIK program participation but not made permanent. Had it not been resolved, a potential existed for additional tax liability from recapture. The legislative solution did not deal with the effects of cash-paid land diversion, only land diverted with payments of commodities in kind. However, in early 1983, IRS announced that no participation in a government land diversion program should jeopardize special use valuation eligibility or cause recapture of special use valuation benefits.

IRS private letter rulings in 1987 and 1988 have indicated that participation in the 10-year Conservation Reserve Program should not trigger recapture of special use valuation benefits.

Absence of Material Participation. Absence of material participation for more than three years during any eight-year period ending after the decedent's death triggers recapture.

Note that says "… during any eight-year period ending after the decedent's death." It does not appear that the family has eight years after death to accomplish five years of material participation. If the deceased was not participating materially in the production of income in the year immediately prior to death, two more years of non-material participation immediately after death could place the qualified heir on the verge of recapture of benefits. Hence, action could be required soon after death to revise the farm lease – for land rented to a tenant – if recapture is to be avoided.

EXAMPLE: Elmer Black left active farming on March 1, 1993 (but not because of disability or retirement), and held a closing out sale for the machinery and livestock. The farmland was retained and rented to an unrelated neighbor under a non-material participation crop share lease. Black died on March 1, 1996, with three years of non-material participation under the lease. If the same type of non-material participation crop share lease continues beyond March 1, 1996, the federal estate tax benefit from

53

special use valuation is recaptured. There would be absence of material participation for more than three years in an eight-year period ending after death. Note that the eight-year test period can end *any* time after death.

Remember, material participation before retirement or disability may be counted as though it had occurred immediately before death in order to avoid recapture after death.

Keep in mind that material participation can be attained directly (rather than through the lease) if the qualified heir or member of the family of the qualified heir is the farm tenant or operator. A key point to note: material participation is to be by the qualified heir – or any member of the qualified heir's family – for the period during which the property was held by the qualified heir. And material participation is to be by the decedent or member of the decedent's family during the time the property was held by the decedent.

EXAMPLE 1: Grandmother died in early 1996 leaving 640 acres of farmland to her three children, A, B and C, and to the two children (X and Y) of a deceased child, D. The farm had been operated for several years by A under a crop-share lease. The material participation requirement could be met by A for A, B and C. But A is *not a member of the family of X and Y*, the children of D. Therefore, A could not meet the material participation test for X and Y. Unless X or Y or a *member of their family* meets the material participation test, recapture would occur *as to X and Y* after the grace period (a maximum of three years of absence of material participation). If X and Y were disabled or full-time students or under age 21, only "active management" would be needed as discussed below.

EXAMPLE 2: Parents die and the farmland is inherited by the four children – all are qualified heirs. The farming son agrees to be the material participator for all four. If, during the recapture period after death, the farming son dies, there's no further worry about recapture of tax benefits *as to his 25 percent interest*. But the other three would suffer recapture of benefits within three years unless material participation were to be provided by another eligible material participator. That could be the qualified heir or member of the qualified heir's family.

EXAMPLE 3: Same facts as above except that the farming son becomes disabled and cannot be the material participator. In that event, recapture may occur within three years as to the other three – unless material participation is provided by another eligible individual. As noted below, only active management is required of those who are disabled.

Off-farm heirs are obviously vulnerable to recapture of tax benefits based on lack of material participation. This may lead to a desire by off-farm heirs for a contractual commitment by the on-farm heir to assure material participation for the recapture period after death. Before undertaking such a commitment, non-farm heirs should assess the consequences if death or disability were to occur – and they couldn't participate materially.

Planning to assure the necessary material participation both before and after death may, in some instances, lead to conflicts with eligibility for social security benefits. Material participation is necessary before retirement to assure that earnings count for social security benefit purposes. Then, after retirement, non-material participation is required if rents received under a lease are not to be treated as earned income and reduce social security benefit levels above the allowable earned income amount, $12,500 in 1996 for those 65 or older.

Thus, a person retiring at age 65 might shift to a crop share lease that does not involve material participation. Upon reaching age 70, beyond which earned income no longer reduces social security benefits, the individual could return to material participation under a lease. But it would take five years in that status before the person had been participating materially for five of the last eight years before death – as required for special use valuation. Therefore, after age 75 eligibility for special use valuation could be restored in this example, at least as to material participation.

A cynic might conclude that an uncommon amount of orchestration of life's processes would be necessary to qualify for maximum social security benefits and also for the heirs to enjoy special use valuation at death.

Remember this – special use value eligibility may be more important in terms of total dollars. But reduced social security benefits from continued material participation status are suffered by the individual in retirement; the advantages of special use valuation rest with the heirs. Thus, it is possible to see how the social security side of the problem might dominate decision making.

But the picture is not quite that grim. Note that material participation before death can be by the decedent-to-be or a member of the family of the decedent-to-be. It is not necessary for the decedent-to-be to have qualified personally under the material participation rules. That suggests that a son farming the land would meet the requirement even though it is under a non-material participation crop share lease with the parents. If neither the decedent-to-be nor a member of the family of the decedent-to-be is involved in farming the land, the nature of the lease – from the decedent-to-be as landlord or from a member of the family – assumes major importance as discussed above.

Moreover, for deaths after 1981, it's sufficient for material participation for the requirement to have been met for five or more of the last eight years before the earlier of retirement, disability or death as noted earlier.

The material participation requirement has been eased in the recapture period after death for a qualified heir who is the surviving spouse of the decedent, person who has not reached age 21, disabled individual or full-time student. The material participation test may be met by "active management" by the qualified heir or by a fiduciary (such as a conservator) if the qualified heir is a person under age 21 or a disabled individual. Note, however, that the "active management" test, as an alternative to material participation, is not open to a member of the qualified heir's *fam-*

ily or a member of the *decedent's family* as is the material participation test.

In the case of qualified woodlands, disposition or severance of the standing timber is treated as a recapture event if the election had been made to treat the timber as part of the land. The additional estate tax from recapture is determined by treating the timber as an interest in real property on which the timber stood.

Bankruptcy. In the 1980s, one of the more perplexing questions was whether bankruptcy causes special use valuation recapture. Some answers are relatively clear but others await rulings or litigated cases.

• It is relatively clear that the transfer of property to the bankruptcy estate under Chapter 7 or 11 bankruptcy by an individual is not a taxable disposition and does not cause recapture under special use valuation rules. A new tax entity is created in the event of Chapter 7 or 11 bankruptcy filing by an individual. Specific provisions enacted in 1980 indicate that mere bankruptcy filing should not lead to recapture.

For Chapter 12 bankruptcy, applicable to eligible family farmers, a new tax entity is not created upon bankruptcy filing and the 1980 rules involving the creation of a new tax entity do not apply. With no transfer occurring, it is generally believed that special use valuation benefits should not be recaptured.

• If special use valuation property is returned to the debtor after bankruptcy, no recapture should occur, at least for Chapter 7 or 11 bankruptcy filings.

• In the event special use value property is transferred by the bankruptcy estate to a member of the debtor's family, no recapture of special use valuation benefits should occur.

• If special use valuation property is transferred to someone other than a member of the debtor's family, recapture occurs.

• For Chapter 7 and 11 filers, the responsibility for payment of the recapture tax rests with the bankruptcy estate. If there are insufficient assets in the bankruptcy estate, it is not clear whether the debtor continues to be liable for the recapture tax. Arguably, the debtor's contingent liability to pay the recapture tax (arising from the agreement of personal liability) is discharged in bankruptcy but that is not clear.

Foreclosure. In a 1989 ruling, the Internal Revenue Service indicated that where land under special use valuation was sold to individuals other than members of the debtor's family to pay off outstanding debt on other special use valued property, both under threat of foreclosure, special use valuation tax benefits were recaptured.

Amount Recaptured. If recapture is triggered because of lack of material participation, a change of land use, failure to meet the qualified use test or a transfer outside the family, the "adjusted tax difference" must be repaid. In general, that's the extra estate tax liability that would have been incurred had special use valuation not been used. The recaptured amount would be less if the gain on disposition (or excess of fair market value over special use valuation in the event of a non-sale disposition) was less.

EXAMPLE 1: At Grandmother's death in 1981, 320 acres of farmland with a fair market value at that time of $3,000 per acre were valued at $1,250 per acre under special use valuation. In 1986, the land was sold by the qualified heirs to an unrelated neighbor for $1,100 per acre. There should be no recapture of special use valuation benefits. That's because the fair market value had dropped below special use value and there was no gain on sale.

Because of this rule, it may be tempting to trigger recapture if fair market value drops below special use value. If that is done, a later increase in fair market value to levels above special use value would not encounter recapture. Before triggering recapture of special use valuation deliberately, there should be solid proof that fair market value is less than special use value.

EXAMPLE 2: At Grandfather's death in 1979, 320 acres of farmland with a fair market value of $2,000 per acre were valued under special use valuation at $800 per acre. The election saved $100,000 of federal estate tax. In 1988, the land was sold for $1,500 per acre. The $100,000 of federal estate tax saved because of special use valuation would have to be paid as a result of the recapture event.

In the event of a disposition of only part of the land held by a qualified heir under special use valuation (or upon failure of only a portion of the land to meet the post-death requirements), the amount of recapture is proportionate to the total amount of special use value land involved. That has not always been the case. For several years, the IRS position was that the entire amount of federal estate tax saved from special use valuation was recaptured unless the gain or potential gain on the property failing to meet the requirements was less, in which case the lesser amount was recaptured.

In late 1983, however, IRS changed its position to require only *proportionate* recapture in the event of a partial disposition. The change of position came in a private letter ruling involving construction of a personal residence on two acres of land, resulting in recapture as to the two acre tract after expiration of the two-year grace period after death. The land involved was owned by two qualified heirs, each with an undivided one-half interest. Each undivided one-half interest in the two acres had a fair market value at death of $2,250 with a special use value of $584. All land under special use valuation had a fair market value at death of $704,000 and a special use value of $211,400. The total amount of federal estate tax saved was $127,000. The formula for recapture used by IRS was –

$$\text{Amount recaptured} = \frac{\$2,250 - \$584}{\$704,000 - \$211,400} \times \$127,000$$

$$= \frac{1,666}{492,000} \times 127,000$$

$$= \$429.52$$

The change of position by IRS removed an extremely dangerous trap for the unwary.

Payment of any recaptured tax benefit is the responsibility of the qualified heir, not necessarily those who benefited from the special use value.

If a qualified heir transfers land to another family member who assumes personal liability for any recapture tax, as is required, the qualified heir making the transfer is relieved from any further recapture liability as to the land transferred.

New Basis on Recapture. The value used for federal estate tax purposes fixes the income tax basis of property involved. Thus, the value set under the special use valuation rules determines the basis. Even though recapture occurs, the general rule has been – and is – that there is no adjustment in income tax basis of the property.

However, the general rule has been modified for deaths after 1981. Upon recapture a qualified heir may make an election to increase the income tax basis of the property by the amount that date of death fair market value (or the fair market value on the alternate valuation date) exceeds the special use value. Essentially, the increase in income tax basis is to the basis the qualified heir would have received had special use valuation not been elected for the decedent's estate. If the election is made to obtain the higher basis, interest must be paid on the tax recaptured at the regular rate of interest on unpaid federal taxes from nine months after the decedent's death to the date of the recapture tax payment. The increase in income tax basis is considered to have occurred immediately before the recapture event. The increased basis may be used for determining gain or loss from disposition of the property but cannot be used for retroactive depreciation or depletion calculations.

If the qualified heir does not make the election and pay the interest, no adjustment is made to the basis of the property.

SPECIAL USE VALUE FOR PARTNERSHIPS, CORPORA-TIONS AND TRUSTS. The Tax Reform Act of 1976 did not go into detail on how the special valuation provision was to work for property interests held in a partnership, corporation or trust.

However, reports of Congressional committees indicated an intent by Congress for special use value to be reflected in the value of partnership shares, corporate stock or interests of beneficiaries in trusts if the special use value requirements were met. The legislation placed responsibility on the Secretary of the Treasury to issue regulations on that point.

Application of special use valuation to partnerships, corporations and trusts is fairly straightforward if the entity has one type of ownership interest. Presumably, the benefits of special use valuation will be appropriately reflected in the valuation of corporate stock, partnership shares and trust interests. In the event that an entity has more than one type of ownership interest, the situation is more complex. If a corporation, for example, has more than one class of stock or has debt securities as well as stock, the question becomes – (1) what assets of the corporation can be used to meet the threshold requirements for special use valuation (the 50 percent and 25 percent tests) and (2) what part of the land is eligible for special use valuation?

The statute specifies that, for an interest in a partnership to be eligible, the partnership must have 15 or fewer partners or 20 percent or more of the partnership capital interest must be included in the deceased's estate. For a corporation, the requirement is 15 or fewer shareholders or 20 percent or more of the *voting* stock included in the deceased's estate. Note that neither debt securities nor preferred stock count toward the alternative for meeting this "Tier I" test based on 20 percent or more of the business included in the deceased's estate. Trusts do not face comparable requirements.

• Debt securities (notes, bonds or debentures) don't count as an interest in a closely held business for purposes of the Tier I test of basic eligibility. Moreover, it would seem that the assets *represented* by the debt securities don't count for purposes of the 50 percent and 25 percent tests (these are discussed below as the Tier II and Tier III tests).

• Any property represented by fixed principal equity securities (such as preferred stock in a corporation or a fixed principal interest in a limited partnership) *should* count toward the 50 percent or Tier II test. The big problem is that fixed principal interests may not be viewed by IRS as "at risk" which has generally been considered as essential for property meeting the qualified use test. And that test must be met for property meeting the 50 percent test. However, if all common stock is held by members of the family, the qualified use test should be met.

It has been thought that a decedent must have a "pure" equity interest in a partnership, corporation or trust for the land represented by that ownership interest to be able to affect the federal estate tax value of the ownership interest. Unless the value of an ownership interest changes as land values change, special use valuation of the land in an entity seems unlikely. However, in a 1992 private letter ruling, preferred stock in a ranch corporation was treated as an equity interest for purposes of special use valuation.

• For a decedent owning an interest in a partnership, corporation or trust, the entity will be stripped away to see what farm real and personal property is owned by the decedent indirectly. Excess cash and non-farm assets are not likely to count as farm real or personal property.

Therefore, for a decedent owning an interest in a partnership, corporation or trust, at least 50 percent of the decedent's gross estate adjusted for secured indebtedness must be made up of farm real and personal property. This is the "Tier II" test.

At least 25 percent of the decedent's gross estate adjusted for secured indebtedness must be made up of farm real property. This is the "Tier III" test.

Table 2 shows how the above points could be applied, using as an example a farm corporation with a $2,000,000 net worth which is represented by debt securities ($200,000 face value), preferred stock ($600,000 principal value) and common stock (valued at $1,200,000). The corporation owns land valued at $1,000,000, machinery and equipment valued at $200,000, livestock valued at $250,000, cash needed in the business of $50,000 and non-

62

farm assets of $500,000. The farm real and personal property represented by the $200,000 of debt securities would seem not to be eligible for the Tier I or Tier II tests. The farm real and personal property represented by the $600,000 of preferred stock may be eligible for the Tier II test. The 1992 IRS ruling noted above suggests that the $300,000 of farmland represented by the preferred stock should be eligible for special use valuation. Clearly, the farm real property represented by the common stock ($600,000 in value) would be eligible for special use valuation for any shareholder. If a shareholder died owning 40 percent of the common stock, 40 percent of the $600,000 of farm real property or $240,000 in amount would be eligible for special use valuation.

Table 2. Determination of corporation-owned land eligible for special use valuation at death of shareholder.

	Farmland	Machinery	Livestock	Cash Needed in Business	Non-Business Assets	Total Value
Common Stock	$600,000	$120,000	$150,000	$30,000	$300,000	$1,200,000
Preferred Stock	300,000	60,000	75,000	15,000	150,000	600,000
Debt Securities	100,000	20,000	25,000	5,000	50,000	200,000
Total	1,000,000	200,000	250,000	50,000	500,000	2,000,000

If special use valuation produces a value at 50 percent of fair market value, the estate of the shareholder would be reduced by $120,000. Again, it is emphasized that regulations have not yet been issued in this area but the above approach is one likely interpretation of the rules.

It is important to note, based upon the above assumptions, that heavy use of debt securities and of fixed principal equity securities (such as preferred stock) can be costly in terms of special use valuation eligibility. However, the 1992 private letter ruling permitted special use valuation for the land represented by preferred stock although how that was to be determined was unclear.

A 1989 Tax Court case indicated that, for corporate stock valued at a discount by virtue of special use valuation, a discount for minority interest and non-marketability is not also available. However, a 1995 case allowed both special use valuation and a discount for a minority interest and non-marketability where the estate was large enough to bump up against the $750,000 maximum reduction of gross estate from special use valuation. The estate involved a 26 percent interest in a large New Mexico ranch. If the estate is under the $750,000 maximum for special use valuation, it appears that an estate can choose special use valuation *or* a discount in stock value for a minority interest in the corporation (and for non-marketability of the stock) but not for both.

Until regulations become final spelling out the Internal Revenue Service view of how the material participation requirements are to be met for trusts, partnerships and corporations, it would seem wise to approach the matter with caution. An important question is whether sufficient farm management decisions or other involvement in a trust, corporation or partnership are made by the deceased or member of the deceased's family to assure that the material participation requirement is met. A similar question exists for material participation after death. For trusts, material participation may, according to regulations, be achieved by – (1) service as a trustee, (2) a contractual arrangement with the trustee to manage – or take part in managing – the real property for the trust, (3) employment by a qualified closely held business in a position requiring material participation in its activities or (4) an express provision in the trust agreement granting management rights to the beneficiaries of the trust. If serving as a co-trustee with a non-eligible individual or a bank or trust company, it would seem wise to provide clearly in a formal written arrangement that farm management decisions would rest with the decedent-to-be or a member of the family. The same degree of caution would seem wise in terms of partnership or corporation decision making until the matter is clarified.

An estate poses special problems. For purposes of material participation after death, unless a member of the family is the farm tenant, the material participation requirement may not be met unless the estate executor or administrator is an eligible material participator or retains an eligible manager. There is, of course, the grace period permitting some absence of material participation in the period after death as noted above (absence of material participation for more than three years in any eight year period after death triggers recapture).

MATERIAL PARTICIPATION FOR LEASE ARRANGE-MENTS. What constitutes "material participation?" The special use valuation statute specifies that the term is to be defined in a manner similar to the way it is defined for social security purposes. In the past, the Social Security Administration and the Internal Revenue Service have used four tests to determine material participation through physical work, management decisions or both for social security purposes. *Test No. 1* – any three (or more) of the following – (l) advance, pay or stand good for a significant part (half or more) of the direct costs of producing a crop; (2) furnish a significant part (half or more) of the tools, equipment and livestock used; (3) advise and consult with the tenant periodically; and (4) inspect production activities periodically. *Test No. 2* – regularly and frequently make decisions which significantly affect the success of the enterprise. *Test No. 3* – work at least 100 hours spread over a period of five weeks or more in activities connected with producing a crop. The work periods need not necessarily be consecutive. *Test No. 4* – do those things which, in total, show that the landlord is materially and significantly involved in production.

The special use valuation regulations suggest that Test No. 3 *may not be acceptable* and that whether someone is materially participating for purposes of special use valuation depends on the facts of each case.

Specifically, the regulations point out that –

"No single factor is determinative of the presence of material participation, but physical work and participation in management decisions are the principal factors to be considered. As a minimum, the decedent and/or a family member must regularly advise or consult with the other managing party on the operation of the business. While they need not make all final management decisions alone, the decedent and/or family members must participate in making a substantial number of these decisions. Additionally, production activities on the land should be inspected regularly by the family participant, and funds should be advanced or financial responsibility assumed for a substantial portion of the expense involved in the operation of the farm or other business in which the real property is used. In the case of a farm, the furnishing by the owner or other family members of a substantial portion of the machinery, implements, and livestock used in the production activities is an important factor to consider in finding material participation."

The last sentence, depending upon the emphasis placed upon it, could be troublesome. Read literally, it could preclude all leased land except that under livestock share leases from participating in special use valuation. In general, crop share leases involve no ownership of livestock by the landowner and little, if any, ownership of machinery by the landowner. And not all livestock share leases involve substantial ownership of machinery by the landowner.

Material participation cannot be achieved through an agent – such as a farm manager. That's because of a 1974 amendment to federal rules for determining net earnings from self-employment for social security purposes. This is discussed in Chapter 1 as the "Section 1402" rule governing the relationship of agents (such as farm managers) to property owners. Those same rules are borrowed for purposes of determining material participation for special use valuation of land. It is possible to achieve material participation *despite the presence of an agent* through direct involvement in decision making, property management and the other elements that go to make up material participation.

An important point – if the status of a family member is that of an agent, the family member characteristic prevails and the individual can be an eligible material participator.

If material participation is to be achieved under a crop share or livestock share lease, the lease should be drafted with care. Specifically, it is suggested that the lease be drawn to require involvement by the landowner – or other material participator – in decisions relating to – (1) cropping patterns and the rotation to be followed; (2) levels of fertilization and formulae of fertilizer to be applied (nitrogen, phosphorous and potash); (3) participation or non-participation in government price (income) support programs; (4) plans for chemical weed and insect control including type of chemical, rate of application and type of application (broadcast or band); (5) soil and water conservation practices to be followed; (6) scheduling of repairs to buildings, fences and tile lines; (7) decisions on use of storage facilities as between the landlord and tenant; (8) changes in basic tillage practices (such as a shift to minimum tillage); (9) varieties of seed to be purchased; (10) marketing strategies for the landlord's share of the crop and delivery responsibilities of the tenant; and (11) for livestock share leases, decisions relative to type of livestock production to be undertaken, level of production planned, nutrition and animal health plans and marketing strategies.

It is also suggested that the landowner (or other material participator) keep a daily, diary-type record of activities related to participation in the production of income under the lease.

In general, it's doubted that material participation can be achieved through a cash rent lease (except, of course, where material participation is by a farm tenant who is a member of the family). Material participation seems possible with livestock share and crop share leases if attention is given to meeting the tests for material participation. In a Tax Court case, IRS argued successfully that the management activities of a brother of an elderly landowner were insufficient for material participation. The court found that most management decisions were made by the tenants under crop share leases (with the tenants providing the machinery) with only limited involvement by the decedent's brother.

Many different types of arrangements are in common use in farm businesses. In terms of eligibility for special use valuation, lease arrangements may be evaluated in terms of whether – (1) the material participation requirement is met and (2) the qualified use test is satisfied. Keep in mind that, for landowners who are disabled or retired and receiving social security benefits, the material participation test must be met only for five or more of the last eight years before disability, retirement or death, whichever comes earlier. On those bases, it appears reasonable to classify the various arrangements in use for the period before the decedent's death as follows:

Reasonably safe:

• The decedent for at least five years before death had been renting farmland to a member of the family as farm tenant under a non-material participation lease. Because both the qualified use test and the material participation test are met by the member of the family as farm tenant, even a cash rent lease would be acceptable in the pre-death period.

• The decedent for at least five years before death had been renting farmland to an unrelated farm tenant under a material participation farm lease. Both the qualified use test and the material participation test must be met by the decedent-to-be. That would require, as a minimum for a retired landowner, a non-material participation crop share lease for the qualified use test at the time of death and for five or more of the last eight years before death. It would require a material participation crop share lease for the material participation test for five or more of the last eight years before retirement, disability or death.

• The decedent had been operating a farm involving the land in question for at least five years before death.

Less clear but still reasonably safe:

• The decedent for at least five years before death had been renting the farmland to a family owned and controlled partnership or corporation under a non-material participation share lease. Regulations haven't been published, but it's been generally assumed that a family owned and controlled partnership or corporation as a farm tenant would be treated in the same manner as a family member as tenant. Therefore, even a cash rent lease should meet the tests.

• The decedent for at least five years before death had been renting farmland to a member of the family under a non-material participation crop share (or cash) lease with the member of the family subleasing the land to an unrelated farm tenant under a material participation farm lease (the facts should support a bona fide material participation arrangement or it may be disregarded).

• A family owned and controlled partnership or corporation owns the land and for a least five years before the decedent's death had been renting the land to a member of the family under a crop share farm lease (the land should be eligible for special use valuation to the extent of the decedent's proportionate ownership of an equity interest in the partnership or corporation). With a cash rent lease, there is a question whether the partnership or corporation is engaged in a trade or business.

• A family owned and controlled partnership or corporation owns the land and for at least five years before the decedent's death had been renting the land to an unrelated farm tenant under a material participation farm lease (the land should be eligible for special use valuation to the extent of the decedent's proportionate ownership of an equity interest in the partnership or corporation).

• A family owned and controlled partnership or corporation owns the land and for at least five years before the decedent's death had been carrying on a farm business involving the land in question (the land should be eligible for special use valuation to the extent of the decedent's proportionate ownership of an equity interest in the partnership or corporation).

Even less clear (wait for regulations or rulings):

• A partnership or corporation, only partly owned and controlled by family members, owns the land and for at least five years before the decedent's death had been renting the land to a family member as farm tenant under a non-material participation farm lease.

Even less clear than that (could eventually be viewed as eligible arrangements but don't get hopes up):

• A partnership or corporation, only partly owned and controlled by family members, owns the land and for at least five years before the decedent's death had been renting the land to an unrelated farm tenant under a material participation farm lease.

• A partnership or corporation, only partly owned and controlled by family members, owns the land and for at least five years before the decedent's death had been carrying on a farm business involving the land in question.

Special Use Value Lien. A special lien is imposed on the land subject to special use valuation. The lien continues until the qualified heir dies, the tax benefit is recaptured or the recapture period has elapsed. The term of the lien was 15 years after death until it was changed in 1981 to 10 years for deaths after 1981. Once filed, the lien takes priority over subsequent obligations such as a mortgage entered into some time after death. But the lien is subordinate to "super priority" obligations – real property taxes and special assessments, mechanic's liens for property repair or improvement, obligations involving construction or improvement of the property and farm production credit for crops and livestock. For other loans, the Department of the Treasury may be willing to subordinate the tax lien if sufficient collateral exists to protect adequately the Treasury's interest.

Making the Election. To take advantage of special use valuation, a statement must be attached to a federal estate tax return. Originally, the election had to be filed within nine months after death or within an extension of time granted for filing. In 1981, however, an amendment was adopted removing the bar for late filing for deaths after 1981. The statement must include an agreement signed by all parties with an interest in the property consenting to personal liability for any additional estate tax on recapture. For minors and those who are incompetent, a representative should be appointed by the local court to sign the agreement.

The statement of special use value election must contain 14 items of information specified in the regulations.

If some items were omitted from the special use valuation election, but substantially all of the information required was submitted, the additional items can be provided within 90 days after the information is requested by the Internal Revenue Service. Some items cannot be submitted late including the notice of election or a signed recapture agreement.

A *protective* election may be made with a timely filed federal estate tax return, pending final determination of property values and eligibility to elect special use valuation. If a protective election is filed, and circumstances later develop – perhaps after audit of the federal estate tax return – that would make special use valuation desirable (or possible), the election can be finalized. Otherwise, a late election may not be permitted without IRS approval. In late 1989 IRS took the position in a private letter ruling that a protective election is available only in two circumstances – (1) when the taxpayer does not have sufficient information at the due date of the federal estate tax return to determine the availability and consequences of the election, or (2) when the estate, after a good faith effort at valuing the assets, encounters a deficiency because of changes in the value of assets as the result of an IRS examination of the federal estate tax return. The restrictive IRS position has been criticized.

One final point on special use value: it only applies to valuation for federal estate tax purposes. It's not applicable to gift transactions or to dispositions by sale. And in most states, it's not applicable for state inheritance or state estate tax purposes. However a few states provide rules similar to special use valuation for state death tax purposes.

GIFTS WITHIN THREE YEARS OF DEATH. Depending upon the circumstances and the date of death, the value of property transferred by gift within three years of death has run the risk of being included in the gross estate and subjected to federal estate tax. The basic idea behind this rule is that individuals should not be able to avoid the tax by making gifts of their property to others shortly before death.

A major change in the rules governing gifts made within three years of death was made in 1981. Under the 1981 amendments, gifts of property within three years of death (with four exceptions) are not included in the estates of those dying after 1981. The net effect of the change is to exclude from taxation any increase in value after the date of the gift; the value at the date of the gift is already taken into account in reducing the unified credit or incurring a gift tax.

The 1981 change does not affect transfers of property included in the decedent's gross estate because – (1) the decedent retained a life estate in the property, (2) the transfer is to take effect at death, (3) the transfer is revocable, or (4) the transfer involves life insurance policies. As a practical matter, no part of life insurance proceeds from policies passing by gift from the insured within three years of the insured's death is shielded from federal estate tax. Thus, if a husband takes out a policy of life insurance on his life, promptly transfers the policy to his wife and dies a month later, the proceeds would be includible in the husband's estate. Also, it appears that approximately the cash value of policies on the life of another that are transferred within three years of the transferor's death are included in the transferor's gross estate.

If the husband makes a cash gift of $10,000 to his wife (no gift tax return required), she happens to use the cash to acquire a policy on his life and he dies shortly thereafter, the rule as to gifts of cash should apply, not the exception for gifts of life insurance, so the policy proceeds should not be included in the husband's gross estate. That's under the assumption that the gift of cash was not a "transfer with respect to a life insurance policy." That's the language used in a 1978 amendment. Suggestion – to be on the safe side, the gift of cash should not be the same amount as needed for the insurance premium payment and should not be given immediately prior to when the premium is due.

If the wife takes out the policy on the husband's life but he supplies funds for the premium payment each year on the policy, the question of whether the policy premiums should be includible in the husband's gross estate depends upon whether supplying funds for premium payment is a "transfer with respect to a life insurance policy." Again, to be on the safe side, be sure the gifts of cash exceed substantially the amounts required each year for premium payments and aren't otherwise linked to the policy.

Where possible, avoid having new policies taken out by the insured with transfer soon thereafter to a new owner. It is generally better to have the new owner take out the policy initially.

With greater use of the revocable living trust in recent years has come the question of whether gifts from the trust to another come within the three year rule. A few cases and several IRS rulings have subjected distributions from the trust to taxation at death where the trustee was directed by the person who set up the trust, the grantor, to make the gifts and the gifts occurred within three years of death. The safe approach is to use a two-step procedure: (1) a distribution is requested from the trust to the grantor and (2) the gift is made by the grantor.

For purposes of determining eligibility for redemptions of stock to pay death taxes and estate settlement costs, special use valuation of land and installment payment of federal estate tax, property transfers by gift within three years of death are included in the gross estate for the limited purpose of determining whether those requirements are met.

LIFE INSURANCE. The general rule is that life insurance proceeds are included in the gross estate if payable to the estate, or if payable to others from policies in which the decedent retained "incidents of ownership." These include the right to

73

change beneficiaries, borrow on the policy, or surrender or cancel the policy. Thus, to avoid federal estate tax consequences at death, the insured must not be the owner and the insured's estate must not be the beneficiary.

If a wife owns a policy on her husband's life, and is also named as the beneficiary, the proceeds would not be taxable upon the husband's death if she had held the policy for more than three years before death. Of course, if the wife died first, the approximate cash value would be included in her estate. But wives typically have smaller estates than husbands, so adding the cash value to her estate may not increase the tax greatly. Another problem, if the wife dies first, is what becomes of policy ownership. If it passes to the husband, a situation is created that could result in taxability of the policy proceeds at his death later for federal estate tax purposes.

Placing ownership of an insurance policy in the spouse's name may create a gift to the spouse. However, the 100 percent federal gift tax marital deduction covers the amount of any gift to the spouse for federal gift tax purposes. If a wife is named as the owner of a new policy on the husband's life, with the husband paying the premiums, the only gift would be the amount of insurance premiums paid by the husband. For old policies transferred to the wife, a gift is incurred at the time of the transfer based upon roughly the cash value of the policy. Later premium payments by the husband would also be gifts.

For planning purposes, it is generally advisable for the insured not to pay policy premiums after transfer of the policy to another. The new owner, for example, could pay the premiums from his or her own funds, from borrowing on the policy (if it is a whole life policy), or from income from a separate gift of income producing property. Another possibility would be for the insured to prepay three years' premiums before transfer of the policy with the insured making annual prepayments thereafter. Under this method, the premiums would be paid with money given away more than three years before, assuming the insured lived more than three years after the transfer.

JOINT TENANCY. Under the "consideration furnished" rule, property is fully includible in the gross estate, except to the extent that the surviving joint tenant could prove that he or she provided part of the consideration when the property was acquired or mortgage paid off. For deaths after 1981, only half the value of joint tenancy property owned by a husband and wife is taxed for federal estate tax purposes at the death of the first joint tenant to die. This is the "fractional share" rule.

Where the fractional share rule does not apply, the consideration furnished rule provides the guidance for taxing joint tenancy or tenancy by the entirety property at death.

Both the "consideration furnished" rule and the "fractional share" rule are discussed in Chapter 2. A case is also discussed in Chapter 2 permitting the consideration furnished rule to be applied to husband-wife joint tenancies (for greater advantage from the rule giving property a new income tax basis at death) for deaths after 1981.

TRANSFERS WITH RETAINED POWERS. Property transferred during life over which the decedent retained an interest is also subject to the federal estate tax. If property is transferred with strings attached, the full value of the property is likely to be included in the gross estate.

For example, if a parent transfers a farm to a child but retains the right to income for life, the entire value of the farm is taxable in the estate of the parent. The retained life estate, or right to income for life, is generally obvious. The retention of other powers, rights or controls over transferred property may be less obvious but no less devastating tax-wise.

In one case, the transfer of a farm from husband to wife was held to be a transfer with a retained life estate – making the value of the farm taxable in the husband's estate – where he continued to maintain effective control over farm income. Therefore, in situations where the wife owns land (in her name alone or in co-ownership), it may be wise to develop a formal lease that involves rental payments to the wife. Whether the lease should be cash or crop share and whether the wife should be a "material participator" under the lease (creating self-employment income or investment income) or involved sufficiently for "active management" depends, in addition to non-tax factors, upon her willingness to pay social security tax on self-employment income, the effect of such income on her social security benefits in retirement, plans for using installment payment of federal estate tax at her death and eligibility for special use valuation of the land.

In recent years, several transfers of residences from husband to wife ownership have been challenged by the Internal Revenue Service (most unsuccessfully) on the ground of retained interest by the husband where he continued to live in his wife's house until his death. In general, if the husband had not insisted on an agreement assuring the husband's occupancy of the residence, the value of the residence has not been included in his gross estate. IRS has been more successful in challenging transfers of residences to children with the parent retaining the right of occupancy until death. To minimize challenge, a parent-child transfer should assure control and enjoyment to the child after the transfer. If the residence is occupied by the parent, the arrangement should match other lease arrangements in the community with rental actually paid.

Sale of a residence to the children (or a trust for the children) with a lease back to the parents and with continued occupancy by the transferor was ineffective in a 1992 case in keeping the residence out of the gross estate. In that case, the evidence indicated there was no intent that the obligation resulting from the sale would ever be paid.

Transfers of farms by gift from parents to children are subject to similar rules if rented back to the parents. The lease should be comparable to other lease arrangements in the community. If the lease requires less or more of the parents than is typical in the community, the possibility for challenge on the grounds of a retained income interest by the parents becomes much higher.

The Tax Reform Act of 1976 added a new rule to the "retained powers" concept. The value of corporate stock transferred after June 22, 1976, over which voting rights were retained, is included in the gross estate. That provision was clarified in the Revenue Act of 1978 to provide that it only applied to transfers of stock in controlled corporations in which the decedent and members of the family owned 20 percent or more of the corporation. A ruling in 1981 indicated that stock in a family corporation passed by a parent to children as a gift will not be included in the parent's estate if the parent did not retain the right to vote the transferred stock.

Estate freezes. The Revenue Act of 1987 added "estate freezes" to the list of property transfers subject to inclusion in the gross estate under the retained power rule. With estate freezes, property or an interest in a business is transferred with retention of an interest that is fixed or frozen in value. Often, the rest of the ownership interest – which can fluctuate in value – was held by a family member.

EXAMPLE: A family held farm corporation is set up by the parents with common stock and preferred stock. The parents retain the preferred stock (which is fixed in value no matter what happens to asset values) and give the common stock (which has little value) to the children. The retention of the preferred stock would activate the freeze rules and, under the 1987 legislation, the common stock transferred to the children would be pulled back into the parents' estates.

However, the "freeze" rules were repealed in 1990 retroactive to the time of enactment and were replaced by a set of rules governing the valuation of transferred interests subject to a valuation "freeze" for federal gift tax purposes. The 1990 legislation is discussed in Chapter 6.

POWERS OF APPOINTMENT. Occasionally, an individual is given the power to direct the distribution of property that does not otherwise belong to him or her. This kind of power is called a "power of appointment." If a decedent had a general power of

77

appointment which could be exercised in favor of the decedent, the decedent's estate, the creditors of the decedent or the creditors of the decedent's estate, property subject to the power of appointment would be taxable in the decedent's estate. Property subject to a special power of appointment is not taxable in the estate of the holder of the power. A special power of appointment is one not exercisable in favor of the decedent, the decedent's estate, the creditors of the decedent or the creditors of the decedent's estate. But it is exercisable in favor of anyone else.

A power to consume property for the benefit of a decedent which is limited by an ascertainable standard (relating to health, education, support or maintenance) is not considered a general power of appointment. Such powers are used in many trusts.

Allowable deductions

Once the amount of the gross estate is determined, attention shifts to allowable deductions. These deductions are subtracted from the gross estate.

A deduction may be claimed for debts of the decedent, funeral costs and losses from fire, storm or other casualty or theft during settlement of the estate that are not compensated by insurance or otherwise. Unless claimed as deductions for income tax purposes (which is optional), the costs of administering the estate, losses and medical expenses may also be deducted from the gross estate. It may be possible to deduct interest on deferred federal estate tax as an expense of estate administration if such a deduction is allowed under state law. More on this point in Chapter 5.

In general, expenses of administering the estate are deductible if allowable under state law and represent reasonable and necessary administrative expenses. Expenses incurred primarily to benefit the beneficiaries of the estate, rather than the estate itself, may not be deductible. Also, expenses may be disallowed unless based on adequate records. Operating expenses of the decedent's business after death are not allowable administrative expenses.

Costs incurred for the decedent's pets may be disallowed

A deduction may be claimed for taxes paid by the estate including income taxes on income received by the decedent and included in the decedent's final income tax return. A 1992 ruling permitted an income tax deduction for income tax paid because the estate representative elected to include accrued interest on government bonds in the decedent's final income tax return.

If an income tax deduction is claimed for expenses of estate administration, the estate must file a statement with the estate's income tax return showing that the items have not been allowed for federal estate tax purposes.

The rule barring the same deduction for costs on both the estate tax return and for income tax purposes does not apply to deductions for interest, taxes, business expenses and other deductible amounts accrued at the decedent's death. The IRS has taken the position that the portion of medical expenses not deductible for income tax purposes is not deductible from the gross estate, either.

The funeral expense deduction must be reduced by the amount of Veteran's Administration death benefits and social security death benefits paid other than to a surviving spouse.

The deduction for the deceased's debts is allowed if the claims represent bona fide obligations with economic substance. Promissory notes given by the decedent-to-be to relatives before death are not deductible where no loan is involved. This has been the outcome even where interest was paid on the "obligation" and even where a mortgage had been executed to secure the repayment of the "loan."

The amounts of mortgages or other claims against property included in the gross estate are deductible. In one 1995 farm estate in the Midwest, the husband had purchased $225,000 of new machinery and financed the purchase with a mortgage on the land owned in joint tenancy with his wife. At his death a few weeks later, quite unexpectedly, one-half the value of the joint tenancy land was included in his estate for federal tax purposes.

This was consistent with the "fractional share" rule for joint tenancies owned by spouses. The problem was that only one-half of the mortgage was deductible, also. The new machinery, of course, was fully includible in the husband's estate. An important point: if the other one-half of the mortgage amount had been a personal obligation of the husband, which it was, that half could also be deducted as an obligation of the decedent. This suggests careful attention to how purchases are made and financed.

For expenses relating to sale of property, if claimed for federal estate tax purposes, the expenses may not be used to offset gain on sale, also.

The marital deduction

Probably the greatest federal estate tax savings device has been the marital deduction. Since 1948, individuals have been eligible for tax saving opportunities (linked to property passing to the surviving spouse) that were previously available only in community property states.

In brief, the marital deduction is a deduction from the adjusted gross estate for property passing to the surviving spouse. Since the marital deduction applies only to property passing to a surviving husband or wife, it is not available in the estate of a widow, widower or an unmarried person.

Through 1976, the amount of the marital deduction was limited to the lesser of (1) 50 percent of the adjusted gross estate, or (2) the amount of property passing to the surviving spouse and qualifying for the marital deduction. For deaths after 1976 and through 1981, the maximum marital deduction was increased to the *greater* of $250,000 or 50 percent of the adjusted gross estate. For estates above the $500,000 level, the former 50 percent rule continued to be the upper limit on the marital deduction. Of course, the 1976 rule was also subject to the further limitation that the marital deduction could not exceed the amount of property passing to the surviving spouse and qualifying for the marital deduction.

Effective in 1982, the marital deduction was increased to 100 percent of the value of qualifying property interests passing to a surviving spouse.

In general, to qualify for the federal estate tax marital deduction, property interests must not be non-deductible "terminable" interests. Eligible property may pass to the spouse by will, as insurance proceeds, by joint tenancy survivorship, or under state law of property distribution applicable if an individual dies without a will.

Property passing outright to the spouse in absolute ownership qualifies for the marital deduction. Before 1982, an ordinary life estate to the spouse would not qualify. At a minimum, the surviving spouse had to be given at least a life estate plus a general power of appointment for the marital deduction to be available. That meant the *surviving* spouse had ultimate control over the dispositions of the property, not the property-owning spouse. Giving the surviving spouse control over the disposition of the property often wasn't a major issue for couples whose marriages remained intact. The typical result was that the surviving spouse would leave the property to their children.

But with more and more multiple marriages, the question of who had ultimate control over the property assumed much greater importance. The second or third spouse's list of beneficiaries rarely would include the children of the first marriage. And so property owners began to question whether to use a marital deduction and risk losing control over the ultimate distribution of the property. In 1981, Congress provided a solution.

The 1981 amendments authorizing a 100 percent marital deduction for property passing to a spouse for deaths after 1981 permit an executor to elect to treat life estates passing to the surviving spouse as qualified terminable interests (sometimes referred to as QTIP arrangements for "qualified terminable interest property"). The property-owning spouse could leave the property (or some of it) to the current spouse for life and then designate who would ultimately receive the property (the remainder interest). Usually, the remainder interest is set to pass to the children of the first marriage or a favorite charity. The surviving spouse has the income but not the power to dispose of the property.

Property under a QTIP arrangement is eligible for the federal estate tax marital deduction if the surviving spouse is entitled to all of the income from the property and there isn't a right or power held by anyone else that could diminish the surviving spouse's interest in the property. If the election is made, the entire value of the property interest is included in the estate of the surviving spouse at the surviving spouse's death. It is possible for the spouse's estate to seek reimbursement for the part of the federal estate tax attributable to the remainder interest from the holder of the remainder interest. Moreover, the full amount of the property value is subject to federal gift tax if given away during life. In a manner parallel to the treatment at death for federal estate tax purposes, reimbursement can be sought for the portion of federal gift tax attributable to the remainder interest from the holder of the remainder interest. A major reason for electing to treat life estates as eligible for the marital deduction is for the property-owning spouse to be able to exercise greater control over the ultimate disposition of the property.

The rules authorizing a 100 percent marital deduction for deaths after 1981 have a transitional provision for wills and trusts containing a formula marital deduction clause expressly providing that the surviving spouse is to receive the "maximum" marital deduction. Under the transitional rule, "maximum" means maximum under the pre-1982 law and not maximum under the law applicable to deaths after 1981 if –

• The marital deduction clause was not amended after 30 days following the date the 1981 legislation became law,

• The decedent dies after 1981, and

• The state does not move to define "maximum" by statute as maximum under the new law.

Thus, if a will *does* come under the transitional rule – because it refers expressly to a maximum marital deduction – the will should be changed if a greater (or lesser) marital deduction is desired. For wills that *don't* come under the transitional rule, and many do not for technical reasons, the will should be reviewed and amended if the marital deduction clause will produce an unsatisfactory result in terms of size of marital deduction.

Another point: the 1981 tax law in creating the 100 percent federal estate tax marital deduction, repealed the definition of "adjusted gross estate." That term is used in many, many wills as part of the marital deduction clause. Unless clearly under the transitional rule, all such wills should be reviewed and revised. If the term "adjusted gross estate" is used in the revised will, the term should be defined in the will itself unless the term "adjusted gross estate" is defined under state law as it is in Iowa.

The marital deduction is reduced by the amount of death taxes apportioned to the marital deduction share under local law. To preserve the maximum marital deduction, wills often specify that death taxes are to be paid from other property of the decedent.

The maximum marital deduction in a community property state has been subject to a special limitation. The marital deduction has been limited essentially to one-half of the decedent's separate property minus its share of debts and expenses. However, the 1976 tax legislation permitted a partial marital deduction from community property to maintain parity of treatment with other states where the larger marital deduction – up to $250,000 on estates under $500,000 – was available. The 100 percent marital deduction is effective in community property states also, commencing with deaths in 1982.

Artful use of the marital deduction requires a look at the estates of both spouses and at the probabilities of order of death of the spouses. Especially for estates under $600,000, the optimal strategy may be to assure full use of the decedent's unified credit and not claim a maximum marital deduction. This approach may reduce the tax bill at the death of the surviving spouse.

Even for those with estates above $600,000, if it's desired to minimize death tax at the deaths of both spouses, it may be preferable to claim less than the maximum allowable marital deduction. For a husband and wife with estates that are perfectly balanced in size, up to $600,000 each could pass free of federal estate tax with no marital deduction claimed. Up to $1,200,000 in family wealth could pass at the death of the first of a couple to die if one half or $600,000 were to qualify for the marital deduction and up to $600,000 could pass free of federal estate tax at the death of the survivor. This is explained in Chapter 4.

Optimal use of the marital deduction may require property shifts by gift between the husband and wife. The federal gift tax aspects of that type of move are discussed in Chapter 6.

Charitable deduction

Amounts may be deducted from the portion of the gross estate remaining (after subtracting the marital deduction) for transfers by the decedent to qualified charities. The charitable deduction must be reduced by the amount of death taxes apportioned to the property passing to the charity under local law. That's why it may be wise to specify by will that death taxes be paid from other property if it's desired for the charitable transfer to be fully deductible.

Not all charities are qualified in the sense that transfers at death are deductible for federal estate tax purposes. Bequests to governmental units and churches qualify. And transfers to organizations holding an "exemption letter" from the Internal Revenue Service under Section 501(c)(3) of the Internal Revenue Code meet the test. But a bequest to a poverty line nephew wouldn't be deductible even though he looks like a charitable case.

The estate tax charitable deduction is not limited in amount or percentage of the estate.

With two exceptions, the value of a remainder interest or other limited interest in property transferred to even a qualified charity may not be allowed as a federal estate tax deduction. The bar against deductibility of a limited interest passing to charity applies if there is a non-charitable income beneficiary unless the transfer of the limited interest is in trust and meets the requirements to be a charitable remainder annuity trust, unitrust or pooled income fund.

EXAMPLE: A husband leaves corporate securities to his wife for her life with the securities to pass to their church at her death. There would be no federal estate tax deduction in his estate for the value of the remainder interest passing to the church at his death unless the securities were left in one of the varieties of trust mentioned above.

But there are two exceptions to that general rule. A federal estate tax charitable deduction may be claimed for the value of a remainder interest in a farm or personal residence passing to charity. The requirements for an annuity trust, unitrust or pooled income fund do not apply. For farms and residences, the transaction can be relatively simple. By deed during life or in the will, the property can be left to someone for life with the remainder to a charity.

Thus, in the preceding example, it would be possible for the husband to leave a farm to his wife for her life with the farm passing to their church at her death. And his estate would be entitled to a federal estate tax charitable deduction for the value of the remainder interest. The amount of the deduction would depend, of course, on the wife's life expectancy. The older the wife, the smaller the value of her life estate and the larger the charitable deduction.

A farm, for this purpose, includes the improvements and is defined as "any land used by the decedent or his tenant for the production of crops, fruits, or other agricultural products or for the sustenance of livestock."

These rules on deductibility of limited interests apply also for federal income tax and federal gift tax purposes. Thus, a farm could be left by a husband by deed during life to a charity with a life estate to his wife. The value of the remainder interest could be claimed as an income tax deduction within allowable limits for amounts passing to charitable recipients. The value of the remainder interest must be adjusted for depreciation or depletion on the property involved for purposes of income tax deductibility.

A relatively recent development, the charitable lead trust, can be used to give an income interest to a designated charity for a period of years with ownership ultimately passing back to the family. The income interest to the charity should be eligible for a tax deduction which reduces the value of the remainder interest taxed to the family.

More on charitable giving in Chapter 13.

Calculating the tax

Several changes were made in federal estate tax calculations by the Tax Reform Act of 1976. That legislation eliminated the $60,000 exemption; introduced the concept of a unified credit against the calculated tax as a replacement for the exemption; shifted the federal estate and gift tax to a unified, single rate schedule; and made changes in how the federal estate tax could be paid. Otherwise the former calculation procedures were largely retained under the 1976 law.

Changes in 1981 boosted the size of the unified credit over a six year period and created 100 percent federal gift and estate tax marital deductions but otherwise did not change significantly the procedure for calculating the federal estate tax.

The taxable estate is determined by subtracting from the decedent's gross estate, costs of estate administration, allowable losses, the marital deduction and charitable deduction.

Then, in a calculation designed to take into account the fact that part or all of the unified credit may have been used to cover gifts during life, "adjusted taxable gifts" made since 1976 are added to the taxable estate. The term "adjusted taxable gifts" means gifts after 1976 that were not covered by the federal gift tax annual exclusion, the federal gift tax marital deduction and the federal gift tax charitable deduction.

Thus, taxable gifts during life are brought back into the taxable estate at death. And federal gift tax paid on those gifts – if any – is subtracted from the calculated federal estate tax. This is all part of the "unification" of the federal estate and federal gift tax. The basic idea is to treat gifts during life and property passing at death under equivalent rules. More on this in later paragraphs.

The resulting taxable estate is used to calculate the "tentative tax." Starting in 1977, one single, unified rate schedule has been used for federal estate tax and for federal gift tax. The rates rise as the taxable estate increases (See Appendix A). The tax is imposed at its lowest level – 18 percent – on taxable transfers of $10,000 or less. The rate rises sharply and reaches the 30 percent bracket at the $100,000 level. Because of larger brackets in the tax rate schedule above that level, the tax rate begins to level off with taxable transfers between $750,000 and $1,000,000 subject to tax at the 39 percent rate. The maximum rate is 55 percent and applies to taxable estates over $3 million.

The unified credit (for both federal estate tax and federal gift tax) phased in over a six year period (1982 through 1987) based on the date of death of the decedent (or date of gift) as follows –

	Credit	Equivalent Deduction
1981	$ 47,000	175,625
1982	62,800	225,000
1983	79,300	275,000
1984	96,300	325,000
1985	121,800	400,000
1986	155,800	500,000
1987 and later	192,800	600,000

Legislation pending in Congress in early 1996 would increase the $600,000 figure to $750,000 over a period of several years.

The unified credit available at death may be reduced below the levels indicated. The credit must be reduced by 20 percent of the amount allowed as a federal gift tax lifetime exemption for gifts after September 8, 1976, and before January 1, 1977. The unified credit against the calculated "tentative tax" from the rate table essentially eliminates the lower part of the tax table. For 1987 and later years, the credit of $192,800 means that the tax imposed – above the credit – starts in the 37 percent tax bracket.

Legislation enacted in 1987 phases out the benefit of the unified federal gift and estate tax credit and graduated tax rates for transfers exceeding $10 million but less than $21,040,000 for decedents dying after 1987. The phase-out is accomplished by levying an additional 5 percent tax on those transfers.

Once the tentative federal estate tax has been computed, certain credits may be available to reduce the tax. The unified credit is available, as noted above. Also, a credit is allowed for part or all of the state death tax paid. That credit is figured on a formula using the "adjusted taxable estate" for federal estate tax purposes. The adjusted taxable estate is the taxable estate less $60,000. That's done to preserve the effects of the credit as it operated before the $60,000 estate tax personal exemption was eliminated at the end of 1976. The rate table for the credit appears in Appendix B.

A credit is also allowed for federal estate tax paid if the property had passed through another estate during the 10 years before or within two years after the death of a decedent whose estate is claiming the credit. This credit varies with the number of years separating the deaths. If the present decedent died within two years of the prior decedent who had owned the property, the credit is 100 percent. For each additional two years between deaths, the credit is 20 percent less, i.e. 3 or 4 years apart, 80 percent; 5 or 6 years, 60 percent; 7 or 8 years, 40 percent; and, if 9 or 10 years apart, the credit is 20 percent. Beyond 10 years, no credit is allowed.

A credit is permitted for death taxes, if any, paid to a foreign government.

Illustrative calculation

The calculation procedure explained in the preceding paragraphs can be illustrated with an example.

Assume a husband dies in 1996 with a gross estate of $515,000. Allowable deductions total $15,000. One-half of the adjusted gross estate is left to the surviving spouse. In 1977, the decedent had made taxable gifts of $20,000.

Here's how the calculations would look –

Gross estate		$515,000
Deductions	15,000	
Marital deduction	250,000	
Total deductions	$265,000	(265,000)
		250,000
Adjusted taxable gifts		20,000
Taxable estate	270,000	270,000
Tentative tax (See Appendix A)	77,600	
Unified credit	192,800	
Federal gift tax due	-0-	

Thus, the allowable estate settlement costs, the marital deduction and the unified credit reduce the tax bill to zero. In fact, the estate could have been considerably larger and still no federal estate tax would have been due. If necessary, a larger marital deduction could have been claimed at the husband's death (up to 100 percent of the property passing to the surviving spouse) although that might have increased the tax at the surviving spouse's death.

The credit of $192,800 is equivalent to an exemption of $600,000, for someone with a taxable estate in that range.

Table 3 shows calculations for five estates of different sizes, again assuming the maximum marital deduction claimed.

The big tax bite nearly always comes at the death of the surviving spouse. There's no marital deduction that time around unless the surviving spouse had remarried. (As some have observed, this may provide a good rationalization for a second marriage – it saves tax!)

Table 3. Federal estate tax calculations for death of property-owning spouse in 1996, leaving all to surviving spouse outright.

	A	B	C	D	E
Gross estate	$200,000	$300,000	$400,000	$500,000	$1,000,000
Deductions	10,000	15,000	20,000	25,000	50,000
Marital deduction	190,000	285,000	380,000	475,000	950,000
Total deductions	200,000	300,000	400,000	500,000	1,000,000
Taxable estate	-0-	-0-	-0-	-0-	-0-
Tentative tax	-0-	-0-	-0-	-0-	-0-
Unified credit	192,800	192,800	192,800	192,800	192,800
Credit for state death tax	-0-	-0-	-0-	-0-	-0-
Federal estate tax due	-0-	-0-	-0-	-0-	-0-

Table 4 shows the results of the death of the surviving spouse in 2005 for the estates listed in Table 3. In all of these calculations, it is assumed that assets increase in value by 8 percent per year and that deductions at death for debts and estate settlement costs (other than death taxes) are 5 percent of the gross estate – that may be wide of the mark for a specific estate of that size.

With these points in mind, examine Table 4 and compare with the tax due at the death of the first spouse to die. Note that the estate of the surviving spouse is reduced by the amount of estate settlement costs and federal estate tax due. These computations do not include state inheritance tax or state estate tax figures since those vary by state.

Note that, for a $400,000 estate, there was no federal estate tax at the death of the property-owning spouse in 1996 but, under the assumptions stated above, there would be federal estate tax liability of $25,956 at death of the surviving spouse in 2006. For the $1,000,000 estate, death in 1996 resulted in no federal estate tax but death of the surviving spouse 10 years later would mean federal estate tax liability of $468,906 under these assumptions.

Table 4. Federal estate tax calculations for death of surviving spouse in 2006.

	A	**B**	**C**	**D**	**E**
Gross estate	$379,791	$569,687	$759,582	$1,025,488	$2,050,978
Deductions	18,990	28,484	37,979	51,274	102,549
Marital deduction	- 0 -	- 0 -	- 0 -	- 0 -	- 0 -
Total deductions	18,990	28,484	37,979	51,274	102,549
Taxable estate	360,801	541,203	721,603	974,214	1,948,429
Tentative tax	108,472	171,045	237,793	335,743	757,593
Unified credit	192,800	192,800	192,800	192,800	192,800
	- 0 -	- 0 -	44,993	142,943	564,793
Credit for state death tax	- 0 -	- 0 -	19,037	31,756	95,887
Federal estate tax due	- 0 -	- 0 -	25,956	111,187	468,906

These calculations suggest four rules of thumb:

Unless the gross estate exceeds $600,000 (for death in 1996 or later), the federal estate tax should be of little or no concern. Keep in mind that if assets increase in value, or the estate grows through saving, gifts or inheritances, even an estate of modest size can move into tax territory rather quickly.

• If full advantage is taken of the marital deduction (which may or may not be wise tax planning), there should be no federal estate tax due at the death of the first to die.

• The greatest federal estate tax liability nearly always comes at the death of the surviving spouse. The death tax saving aspects of estate planning tend to focus, therefore, on the possibilities for death tax saving at the death of the surviving spouse.

• For greatest tax saving, it may be wise to make full use of the unified credit at the death of the first of the couple to die, reducing the marital deduction accordingly. This could soften the tax burden at the death of the surviving spouse later. Tax savings from such a move would be possible in examples C, D and E.

Making full use of the unified credit

For those with assets of more than $600,000, death tax savings can be substantial if full advantage is taken of the credits available (especially the unified credit) in the estate of the first spouse to die with the marital deduction adjusted accordingly.

EXAMPLE: Assume the husband's gross estate totals $400,000; he dies first and leaves the property to the surviving spouse outright as shown in Table 5.

It's obvious that full advantage is not taken of the $192,800 unified credit in the husband's estate.

By limiting the marital deduction at the first death, death taxes can be saved in the surviving spouse's estate, as shown in Table 6.

In addition to saving $38,377 in federal estate tax, the estates are structured to accommodate a substantial increase in size of the wife's estate beyond the assumed inflation rate of 8 percent for 10 years *before it would become subject to federal estate tax.* This feature affords substantial protection against effects of inflation. Note that even though the size of the marital deduction is reduced, the surviving spouse is still assured of all the income from the entire estate.

The major death tax saving approaches – referred to in the following chapter as Model I, Model II and Modified Model II, involve careful consideration of how the property is owned as between the spouses and the best use of the marital deduction.

Table 5. Death of property-owning spouse in 1996, with full marital deduction claimed, with death of surviving spouse 10 years later.

	Estate of Property Owning Spouse	Estate of Surviving Spouse
Gross estate	$400,000	$799,560
Deductions	20,000	39,978
Marital deduction	380,000	- 0 -
Total deductions	400,000	39,978
Taxable estate	- 0 -	759,582
Tentative tax	- 0 -	252,037
Unified credit	192,800	192,800
Federal estate tax	- 0 -	59,237
Credit for state death tax	- 0 -	20,860
Federal estate tax due	- 0 -	38,377

Table 6. Death of property-owning spouse in 1996, with partial marital deduction and full use of credits, with death of surviving spouse 10 years later.

	Estate of Property Owning Spouse	Estate of Surviving Spouse
Gross estate	$400,000	$118,741
Deductions	20,000	5,937
Marital deduction	55,000	- 0 -
Total deductions	75,000	5,937
Taxable estate	325,000	112,804
Tentative tax	192,800	27,641
Unified credit	192,800	192,800
Federal estate tax	- 0 -	- 0 -
Credit for state death tax	- 0 -	- 0 -
Federal estate tax due	- 0 -	- 0 -
Tax saving by limiting marital deduction		$ 38,377

93

Generation skipping transfer tax

Since 1976, generation skipping transfers have been subject to some form of additional tax. In 1986, the original provision was repealed and the present generation skipping transfer tax (GSTT) was enacted.

In a typical generation skipping transfer, a grandparent transfers property at death to a child for life with the remainder interest to a grandchild. A major advantage of such an arrangement, before the advent of the generation skipping tax, was that the property involved would be subject to federal estate tax in the grandparent's estate, but would not be taxed again until the death of the grandchild. Even though the child had the income from the property for the child's life, no part of the property value would be taxed in the child's estate.

Generation skipping transfers are a way to keep certain assets (such as farmland) in the family. Some view it as a way to discourage irresponsible sale of family assets and consumption of the proceeds.

The generation skipping transfer tax (GSTT) was designed to levy a tax on such generation skipping transfers. The tax is imposed at a flat rate equal to the maximum federal estate and gift tax rate.

Transfers subject to the tax. The GSTT reaches three types of transfers – (1) direct skips, (2) taxable terminations and (3) taxable distributions.

• A direct skip is a transfer to a skip person. A skip person is an individual at least two generations after the individual making the transfer or a trust in which all beneficiaries are two generations after the individual creating the trust. Any lifetime transfer exempt from federal gift tax because of the federal gift tax annual exclusion or the exclusion for tuition or medical payments is not a direct skip subject to tax. Moreover, all direct skips to a grandchild when the child is not living are exempt.

• A taxable termination is a transfer of an interest in trust from the trust to a skip person. For example, in a trust providing that income be paid to a child for life, remainder to a grandchild, the child's death would result in a taxable termination.

• A taxable distribution is a distribution from a trust to a skip person. For example, in a trust with a power in the trustee to distribute income or principal to children or grandchildren, any distribution to a grandchild is a taxable distribution.

Assigning individuals to generations. Individuals who are descendants of the grandparents of either the transferor or a spouse of the transferor are assigned to generations on the basis of their place in the family tree. Any spouse or former spouse of the transferor or of any individual on the family tree is assigned to the generation of the family member to whom the person is married. Those two rules take care of most situations.

In addition, unrelated persons and those more remotely related are assigned to generations by date of birth –

• Anyone not more than 12½ years younger than the transferor is assigned to the transferor's generation.

•A person whose birth date is between 12½ and 37½ years after the transferor's is assigned to the first generation below the transferor.

• Subsequent generations are assigned by additional 25-year intervals.

$1 million exemption. An exemption of $1 million of property is allowed per transferor. Thus, a transferor not leaving more than $1 million in total need not worry about the GSTT. Moreover, with some planning, a transferor leaving not more than $1 million in generation skipping transfers need not be concerned about the tax.

The exemption may be allocated as the transferor wishes. Once allocated to a transfer, the exemption, in effect, shields all later skip distributions and terminations resulting from that transfer for its entire duration.

The $1 million exemption is allocated by statute if not allocated by the transferor. If done by statute, the exemption is allocated as follows –

• to direct skips during life as they are made,

• to direct skips occurring at death, at any time until the federal estate tax return (with extensions) is due,

• to living trusts and testamentary trusts from which taxable distributions or terminations will or might occur after the transferor's death.

Calculating the tax. Although the tax is levied at the maximum federal estate and gift tax rate, the tax is calculated in a roundabout manner. The key to figuring the tax is in calculating the *inclusion ratio* which is a fraction. The numerator of the fraction is the amount of the $1 million exemption allocated to the disposition. The denominator is the value of the property transferred in that disposition reduced by any federal and state death taxes actually paid on that property and any federal estate or gift tax charitable deduction allowed with respect to that property. The fraction is then subtracted from one to determine the inclusion ratio.

EXAMPLE 1: a total of $600,000 is transferred to a generation skipping trust. The transferor allocates $360,000 of the transferor's $1 million exemption to the trust. The fraction (referred to as the applicable fraction) would be –

$$AF = 360,000 \div 600,000$$
$$= 0.6$$

The inclusion ratio would be

$$IR = 1 - 0.6$$
$$= 0.4$$

Thus, any taxable distributions or terminations from the trust would be subject to tax at a rate of 40 percent of the maximum federal estate and gift tax rate. With a 55 percent rate, generation skipping transfers would be taxed at a rate of 22 percent –

$$= .40 \times .55$$
$$= .22$$

96

EXAMPLE 2: a decedent left all of her assets to her two children except for $200,000 left to grandchildren. The tax would be figured as follows, assuming the decedent allocated $200,000 to cover the transfer to grandchildren –

$$AF = 200{,}000/200{,}000$$
$$= 1.0$$

The inclusion ratio would be –

$$IR = 1 - 1$$
$$= 0$$

Therefore, no tax would be due on the transfer to grandchildren.

Who pays the tax? An important question in planning for generation skipping transfers is who pays the tax. The generation skipping rules make it clear, that as a matter of personal liability –

• For a direct skip not from a trust, the transferor pays the tax.
• For a direct skip from a trust, the tax is paid by the trustee.
• For a taxable termination, the tax is also paid by the trustee.
• For a taxable distribution, the tax is paid by the transferee.

Regardless of liability for payment, the generation skipping transfer tax is a charge on the property involved in the transfer. That's the rule unless the will or trust directs otherwise by making specific reference to the generation skipping transfer tax.

As two 1995 cases have pointed out, it can make an enormous difference whether the tax is paid out of the property involved in the transfer or paid out of the residue of the estate. In drafting wills and trusts, it is important to note what is said in the instrument about liability for paying the tax.

Planning principles. It is clear from the preceding discussion that a great deal of importance is attached to how the $1 million exemption is allocated. Several planning principles should be considered in setting up estate plans involving generation skipping transfers.

• Plan to create separate trusts or make transfers just for skip persons (primarily grandchildren and great-grandchildren) and do not distribute property to others from those trusts or transfers. These amounts should have an inclusion ratio of zero (not subject to tax) until the $1 million exemption is fully used.

• Plan to create separate trusts or make transfers to the spouse, children and anyone else not more than one generation below the transferor. These amounts should have an inclusion ratio of one – but there are no GSTT consequences because the transfer doesn't involve generation skipping.

• In general, allocate the $1 million exemption to longer term trusts (trusts that are multi-generational, up to the maximum length for trusts) as opposed to allocation to short term trusts.

When GSTT effective. The generation skipping transfer tax is effective for death-time transfers after October 22, 1986, and for lifetime transfers after September 25, 1985. Trusts which were irrevocable on September 25, 1985, are excepted from the 1986 legislation if nothing is added to the trust after September 25, 1985. Revocable trusts are treated as death-time transfers for this purpose.

Persons who were mentally disabled on October 22, 1986, and who do not regain competence before death are not subject to the tax if the transfer is by gift or death on or before August 3, 1990.

Disclaimers

Frequently, estate planning is completed years before death. That means plans are developed based on expected values at death.

Disclaimers provide a last minute opportunity to adjust property disposition patterns after death has occurred.

EXAMPLE: Grandfather's will, prepared several years ago, left all of his estate to his only daughter. At his death in 1996, the daughter already had an estate valued at $2 million and was concerned with gift making and other strategies to reduce her estate. By disclaiming her right to her father's $350,000 estate, the property would pass to the six grandchildren, all of whom were in need of funds for college expenses and to get started in business.

Rules for qualified disclaimers. For the property to pass as if the disclaiming person had never possessed a right to the property, four conditions must be met –

• The disclaimer must be in writing.

• The refusal must occur within nine months after the transfer is made.

• The person did not accept the property or any of its benefits before making the disclaimer.

• The interest passed to someone other than the person making the disclaimer as a result of the refusal to accept the property.

Jointly owned property. For years, IRS insisted that disclaimers of property owned in joint tenancy had to be made within nine months after creation of the joint tenancy interest. That is usually months, often years, before death of a joint tenant. IRS now accepts disclaimers of joint bank and brokerage accounts and U.S. Government bonds within nine months of death – the so-called "revocable" joint tenancies. Even joint tenancies in land can now be disclaimed within nine months after death.

However, a qualified disclaimer still cannot be made of tenancy by the entirety property (unless disclaimed within nine months of creation of the interest) because there is no right to sever the joint interest before death.

As for *what* can be disclaimed in the case of death of a joint tenant –

• The entire interest can be disclaimed if done within nine months of creation of the joint tenancy interest.

• Otherwise, one-half could ordinarily be disclaimed.

• It may be possible to disclaim the entire amount if it involves property for which a gift did not occur on creation of the joint tenancy (joint bank or brokerage accounts and U.S. Government bonds owned in joint tenancy).

Retirement plans. A 1993 IRS private letter ruling approved a disclaimer of a qualified retirement plan without triggering adverse income tax consequences for the designated beneficiary. Retirement plan benefits are income in respect of decedent which makes distributions fully taxable to the recipient for income tax purposes. Disclaimer apparently does not trigger the income tax on the plan.

4
Optimal tax saving

The best strategy for saving federal estate tax, state inheritance tax and estate settlement costs depends upon the objectives to be accomplished. More specifically, it depends upon whether saving of death taxes and costs should be emphasized only at the death of the first of a couple to die or at both deaths.

Planning to save death taxes and costs at the first death, leaving the surviving spouse a maximum amount of wealth and maximum latitude in managing that wealth calls for relatively simple planning techniques. Full use of the federal estate tax marital deduction – and all other deductions – with the property left to the survivor outright has been the standard approach.

With the 100 percent federal estate tax marital deduction and the present level of the unified credit, estate planning strategies have been modified. However, it still may be advisable to limit the size of the marital deduction to less than the maximum allowable marital deduction at the first death if the combined wealth of a couple exceeds $600,000. Even with combined estates of less than $600,000, limiting the size of marital deduction at the first death may be wise in anticipation of inflation or saving or both between the two deaths as noted in Tables 4 and 5 of Chapter 3.

For those wishing to minimize death taxes and costs at both deaths, leaving the heirs with a maximum amount of wealth from the second estate, the planning task becomes much more complex. This chapter discusses the two fundamental planning approaches that are appropriate to an objective of maximizing wealth for the heirs – Model I and Model II – as well as a variation of the second, referred to here as Modified Model II.

Before turning to the three models of property ownership and transfer, it is helpful to examine the fundamental guidelines for planning.

The three zones

For planning, the following guidelines may be helpful:

• Zone I – If the combined wealth of husband and wife is expected to be no greater than the equivalent deduction amount from the available unified credit at the death of the surviving spouse, the optimal strategy may be to leave the property outright to the survivor at the death of the first to die. For individuals in this category, however, state death tax and income tax considerations are also important. Income tax aspects may be important because the decedent's property receives a new income tax basis at death. The new basis is the value used for federal estate tax purposes. If no federal estate tax is due, the basis becomes the fair market value at death.

• Zone II – If the combined wealth of husband and wife is expected to be no greater than twice the equivalent deduction from the available unified credit at the death of the surviving spouse, the optimal strategy may be to – (a) divide the property between the spouses equally during life and (b) each leave the other a life estate in the property owned with no marital deduction claimed at the first death. This calls for the Model II approach to property ownership and transfer.

• Zone III – If the combined wealth of husband and wife is expected to be more than twice the equivalent deduction from the available unified credit at the death of the surviving spouse, the optimal strategy may be to – (a) divide the property between the spouses equally during life, (b) create a partial marital deduction at the death of the first spouse to die and (c) leave the remaining property of the first spouse to die in a life estate for the other spouse. This suggests the Modified Model II arrangement for ownership and transfer of the property.

Model I

Probably the most popular plan (in the past) for minimizing federal estate tax on the deaths of both the husband and wife has required concentration of property ownership in the name of one spouse only (usually the husband) during life. Then in his will, if the husband is the owner of the property, he leaves a portion of the property (package A) – usually about one-half – to the surviving spouse outright (or nearly outright) with the rest of the property – package B – left to her for her life as shown in Figure 1A.

Figure 1A. Model I: husband dies first.

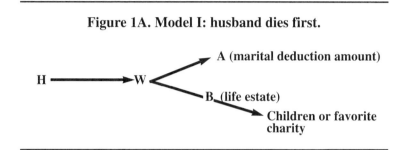

Typically, the children or a favorite charity or both are designated to receive the remainder interest in package B and to acquire the property at the termination of the wife's life estate. If desired, the wife's interest in package A could be reduced to a life estate plus a general power of appointment without loss of the tax-saving features of Model I.

At death of the husband, the package A amount is set to equal the desired marital deduction. By design, package B does not qualify for the marital deduction. A mere life estate is a terminable interest and property held in a life estate is normally not eligible for the marital deduction. With advantage taken of the marital deduction, the federal estate tax is minimized in the husband's estate.

During her remaining life, the widow receives the income from both package A and package B. And she may have the right to use or invade the principal of package A. If package B is held in trust, the trustee may have a limited right to invade the principal in package B on behalf of the widow. The right to invade the

103

principal of package B on behalf of the widow is severely limited. The widow could be given the non-cumulative right to request the withdrawal of up to $5,000 or 5 percent of the trust principal each year in package B. And the trustee of package B could be given the discretion to apply the trust principal for her care, support and maintenance – limited by an ascertainable standard.

At the death of the widow, only the property remaining in package A would be included in her gross estate. The package B property passes to the remainder person (usually the children but it could be a favorite charitable organization) at her death without further federal estate tax.

In effect, part of the property – represented by package B – is taxed at the husband's death. Package A is deductible in his estate. Then package A is taxed at her death later. In effect, one-half the family wealth is taxed at the death of the first of the couple to die. The other half is taxed at the death of the survivor. Traditionally, package A has been set at one-half the adjusted gross estate. The rest of the property passes into package B.

Package A can be set at any level up to 100 percent of the amount passing to the other spouse. Determining the optimal size marital deduction requires careful planning, taking into consideration the fact that a larger marital deduction at the death of the husband reduces the husband's taxable estate and the tax paid. However, the estate of the surviving spouse is increased. Up to a point, if the surviving spouse owns no other property, "creating" an estate through the use of the marital deduction at the death of the first spouse carries positive economic benefits. The overall tax bill may be reduced. But if the surviving spouse has other property, or if full use of the marital deduction would otherwise place the surviving spouse in a high enough tax bracket to call into serious question the full use of the marital deduction, attention to the same four factors identified below under the heading "Modified Model II" may be warranted. Claiming the maximum marital deduction does not always lead to maximum remaining wealth passing from the survivor.

With the advent of a 100 percent federal estate tax marital deduction in 1982, a strategy of claiming the full marital deduction at the death of the first spouse to die may appear attractive. That would reduce the federal estate tax liability at the first death to zero as shown in Table 7 for estates of five different sizes. However, federal estate tax liability at the death of the survivor could be quite substantial as shown in Table 8. All calculations assume deductions of 5 percent of the gross estate for estate settlement costs and debts and an 8 percent annual increase in the value of assets between the two deaths.

Tables 9 and 10 show the results in direct savings of federal estate tax and estate settlement costs of applying a Model I solution to estates of five different sizes. Table 9 gives the figures for death of the first spouse (the one owning the property). Table 10 provides figures for the death of the surviving spouse, assuming the surviving spouse had no property other than that left in the Model I plan and assuming 8 percent inflation.

Table 11 shows the savings in federal estate tax (under the assumptions noted) from implementing a Model I plan over leaving all property to the survivor outright. As a percentage of the initial estate, savings range from above 6 percent for a $400,000 estate up to more than 25 percent for an estate at the $2,000,000 level. Again, these figures do not reflect state death tax calculations or estate settlement costs.

Satisfactory use of a "pure" Model I rests on two basic assumptions: (1) that one of the spouses, usually the husband, owns all or most of the property in that person's name, and (2) that the person owning the property dies first. These assumptions are not always met – or acceptable. In some families, wives may object to title shifts late in life to make the husband the sole owner of the property. And there's always the possibility that the husband may utterly refuse to cooperate in dying first. Therefore, some couples may prefer Model II instead.

Under a variation of the traditional Model I plan, sufficient property is left in a "credit shelter" trust to equal the equivalent value of the unified credit for the year of anticipated death. The income from that amount is left to the surviving spouse for life with the remainder interest typically left to children or a favorite charitable organization. As shown in Figure 1B, the remaining property is left in a manner to qualify for the federal estate tax marital deduction or a portion qualifies for the marital deduction and the rest is left in a life estate/remainder arrangement if the outcome would be more desirable with less than the maximum marital deduction claimed at the first death. In the latter instance, some federal estate tax would likely be paid in the estate of the first of the couple to die.

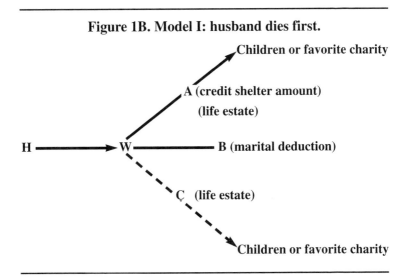

Figure 1B. Model I: husband dies first.

Children or favorite charity

A (credit shelter amount)
(life estate)

H   W   B (marital deduction)

C (life estate)

Children or favorite charity

The message from Tables 7 through 11 is rather clear: for an estate of substantial size (roughly $600,000 or greater) the costs of leaving property outright to the surviving spouse can be significant in terms of additional estate tax. The costs are particularly notable if the survivor lives for a substantial period in a time of inflation.

Table 7. Federal estate tax calculations for death of property-owning spouse in 1996, with 100% marital deduction.

	A	B	C	D	E
Gross estate	$400,000	$500,000	$1,000,000	$1,500,000	$2,000,000
Deductions	20,000	25,000	50,000	75,000	100,000
Marital deduction	380,000	475,500	950,000	1,425,000	1,900,000
Total deductions	400,000	500,000	1,000,000	1,500,000	2,000,000
Taxable estate	- 0 -	- 0 -	- 0 -	- 0 -	- 0 -
Tentative tax	- 0 -	- 0 -	- 0 -	- 0 -	- 0 -
Unified credit	192,800	192,800	192,800	192,800	192,800
Credit for state death tax	- 0 -	- 0 -	- 0 -	- 0 -	- 0 -
Federal estate tax due	- 0 -	- 0 -	- 0 -	- 0 -	- 0 -

Table 8. Federal estate tax calculations for death of the surviving spouse in 2006.

	A	B	C	D	E
Gross estate	$759,582	$949,478	$1,898,955	$2,848,433	$3,797,910
Deductions	37,979	47,474	94,948	142,422	189,896
Marital deduction	- 0 -	- 0 -	- 0 -	- 0 -	- 0 -
Total deductions	37,979	47,474	94,948	142,422	189,896
Taxable estate	721,603	902,004	1,804,007	2,706,011	3,608,014
Tentative tax	237,793	307,582	692,603	1,128,806	1,579,807
Unified credit	192,800	192,800	192,800	192,800	192,800
	44,993	114,782	499,803	936,006	1,387,007
Credit for state death tax	19,037	27,712	85,489	156,129	239,633
Federal estate tax due	25,956	87,070	414,314	779,877	1,147,374

Table 9. Federal estate tax calculations for death of property-owning spouse in 1996, with 50% marital deduction.

	A	B	C	D	E
Gross estate	$400,000	$500,000	$1,000,000	$1,500,000	$2,000,000
Deductions	20,000	25,000	50,000	75,000	100,000
Marital deduction	190,000	237,500	475,000	712,500	950,000
Total deductions	210,000	262,500	525,000	787,500	1,050,000
Taxable estate	190,000	237,500	475,000	712,500	950,000
Tentative tax	51,600	66,800	147,300	234,425	326,300
Unified credit	192,800	192,800	192,800	192,800	192,800
	- 0 -	- 0 -	- 0 -	41,625	133,500
Credit for state death tax	- 0 -	- 0 -	- 0 -	18,600	30,400
Federal estate tax due	- 0 -	- 0 -	- 0 -	23,025	103,100

Table 10. Federal estate tax calculations for death of the surviving spouse in 2006.

	A	**B**	**C**	**D**	**E**
Gross estate	$379,791	$512,746	$1,025,492	$1,538,238	$2,050,984
Deductions	18,990	25,637	51,275	76,912	102,549
Marital deduction	- 0 -	- 0 -	- 0 -	- 0 -	- 0 -
Total deductions	18,990	25,637	51,275	76,912	102,549
Taxable estate	360,801	487,109	974,217	1,461,326	1,948,435
Tentative tax	108,472	151,417	335,745	539,170	757,596
Unified credit	192,800	192,800	192,800	192,800	192,800
	- 0 -	- 0 -	142,945	346,370	564,796
Credit for state death tax	- 0 -	- 0 -	31,756	61,925	95,887
Federal estate tax due	- 0 -	- 0 -	111,189	284,445	468,909

Table 11. Savings in federal estate tax from Model I plan for deaths of both spouses.

	A	**B**	**C**	**D**	**E**
Size of estate (at first death)	$400,000	$500,000	$1,000,000	$1,500,000	$2,000,000
All to survivor outright	25,956	87,070	414,314	779,877	1,147,374
Model I plan	- 0 -	- 0 -	111,189	307,470	572,009
Savings	25,956	85,070	303,125	472,407	575,365

Model II

The other fundamental approach to federal estate tax saving (assuming a given size of estate) suggests equal property ownership between the husband and wife. Equal ownership may be accomplished by using tenancy in common on each item of property, producing estates of precisely equal size. Or, equal ownership could be attained by individual ownership of specific assets with continuing attention to maintaining a balance in property value between the husband and wife.

Model II plans have always been an attractive choice from the standpoint of saving death taxes. However, the problem with

Model II plans has been in achieving balanced property ownership as between the spouses.

With a 100 percent federal gift tax marital deduction available, the potential gift tax problems of balancing estate size have been completely eliminated. If equal ownership is acceptable to a couple philosophically, shifting property ownership to create estates of approximately equal size would be in accord with an objective of minimizing death taxes.

Model II functions with each spouse, by will, leaving his or her property to the other for life as shown in Figures 2 and 3. Typically, the remainder interest in both instances is left to the children. The survivor would be entitled (1) to the income from the property left by the deceased spouse, (2) to the income from his or her property and (3) to sell, mortgage or consume the principal of his or her own property.

Figure 2. Model II: husband dies first.

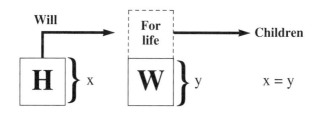

Figure 3. Model II: wife dies first.

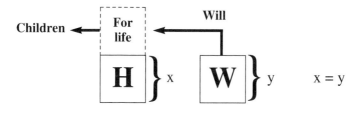

On the death of the surviving spouse, only the property owned by that person would be included in the gross estate. The property received earlier from the predeceased spouse and held in a life estate would not be included in the gross estate of the surviving spouse. That property would pass to the remainder person without further federal estate tax. Granted life estates are not taxable in the estate of the recipient.

Thus, in a Model II, one-half the family wealth is taxed at the first death (and gets a new income tax basis). The other half is taxed and obtains a new basis at the death of the survivor. The order of death is unimportant from a tax-saving perspective.

A pure Model II deliberately avoids qualifying property for the marital deduction. If some of the property at the death of the first spouse qualifies for the marital deduction, the tax burden would be higher at the death of the survivor. And this might occur unless the implementation of Model II has been carefully planned because (1) the surviving spouse usually has the right to elect to take against the will and thus receive outright the amount of property that spouse would have been entitled to receive had there been no will, (2) some property may have been held in joint tenancy, or (3) some life insurance proceeds taxable in the estate of the first to die may pass to the surviving spouse, all of which would generally qualify for the marital deduction.

The assumptions of Model II are quite different from Model I. Under Model II, equal property ownership is assumed. And it matters not who dies first. The plan works equally well if the husband survives or if the wife survives. For deaths in 1987 or later, a total of $1,200,000 of property ($600,000 in each spouse's name) could pass free of federal estate tax in a Model II plan.

Tables 12 and 13 portray the effects of imposing a Model II plan on the five estate sizes in Tables 7-11. In each instance, no marital deduction is claimed at the first death; property remaining after payment of costs and taxes at the first death is left in a life estate to the surviving spouse. It is assumed that no election is made to treat the life estate as eligible for the marital deduc-

Table 12. Federal estate tax calculations for death of first spouse to die in 1996, leaving property in Model II plan (no marital deduction) with estates balanced in size.

	A	B	C	D	E
Gross estate	$200,000	$250,000	$500,000	$750,000	$1,000,000
Deductions	10,000	12,500	25,000	37,500	50,000
Marital deduction	- 0 -	- 0 -	- 0 -	- 0 -	- 0 -
Total deductions	10,000	12,500	25,000	37,500	50,000
Taxable estate	190,000	237,500	475,000	712,500	950,000
Tentative tax	51,600	66,800	147,300	234,425	326,300
Unified credit	192,800	192,800	192,800	192,800	192,800
	- 0 -	- 0 -	- 0 -	41,625	133,500
Credit for state death tax	- 0 -	- 0 -	- 0 -	18,600	30,400
Federal estate tax due	- 0 -	- 0 -	- 0 -	23,025	103,100

Table 13. Federal estate tax calculations for death of surviving spouse in 2006, with property in a Model II plan.

	A	B	C	D	E
Gross estate	$399,780	$499,725	$999,450	$1,499,175	$1,998,900
Deductions	19,989	24,986	49,973	74,957	99,945
Marital deduction	- 0 -	- 0 -	- 0 -	- 0 -	- 0 -
Total deductions	19,989	24,986	49,973	74,957	99,945
Taxable estate	379,791	474,739	949,477	1,424,218	1,898,955
Tentative tax	114,929	142,211	326,096	523,214	735,330
Unified credit	192,800	192,800	192,800	192,800	192,800
	- 0 -	- 0 -	133,296	330,414	542,530
Credit for state death tax	- 0 -	- 0 -	30,371	59,550	92,325
Federal estate tax due	- 0 -	- 0 -	102,925	270,864	450,205

Table 14. Savings in federal estate tax from Model II plan for deaths of both spouses.

	A	B	C	D	E
Size of estate	$400,000	$500,000	$1,000,000	$1,500,000	$2,000,000
All to survivor outright	25,956	87,070	414,314	779,877	1,147,374
Model I plan	- 0 -	- 0 -	111,189	307,470	572,009
Model II plan	- 0 -	- 0 -	102,925	293,889	553,305

111

tion. All calculations assume 8 percent inflation in the period between the two deaths.

A Model I plan and a Model II plan produce about the same results for all estate sizes *if the property-owning spouse with a Model I plan dies with a spouse surviving.* If the non-property-owning spouse dies first where a Model I plan is in effect, the federal estate tax liability is much higher than a Model II plan with the costs the same as though the property-owning spouse had died first and left the property outright to the surviving spouse (Tables 7 and 8). Thus, the tax saving feature of a Model I plan is totally dependent upon a particular order of death. For many, that risk is unacceptably high now that estates can be balanced into a Model II plan with no federal gift tax liability.

Modified Model II

Because of the economic advantage of delaying tax payment, some motivation exists to qualify some property for the marital deduction in the estate of the first to die. This would reduce the tax somewhat in that estate and permit interest-free use of the tax dollars saved until the day of reckoning following death of the survivor. The use of Modified Model II is illustrated in Figure 4. For most couples, this may be the optimal plan as balanced estates are "unbalanced" at the death of the first to die by qualifying some property for the marital deduction. Because it operates from a basic assumption of balanced estates before death of either spouse, this approach is referred to as Modified Model II.

The amount of property to qualify for the marital deduction for optimal overall death tax saving depends upon the life expectancy of the surviving spouse at the death of the first spouse to die, the rate of return expected on deferred tax dollars, expectations as to inflation or deflation and expected changes in tax rates.

Life expectancy is a key variable. In general, the longer the life expectancy, the larger the desired marital deduction. The value of

112

interest-free use of deferred tax dollars at the first death is weighed against the larger tax later in the survivor's estate (because the survivor's estate may be moved to a higher tax bracket as a result of the property qualifying for the marital deduction). The marital deduction may be created in rather precise terms with an appropriate provision in the will, by the surviving spouse disclaiming property after death of the first spouse or it can be approximated with some property left or placed in joint tenancy between the spouses. As an example of the results in terms of federal estate tax payment, assume that application of a pure Model II approach would result in $50,000 in tax at the death of the first to die and $50,000 at the death of the survivor. If the survivor has some significant life expectancy remaining, this plan would be optimal only if money is costless and would

Figure 4. Modified Model II: husband dies first.

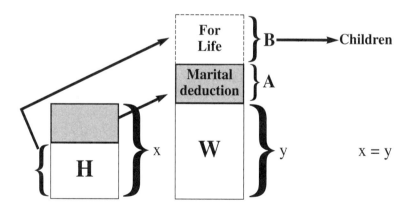

earn no interest and if neither inflation or deflation was expected. Otherwise, it could be advantageous, for example, to reduce the tax at the first death to $30,000, through use of the marital deduction, even though the tax at the death of the survivor might rise to $75,000. The extra $5,000 in tax paid overall could well be less than the value of deferring payment of $20,000 in tax for a period of years. The $20,000 in deferred taxes could, in effect, be used interest-free for the period between the two deaths.

The individual effects of the key variables influencing the size of the optimal marital deduction – in terms of wealth passing from the estate of the surviving spouse – may be summarized as follows:

• The greater the life expectancy of the surviving spouse, all else being equal, the greater the desired marital deduction.

Life expectancy should be taken from the actuarial tables unless the state of health of the surviving spouse is abnormally poor for age, in which event a subjective estimate of life expectancy should be used.

• The greater the expected return on deferred tax dollars, the larger the optimal marital deduction.

• The higher the rate of inflation expected (or increase in asset value otherwise), the lower the optimal marital deduction. Inflation increases the survivor's estate and runs up the tax bill at the survivor's death. Deflation would have the opposite effect, assuming no change in tax rates.

• If death tax rates are expected to rise during the time between the two deaths, an optimal marital deduction would be smaller than would be the case if tax rates were expected to remain unchanged or decrease.

Obviously, consideration of the effects of each variable individually does not produce the optimal marital deduction. All four factors must be taken into account. To accomplish simultaneous consideration of all four variables with an objective of maximizing wealth passing from the survivor's estate requires computer assistance if the task is to be done with precision although useful approximations can be obtained with a series of manual calculations. For those with estates of $1,200,000 or greater, the extra effort involved may be worthwhile in terms of capital conserved over both deaths. Even smaller estates may benefit from a Modified Model II plan if inflation is expected after planning takes place.

5
Liquidity considerations

In the 1970s, as land values rose rapidly and farm estates increased in size, the handling of cash or "liquidity" needs of the estate after death grew considerably in importance. The alternatives for reducing the amount to be paid – or delaying the time of payment – increased the importance of specific planning to handle liquidity needs. In the 1980s, emphasis in liquidity planning shifted toward handling the short and long-term debt obligations in the estate. For many farm estates, reduced land values and diminished death tax liability coupled with high interest rates and heavy debt loads meant that the "debt" side of liquidity planning was of equal or even greater importance than the "costs" side of liquidity planning. Clearly, liquidity planning – for whatever reason it is important – continues to be an integral part of estate and business planning. That's why it's strongly urged that a *liquidity plan* be developed as part of the overall estate plan.

The question of how – and when – the various costs and taxes that come due after death are to be paid should be part of the overall liquidity plan. Attention is focused on the best approaches for payment of federal estate tax, state inheritance or state estate taxes, estate settlement costs and inherited shares to off-farm heirs. Developing strategies for paying off accumulated debt is likewise an integral part of the liquidity plan.

Pre- and post-death funding

The liquidity plan may include one or more of several *pre-death* funding possibilities including life insurance, flower bonds, creation of savings accounts and other highly liquid items and investments in tangible assets with sale of inventory items or sale or mortgage of land and other assets used in the business after death. As shown in Figure 5, the major economic questions are the projected liquidity needs and the expected rate of return on funds among the various pre-death funding choices.

Another basic option involves discharging obligations for death taxes and estate settlement costs over a period of years after death. Among the possibilities in this category are post-death borrowing, the use of 15-year installment payment of federal estate tax, extensions of time to pay federal estate tax and, for those operating in corporate form, redemption of corporate stock after death. Here, the key economic questions are the projected amount of liquidity needed and the interest rate paid as the obligation is being discharged. The economic impact of the choice among liquidity augmenting alternatives can be substantial, indeed.

For many, the key objective in liquidity planning is to select those liquidity-augmenting options likely to produce the greatest amount of wealth after payment of death taxes and costs. This is shown by the wealth line in Figure 5. For example, with strategy A, involving pre-death accumulation of savings, amounts are piled up to pay death taxes and costs in the years before death with amounts remaining after death invested in the farm business. The result is a certain level of wealth n years after death.

Strategy B involves a contrasting strategy with liquidity funds invested in the farm business with the farm business simply reduced in scale at death (or saddled with an additional obligation) to pay the death taxes and estate settlement costs, again with the remaining funds invested in the farm business. Very likely, the result would be a different point reached on the wealth line n years after death.

With Strategy C, there's a variation: funds are invested in the business before death with use made of 15-year installment payment of federal estate tax after death to the extent of federal estate tax attributable to the business. The post-death growth curve is damped slightly because of interest paid on the deferred tax amount. The result, as would be expected, is a different point on the wealth line after death.

Figure 5. Pre- and post-death funding of liquidity needs.

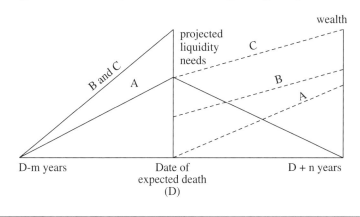

All this assumes we know when death will occur – right on schedule according to the life expectancy tables. In reality, deaths rarely occur on schedule. Rather, deaths tend to be premature or come at a later-than-expected time. The impact of such a departure from the time of expected death should be part of the overall liquidity planning effort. Some of the liquidity planning techniques, such as life insurance, are not affected adversely by premature death. Other options such as accumulation of savings might produce insufficient liquidity if death occurred prematurely.

The liquidity plan

Because of the high stakes involved, the number of options available to add to estate liquidity, and the differences among farm businesses in terms of liquidity needs, it has become apparent in recent years that many farm families should have a liquidity plan as a subpart of their overall estate plan. The liquidity plan is designed to come to grips with the choices among the alternatives.

It is believed that every liquidity plan should have four components:

119

• The first component is a realistic appraisal of liquidity needs for the farm estate. It is usually wise to calculate the liquidity needs on the basis of projected property values and projected debt loads. In general, it's a good idea to plan ahead five and 10 years, using the property values and debt loads expected to exist at that time.

The most severe liquidity problems are faced by farm businesses that expect to continue as an economic entity into the next generation. Farm businesses expected to terminate at the retirement or death of the parents can usually squeeze liquidity out of numerous assets in the estate. Land can be mortgaged or sold, inventory can be liquidated and funds can generally be borrowed. Only if it is felt some assets should not be sold or some property should not be mortgaged would these options not be available.

For those struggling with heavy debt loads, liquidation of assets after death to pay the debt may leave an insufficient amount of wealth for support of the survivors. In some instances, there may be a question whether asset values at death will be sufficient to cover debt obligations and estate settlement costs.

• The second part of the liquidity plan involves a review of the choices reasonably open for liquidity augmentation. As noted above, this typically includes pre-death savings, investment of additional capital in the farm business, the use of life insurance, 15-year installment payment of federal estate tax, and post-death redemption of corporate stock to pay death taxes and estate settlement costs.

• Third, the liquidity plan should involve a choice from among the liquidity-augmenting alternatives available. For many farm families, the choice is an economic one with attention given to the alternative or alternatives expected to produce the largest amount of wealth a specified number of years after the death of the parents. Some families, however, may object to some choices as a matter of principle. For example, some may reject the idea of borrowing after death to pay death taxes and estate settlement costs.

• Finally, the liquidity plan should include a careful listing of all requirements that must be met, either on a continuing basis or in the period immediately prior to death, for availability to be assured of the selected liquidity-augmenting techniques. It is especially important to recognize that pre-death gifting or sale of farm property and the structuring of property ownership and handling of management in the period prior to death may influence the availability of some alternatives. In particular, gift or sale of business assets late in life can drop the estate below the eligibility level for several provisions available to ease the liquidity problem. Likewise, a shift away from a crop-share lease to a cash rent lease can result in loss of eligibility for several provisions requiring a minimum percentage of business assets. For example, a shift to a cash rent farm lease in retirement could cause serious problems of eligibility for installment payment of federal estate tax and special use valuation of land.

Pre-death funding choices

The list of possibilities is lengthy for adding to liquidity by accumulating capital before death. Two of the major choices, life insurance and "flower" bonds, are discussed in the paragraphs following. There's also the choice of accumulating savings before death plus the option of simply plowing all available capital into the farm business with the realization that liquidity would then necessarily be squeezed from the business after death.

LIFE INSURANCE. As one of the more traditional liquidity-augmenting alternatives, life insurance involves basically pre-death funding for death taxes and estate settlement costs. Life insurance carries the advantage of providing for funding if the time of death is premature. Life insurance may also be the most practical alternative for planning to cover heavy debt loads at death.

One current area of challenge in conjunction with liquidity

funding by life insurance involves how to set up policy ownership and beneficiary designations so the proceeds would be
available for payment of the death taxes and costs, but without
subjecting the life insurance proceeds to federal estate tax and, in
some states, state inheritance tax.

• Life insurance proceeds could be made payable to whomever
has the burden of paying the death taxes and estate settlement
costs. This is often the surviving spouse.

• The proceeds could be made payable to a trust authorized to
loan funds to the estate. But then there's the question of how to
discharge that obligation.

• The proceeds could be made payable to a trust with the
trustee empowered to purchase assets from the estate. This could
lead to some income tax liability, however.

• The proceeds might be made payable to a "liquidity trust"
that makes the funds available to the estate. Life insurance is discussed also in Chapter 12; life insurance trusts are discussed in
Chapter 11.

"FLOWER BONDS." United States treasury bonds of certain
issues outstanding on March 3, 1971, may be applied in payment
of the federal estate tax owed. Eligible bonds, to the extent of the
federal estate tax liability, are redeemable at par, which is often
higher than the purchase price. This method of funding for payment of federal estate tax may produce a benefit in the form of
profit on the bonds.

For analytical purposes, a great deal of importance attaches to
the tax treatment of the profit on the bonds. It is assumed the
purchase price of the bonds would have been included in the
deceased's estate in any event. Therefore, the major concern
relates to whether the profit on the bonds would be subject to
income and death taxes.

In some (but not all) states, only the date of death value (and
not the redemption value) is subject to state inheritance tax.
Where that is the case, imposition of state inheritance tax does
not affect the attractiveness of flower bonds as a liquidity-aug-

menting alternative. The par value of the bonds redeemed to pay federal estate tax, or the market value, whichever is higher, plus accrued interest, is includible in the gross estate for federal estate tax purposes. Therefore, the apparent profit in the bonds is reduced by the amount of federal estate tax imposed.

EXAMPLE: Bonds are purchased on the market at 94, death occurs two months later, and the bonds are redeemable at par (100) to pay federal estate tax. The difference between the purchase price and par is viewed properly as profit, subject to payment of federal estate tax (and state death tax in those states taxing par value).

The economic advantage of flower bonds is heavily influenced by the income tax treatment of the gain or profit on the bonds at death. Gain on such bonds is eliminated at death with no income tax liability on bond redemption to pay federal estate tax. If gain on such bonds were to become subject to income tax, their attractiveness for augmenting liquidity would be lessened.

In a community property state, only one-half of the bonds are redeemable at par at the death of the first spouse to die unless it can be shown that the bonds were purchased with separate property of the deceased spouse.

One word of caution: it can be economically hazardous to over purchase flower bonds.

EXAMPLE: Estimated federal estate tax in S's estate was $145,000 so that amount (par value) of flower bonds was purchased after death, federal estate tax was calculated at $127,000 and that amount of bonds was redeemed to pay the tax. The remaining bonds, par value of $18,000, were sold promptly for $13,500 because of the low interest rate on the bonds. A year later, on audit of the federal estate tax return, the federal estate tax liability was refigured at $135,000. That alone was a major blow. It was an even larger blow when IRS insisted (and eventually won the argument) that the $8,000 deficiency could have been paid with flower bonds – had they not been sold. Result: $8,000 of the bonds were revalued – at par – as though they had not been sold.

123

MORAL: Either don't over purchase flower bonds or retain enough bonds past the audit stage so any likely deficiency could be covered.

These bonds, popularly known as "flower bonds," must be acquired during the life of the decedent to be eligible for redemption to pay federal estate tax. Late pre-death purchases of "flower bonds" under conventional powers of attorney have been questioned where the person for whom the bonds were purchased was of doubtful competence at the time. Conventional powers of attorney are generally no longer valid if the person giving the power of attorney becomes incompetent. In response, some states have adopted legislation creating so-called "durable" powers of attorney that purport to survive incompetency. Even under the older power of attorney provisions, IRS has not been very successful in its challenges to redemption of flower bonds purchased while the decedent was incompetent to make the purchase. The best advice: Don't wait too long to buy the bonds.

No new bonds are being issued for this purpose. So as the supply of the special series eligible for federal estate tax payment dwindles, expect the traded price to rise toward par. Eventually, all such bonds will be redeemed with none available for purchase.

Post-death funding possibilities

Several choices are available for paying death taxes and estate settlement costs with the obligation incurred paid off after death.

Installment payment of federal estate tax over 15 years

BASIC RULES OF ELIGIBILITY. The 15-year option for installment payment of part of the federal estate tax bill differs sharply from the 10-year election that was around for years and which was repealed in 1981 effective for deaths after 1981. The 15-year provision was amended substantially in 1981 effective for deaths after 1981 to ease the eligibility rules.

If a closely held farm – or other business – makes up more than 35 percent of the adjusted gross estate, the federal estate tax on the closely held business part of the estate can be totally deferred for more than five years after death, with the tax paid in up to 10 equal annual installments thereafter. This is the basic eligibility requirement for the currently available 15-year installment payment provision.

Interest must be paid, of course, on the unpaid tax balance – even during the first five years. But the interest rate is only 4 percent (compounded daily) on the first $1 million of taxable estate attributable to the business. Actually, it's the first $345,800 of tax – less the allowable unified credit – that's eligible for 4 percent interest. And $345,800 is the federal estate tax on $1 million of taxable estate. The net amount deferred is $345,800 minus the available unified credit of $192,800 or $153,000.

Amounts of tax beyond that level are subject to interest at the regular rate for unpaid federal taxes. For underpayments of tax,

Table 15. Interest rates paid by taxpayers for unpaid federal tax.

Period	Rate (percent)	Period	Rate (percent)
Jan. 1-June 30, 1983	16	Apr. 1-Sept. 30, 1989	12
July 1, 1983-Dec. 31, 1984	11	Oct. 1, 1989-Mar. 31, 1991	11
Jan. 1-June 30, 1985	13	Apr. 1-Dec. 31, 1991	10
July 1-Dec. 31, 1985	11	Jan. 1-Mar. 31, 1992	9
Jan. 1-Dec. 31, 1986	9	Apr. 1-Sept. 30, 1992	8
Jan. 1-Sept. 30, 1987	9	Oct. 1, 1992-June 30, 1994	7
Oct. 1-Dec. 31, 1987	10	July 1-Sept. 30, 1994	8
Jan. 1-Mar. 31, 1988	11	Oct. 1, 1994-Mar. 31, 1995	9
Apr. 1-Sept. 30, 1988	10	Apr. 1-June 30, 1995	10
Oct. 1, 1988-Mar. 31, 1989	11	July 1, 1995-Mar. 31, 1996	9
		Apr. 1, 1996-June 30, 1996	8

since the beginning of 1987 taxpayers have been obligated to pay the federal short-term rate plus three percentage points. Prior to that time, a different formula was used. Before 1987, the rate was set at 100 percent of the average prime rate charged by commercial banks and was changed every six months, on January 1 and July 1. The federal short-term interest rate, applicable beginning in 1987, is based on the average market yield on outstanding marketable obligations of the United States with remaining periods to maturity of three years or less. The interest rates are adjusted quarterly, determined during the first month of a calendar quarter and effective for the following calendar quarter. The rates are rounded to the nearest full percentage point. Table 15 shows the rates in effect in recent years.

For overpayments of tax, the Internal Revenue Service is obligated to pay the federal short-term interest rate plus two percentage points.

Legislation was proposed in 1995 and again in early 1996 to increase the amount subject to deferred installment payment to the first $2.5 million of value of the business and to reduce the interest rate on the amount from four percent to two percent. The rate on values above $2.5 million would be reduced to 45 percent of the IRS rate on underpayments of tax. These proposals had not been enacted as of mid-May 1996.

For purposes of meeting the 35 percent requirement, the farm residence – and other improvements on the farm – are included if occupied on a regular basis by the owner of the farm, a farm tenant or farm employee. This factor may be important – if it's a close case of meeting the minimum percentage – in deciding whether to rent the farm to a resident tenant, or to rent the land to nearby farm operators and rent the house and buildings to someone working in town.

The minimum percentage rules also mean that every proposed gift or sale of farm property should be checked to assure that the transaction wouldn't jeopardize installment payment of tax, if it looks attractive. That's another reason for a liquidity plan – to

126

call attention to the eligibility requirements on a continuing basis.

BENEFITS FROM INSTALLMENT PAYMENT. The economic benefit from paying interest at 4 percent on unpaid federal estate tax attributable to the business is shown in Table 16. Column 2 shows the schedule of principal payments and column 3 the interest payments under the 15-year installment of federal estate tax with an assumed tax bill of $100,000 for the "business" part of the estate. The savings over the payment period (actually 14 years, 9 months) depend upon the rate of return on capital within the firm. Table 16 reflects simple annual interest at 4 percent on the unpaid tax. Daily compounding is required of all interest on unpaid tax (other than for underpayment of estimated tax). IRS has published tables for daily compounding of the 4 percent interest amount.

At an assumed 5 percent rate of return on deferred tax dollars (after income tax has been paid) a net amount of 1 percent is available for investment each year above the required 4 percent interest on unpaid tax. Compounded annually at 5 percent, the savings total $14,443 for the payment period. This reduces the overall tax bill by 14.4 percent.

For an 8 percent after-tax return on deferred tax dollars, the results are more dramatic. A net of 4 percent is available for investment. Over the 15 years, this yields a total saving of $74,427 or 74.4 percent of the total tax bill.

Obviously, the higher the rate of return on deferred tax amounts, the greater the advantage from installment payment. For those expecting a 10 percent return – net of income taxes – the total saving runs to almost $132,225. The savings more than pay the tax bill compared to payment of the $100,000 when due with the federal estate tax return within nine months after death.

A 10 percent rate of return – after income taxes – may look high. But farm operations facing capital rationing because of limits on borrowing could be generating a return that high or perhaps even higher.

Table 15 suggests that installment payment of federal estate tax would be economically wise – any time extra funds could be invested at a rate greater than 4 percent. Thus installment payment may make sense at a time of high interest rates even if no capital is being borrowed.

• The calculations in this table do not reflect daily compounding of the 4 percent interest rate which is required.

IS INTEREST DEDUCTIBLE? Interest paid is deductible for income tax purposes. But for some time, the Internal Revenue

---

Table 16. Net savings from installment payment of federal estate tax under varying rates of return.

(Assumed Tax Bill of $100,000)

(1) months after death	(2) principal	(3) * interest	(4) total payment	(5) 5% return on capital	(6) 8% return on capital	(7) 10% return on capital
9	0	0	0	0	0	0
21	0	4,000	4,000	1,000	4,000	6,000
33	0	4,000	4,000	1,050	4,320	6,600
45	0	4,000	4,000	1,102	4,666	7,260
57	0	4,000	4,000	1,158	5,039	7,986
69	10,000	4,000	14,000	1,216	5,442	8,785
81	10,000	3,600	13,600	1,176	5,471	9,063
93	10,000	3,200	13,200	1,135	5,515	9,369
105	10,000	2,800	12,800	1,092	5,557	9,706
117	10,000	2,400	12,400	1,046	5,601	10,077
129	10,000	2,000	12,000	999	5,649	10,485
141	10,000	1,600	11,600	949	5,701	10,933
153	10,000	1,200	11,200	896	5,757	11,426
165	10,000	800	10,800	841	5,818	11,969
177	10,000	400	10,400	783	5,883	12,566
	100,000	38,000	138,000	14,443	74,427	132,225

*The calculations in this table do not reflect daily compounding of the 4 percent interest rate which is required by the Tax Equity and Fiscal Responsibility Act of 1982.

128

Service took the position that interest on deferred federal estate tax was not deductible as an administration expense in the estate. However, a 1977 Tax Court case permitted a deduction where authorized by state law and IRS has agreed with that decision if interest is deductible under state law and the interest expense is "actually and necessarily" incurred.

The interest amount must be calculated for each year because the amount of interest deducted for federal estate tax purposes affects the amount of tax paid and thus the amount of interest for the following year. Deductibility of interest is, of course, a major factor in the calculation of economic advantage from installment payment of tax. Detailed calculations may be necessary before it is known whether deducting interest paid on deferred federal estate tax would be more advantageous as an estate tax deduction or as an income tax deduction.

If the estate executor claims the initial interest payments for income tax purposes, later payments may, nonetheless, be deducted for federal estate tax purposes.

In a 1994 private letter ruling, IRS agreed that interest on a bank loan was deductible if the District Director of Internal Revenue determines that the loan was necessary to avoid forced sale of the assets. IRS concluded that interest not claimed as an expense of estate administration is non deductible personal interest for income tax purposes and is apparently not deductible as investment interest.

WHAT IS A "BUSINESS"? It's only the part of the total federal estate tax bill attributable to a closely held business that's eligible for installment payment. A major question for retired farmers planning to make use of installment payment of federal estate tax is what constitutes "an interest in a closely held business." This we refer to as the *Tier I* test.

Partnerships and corporations. If the farm business is operating as a partnership, 20 percent or more of the capital interest in the partnership must be included in the decedent's gross estate or the partnership must have 15 or fewer partners. That's for 15-

year installment payment eligibility.

Similar requirements are imposed if the farm business functions as a corporation – 15 or fewer shareholders or 20 percent or more of the corporation's *voting* stock included in the deceased shareholder's estate. Only voting stock is an "interest in a closely held business" and thus eligible for deferral of federal estate tax. Corporate debt securities – notes, bonds or debentures – are not an interest in a closely held business for this purpose. Ownership of stock in a corporation carrying on an active business is sufficient for eligibility. It is not necessary for the shareholder to be personally involved in the business. Ownership of stock in a corporation functioning as a passive investor in property does not satisfy the requirement, however.

Corporate stock or a partnership interest held by a husband and wife as community property or in joint tenancy, tenancy by the entirety or tenancy in common is treated as owned by one individual for purposes of meeting the above requirements. And *stock and partnership interests* held by the decedent and by brothers, sisters, spouse, ancestors and lineal descendants are treated as owned by the decedent for purposes of meeting the above requirements. Interests held in two or more businesses can be counted toward the 35 percent requirement if 20 percent or more of each is included in the deceased's estate. For purposes of the 20 percent requirement, a surviving spouse's interest can be counted if held by the deceased and the surviving spouse as joint tenants, tenants by the entirety, tenants in common or as community property.

An election may be made to treat interests in a partnership and non-readily tradable stock in a corporation that are held by family members as though owned by the decedent for purposes of the 20 percent requirement and the aggregation of interests for two or more businesses. That includes partnership interests or stock held by a spouse, brothers, sisters, ancestors and lineal descendants. It's designed to help family operations where ownership of the business is spread over more than 15 owners. But the 4 percent interest rate is not available if such an election is made to meet the 20 percent requirement by counting family ownership interests. And the "interest only" period (five years after the federal estate tax return is due) is not applicable.

Sole proprietorships. For a farm or ranch business organized as a sole proprietorship, the net value of the interest is treated as an interest in a closely held business. Grain stored on the farm and at a local elevator was viewed in a 1982 IRS letter ruling as an interest in a sole proprietorship for purposes of installment payment of federal estate tax. The ruling left the question of the amount of cash to be considered to be working capital left to be determined by the local District Director of Internal Revenue. In a 1992 ruling, cash accumulations met the interest of reasonableness for purposes of meeting the working capital needs of the business. In determining what is a reasonable accumulation, IRS relied on the rules for figuring the accumulated earnings tax.

Trusts. The installment payment rules do not refer specifically to trust ownership of an interest in a closely held business. However, in several rulings the business interest was eligible for installment payment of federal estate tax even though held in a revocable living trust at death.

Lease arrangements. Perhaps the most difficult determination of what is a "business" involves farmland leased to tenants. In an Internal Revenue Service ruling in 1975, a crop share lease arrangement was held to be a business for a deceased landlord.

Under the lease, the landlord received 40 percent of the crops and paid 40 percent of the expenses. The landlord participated in important management decisions and made almost daily visits to inspect the farms and discuss operations although the landlord lived several miles away. The ruling states that a cash rent lease would not qualify the arrangement as a business for purposes of installment payment of the federal estate tax. Keep in mind that the 1975 ruling was issued for the 10-year installment payment provision that was repealed effective at the end of 1981. However, the ruling is believed to be fully applicable to 15-year payment.

131

In two other rulings issued at the same time as the 1975 ruling, rental of properties to tenants for human habitation did not constitute businesses even though, in one instance, the landlord maintained a fully equipped business office to collect rental payments, negotiate leases and, by contract, direct the maintenance of the properties. The arrangement was held to be "merely that of an owner managing investment assets to obtain the income ordinarily expected from them."

The 1975 rulings left several questions unanswered including the issue of whether the necessary involvement in the business could come from agents or employees of the decedent. In several letter rulings issued in 1981, it was acceptable for a member of the family to be the individual involved in management under the lease as an agent of the decedent-to-be as the landowner. In another ruling issued in 1981, the activities of a bank as agent were sufficient to qualify the decedent's interest for installment payment of federal estate tax. It seems reasonably clear from the rulings that the decedent's agent or employee can supply the necessary involvement in management to qualify a crop share or livestock share lease as an interest in a closely held business. This is the general rule on the relationship of agents and employees to the property owner as discussed in Chapter 1.

One highly important feature of lease arrangements is that property under a cash rent farm lease does not constitute a business interest for this purpose.

Whether a non-material participation crop share or livestock share lease qualifies the property as a business interest is not completely clear. One 1980 letter ruling (the least authoritative type of ruling) intimated that property under a crop share lease was eligible for installment payment of federal estate tax even though the income under the lease was reported as "rent" for income tax purposes, thus suggesting that it involved a nonmaterial participation lease. A 1984 letter ruling indicated that failure to pay self-employment tax was not a bar to eligibility for installment payment of federal estate tax.

Participation in government acreage diversion programs apparently does not make the idled land ineligible for installment payment of federal estate tax. Receiving annual land diversion payments in return for idling land is not viewed the same as a cash rental arrangement.

The line between what is and what is not a business is a fine one. Landlords planning on installment payment of federal estate tax as an important part of their liquidity plan should build a strong record of eligibility including – (1) a farm lease that specifically involves the owner (or an agent or employee of the landowner) in the risks of production and the risks of price change and (2) a good, daily, diary-type record of involvement in decision making, physical work or both. It is clear that assets are not eligible for installment payment of federal estate tax if neither the decedent nor an agent or employee of the decedent was actively involved in the business.

The required involvement for installment payment purposes can be contrasted with the "material participation" requirement for special use valuation of land as discussed in Chapter 3. There are two additional differences between material participation for purposes of special use valuation and the necessary involvement for purposes of installment payment of federal estate tax:

• For purposes of installment payment of federal estate tax, the question of whether the operation amounts to a "business" is determined as of immediately prior to death. For special use value purposes, material participation is required for five or more of the last eight years before the earlier of retirement, disability or death.

• For special use valuation purposes, material participation cannot be gained through the services of an agent, such as a farm manager. Even an unrelated agent can assure the necessary degree of involvement for purposes of installment payment of federal estate tax.

"Passive assets." For decedents dying after July 18, 1984, "passive assets" held by any business are disregarded for purpos-

es of eligibility and for purposes of figuring the amount of federal estate tax that may be deferred. The term "passive asset" means any asset other than an asset used in carrying on the trade or business. The term includes stock owned in another corporation unless the corporation comes under the rule making holding company stock eligible for installment payment of federal estate tax. Under the holding company rule, businesses held by holding companies involving non-readily tradable stock may be eligible for installment payment of federal estate tax. If the election is made, the 4 percent interest rate and the 5-year deferral of payment of the principal amount of tax are not available.

An exception is made to the "passive asset" rule for an active corporation if the corporation owns 20 percent or more in value of the voting stock of another corporation, or the other corporation has 15 or fewer shareholders, and assets totalling 80 percent or more in value in the other corporation are used in carrying on a trade or business. In that event, the corporation is treated as one corporation.

Size of business relative to estate. To be eligible for installment payment of federal estate tax, the "interest in a closely held business" must make up more than 35 percent of the gross estate less deductions allowable for purposes of figuring federal estate tax. This we refer to as the *Tier II* test. The determination of what constitutes an interest in a closely held business is made as of the time immediately prior to death. In a 1982 ruling, a rancher and his wife were involved in an airplane crash. The rancher (who owned the property) was killed instantly. He left part of the ranch property to his wife who lived about an hour. The ruling indicated that her estate (as well as his estate) was eligible for installment payment of federal estate tax. At the time of her death, she held an interest in a closely held business.

What is required to meet the Tier II test differs from the requirements for the Tier I test:

• For a corporation, corporate stock in a corporation carrying on a business counts for purposes of the 35 percent requirement.

Debt securities are not considered to be an interest in a closely held business but any kind of stock is eligible.

• For a partnership, an interest as a partner in a partnership carrying on a business counts toward the Tier II requirement.

• The net value of an interest in a sole proprietorship is eligible to meet the 35 percent requirement.

• For leased property and for trusts, the same rules appear to apply as for the Tier I test.

DISPOSITIONS THAT MAKE TAX DUE. Under 15-year installment payment of federal estate tax, disposition or withdrawal of 50 percent or more of the interest in the closely held business – with a few exceptions – makes the remaining installments become due. This bears close watching. Death-time transfer to members of the family don't count against the 50 percent limit. But in a 1975 ruling, a big dividend payment after death was considered a withdrawal to the extent of pre-death accumulations of earnings and profits. A change in organizational form does not result in termination of the installment payment right if it does not materially alter the business. Thus, incorporation of a sole proprietorship, a shift from sole proprietorship to partnership, liquidation of a corporation or transfer of a sole proprietorship to a limited partnership has been held not to accelerate payment of federal estate tax being paid in installments. However, IRS has indicated that incorporation of a sole proprietorship *with issuance of corporate debentures* would be a disposition as to the debt securities issued.

In a reversal of an earlier ruling, IRS held in 1980 that the transfer of assets in a tax-free exchange did not accelerate tax payment. However, an installment sale of property terminates installment payment even though the sale is to family members if the 50 percent limit is reached.

Mortgaging property is not a disposition, at least so long as funds obtained are used to pay the costs of refinancing and the old lien on the property. To date, IRS has not ruled on whether mortgaging property is a disposition if funds obtained exceed that necessary to pay the costs of refinancing but are used within the business. In 1989, IRS ruled that where estate property is sold to pay off outstanding debt on that and other estate property, both under threat of foreclosure, the sale does not cause acceleration of installment payment of federal estate tax unless the sale proceeds exceed the debt payment on the properties. IRS noted that the value of the closely held business included in the estate would not decrease in such a transaction, except to the extent the sale proceeds are in excess of that needed to pay off the debt against the remaining property.

Apparently, cash renting farmland during the period of installment payment of tax is treated as a disposition.

Execution of an oil and gas lease does not cause acceleration. However, parcels of land on which farming is discontinued as a result of oil and gas exploration and production activities are considered to be disposed of for purposes of acceleration of tax payment.

Transfer of property to a bankruptcy estate by an individual in a Chapter 7 or 11 bankruptcy filing is not treated as a disposition for tax purposes, apparently including installment payment of federal estate tax. The bankruptcy estate steps into the shoes of the debtor. Transfer of property to the debtor at the termination of the bankruptcy estate should not be treated as a disposition, either. However, any disposition otherwise by the trustee in bankruptcy or debtor in possession presumably runs the risk of being treated as a disposition for purposes of acceleration of payment. It is not believed that a transfer occurs for purposes of acceleration of payment of federal estate tax on the filing of Chapter 12 bankruptcy for family farmers. Chapter 12 filers have not been made eligible for the same tax treatment accorded individuals filing under Chapter 7 or 11 bankruptcy. For individuals filing under Chapters 7 or 11, a new tax entity is created. That does not occur in the case of a Chapter 12 bankruptcy.

It's especially important to watch transfers of property during life by gift or sale after the estate has elected installment payment of federal estate tax. *Such transfers count toward the 50 percent limit.*

For transfers (not deaths) after 1981, the transfer of the decedent's interest in a closely held business at the death of the original heir – or at the death of any subsequent transferee receiving the interest as a result of the transferor's death – does not cause acceleration of payment if each subsequent transferee is a family member of the transferor.

The rules for 15-year installment payment of federal estate tax were amended in 1981 relative to the effect of late payments. For deaths after 1981, late payments of tax or interest made up to six months after the due date do not terminate installment reporting, but do incur a penalty of 5 percent of the late payment for each month or fraction of a month the payment is late. Moreover, the late payment loses eligibility for the 4 percent interest rate. For deaths before 1982, failure to make a timely interest payment during the first five year deferral period did not accelerate the deferred tax. IRS had insisted that late payment of tax terminated the installment payment right but the courts had not gone along completely with the IRS position.

MAKING THE ELECTION. The notice of election to use installment payment of federal estate tax must be attached to a timely filed federal estate tax return. *A protective election* can be included when the estate tax return is filed. A protective election can be relied upon later if installment payment of federal estate tax becomes advantageous – and that might occur if property values were increased on audit of the federal estate tax return by the Internal Revenue Service.

Even if a regular or protective election was not filed, an election may be made to pay tax deficiencies in installments.

THE LIEN TO SECURE TAX PAYMENT. One factor that discouraged use of installment payment of federal estate tax for years was the continued liability of the estate representative for payment of the tax. For deaths after 1976 an executor or administrator seeking discharge of liability may file an agreement giving rise to a special estate tax lien. The lien is against "real and other property" expected to survive the deferral period. The maximum amount subject to the lien is the amount of deferred tax plus the first four years of interest.

All parties having any interest in the property to which the lien is to attach must sign an agreement to creation of the lien.

Once filed the lien is a priority claim against the property – as against subsequent creditors – with several exceptions. The lien does not take priority over specified "super priority" type obligations entered into later – (1) real property tax and special assessment liens (2) mechanic's liens for repair or improvement of real property and (3) real estate construction or improvement financing agreements to finance the construction or improvement of real property, a contract to construct or improve the real property or financing for the "raising or harvesting of a farm crop or the raising of livestock or other animals." This opens the way to production credit financing and financing for buildings or other improvements.

For loans that don't fit into the super priority category – such as borrowing to pay state inheritance tax or to purchase interests of off-farm heirs – the Department of the Treasury has indicated a willingness to subordinate the special tax lien. That may be possible if there's enough collateral to secure the loan and the special tax lien so the Treasury's interest is protected.

The District Director of Internal Revenue has authority to discharge part of the assets from the lien so long as the property remaining subject to the lien is at least double the amount of the unpaid tax liability.

IN SUMMARY. For those with significant potential federal estate tax liability 15-year installment payment of federal estate tax is a likely candidate for inclusion in the liquidity plan. Even those not expecting serious liquidity problems may find the 4 percent interest (on roughly the first million dollars of taxable estate attributable to a closely held business) to be too attractive to turn down.

But it takes planning to assure that the requirements are met.

If installment payment of federal estate tax looks promising, be sure the liquidity plan identifies the pre-death requirements that must be met and stakes out the danger signals on disposition of farm property before death or shifts in lease arrangements that would likely destroy eligibility.

Installment payment of federal estate tax over 10 years

The "l0-year" installment payment option has been repealed, effective for deaths after 1981. As with the 15-year option, 10-year installment payment permitted the portion of federal estate tax attributable to a closely held business – including a farm business – to be paid in up to 10 annual installments. Interest, adjusted periodically as explained above, was due on the unpaid balance. The 4 percent rate, available for 15-year installment payment, was not open for the 10-year payment election.

As noted, the 10-year option for installment payment of federal estate tax has been repealed effective for deaths after 1981.

Extensions of time for payment of federal estate tax

The 1976 changes also altered the rules for one-year extensions of time to pay the federal estate tax. Through 1976, it required proof of "undue hardship." For deaths after 1976, the "undue hardship" rule was changed to "reasonable cause." If that test is met, the time of payment may be extended for a period of up to one year for each extension or up to 10 years for all extension periods. Again, interest at regular rates is figured on the unpaid amount due.

Stock redemption after death

For farm businesses organized as a corporation, a special provision for stock redemption after death may be an attractive addition to the liquidity plan for the shareholders. In general, partial redemptions of stock in a closely held corporation are treated as a dividend – all ordinary income. But under a "Section 303" stock redemption, the gain in the stock, if any, is capital gain. The part of each redeemed share of stock that represents the income tax basis in the stock is non-taxable. With corporate stock receiving a new income tax basis at death equal to the value set for federal estate tax purposes, there should be slight gain on redemption of the stock except – (1) where stock redemption is continued over a period of years, or (2) special use valuation of corporation-owned land reduces the federal estate tax value (and hence the income tax basis) of corporate stock.

To be eligible for Section 303 stock redemption, the value of the stock included in the deceased's estate must exceed 35 percent of the decedent's adjusted gross estate. If two or more corporations are involved, as might be the case if one corporation owns the land as an incorporated landlord and another carries on the farming operation, the stock of both may be counted toward the 35 percent requirement if the deceased's gross estate included 20 percent or more of the stock of each one. Careful attention is suggested as to the structuring of the farm business and to programs of gifts or sale of stock before death if stock redemption after death would be helpful. As an example of the need for careful planning, if land is retained in individual ownership at the time the corporation is formed, it is unlikely that the value of the corporate stock would exceed 35 percent of the adjusted gross estate as required.

The capital gains treatment for a Section 303 stock redemption is limited to stock redeemed to the extent of federal estate tax, state estate and inheritance taxes and funeral and administration expenses allowable for federal estate tax purposes. Note that Section 303 redemption cannot be used to pay any income tax liability on redemption. A key point: the benefits of Section 303 redemption are only available if stock is redeemed from those who suffered the pain of paying – or suffered a reduction of interest because of payment – of the taxes and costs. That means for stock left to one individual – for example a surviving spouse – with the portion left to the children bearing the burden of the taxes and costs, Section 303 redemption might not be available. Careful attention to drafting the will – and any trusts involved – has high priority if Section 303 redemption looks helpful.

Generally, Section 303 redemptions must be made within 48 months after death. However, if installment payment of the federal estate tax on the business part of the estate is elected, the redemption can continue for the duration of the installment payments. This lets the business gradually generate the cash needed to pay the federal estate tax on the business part of the estate.

Because of potential death tax and estate settlement cost liability, the need to buy out business interests held by off-farm heirs and the size of the debt load, the liquidity issue takes on considerable significance, especially for larger farm estates. Like any major business decision, it merits planning attention. Making a wrong move in this area can affect the amount of wealth passed to the survivors – or a favorite charity.

6
Gifts in estate planning

Frequently, estate planning is viewed as a process of arranging for an orderly transfer of property at death. Transfers of property by will or under state rules of inheritance are important estate planning techniques. But the transfer of property during life – by gift – may also be part of a carefully drawn estate plan.

Pros and cons of gifts

Gifts during life may be used to (1) reduce death taxes (federal estate and state inheritance or state estate taxes), (2) cut estate settlement costs, (3) ease the total family income tax burden by moving property into the hands of family members in low income tax brackets, (4) transfer a going family business to successors and, (5) perhaps most importantly, benefit family members and charitable organizations that occupy a special place in your priorities.

However, gift-making has its disadvantages. Property given away is not available to provide income in the later years. Control over the gift property is normally given up when the transfer is made. And the recipients are generally free to sell, mortgage or give the property to others.

Property given away during life may encounter an *income tax* disadvantage. Gift property retains the giver's (donor's) income tax basis in the hands of the recipient (donee). But property held until death receives a new income tax basis at death equal to the value used for federal estate tax purposes. That difference can be enormously important for farm property if the income tax basis is low as discussed in Chapter 7. For property with an income tax basis above fair market value, a sale during life to an unrelated purchaser may be the most attractive disposition option with the resulting loss reported by the seller. Sales to closely related purchasers do not trigger deductible losses.

Another disadvantage of gifts of *farmland* during life is that gifts are valued at fair market value for federal gift tax purposes. But land held until death may be eligible for special use valuation at a much lower value per acre for federal estate tax purposes as discussed in Chapter 3.

Gift taxes

Although no limit is placed on how much property *may* be given, federal gift tax laws (and state gift tax rules in less than one-fourth of the states) limit the amount the donor generally *wants* to give. The discussion in the rest of this chapter is limited to federal gift tax.

ANNUAL EXCLUSION. Under federal gift tax laws, the gift tax annual exclusion permits a donor to give up to $10,000 per beneficiary per year. The exclusion becomes $20,000 per beneficiary per year for a husband and wife making gifts even though only one of them owns the gift property.

Only *present* interests in property qualify for the annual exclusion. That means gifts of *future* interests like a remainder (following a life estate) would not be eligible for the annual exclusion. Cases involving gifts in trust of corporate stock subject to tough stock transfer restrictions and with a history of no dividend declaration have held the transfers to be gifts of future interests and thus not eligible for the gift tax annual exclusion. It would seem wise to build a history of dividend declarations even though modest in amount and even though dividends are not declared every year.

MARITAL DEDUCTION. Through 1981, the federal gift tax marital deduction covered the first $100,000 of gifts to a spouse during life and one-half of aggregate gifts above $200,000.

The federal gift tax marital deduction was changed to 100 percent of gifts made to a spouse after 1981.

Between 1976 and 1982, the *estate tax* marital deduction

available after death was reduced to the extent the gift tax marital deduction claimed exceeded what the gift tax marital deduction would have been had it been set at the 50 percent level.

For gifts after 1981, the federal gift tax marital deduction is 100 percent of gifts to a spouse with no reduction in the federal estate tax marital deduction. Also, since 1981 gifts to a spouse for life followed by a remainder interest to others have been eligible for the federal gift tax marital deduction under the QTIP rules discussed in Chapter 3.

CHARITABLE DEDUCTION. Gifts to qualified charitable, religious and educational institutions are deductible without limit. As with the federal estate tax charitable deduction, look for the exemption letter from the Internal Revenue Service indicating charitable status of the organization for gift tax purposes except for gifts to churches and subdivisions of government.

GIFT TAX CALCULATION. Gifts are valued at fair market value for federal gift tax purposes. That means the price at which the property would change hands between a willing buyer and a willing seller, neither being under a compulsion to buy or to sell and both having reasonable knowledge of the facts.

Special use value for real estate, which may be used for federal estate tax purposes if the real property is used in a farm or other business, is not authorized for valuing land transferred by gift. This is an additional reason for holding real property eligible for special use valuation until death.

The federal gift tax is figured on the same rate schedule as the federal estate tax. See Appendix A for rates. Until 1977, the federal gift tax rate was three-fourths the federal estate tax rate through the entire rate schedule. The "unification" of the federal estate and federal gift tax in the Tax Reform Act of 1976 eliminated the rate differences and also introduced the unified credit.

The unified credit, as discussed in Chapter 3, may be used to offset federal gift tax levied before death. Any use of the credit during life is taken into account after death by adding taxable gifts after 1976 to the taxable estate for federal estate tax purposes.

Any gift tax paid is then subtracted from federal estate tax due. In effect, the federal estate tax after death is calculated as though the taxable gifts had not been made during life. The unified credit as originally enacted in 1976 phased in over a five-year period as follows –

When gift made	Unified Credit
Gifts in 1977	$30,000
(Gifts during the first half of 1977 were limited to a credit of $6,000)	
Gifts in 1978	34,000
Gifts in 1979	38,000
Gifts in 1980	42,500
Gifts in 1981	47,000

The unified credit was increased substantially in 1981, with the increased credit phased in over a six year period as follows

When gift made	Unified Credit	Deduction Equivalent
Gifts in 1982	$ 62,800	$225,000
Gifts in 1983	79,300	275,000
Gifts in 1984	96,300	325,000
Gifts in 1985	121,800	400,000
Gifts in 1986	155,800	500,000
Gifts in 1987 and thereafter	192,800	600,000

EXAMPLE: Mother T made a gift in 1981 of 80 acres of land valued at $150,000 to her four children (the father is deceased). The federal gift tax would be handled as follows:

Value of gift	$150,000
Less annual exclusions (4 @ $3,000 each)	12,000
Taxable gifts	138,000
Tentative tax (See Appendix A for rates)	35,200
Unified credit (maximum of $47,000 in 1981)	35,200
Federal gift tax due	-0-

ANOTHER EXAMPLE: Mother T made a gift of another 80 acres of land in 1982 to her four children. The land was valued at $160,000. The federal gift tax would be handled as follows:

Value of gift	$160,000
Less annual exclusions (4 @ 10,000)	40,000
Taxable gifts	120,000
Tentative tax (See Appendix A for rates)	29,800
Unified credit available (maximum of $62,800 in 1982 but $35,200 used in 1981)	27,600
Federal gift tax due	$2,200

If Mother T dies in 1996, the taxable gifts of $258,000 ($138,000 plus $120,000) would be included in her estate and the $2,200 in federal gift tax paid would be subtracted from her federal estate tax due. With the unified estate and gift tax credit fully phased in, taxable amounts are taxed beginning at a 37 percent tax rate.

Thus, covering gifts during life with the unified credit does not come free – *it just looks that way at the time.* You pay the price at death with higher federal estate tax rates. Taxable gifts during life levy a "phantom" tax by moving the donor up the tax rate scale at death. Therefore, if the unified credit is to be used to cover gifts during life, it's good tax planning to use the credit to cover gifts to grandchildren. Then the gift property is not likely to be taxed again for years. If the unified credit is used to cover gifts to a child, a "phantom" tax is exacted from the donor's estate and the property may be hit again with tax in the donee's estate in a few years. In effect, there are two tax bites imposed in a span of a couple or three decades.

One final note on taxable gifts – the IRS position has been that prior taxable gifts can be revalued even though the three-year period for challenging the assessment of gift tax has expired. Most courts have agreed with IRS; only one has not.

GIFT TAX RETURN. The rule is that a gift of more than the

federal gift tax annual exclusion to any one beneficiary in a year requires the filing of a federal gift tax return – Form 709 – even though no tax is due. That is, if the gift is of a *present* interest. A gift of a *future* interest requires the filing of a gift tax return regardless of amount involved. A federal gift tax return is not required for gifts to a spouse.

Gift tax returns are filed and gift tax is paid on an annual calendar year basis with the return due April 15 of the following year. An extension of time to file the income tax return is deemed also an extension of time to file the gift tax return. If the donor dies, the gift tax return is not due until the federal estate tax return is due (including extensions).

The donor is liable for any tax due.

If the gift tax is paid by the donee, the amount of the gift may be reduced by the gift tax due if it is expressly shown that payment of the tax by the donee was a condition of the transfer. If the gift tax is paid by the donee it is income to the donor to the extent the federal gift tax liability exceeds the income tax basis of the property. The IRS has taken the position that a gift of property subject to the obligation of the donee to pay the federal gift tax requires that the donor's unified credit be used in computing the federal gift tax. The use of the unified credit to cover gifts is mandatory.

Gifts of farmland

One of the more difficult aspects of gift making using farmland is how to handle the gift and make systematic use of the federal gift tax annual exclusion. It's possible to give undivided interests in a tract of land. And it's feasible simply to deed an acre or two at a time. But both approaches leave something to be desired.

For those using the corporation as the landowner, gifts of stock can be made. With stock value set initially at $1, $5, or $100 per share and adjusted periodically as values change, it's relatively easy to make gifts within the exclusion amounts.

Another possibility is to give a relatively small tract at a time, using the annual exclusions so far as they go, and then to use the unified credit to cover the rest of the gift.

EXAMPLE: Parents wish to give 160 acres to their three children. The land is valued at $1,500 per acre or $240,000 in total. By giving 40 acres to the three children in 1996, each receiving an undivided one-third interest, the gift tax aspects could be handled as follows –

Value of gift – 40 acres @ $1,500	$60,000
Less annual exclusions – 3 @ $20,000	60,000
Taxable gifts	-0-
Tentative tax (See Appendix A for rates)	-0-
Unified credit (assuming gift in 1996)	-0-
Federal gift tax due	-0-

The same procedure could be followed in the second, third, and fourth years. Assuming the land does not change in value – which is unlikely, the entire 160 acres would have passed to the children with no loss of the unified credit to cover the total amount of gifts.

Gifts of life insurance

Many estate plans call for transfers of ownership of life insurance policies away from the insured individual. This is done in an attempt to avoid including the policy proceeds in the insured's estate for federal estate tax purposes later. For term insurance, with no cash value, there's no gift on policy transfer. It's a different matter with whole life or ordinary life insurance. And keep in mind that payment of premiums by the insured would be a gift of the premium amount with the policy owned by someone else.

VALUING THE GIFT. For a life insurance policy paid up at the time of the gift, the amount of the gift is the value that would be charged for a single premium policy on the individual. If the

149

policy is not paid up, it's roughly the cash value (technically the interpolated reserve at the time of the gift) plus a part of the last premium paid.

But don't worry about the calculations. On request, the insurance company will do the figuring and provide a Form 712, Life Insurance Statement, showing the amount of gift. The form is to be filed with the gift tax return.

BEWARE OF MULTIPLE OWNERS. Normally, a transfer of a policy to a new owner qualifies for the federal gift tax annual exclusion. However, if the transfer is to two or more policy owners, the transfer may not qualify for the annual exclusion – it may be a future interest.

There's a solution: ask the insurance company to split the policy and give each new owner a separate policy. Then it's a present interest and would qualify for the federal gift tax annual exclusion.

Gift at death of insured. If the ownership of a life insurance policy is held by someone other than the insured, and the beneficiary is someone else, there's likely to be a gift at the death of the insured individual.

Example: a policy on the husband's life is transferred to the wife who becomes the new owner. The wife then makes their two children equal beneficiaries under the policy. At the husband's death, the wife would be deemed to have made a gift of one half the proceeds to each of the children.

Therefore, caution should be exercised in making beneficiary designations whenever policy ownership is held by someone other than the insured.

Unusual gift tax situations

Most planned gifts involve transfers of property from parents to children or grandchildren. But gifts may occur with change of title or ownership between a husband and wife, other individuals or between an individual and a newly formed partnership or corporation – and often go unrecognized as gifts.

For example, if a husband uses $50,000 of his own money to buy stock in his name and his wife's name (joint tenancy or tenancy in common) he has made a gift to his wife. If she ends up with an undivided one-half interest in the stock, the gift would be $25,000. Federal gift tax would not be due because of the federal gift tax marital deduction.

There have been three important exceptions to the general rule that a gift takes place when one person's money passes into property held in co-ownership.

BANK ACCOUNT – No gift occurs when one person deposits money in a joint bank account. The gift arises when the person not providing the money makes a withdrawal without responsibility to account for expenditure of the funds to the one making the deposit. The importance of this exception was eliminated, in effect, in 1981 *for joint accounts owned by husbands and wives* because of the 100 percent federal gift tax marital deduction for transfers after 1981. The exception still applies to bank accounts owned in joint tenancy other than by husbands and wives.

U.S. GOVERNMENT SAVINGS BONDS – Similarly, it has not been a gift for a person to purchase a U.S. savings bond with title taken in joint tenancy with one not providing money for the purchase. A gift was made when the one not providing the money redeemed the bond during their joint lives without responsibility to account for the proceeds to the one providing the money initially. Again, the importance of this exception was reduced in 1981 *for bond acquisitions after 1981 by husbands and wives together* because of the 100 percent federal gift tax marital deduction. The exception still applies to U.S. Government savings bonds acquired in joint tenancy other than by husbands and wives.

LAND IN JOINT TENANCY – Before January 1, 1955, a gift was made whenever land was paid for out of one spouse's funds but with title taken in the husband's and wife's names as joint tenants or tenants in common. That's in accord with the general rule. But, for purchases of real property (1) after December 31, 1954, and before January 1, 1982, (2) by husband and wife, and (3) in joint tenancy, a gift did not occur upon purchase unless a special election was made to treat the transaction as a gift. Instead, the gift occurred when the joint tenancy was terminated (other than by death). Tenancies by the entirety (similar to joint tenancies but limited to husband-wife co-ownership) were treated in comparable fashion.

The general rule. The application of this rule meant that for land bought and paid for before 1955, the general rule applied – it was a gift to the wife on acquisition. For a purchase of land in joint tenancy by a husband and wife where one spouse provided the funds, it was a gift of one-half the amount *at the time of purchase.* And the joint tenancy could be severed into a tenancy in common later with no federal gift tax liability. However, severance into the husband's name alone would trigger a gift of half the current value. Likewise, severance into the wife's name alone would result in a gift of half the current value of the property. *Special note:* discharge of indebtedness or improvements made after 1954 and before 1982 (on land acquired in joint tenancy before 1955) may not have involved a gift.

The third exception. The rule on gifts involving joint tenancy property was changed for land acquired after 1954 and before 1982. For land acquired by a husband and wife in joint tenancy, it's not been a gift – even though contributions were all by one spouse, for example – unless reported as a gift on a federal gift tax return filed on time. And apparently very few did that.

So if the husband had provided all of the funds on acquisition of land between 1954 and 1982, and it was not reported then as a gift, for gift tax purposes it was still viewed as the husband's property. Therefore, the only "safe harbor" would have been to sever the joint tenancy with title transferred to the husband's name alone.

A shift to tenancy in common would have meant a gift of 50

percent of the value of the property from husband to wife. Severance to the wife's name alone would trigger a gift of 100 percent of the current value.

Under the 1981 change, acquisitions of land by a husband and wife in joint tenancy are treated as gifts. But because of the 100 percent federal gift tax marital deduction, joint tenancies involving husband-wife ownership can be terminated into any ownership form – with the property owned by either or both of the spouses – with no federal gift tax due.

Careful attention to gift tax aspects of co-ownership patterns is warranted whenever land is transferred. *Any adjustment of titles should be undertaken only after the gift tax implications have been considered.* Remember, transfers between a husband and wife after 1981 should generally be eligible for the 100 percent federal gift tax marital deduction. To complicate matters, several states impose gift taxes. And breakup of joint tenancies (or tenancies by the entirety) could trigger a state gift tax. Unfortunately, some state gift tax rules do not parallel the federal provisions.

Below-market interest rates on installment sales

For years, the Internal Revenue Service has maintained that a sale of property with installment payment of the principal and with interest figured at a rate other than the prevailing market rate of interest produced a gift. The gift was the present value of the difference between the market rate and the lower interest rate actually used. This often happens when land transactions are set up between family members calling for 6 percent interest. The 6 percent rate is permitted for income tax purposes for sales of land between family members up to $500,000 in sales per year.

In a 1988 case, an appellate court reversed the Tax Court that had upheld the IRS position and held that if a transaction uses an interest rate acceptable for federal income tax purposes, there would be no gift for federal gift tax purposes. However, in a 1990 case the Tax Court again upheld the IRS view and that case was upheld on appeal in 1991 by the Eighth Circuit Court of Appeal. The U.S. Supreme Court declined to resolve the conflict between the two courts. A 1995 Tenth Circuit Court of Appeal decision agrees with the IRS position (and the Eighth Circuit).

The 1988 appellate decision only binds the Tax Court in the Seventh Court of Appeal area headquartered in Chicago. Therefore, taxpayers outside the Seventh Court of Appeal area (Illinois, Indiana and Wisconsin) should be mindful of the IRS position inasmuch as the Tax Court agrees with the IRS position.

A gift can be avoided if the selling price is adjusted to account for the effect of the below-market (or above-market) interest rate used in the transaction. Few family transactions contain such an adjustment.

Transfer of property subject to valuation "freezes"

In 1990, a provision was repealed that imposed federal estate tax if interests in property subject to a "freeze" in values were transferred and a fixed-value interest was retained. With a typical freeze, parents transfer common stock in a family-held farm or ranch corporation to children and retain preferred stock. The preferred stock is fixed in value no matter what happens to specific asset values. The common stock changes in value as the values of underlying assets change.

The 1990 legislation replaced the original rule, enacted in 1987, with a provision focusing on the proper valuation of the retained and transferred interests. Thus, the 1990 approach shifted the focus on the problem from federal *estate* tax to federal *gift* tax. The federal gift tax rules on valuation of interests apply to gifts and transfers after October 8, 1990.

The 1990 rules apply to buy-sell agreements and first options as well as to more conventional "freeze" situations. In addition, the 1990 valuation provisions apply to the joint purchase of an asset such as a farm by related individuals. In a typical joint purchase, a parent would purchase a life estate or term interest in a farm and a child would buy the remainder interest. The 1990 law treats the person acquiring the life or term interest as having acquired the entire interest with a transfer of the remainder interest to the other related person.

Relative to buy-sell agreements and first options, the freeze rules provide that the value of property is determined without regard to the agreement or option unless – (1) the agreement or option is a bona fide business arrangement; (2) the agreement or option is not a device to transfer the property to members of the family for less than full value; and (3) the terms of the agreement or option are comparable to those expected in similar arrangements between unrelated parties in arm's length transactions. The regulations point out that a binding agreement among persons who are not natural objects of each other's bounty would meet the three tests. That, of course, is a difficult condition to meet in a closely held farm or ranch corporation. Accordingly, buy-sell agreements or first option arrangements may have no influence on the valuation of property.

The 1990 freeze rules have focused attention on the use of various planning techniques where property is placed in trust with an interest retained by the grantor. These are discussed in Chapter 11.

Gifts to minors

Traditionally, gifts of property to minors have created problems. Minors are not competent to manage their property until they are of age. Minors may be legally incapable of selling the property, giving a mortgage or exercising management prerogatives.

If steps are not otherwise taken, the transfer of property to a minor might occasion the establishment of a legal guardianship or conservatorship in the local court. Although assuring management and protection of the minor's property, a guardianship or conservatorship is normally somewhat restrictive and may involve considerable expense.

A trust may be set up to handle gifts made to minors. If relatively large amounts are to be given a minor or group of minors, a trust may be a very useful device. However, the expense and formality of a trust may make it less suitable for small gifts.

In recent years, each state has adopted a uniform law setting up a simple, trust-like device to be used in making gifts to minors. The property is held by a custodian, rather than a trustee. The custodian has responsibility for handling the investment and management of funds and the appropriate distribution of funds to the minor. The custodian may be an adult person or a bank. When the minor reaches the age for distribution (usually the age of majority), the funds held in the simple trust must be paid out.

These uniform laws, referred to as "Gifts to Minors Acts," are relatively easy to use, inexpensive and involve surprisingly little red tape. However, in many states, only gifts of stock securities or money are eligible for transfer to minors under the uniform acts. Gifts of livestock, machinery and equipment, by contrast, are not eligible for transfer to minors under the uniform acts in many (but not all) jurisdictions. Some states have extended the rules to gifts of other property and refer to the concept as a "Transfers to Minors Act." In those states, property other than stock, securities or money can be held in the custodianship.

One point to observe: if the donor is also the custodian and dies before the child reaches majority, the amount of the property held would likely be included in the donor's estate for death tax purposes. Therefore, the custodian is usually someone other than the donor.

7
Income tax considerations

Estate and business planning frequently involves sale of part of the assets during life or after death. The choice between gift and sale should include consideration of income tax, death tax and gift tax liability as well as consideration of income needs and vulnerability to inflation (or deflation). Finally, the decision to sell for cash, with installment reporting of gain or under a private annuity merits planning attention.

Any sale of inventory or machinery, livestock or land used in the farm business raises important income tax questions. In this section, the income tax aspects of outright sale are considered. Income tax treatment of installment sales is discussed in Chapter 8. The use of private annuities is covered in Chapter 10.

For retiring farmers, the potential gain on sale of assets is typically quite large although in some instances the gain may be modest and in a few cases there may be a loss to be reported. The difference between the income tax basis for each asset and its selling price is taxable gain or loss – either as ordinary income or loss or capital gain or loss.

More than 97 percent of the farmers use the cash method of accounting. For them, raised livestock, grain and feed have a zero basis. Besides, the use of accelerated depreciation may have dropped the income tax basis of machinery (undepreciated value) below fair market value. And increases in values of farmland may have assured gain on sale of that asset.

For assets that have declined in value, sale may involve a loss. Losses involving inventory property are ordinary losses. The same treatment is accorded net losses from property used in the business of farming such as machinery, breeding stock and land. Capital assets generate capital losses which can offset capital gains and up to $3,000 of ordinary income each year for individual taxpayers. Land that has been cash rented for an extended period may be treated as a capital asset. Remember, gains on property used in the business of farming (section 1231 assets) are reported as capital gains even though net losses are ordinary losses. It's important to note that losses triggered on sales between related parties are not reportable for income tax purposes. This is highly important for those with high basis land – that has declined in value – who would like to obtain the income tax benefit from a loss on the property.

A closing out sale does not constitute the sale of a single asset – the farm business. Separate computations must be made of the gain or loss with respect to each asset sold for the purpose of determining whether gain or loss is capital gain or loss or ordinary income or ordinary loss. And separate calculations must be made for depreciation recapture on sale.

Income tax basis

Fundamental to an understanding of the sale option for property disposition is the matter of *income tax basis.* That's the part of asset value that's already been through the income tax mill once. Once subject to income tax, it's not again subjected to income taxation for that taxpayer.

The income tax basis thus becomes the beginning point for figuring income tax liability on sale as well as the ultimate income tax liability to the recipients if property is given during life or held until death. Thus, property typically has two values and may have three – (1) fair market value for figuring federal gift tax liability and in judging whether a selling price between related parties is adequate, (2) income tax basis for determining current or eventual income tax liability on sale and (3) special use value for eligible land (see Chapter 3) for determining federal estate tax liability – *but not income tax or gift tax liability except as special use value establishes the income tax basis at death.*

The search for the income tax basis of specific assets may be quite involved for some property and depends upon how the property was acquired.

PROPERTY ACQUIRED BY GIFT. The general rule is that the donor's income tax basis carries over to the donee. Gift property does not receive a new income tax basis at the time of the gift.

For purposes of figuring loss, the income tax basis is the donor's basis or the fair market value of the property at the time of the gift, whichever is less. After 1976, gift tax attributable to the appreciation in value of the property may be added to the donee's income tax basis unless that would raise the basis above fair market value.

EXAMPLE: Father owns a tract of bare land purchased in 1940 for $20,000. Current value is estimated at $100,000. The father's wish is for the land to go to his son.

If the land were transferred to the son by gift during the father's life, the father's old $20,000 basis would carry over to the son and become the son's basis for purpose of figuring gain (or loss) on sale and for purposes of figuring depreciation, if any, that could be claimed.

Improvements made after the date of the gift increase the income tax basis. Depreciation (or depletion) reduces the basis.

The income tax basis rule for gifts means that the donee shoulders the donor's potential income tax liability. It's never so great as to justify refusal to accept the gift. But it can take some of the fun out of gifts and suggests attention to establishing a record of the income tax basis at the time of the gift.

PROPERTY ACQUIRED BY PURCHASE. If assets are sold, the seller is charged with paying income tax on the gain or reporting any loss. If it is a capital asset or asset used in the business, the gain should be eligible for capital gain treatment Thus, in the above example, if the land passed by sale for $100,000, the father would have $80,000 of gain ($100,000 selling price less $20,000 basis). The son's new basis would be $100,000 – the purchase price. This amount becomes the figure for calculating depreciation and for computing gain or loss on later sale.

Again, improvements made after the date of the purchase increase the income tax basis; depreciation or depletion reduces the basis.

There's an exception to the purchase price becoming the income tax basis for the purchaser. The exception is for land under special use valuation that is purchased from the estate. In that situation, the purchaser's income tax basis is equal to special use value plus the difference between fair market value of the land at death and fair market value of the land at the time of sale. This exception to the usual rules for income tax basis for purchased assets is discussed in detail in Chapter 3.

PROPERTY ACQUIRED BY INHERITANCE. If property is held until death, yet a third rule is invoked. Retention of assets until death subjects the property to federal estate tax. But the potential gain or loss on the property is eliminated and the estate or heirs take the property with an income tax basis equal to its value in the estate for federal estate tax purposes.

EXAMPLE: A farm was bought in 1940 for $20,000 with $32,000 of improvements made and $12,000 of depreciation claimed. The income tax basis would be –

Original cost	$20,000
Improvements	+ 32,000
	$52,000
Depreciation	–12,000
Adjusted basis	40,000

If the land were sold for $100,000, there would be $60,000 of gain. But if the owner died in 1996 with the land valued at $100,000, the $60,000 of gain would be eliminated, wiped off the books.

EXAMPLE: A farmer on the cash method of accounting died in 1996 owning $100,000 of stored grain, an inventory of $50,000 of hogs and $105,000 of cattle. All animals were raised

160

except for a $5,000 bull that was purchased. Had the farmer sold out before death, $250,000 of the $255,000 (all but the income tax basis on the purchased bull) would have been subject to income tax, much of the gain as ordinary income. But by holding the property until death, the $250,000 of gain is eliminated.

This rule on handling gain at death dates back to the beginning of the income tax. And it's been an enormous tax saver in agriculture. That's because – (1) the income tax basis for raised animals is zero for a farmer on cash accounting, (2) inventories of raised grain and feed likewise have a zero income tax basis, (3) machinery and equipment are often depreciated at a faster rate than the items decline in value (and, for older farmers, much of it may be depreciated out at death), and (4) land, for many farmers, has a low income tax basis relative to fair market value.

But the rule providing a new income tax basis at death is a two-edged sword. It can eliminate potential losses, as well.

EXAMPLE: A farm bought in 1980 for $720,000 was valued at death in 1996 for $370,000. The farmer had claimed $120,000 of depreciation and had added $15,000 in improvements. Had the farm been sold in 1996, the farmer would have had a $245,000 ordinary loss –

$$= (720,000 + 15,000 - 120,000) - 370,000$$
$$= 245,000$$

By holding the land until death, the potential loss was eliminated in a "step down" of basis. Obviously, dying with a potential loss is unwise. A sale to an unrelated purchaser during life would have triggered the loss. For an operating farmer, or share-rent landlord, a loss on sale of a farm can usually be used to off-set ordinary income.

An exception to the rule of a new income tax basis for property held until death was added in 1981. For deaths after 1981, with respect to property acquired after 1981, gifts of appreciated property transferred within one year of death do not receive a new income tax basis at death. That's the rule if the property is acquired after the decedent's death by the donor of the property or the spouse of the donor. The same treatment applies if the property is sold by the decedent's estate if the donor or spouse of the donor is entitled to the proceeds from sale of the property. The rule was enacted to discourage the transfer of appreciated property to a spouse shortly before death to accomplish a wipe out of gain at no cost because of the 100 percent gift tax and estate tax marital deductions.

Allocating basis on purchase

Upon purchase of farmland or other assets where there are several assets involved, it is necessary to allocate the purchase price among the various assets. The allocation is to be made on the basis of relative fair market values of the items.

Under a 1986 amendment, a more detailed rule applies to multiple asset acquisitions. For acquisitions after May 6, 1986, involving "assets which constitute a trade or business" the allocation is to be made in a specified manner. First, the purchase price is to be allocated to cash and cash-like items (certificates of deposit, government securities, and other marketable stock or securities). Second, the purchase price is to be allocated to tangible and intangible assets. Finally, any remaining purchase price is to be allocated to goodwill and going concern value (if any). Intangibles such as good will and going concern value may be eligible for a special 15-year amortization. All allocations are to be made on the basis of fair market values.

Most farmland purchases do not involve the purchase of cash or cash-like items, intangible assets, or goodwill or going concern value. That means the purchase price is allocated among the tangible assets. Thus, even if farmland purchase is considered the purchase of a trade or business, which is far from clear, the allocation process is essentially unchanged by the 1986 amendment. The purchase price is still allocated among tangible assets at relative fair market values.

162

Carry-over basis rules

The rule of a new income tax basis for property held until death was changed in 1976, to be effective in 1977. The new rule, known as "carry-over basis," would have subjected gain accruing after 1976 to income tax on sale after death. The carry-over basis concept proved to be highly controversial, was subjected to a three-year moratorium, and was repealed in 1980 except for a special election for deaths after December 31, 1976, and before November 7, 1978.

Income in respect of decedent

One category of property – referred to as producing "income in respect of decedent" – merits special planning effort. Essentially, income from this category of asset continues to be taxable income after death with no adjustment in income tax basis. The idea is that the income is so close to being earned that it retains its taxable character. One example: The last paycheck of the decedent.

For farm estates, there are three common categories of income in respect of decedent.

SHARE RENTS. Crop share and livestock share rents held by the decedent at death are income in respect of decedent and are taxable on later sale by the estate or heirs. This is the treatment if the landlord was a *non-materially participating* landlord at the time of death. And many are, for social security reasons.

If the landlord was participating materially in the production of income under the lease, the share rents are treated as other property with the usual adjustments to income tax basis at death.

For death of a non-materially participating farm landlord during a rent period, with crops and livestock sold after death, the portion of the proceeds allocable to the period before death is income in respect of decedent. That portion is also includible in the gross estate for federal estate tax purposes. The remaining amount represents ordinary income earned by the estate after the landlord's death. The proceeds of sale are apportioned according to the number of days in the rental period before and after death.

For share rents held by the landlord at the time of death, which are later sold, the proceeds of sale are similarly allocated between income in respect of decedent and ordinary income.

Many retired farmers rent out their land under a cash or non-materially participating crop share lease. Some also maintain a modest livestock enterprise of their own – such as a small cow-calf operation. A cattle enterprise is especially attractive because sale of some animals may qualify for capital gain treatment. And the objective usually is to keep self-employment income below the maximum allowed for social security purposes before benefits are reduced.

In such a situation, at the time of death some hay and grain that would otherwise be income in respect of decedent is being held for use in the livestock enterprise. It's not entirely clear when such crops cease being income in respect of decedent. But it would appear that intent to hold the crops for use in the livestock venture should be a major factor.

If a landowner is retired and receiving social security benefits under a non-material participation lease, it may be possible to achieve material participation through an agent (such as a child or farm manager) which would eliminate the problem of income in respect of decedent. This involves application of the general rule in the relationship of agent to property owner as discussed in Chapter 1. Yet because an agent's activity level is irrelevant for purposes of liability for social security tax (as under the "Section 1402" rule) the presence of a materially participating agent does not jeopardize the receipt of social security benefits.

SERIES E BOND INTEREST. Accrued, untaxed interest on U.S. Government Savings Bonds, Series E, is income in respect of decedent. H bonds issued for E bonds are similarly treated. There are three possible strategies for handling such interest –

• The executor or administrator could elect to report the interest increment on the Series E bonds on the final return of the decedent even though the decedent held the bonds uncashed at death.

• The interest could be reported as income by the estate.

• The bonds could pass through the estate uncashed with the ultimate beneficiary reporting the interest as taxable income.

INSTALLMENT SALES. Assets, such as land, that are sold under installment reporting rules are also income in respect of decedent as noted in Chapter 8. The recipient of payments after death reports the income in the same manner as the decedent would have done if living. Thus, part of each payment is return of basis, part is taxable gain (capital gain if the asset sold was a capital asset or asset held for use in the business) and part is interest which is taxable as ordinary income.

Sales contracts for farm products such as livestock also produce income in respect of decedent. But in a case involving sale of feeder calves before death, the sale did not produce income in respect of decedent because the calves were too light at the time of death. It was necessary to keep the calves for several weeks after death. That removed the transaction from the category of income in respect of decedent and the calves received a new income tax basis at death.

For sales of property, if only ministerial acts or mere formalities remain to be carried out at death, the transaction ordinarily produces income in respect of decedent. But, if more important and substantive tasks remain to be performed, it may not be a transaction generating income in respect of decedent.

RETIREMENT PLANS. Amounts held in retirement plans and accounts at death also produce income in respect of decedent. Distributions from the fund after death are taxed in the same manner as if paid out before death. Death does not give the assets a new income tax basis.

Disposition of IRD items

The transfer of an item of income in respect of decedent ordinarily triggers gain. That includes a transfer by sale, gift or other type of exchange. However, if property is paid or distributed in kind, no gain or loss is triggered unless the distribution is in satisfaction of a right to a specific dollar amount or specific property other than that distributed. In 1995, IRS ruled that Series E US Government bonds could be transferred in kind to a charitable beneficiary without triggering gain on the unreported interest.

If an installment obligation passes into an estate and in turn is transferred to a beneficiary of the estate, the gain in the installment obligation is not immediately taxable unless the obligor under the obligation is also a beneficiary of the estate.

INCOME TAX DEDUCTION. Because property producing income in respect of decedent is also included in the gross estate for federal estate tax purposes, the income part of the asset would appear to be taxed twice – federal estate tax and income tax. To avoid the double tax, the taxpayer reporting income in respect of decedent is entitled to an income tax deduction for the federal estate tax, if any, on the income in respect of decedent amount.

The deduction is figured at the highest marginal federal estate tax rate imposed in the estate. For estates of retired farmers and others leasing farmland under non-material participation leases, stored crops often constitute a considerable amount of income in respect of decedent. Likewise, those inheriting the right to receive installment land contract payments also can benefit from the income tax deduction available as installment contract payments are reported for income tax purposes. Thus, the deduction against income tax for part of the federal estate tax paid can be a major item. Appendix F illustrates how the income tax deduction is calculated.

Transferring residences

Estate planning often involves a change of residences as the shift is made from full-time farming to part-time or fully retired status. The capital needs and financial adjustments required are important estate planning considerations.

SALE AFTER AGE 65. For sale of a residence before July 27, 1978, part or all of the gain from sale of the old residence could be excluded from income by a person age 65 or older once during the individual's (or the spouse's) lifetime. If the sale price was $35,000 or less, all gain could be excluded. For residences over $35,000 a fraction of the gain could be excluded (fraction derived by dividing $35,000 by the sale price).

To be eligible for the special over-65 treatment, the residence must have been used as the principal residence for at least five of the last eight years before sale. This meant that a retiring farmer who moved off the farm had only three years to make the sale in order to qualify.

SALE AFTER AGE 55. For sale of a residence after July 26, 1978, a much larger exclusion is available. Up to $125,000 of gain ($62,500 on a separate return by a married individual) on sale of a principal residence may be excluded from income for taxpayers age 55 or older for sale or exchange of principal residences. Even if gain had been excluded on the sale of a principal residence before July 27, 1978, by a person age 65 or older, the individual may still elect to exclude up to $125,000 of gain on sale of a principal residence under the current rules.

The election is on a once-in-a-lifetime basis. For a married couple, they can elect to exclude gain on sale of the residence once. If the excluded gain is less than $125,000 on that sale, they can't use the rest of the exclusion on later sale of another residence. This may pose difficult planning problems for the couple.

For husbands and wives owning a residence (or the residence part of a farm) in joint tenancy, tenancy by the entirety or as community property, only one need be age 55 or older and satisfy the other requirements. Note, however, that the same treatment is *not* extended to those owning the residence (or residence part of a farm) in tenancy in common. Therefore, a shift in title for the residence to joint tenancy (or tenancy by the entirety) prior to sale may be advisable if one spouse is under age 55. In general, no federal gift tax should result if such a change is made.

This once-in-a-lifetime election also poses important questions for selecting a spouse. If a prospective spouse had already used the exclusion, this would bar use by the new spouse after remarriage. Some may want to include this item on their checklist of points to consider before a final decision is made on a spouse. It appears, however, that if both individuals had used the exclusion independently before marrying, no recapture is required. But if a couple is divorced after using the exclusion, no further election could be made by either of them – or by their spouses if they should marry again. They're tainted for life!

To be eligible for the $125,000 exclusion the property must have been owned and used as the taxpayer's principal residence for three or more of the last five years before sale. If the old residence was "involuntarily converted" – taken by condemnation, for example, the holding period for the old residence could be "tacked on" to the holding period for the new residence. Otherwise, it's necessary to have owned and used the place as the principal residence for at least three of the last five years before sale.

The $125,000 exclusion was designed, in part, to permit older individuals to sell their larger homes and move to smaller quarters. An additional effect, probably unintended, is to encourage individuals to maneuver as much gain as possible into an expensive residence, live there the minimum three year period, sell the residence and exclude $125,000 of the gain from income tax.

The residence portion of a farm is eligible for the exclusion. In carving out the residence, care must be taken not to include any part of the farm used for business purposes. If an income tax deduction is being claimed for an office in the residence in the year of sale, that part of the residence isn't eligible for the special over 55 sale treatment if a depreciation deduction had been claimed in the year of sale.

If the entire farm is sold, a part of the selling price – and a part of the income tax basis – must be attributed to the residence before the 55 or over calculations may be made. It may be possible to allocate the selling price between the residence and the rest of the farm in the contract of sale.

SALE OF RESIDENCE AND REINVESTMENT. At any age, a retiring farmer may use the rule authorizing the tax-free sale of the old residence and repurchase of a new one. The rule applicable for sales or exchanges is that if the new residence was acquired within two years before or two years after sale of the old one, the gain on the old residence carries over into the new one. However, if the new residence costs less than was received for the old one, part of the gain is recognized for income tax purposes.

Gain from more than one residence during the replacement period may be deferred if the individual relocates for employment purposes. To qualify, the sale must be in connection with commencement of work by an employee or self-employed person at a new principal place of work. And the geographic and length-of-employment requirements must be met for deductibility of moving expenses.

Again, the tax-free sale rules apply to a farm residence. The residence portion of the farm may be carved out for separate treatment if the entire farm is sold. Remember, the sale and reinvestment provision does not extend to parts of the residence used for business purposes such as an office in the home. A ruling, however, indicates that merely because a portion of a residence had been treated as a business asset in a prior year (but not currently) does not preclude the gain on that part of the residence from being eligible for sale and reinvestment treatment.

If spouses sell their residence, file a joint income tax return and then divorce, both are liable if the proceeds aren't reinvested in a new residence in a timely manner. This suggests that filing a separate return could be a prudent move if marital problems loom large.

Part gift-part sale

Some property transfers for estate planning purposes combine a sale with a gift transaction. This is often done in one of three ways. (1) The property to be transferred is divided into two parts, that to be sold and that to be the subject of the gift. (2) The selling price for the property sold may be established on the low side. However, such transactions are subject to challenge as constituting a gift to the extent the selling price is less than fair market value for the property if it involves closely related parties – such as transfers from parents to children. Of course, if the transfer is a good faith, arm's-length transaction, free of any intent to make a gift, the fact of bargain purchase does not create a gift. (3) The property may be sold with installment reporting of gain with periodic forgiveness of part or all of the payments as they come due.

The income tax aspects of forgiveness of installment payments are discussed in Chapter 8. Payments that are canceled or forgiven must be reported into income as though received. Moreover, regular and consistent forgiveness of payments could lead to a recharacterization of the entire transaction as a gift as of the date the "sale" was made. A 1958 Tax Court case so held and a 1977 Revenue Ruling specifically embraced that case and served notice that the Internal Revenue Service would be on the lookout for such transactions. One solution: Because cancellation or forgiveness of installment payments makes the gain on the cancelled or forgiven payment taxable as gain to the seller under the contract, the seller should collect all payments and either pocket the funds or make a completely separate gift of the payment amount.

The way a transaction is characterized has a great deal to do with the current and future income tax liability of the parties involved. If treated as a sale only, the buyer's income tax basis in the property is the purchase price. If treated as a gift only, the donor's income tax basis carries over to the recipient. If it is treated as part gift-part sale, the purchaser-donee's basis is the greater of the purchase price or the transferor's income tax basis.

EXAMPLE: Mother wishes to enter into a bargain purchase

transaction on 160 acres of land with her daughter. The land has a fair market value of $150,000 and an income tax basis of $60,000. If sold to the daughter for $75,000, the daughter's income tax basis would be $75,000. However, if the mother were to sell one 80-acre tract to the daughter for $75,000 and make a gift to the daughter of the other 80-acre tract, the daughter's income tax basis for the 160 acres would be $105,000 ($75,000 purchase price plus one-half of the $60,000 basis of the donor in the entire tract). Obviously, there is an advantage to the daughter in handling the transaction as part gift and part sale rather than as a bargain purchase transaction.

Maintaining the initial characterization of the transaction as a sale may be especially important to the purchaser who may have depreciation deductions at stake and who often is in a higher tax bracket than the seller as a retired parent.

Effect on plans for property transfer

In making decisions to sell property during life, make gifts of property during life or retain property until death, income tax considerations should play a major role. Decisions on transferring property involve, in addition, federal estate tax, state inheritance tax, federal gift tax and state gift tax (in some states) as well as various non-tax considerations. The tax and non-tax considerations are all juggled by the estate planner as decisions are made to transfer the property during life or after death. Seven major rules of thumb are suggested:

1. All else being equal, if gifts are to be made it's still a good idea to make them out of property that has not appreciated in value. Like cash.

2. Retain assets that have increased in value, run those assets through the estate and obtain a "stepped up" basis. For maximum income tax savings, retention of appreciated property until death may be advantageous. Under current law, the recipient of property from the estate receives a new income tax basis at death equal

171

to the value used for federal estate tax purposes. Thus, property held until death is subject to the death taxes – federal estate and state inheritance or state estate tax – but income tax liability on later sale is reduced to the extent of any step-up in basis. And more depreciation may be claimable after the step-up in basis at death. Remember, however, that if land is valued under the special use valuation rules, that same figure becomes the income tax basis. Thus, gain is wiped out at death only up to the value placed on the property for federal estate tax purposes.

Even at that, for property to be sold soon after estate settlement, the income tax advantage of retention until death may outweigh the extra death taxes.

3. For assets that have declined in value, a sale during life may produce a better tax result than a step down in basis at death. A sale during life may produce a loss which can be used to good advantage. That loss is not available for property held until death.

4. For land, remember that it may be possible to apply special use valuation procedures for federal estate tax purposes. But gifts of land are valued at *fair market value.*

5. Be cautious in accepting, uncritically, low valuations of property in an estate. After all, the higher the value used at death the greater the amount of gain eliminated at death. Of course, there may be a trade-off in terms of death taxes due. Keep in mind, also, that the latitude for establishing property values in the estate may be quite limited.

6. Sale of property causes recapture of depreciation, soil and water conservation and land clearing expense deductions (if land was held for less than 10 years) and government cost sharing payments excluded from income (over the past 20 years). Moreover, deductions are disallowed for costs of producing unharvested crops sold with the land. None of these is recaptured on transfer of property at death.

7. The decision to sell major assets such as land during life deserves careful consideration and involves several factors in

addition to income tax liability on sale. Inflation deals sternly with fixed principal, fixed income obligations. So if sale proceeds are received in installments over a period of several years or if the proceeds are received in cash and reinvested in fixed principal, fixed income investments, vulnerability to inflation may become an important factor.

It is entirely possible to outlive the term of an installment contract and medical advances during the next couple of decades could increase life expectancies significantly. Thus, use of principal and interest payments for current consumption could jeopardize long-term security.

Comparison of ways to defer gain on property

A sale of property for cash produces gain or loss in the year of the transaction. That may be acceptable for losses and may even be acceptable for gains if the gains are modest or the seller is concerned about the risks of nonpayment. For those willing to take the risks of nonpayment, a sale of property with a deferral of gain may be a good strategy.

Actually, there are three different ways to defer gain on the sale of property – (1) the installment sale, discussed in Chapters 8 and 9; (2) the private annuity, covered in Chapter 10; and (3) the self-canceling installment note (SCIN) also discussed in Chapter 10. SCINs are similar to installment sales except that, once death of the seller has occurred, all future payments are canceled. The three choices have vastly different tax consequences and can be compared on six bases.

Handling gain at death. For private annuities, payments halt at death if there is a single annuitant and there is no gain at death to be concerned about. With self-canceling installment notes (SCINs), the canceled payments following death must be reported into the estate's first income tax return as though received. That does not happen with an installment sale but payments after death are transformed into income in respect of decedent. The payments continue to be taxable as though received by the decedent.

Security interest retained. With both installment contracts and SCINs, the seller can and usually does retain a security interest in the property sold. That is not possible with a private annuity; retaining a security interest causes the transaction to be treated as a sale.

Outliving payment stream. There is no risk of outliving the payment stream with a private annuity – payments continue until death. It's entirely possible to outlive either an installment contract or a SCIN. Both involve a specified number of payments.

Consequences of repossession. In the event of buyer default under either an installment sale or a SCIN, the property can be repossessed under a special tax provision that softens the tax bite for the seller. In many instances, the seller must report as income only the portion of each payment previously excluded as return of basis. That approach cannot be used with a private annuity. That makes default under a private annuity a more costly matter for the annuitant.

Deductibility of interest. Interest payments are deductible by the buyer under an installment sale or a SCIN. However, there is no interest deduction allowed for a private annuity. All payments are principal and aren't deductible.

Inclusion in gross estate. With an installment sale, the remaining balance is included in the seller's gross estate for federal estate (and state death tax) purposes. There's nothing to be included in the gross estate for either SCINs or private annuities.

Before the final decision is made on a sale of property – or part gift/part sale – it's a good idea to check carefully the consequences for the three basic ways the deal can be handled.

8
The installment contract

The installment contract has become a popular device in recent years for financing the transfer of farmland. For sellers, it provides the opportunity to spread taxable gain over a period of years for tax reporting purposes. For buyers, it offers the possibilities of acquiring property with a low downpayment.

From an estate planning standpoint, the installment land contract can be a handy planning tool. It has application to many estate planning situations.

In the next chapter we'll discuss some of these situations and point out some of the provisions that should be included in a contract. This chapter focuses on several income tax aspects of the land contract that should be considered.

Income tax angles

Despite the sharp declines in farmland values in the 1980s, some landowners still have a great deal of potential gain wrapped up in land. An outright sale, of course, triggers immediate recognition of all of the gain in the year of sale.

However, gain from the transaction may be spread over a period of years if the requirements for installment reporting are met. Actually, the income tax benefits of installment reporting of gain are available whether the instrument used is a land contract or a deed and mortgage so long as the requirements are met for installment reporting.

For installment sales, the recognition of gain (but not loss) may be postponed until the year payments are actually received. Losses are reported in the year of sale.

The requirement that an installment obligation must have two or more payments spread over at least two taxable years and the requirement that the payments in the year of sale not exceed 30 percent of the selling price were repealed in 1980.

Even a sale arrangement calling for a single payment at a specified time in the future can qualify for installment reporting of any gain involved. Likewise, the size of the payment received by the seller in the year of sale no longer affects eligibility for installment reporting for income tax purposes. The amount of payments received does, of course, influence the income tax liability for that year.

Calculation procedure. With installment reporting of gain, the amount of gain to be reported by the seller is spread over the payments received by the seller. It appears that "payments in the year of sale" include downpayments or earnest money paid in a prior year as well as payments in the year that the benefits and burdens of ownership pass to the buyer. This is usually the year of transfer of possession or the year of title passage, whichever occurs first.

EXAMPLE: A farmer agrees to sell the farm for $100,000 on November 1, 1995, and receives $500 in earnest money. Possession is given and $30,000 received on March 1, 1996. Total payments of $30,500 would be reportable in 1996.

The seller, in figuring taxable gain each year, must determine "gross profit" and "total contract price." Gross profit is the selling price less the adjusted basis. "Selling price" includes the cash, notes and other property received by the seller plus the amount of any mortgage or other obligation against the property. Total contract price refers to the cash, notes and other property *paid by the buyer to the seller.* Total contract price does not include any mortgage or other obligation taken over by the buyer. Thus, total contract price is the selling price less the indebtedness taken over by the buyer.

To calculate the amount of gain reportable as income, the payments received by the seller are multiplied by a percentage computed by dividing the gross profit by the total contract price.

$$\text{Gross profit percentage} \quad = \quad \frac{\text{Gross profit}}{\text{Total contract price}}$$

176

In the example above of a sale for $100,000, if the income tax basis for the property was $20,000, the gross profit would be $80,000 and the total contract price would be $100,000 if there is no indebtedness against the property.

$$GPP = \frac{\text{Gross profit}}{\text{Total contract price}} = \frac{\$80,000}{\$100,000}$$
$$= 0.80$$

Thus, 80 percent of each principal payment received would be reportable as capital gain. The other 20 percent would be nontaxable return of capital.

EXAMPLE: A farmer agrees to sell 320 acres of land with an income tax basis of $160,000 and an outstanding mortgage of $80,000 (to be taken over by the buyer) for $320,000. Gross profit would be $160,000 ($320,000 – 160,000), total contract price would be $240,000 (320,000 – 80,000) and the gross profit percentage would be –

$$= \frac{160,000}{240,000}$$
$$= 2/3$$

Thus two-thirds of each principal payment would be reportable as capital gain. One-third of each principal payment would be reported as return of basis which is not taxable.

Reporting Interest. Interest received is reported as ordinary income. Under the unstated interest rules, a part of each principal payment under an installment sale must be treated as interest rather than sales price if interest of less than the prescribed rate is specified. For binding written contracts (including irrevocable written options) entered into before July 24, 1975, the "test rate" was 4 percent. If a lesser rate of interest was specified, the interest to be reported was computed at 5 percent compounded semiannually. For obligations entered into on or after July 24, 1975, the unstated interest "test rate" was 6 percent and unstated interest was computed at 7 percent compounded semi-annually. For obligations entered into on or after July 1, 1981, in general the minimum interest rate was 9 percent; otherwise, interest was figured at 10 percent compounded semi-annually.

For obligations entered into after June 30, 1985, the minimum interest rate is the lesser of 9 percent or the Applicable Federal Rate (AFR) if the amount of seller financing is $2.8 million or less adjusted for inflation ($3,622,500 for 1996). Where the amount of seller financing is more than that, the minimum rate is 100 percent of the AFR.

The AFR is based on the average yield for federal debt obligations of similar maturity. The short-term rate is for obligations with a term of not more than three years, the mid-term rate is for obligations with a term over three years but not more than nine years and the long-term rate is for obligations with a term of more than nine years. The AFR is the interest rate in effect as of the first day on which there is a binding contract for the sale, the rate for the preceding month or the rate for the second preceding month. AFR's are published monthly by the Internal Revenue Service.

Under the 1985 amendments, the imputed rate is the same as the test rate. There is no higher penalty rate as there was before mid-1985.

Under an exception to the general rule on minimum interest rates, an installment sale of land qualifies for a minimum interest rate of 6 percent if the sale is between members of the same family and if the sales price of property sold or exchanged between the same family members during the calendar year does not exceed $500,000. In the event the $500,000 limit is exceeded, the 6 percent rate is available on sales or exchanges up to that limit.

There is some indication that IRS originally intended to define "land" as including only soil and not including depreciable improvements such as buildings. Such an interpretation would

178

have greatly complicated installment sales of real property. If such an interpretation had prevailed, depreciable property would have been subject to the minimum interest rate. With a decade and a half elapsing with no formal statement of that interpretation, the general belief is that the meaning of "land" is based upon the state law definition and generally includes improvements added to or affixed to the land.

Remember, as noted in Chapter 7, there is currently a split among the courts as to whether use of the 6 percent rate (or any rate different from a market rate of interest) produces a gift.

If there is a substantial change in the terms of older contracts, *the current minimum interest rate rules apply.*

The unstated interest rules do not apply if all of the payments under the contract will be made within one year or if the sale price is $3,000 or less. The unstated interest rules apply if a payment is due more than six months after the sale.

Recapture of depreciation. If a sale involves recapture of depreciation, and the installment method of reporting the gain is followed, the income is deemed to have been received in the year of sale. This is the case even if no payments are actually received in the year of the sale.

Claiming depreciation. When can the buyer start a depreciation schedule? The Internal Revenue Service says depreciation (now referred to as "cost recovery") may be claimed by the buyer from the date of possession. If the property is subject to a lease, actual possession is not required, of course.

Handling mortgages

Mortgages on the property may either be paid off by the seller or taken over by the buyer. In general, mortgages taken over by a buyer are not considered as payments in the year of sale or part of the total contract price. Of course, if the buyer pays off the mortgage at the time of sale, the seller must include the mortgage payments in the year of sale.

SPECIAL SITUATION: If the mortgage exceeds the seller's income tax basis for the property, the excess is considered as a payment in the year of sale and as part of the total contract price.

EXAMPLE: In our earlier example of the $100,000 farm with a $20,000 basis, if a mortgage of $55,000 were taken over by the buyer, the $35,000 excess of mortgage over income tax basis would be a payment in the year of sale and a part of the total contract price.

This may happen in farm situations as farms with low income tax basis figures are mortgaged as part of a refinancing effort to keep debt obligations paid or as part of a strategy to create capital for expansion, and then sold.

Reporting the $35,000 into income would elevate the basis to $55,000. As a result, the gross profit would be $45,000, total contract price would be $45,000, the gross profit percentage would be 100 percent and all future payments would be reported as gain. There would be no return of basis as subsequent payments are received.

One way out: If the buyer is not required by the terms of the contract to take over the mortgage until some future year, the excess of the mortgage over the basis would not be treated as a payment in the year of sale. Until the year the buyer is to take over the mortgage, it appears that the buyer should not be making payments on the mortgage. That should be the seller's concern. IRS has taken the position in regulations that "wrap around" indebtedness is deemed to have been taken "subject to" even though title for the property has not passed and even though the seller remains liable for payments on the wrapped indebtedness. With wrap around indebtedness, as part of the sales agreement the buyer issues the seller a note with the principal amount reflecting the existing mortgage. The IRS position has not, however, been sustained by the courts and IRS has recently conceded on the issue.

SELLER'S LIABILITIES. What if the buyer, in the year of sale, makes payments for liabilities against the property – back taxes, accrued interest or amounts backed by liens? These payments generally do not constitute payments in the year of sale if the liabilities were incurred in the ordinary course of business. Of course, if the liabilities exceed the income tax basis of the property, the excess is considered a payment in the year of sale.

The Internal Revenue Service treats liabilities which are directed to be paid out of the original purchase price as payments in the year of sale.

Related party dispositions

The sale of property with installment reporting of gain is subject to two different related party rules. One rule, the "two-year redisposition" rule, applies to all types of property. That rule arose out of efforts to develop escrow arrangements to handle sales to land developers. The second rule is limited to depreciable property.

Two-year redisposition rule. Occasionally, a purchaser prefers to pay the full purchase price for the property and receive title. Land developers are often in this situation as the land is to be resold or mortgaged and title is necessary for those steps to be taken. Yet the seller, usually for income tax reasons, prefers to receive payments in installments and spread the gain over a period of years. An appealing solution, if it succeeds in shielding the seller from income tax liability, has been the escrow arrangement. The purchase price is paid into an escrow account with instructions for installment payments to be made to the seller.

Unfortunately, for the seller, escrow arrangements have rarely been successful in delaying receipt of the selling price. In a number of cases, the seller has been treated as in "constructive receipt" of the amounts in escrow. Even certificates of deposit placed in escrow to mature as payments come due have been unsuccessful in protecting the seller from full tax liability in the year of sale. Likewise, in one case, sale of property in an installment transaction to a spouse who in turn sold the property to a purchaser failed to meet the test of avoiding income tax liability in the year of sale.

The escrow arrangements that have succeeded – and relatively few have – have generally involved situations where the seller had no direct or indirect control over the benefits of the transaction, the escrow was set up entirely by and at the behest of the purchaser and the escrow account was administered by an independent trustee. In a case upholding an escrow arrangement, an installment sale was made to an irrevocable trust with later sale by the independent trustee who had complete control over the property.

Even though the use of sales within families as a type of escrow arrangement has not succeeded in all instances, as noted above, the Congress in 1980 added a rule combatting sales of property to a related person with resale to a land developer or other purchaser. Under the 1980 rule, disposition of property within two years after an installment sale between related parties triggers income tax liability for the original seller. For installment sales of stock or securities, the resale rule applies without regard to the two-year time limit.

The rules taxing gain on resale of property do not apply, however, if the resale (1) is because of loss of the property through condemnation or other "involuntary conversion" such as a casualty loss; (2) occurs after the death of the original installment seller or purchaser; (3) involves sale of stock to the issuing corporation; or (4) did not have as one of its principal purposes income tax avoidance.

For purposes of this related party rule, the definition of "related parties" includes a spouse, children, grandchildren, parents, brothers and sisters. The definition also includes interests held by a related corporation, partnership, trust or estate.

Depreciable property rule. For sales of depreciable property between closely related parties, the deferred payments are deemed to be received in the year of sale. There is an exception if a principal purpose of the transaction was not tax avoidance.

For this rule, the meaning of "related party" is more limited and is confined to entities.

Example: Mother wishes to sell 50 head of raised beef cows to her son with payments over five years. Although never depreciated, it is arguable that the cows are of a nature or character subject to an allowance for depreciation and so would be depreciable property. Because the sale does not involve an entity, only a mother-to-son sale, it would appear that the depreciable property rule would not apply. Because the cows were raised, there would be no depreciation recapture. It should be noted, however, that the "two-year redisposition" rule could apply if the cows are sold within two years unless one of the exceptions applies.

Disposing of installment obligations

The seller should be careful to avoid triggering immediate taxability of the gain in the contract after the contract qualifies for installment reporting. Sale, gift or other disposition or satisfaction of an installment obligation, including exchange for a private annuity, results in immediate recognition of gain to the seller.

The IRS view has been that pledging an installment obligation – or assigning the obligation as collateral on a loan – is also a taxable disposition. IRS has been successful in some cases but less so if the interest rates and maturity dates differ between the installment obligation and the loan and the installment seller did not part with a substantial portion of the ownership rights in the obligation. In 1987, however, an amendment provided backing to the IRS view. The law is effective for dispositions after December 17, 1987, in taxable years ending after that date. The statute applies to indebtedness secured by an installment obligation involving property used in the taxpayer's trade or business or held for the production of rental income with a sales price exceeding $150,000. The statute does not apply to personal use or farm property. For property subject to the 1987 law, the net proceeds of the loan are treated as a payment received on the installment obligation. Thus, care should be exercised in using installment obligations as collateral on a loan. The 1987 law does not apply to the refinancing of indebtedness outstanding on December 17, 1987, if – (1) the taxpayer is required by the creditor to refinance the loan and (2) the refinancing is provided by a person other than the creditor or a person related to the creditor.

Transfer of an installment obligation to a trust may cause immediate taxability of all of the gain unless the seller is considered an owner of the trust consisting of the deferred profit in the installment obligation. Revocable living trusts normally meet that test.

It's alright to substitute a deed and mortgage for an installment contract if the terms and conditions of payment are the same. If the reshuffle only involves a change in the type of security, it's permissible and there are no adverse tax consequences. Likewise, a tax-free exchange to a corporation or partnership does not trigger taxability of installment obligations transferred.

Cancellation or forgiveness of an installment obligation is treated as a disposition and income tax becomes due on any gain involved. Cancellation or forgiveness of payments has been a relatively common practice among farm families selling land to children under installment payment obligations. Until 1980, many did not consider income tax to be due when payments were forgiven or cancelled. Cancellation or forgiveness of installment payments since 1980 has required the seller cancelling or forgiving payments to report the amounts into income as though the payments had been received. For transactions involving unrelated parties, the fair market value of the obligation is used to determine gain. Where related parties are involved, gain must be figured using the face value of the obligation.

Although the rule is broad enough to cover cancellation or forgiveness of principal to assist financially troubled purchasers, a 1987 IRS letter ruling declined to apply the rule to a writedown of principal for a financially strapped purchaser.

Death of the seller

Generally, upon death of a property owner, the property receives a new income tax basis, the potential gain or loss is eliminated, and a new depreciation schedule can be set up. *But on death of a seller within the term of an installment sale transaction, the installment obligation as an asset of the estate does not receive a new basis.* Payments received after death are reported in the same manner, for income tax purposes, as the seller would have done if living. There is a deduction for the estate tax attributable to the obligation. That's some help.

This feature of installment obligation taxation may pose an income tax disadvantage compared with retention of the property until death. The disadvantage is greatest for property that has appreciated substantially in value.

In general, death of the seller holding an installment obligation with passage of the installment obligation through the estate to the heirs does not trigger taxability of gain in the installment obligation at that time. But the heirs (or the estate) must report the payments in the same way the seller would have reported the payments for income tax purposes had the seller lived. The rule is otherwise, however, if an installment obligation is transferred at death to the obligor under the contract. In that event, any previously unreported gain in the installment obligation becomes due and is taxable to the deceased seller's estate.

EXAMPLE: Mother sold 160 acres of farmland to her only son, George, in 1993 for $480,000. After receiving the first two payments under the contract, the mother died with the contract passing to son George by inheritance. All unreported gain in the installment obligation would be taxable to the mother's estate.

There's a different rule if the *estate* is the seller under an installment obligation. In that case, distribution of the installment obligation to the heirs causes immediate taxability of gain in the installment obligation in all instances. For some assets, with a new income tax basis received at death, the amount of gain may be modest. But if the sale involves land that had been valued under special use valuation, *the amount of gain could be substantial.* The new basis at death would be only up to the value set for federal estate tax purposes (special use value) and not up to fair market value. Thus, caution is urged in instances where land is sold by the estate under installment sale arrangements. This problem is discussed in greater detail in Chapter 3.

9
Uses of the installment contract

In using the installment contract, competent legal and tax counsel is a must. And *both* sides should be represented by an attorney. Relying on the attorney for the other side to protect one's interest can be a serious mistake.

Ways to use contracts

In some cases, an installment land contract may be just the ticket if parents wish to begin lifetime transfers of land to particular children. With a contract, here are some of the things the parents can accomplish:

• Retain an interest in the land as security, by keeping the title.

• Receive a steady, annual income for the duration of the contract, with the income neither subject to social security tax nor reducing benefit payments.

• Transfer management responsibility for the property to the buyers.

• Provide an opportunity for the buyer, for example a son, to acquire an interest in land with a low downpayment.

• Reduce the size of their estates by consuming or making gifts of the installment payments. The contract value is fixed, so further increases in land values after the contract is signed do not increase the size of the parents' estates.

The land contract may be particularly attractive to a surviving spouse wanting to avoid heavy involvement in property management, for example.

But, there are problems with installment contracts.

The parents may outlive the term of the contract and then have to depend on other sources of income.

Inflation may elevate the parents' cost of living to the point where they have difficulty living on the fixed contract payments. If continuation of the farm business is an objective, the land contract may not be the whole solution. The contract may be useful for transferring specific assets – such as farmland. But it's less well suited for transfer of interests in machinery, livestock, equipment and miscellaneous assets as a going business.

The installment land contract can be used to generate income for retirement through sale to an outsider. The same advantages of reducing management worries, setting up a fixed income and keeping a security interest are there. And the worries about inflation and outliving the contract may be present, also.

A contract *reduces* the uncertainty of annual income amounts. But it *increases* the uncertainty of outliving one's assets. In general, the older a person becomes, the less he or she likes uncertainty.

Flexibility in drafting contracts

Land contracts are governed by state law. And state contract law varies somewhat from jurisdiction to jurisdiction. Yet in every state, there's considerable flexibility in setting up a land contract.

A printed contract is rarely satisfactory without additions or deletions. Printed or form contracts typically favor the seller. A completely fair and equitable contract usually arises only from careful discussion and negotiation over a range of issues.

There's a great deal of latitude in how a contract can be written. That's why each side should have an attorney.

In the paragraphs following, key issues are mentioned with the suggestion that these be checked out under local law if they're important. The choice of contract provisions may be governed in part by whether the buyer and seller are related, the bargaining positions of the parties, and trade-offs as the issues are negotiated.

Payment plan – The payment schedule may be set up calling for fixed principal payments for the life of the contract plus interest on the unpaid balance. Under this scheme, total annual payments decline each year.

Or, the total annual payments may be fixed with a larger portion of each succeeding payment representing principal and a smaller part representing interest. Tables are available to help make the calculation.

To soften the buyer's immediate payment burden, an increasing payment plan may be used with total annual payments rising over part or all of the contract life. This method may be helpful to buyers anticipating difficulties in meeting payment obligations over the first few years after purchase. But it can also get an optimistic buyer into a tight financial bind.

Occasionally, variable payment plans are used with the size of payment dependent on prices, yields or incomes. These are relatively rare except among closely related buyers and sellers.

Pre-payment privilege – Especially for a contract written in an era of high interest rates, it may be important to the buyer to have the right to make payments in addition to the annual payment due. This enables the buyer to make extra principal payments and reduce the interest bill. If interest rates drop sharply, it would permit the buyer to pay off the seller and refinance.

But sellers may not welcome prepayment clauses with open arms. Extra payments mean extra income tax to pay. This may be especially crucial if the buyer pays off the seller and refinances elsewhere with a mortgage. Sometimes a compromise is reached: the amount of prepayment allowed is limited, or the buyer agrees to pay the seller's extra income tax bill caused by the prepayment.

In some states, extra principal payments are considered to come off the end of the contract. So a buyer in financial difficulty after making extra principal payments may not be able to use prepayments as current principal payments unless that right is reserved in the contract.

Risk of loss – Usually, the contract specifies who bears the risk of loss from wind, fire or other casualty. And the contract normally specifies the amount and type of insurance to be kept in force. Some states shift the risk of loss to the buyer when the contract is signed. In other states, the risk of loss follows possession. It is also important to spell out clearly who receives the proceeds in the event of loss. If the seller receives the insurance proceeds, his or her security interest is protected. But the buyer ends up without either the building or funds to repair or rebuild. If the buyer gets the insurance proceeds, the seller's security interest may be diminished unless the funds are put back into the property as repairs or new construction.

One solution: provide that proceeds may, at the option of the buyer, be used to repair or rebuild, or to reduce the principal due. This assures funds to the buyer and also protects the seller. The seller may also want to reserve the right to approve architectural design and specifications for repairs or new construction.

When title to pass – Although practices vary from state to state, it is customary in many states for the seller under an installment land contract to retain title to the land until part or all of the payments have been made.

To give the buyer flexibility in refinancing and the additional security and certainty that comes with legal title (less likelihood of loss of the property on default, for example) the buyer may argue for a provision that the buyer may request a deed upon payment of 50 percent or so of the purchase price. Such a provision would require the seller to give a deed when the buyer had performed as required and to take back a mortgage for the unpaid balance.

Default by buyer – Until the buyer obtains legal title, his or her rights may not be as great as those of a person who finances a land purchase by mortgage. The buyer stands a greater chance of losing the land if there is a default in making payments.

In some states, a seller can forfeit the rights of a defaulting buyer by giving notice and waiting for a specified time (sometimes as little as 30 days). If the buyer is unable during that time to make payments due, the buyer loses the downpayment, other payments, and improvements made. And, the seller retakes the land. Forfeiture can be a harsh remedy.

Under some circumstances, a defaulting contract buyer is treated under the same foreclosure rules as a defaulting mortgagor. Foreclosure typically requires a judicial sale of the property and payment of the proceeds to the seller to the extent of the amount due. Often, foreclosure requires 12 to 15 months to complete.

A seller confronted by a defaulting buyer can sue for the unpaid balance, obtain a judgment and endeavor to collect the judgment from the non-exempt assets of the buyer. This remedy is rarely used because defaulting buyers often have no assets reachable to satisfy a judgment.

Finally, the buyer and seller could agree to a rescission with the parties returned to their original positions. The property is returned to the seller and all payments are returned to the buyer. This remedy is rarely employed because one or the other of the parties believes another remedy is more advantageous.

Again, there may be room for negotiation in the matter of how to handle default. Form contracts may be unacceptable without modification. That modification may take the form of stretching the period of notice required before forfeiture (from 30 to 60 or 90 days) or replacing forfeiture as a remedy on default with foreclosure.

IN CONCLUSION. The installment land contract is a handy tool in the estate planner's kit. It's not suited to every situation. But, neither is any other estate planning device.

The contract is especially worth considering where the seller is willing to trade the certainties and uncertainties of land ownership for certainty of annual income, the uncertainties of inflation or deflation and the possibility of consuming all of one's principal before death.

10
The private annuity

Most everyone is familiar with commercial annuities, typically issued by insurance companies. With a commercial annuity, the annuitant pays cash in exchange for a promise by the insurer to make periodic payments for the remainder of the annuitant's life or perhaps for the life of the annuitant and the annuitant's spouse.

A private annuity differs from a commercial annuity in two major respects.

1. Ordinarily property other than cash is used to acquire the annuity. For example, farmland may be used in private annuity transactions.

2. The promise to make the payments is usually made by an individual (often a relative) rather than by an insurance company.

In the typical situation, the private annuity transaction involves a parent – as annuitant – and a child as obligor, the one obligated to make the annuity payments.

The annuitant transfers the property to the obligor at the outset. The obligor becomes the owner of the property and promises to make the periodic payments as agreed. Since the obligor's promise is unsecured, the annuitant is left with relatively little protection if the obligor dies or becomes bankrupt.

Unlike an installment sale, which permits retention of title by the seller until part or all of the payments have been made, the tax saving features of a private annuity require that the obligor's promise not be secured by retention of rights over the property involved. And this means some additional risk to the annuitant.

If the obligor's promise to pay is secured, the gain on the property transfer may become taxable as a sale in that year. Hence, the private annuity is more likely to involve an unsecured but firm promise to pay on the part of the obligor. In the paragraphs following, it is assumed that the promise to make payments is unsecured and that the potential gain in the property transferred is recognized over the annuitant's life expectancy.

For a family with several children, one of whom is the obligor, the private annuity is almost inherently unfair. If a parent as the annuitant dies prematurely, the obligor receives a windfall – the property is obtained at a fraction of its value, possibly. And that may make the other children unhappy. On the other hand, a longer than normal life for the annuitant may mean payments by the obligor considerably in excess of the property's value. That may lead to unhappiness on the part of the obligor. Therefore, a private annuity may produce equitable results only if the annuitant dies right on schedule or all children are obligors.

An annuitant may also encounter problems with inflation. The real purchasing power of the agreed-upon payments declines with inflation (or rises with deflation). Thus, uncertainty may exist as to adequacy of the fixed principal payments although the uncertainty of outliving one's income stream is avoided.

The obligor also bears several risks under a private annuity. Some are related to tax treatment as discussed below.

One non-tax risk involves the possibility of premature death of the obligor followed, perhaps, by a longer than normal life for the annuitant. The estate of the obligor remains liable for annuity payments required by terms of the agreement. This could be a substantial burden on the heirs of the obligor. Therefore, it may be desirable for the obligor to take out insurance on his or her own life to protect against loss to the obligor's estate in the event of death before the death of the annuitant.

Private annuities are perhaps best known in estate planning circles for the tax problems involved. The tax problems run the full range – gift tax, income tax and estate tax – and often pose advantages as well as potential pitfalls.

Gift tax problems

In its simplest terms, if the present value of the annuity payments differs from the fair market value of property transferred, a gift may result. And a gift tax may be due.

The fair market value of the property may be easily determined if the property is readily valued – stocks and bonds, for example. For other property, such as land, it may be necessary to have competent appraisers fix the value.

The value of the annuity is figured by multiplying the life expectancy of the annuitant by the annual annuity payments. Tables are available from the Internal Revenue Service for making the calculation of present value. For transfers before May 1, 1989, the present value of annuities was determined using a 10 percent annual interest rate. After April 30, 1989, the interest rate is 120 percent of the midterm applicable federal rate published by IRS for the month of valuation.

EXAMPLE: A 74-year-old widower transfers a $120,000 farm to his son in exchange for the son's promise to pay $1,200 per month for the rest of the father's life. With a life expectancy of 10.1 years for a 74-year-old male annuitant, the expected return would be $145,440 ($14,400 x 10.1 years). For a male, age 74, the present value of the right to receive such an annuity is $81,051, assuming 120 percent of the applicable federal rate produces a 10 percent interest rate. So the difference between the fair market value of $120,000 and the annuity value of $81,051 would be a gift.

In this example, the gift would be $38,949 from the father as annuitant to the son as obligor. This gift would be reported on a federal gift tax return as noted in Chapter 6. Some states also levy gift taxes.

Although it happens less often, a gift could flow the other way. If the present value of the annuity exceeds the fair market value of the property, and there is an intent by the obligor to make a gift, a taxable gift could result. Note, however, that for arm's-length transactions, such as between unrelated parties, a bad bargain doesn't necessarily imply a gift.

A major concern with a private annuity is when the state of

the annuitant's health has deteriorated to the point where the life expectancy tables cannot be used. A series of court cases have allowed the tables to be used if death is not imminent. More recent authority including revised regulations issued in late 1995 suggests that an effort is being made to require departure from the tables if life expectancy is substantially diminished. This is obviously an important issue if the potential annuitant is suffering from the early stages of an incurable disease.

Estate tax aspects

Ordinarily, the value of property transferred in a commercial or private annuity transaction is not included in the annuitant's gross estate for federal estate tax purposes if the right to receive payments terminates upon the death of the annuitant. So with a single annuitant, an annuity transaction removes the property transferred from the annuitant's estate. This is generally a major reason for selecting the private annuity.

However, the value at the annuitant's death of payments receivable by a survivor of the decedent – such as a spouse – would be included in the gross estate to the extent attributable to the decedent's contribution to annuity acquisition.

If not properly set up, a private annuity can have quite different estate tax results. In the event that the annuitant retains control over the property during his or her lifetime, the annuity payments are tied to the income from the property transferred or the obligor's use of the property is contingent upon death of the annuitant, the transaction may be treated as a transfer with a retained interest. And that makes the full value of the property includible in the annuitant's estate for federal estate tax purposes.

In some cases where the value of the property transferred exceeds substantially the present value of the annuity, the transaction has been held to be a transfer of property with a retained life estate. Again, the value of the property involved is included in the annuitant's gross estate at death. Therefore, it's usually wise to separate out the gift portion of an annuity transaction with a separate transfer made of that amount specifically by gift.

Although a private annuity may be motivated by thoughts of estate tax savings, it should be remembered that amounts received under a private annuity may accumulate to increase the value of the annuitant's estate, particularly if the annuitant lives a longer than normal life. The estate tax problem may not be solved unless amounts received are consumed or transferred by gift during life.

Income tax treatment for the annuitant

The income tax impact of a private annuity transaction on the annuitant is figured by spreading the gain over the period of years measured by the annuitant's life expectancy. And the gain is capital gain if the transferred property was a capital asset or an asset used in the business such as farmland.

EXAMPLE: Returning to the earlier example, a transfer of a $120,000 farm by a 74-year-old male annuitant in exchange for payments of $1,200 per month would produce a gift of $38,949. The present value of the annuity would be $81,051.

If the income tax basis for the property is $40,000, the gain realized would be $41,051 ($81,051 – $40,000).

The "investment in the contract" of $40,000 (the adjusted basis for the property) is divided by the expected return of $145,440 to produce the exclusion ratio of 27.5 percent. Out of each $14,400 annual payment, the annuitant would report 27.5 percent or $3,960 as return of capital which is not taxable. This portion of non-taxable return continues for the annuitant's life expectancy – 10.1 years in this example.

The capital gains income of $41,051 total would be spread over the 10.1 years' life expectancy of the annuitant with $4,064 reported as capital gain each year. The remainder would be reportable as ordinary income. For the first 10.1 years, that would amount to $6,376 per year.

197

After the gain has been fully reported ($41,051) and the basis has been recovered, the amount of payments received would be taxable as ordinary income. Thus, after 10.1 years, the full amount of each payment would be ordinary income.

Along with other concerns, the annuitant should keep in mind the possibilities for recapture of depreciation in establishing a private annuity.

Income tax treatment for the obligor

A key distinction between being an obligor under a private annuity and being a buyer under an installment contract is that there's no deduction for interest paid with a private annuity.

Likewise, then, the unstated interest rules do not apply.

The cost of the property is somewhat uncertain to the obligor who may end up making one annuity payment for the property or many. The transaction may or may not turn out to be a bargain. It all depends on how long the annuitant lives. Since the obligor's cost is uncertain, the income tax basis for the property is uncertain, also.

For purposes of starting a depreciation schedule, the obligor's basis is the value of expected annuity payments to be made under the annuity agreement. Excess payments are added to the basis when, and if, made.

After death of the annuitant, subsequent depreciation is computed using the total payments actually made. And the basis for computing gain or loss would be the total of all payments actually made. Therefore, a premature death of the annuitant would mean a "bargain" for the obligor, but the obligor would have a low income tax basis for the property.

If the property is sold before the annuitant's death, the basis for computing gain is more complicated. The obligor then uses as basis the total of payments actually made plus the present value of payments remaining based on the annuitant's life expectancy on the date of disposition of the property. Death of the annuitant after sale of the property may require adjustment in gain previously reported.

A final point ... the private annuity is complex and involves the full range of taxes. Competent tax advice is a must in setting up a private annuity.

Self-cancelling installment notes

Self-cancelling notes bear some resemblance to private annuities and are also similar in some respects to installment contracts. A self-cancelling installment note (SCIN) is a debt obligation which is extinguished at the death of the seller with the remaining note balance cancelled automatically by the terms of the note. Because the seller bears the risk of cancellation of the principal balance before all payments are made, the SCIN must reflect a risk premium. The risk premium may be in the form of an increased sales price or an increased interest rate.

Like a private annuity, payments under a SCIN terminate at the death of the seller. But unlike a private annuity, the seller can retain a security interest in the property involved which is the case also with an installment contract. The major use of SCIN is likely to be as an alternative to the private annuity.

For a SCIN, the value of the obligation cancelled at death is not included in the transferor's gross estate so the outcome in that respect is favorable and is similar to that of a private annuity. For income tax purposes, a SCIN is treated as an installment sale with each payment divided into return of basis, gain and interest income. The most significant negative feature of a SCIN is that all of the deferred gain is taxed to the decedent's estate, apparently on the estate's first income tax return.

Self-cancelling installment notes are not without drawbacks but do offer a useful alternative to the private annuity and the installment contract.

199

11
Trusts and estate planning

The trust is one of the most flexible and among the most under-used estate planning devices today. Trusts are quite commonly used in urban areas, with trust departments of the larger banks playing a major role as trustees. But in many rural communities, the trust is less well known.

Part of this may be due to myths about the trust and what it can do. Some believe, for example, that trusts are only for incompetents and the very elderly. To a considerable extent, infrequent use of the trust may be attributable to lack of familiarity with it as an estate or business planning device.

Professional advisors can do a great deal to promote a better understanding of the tax and property management aspects of the trust. In many situations, it's a highly appropriate estate planning tool.

Nature of a trust

Stripped to its bare essentials, the trust is relatively simple. A person using a trust is trusting someone else (the trustee) to handle property for the benefit of beneficiaries. A trust has three necessary elements: (1) a trustee, (2) property to be held by the trust or the "corpus" and (3) beneficiaries.

The rules guiding the administration of a trust come from three sources – state law, federal law and the trust instrument.

State law. State law provides a set of governing rules, particularly with respect to investment policies and periodic reporting to a court or other state agency. State laws are concerned with placing various limitations on the powers of the trustee and on the length of time property may be held in trust. In most states, a trust can be created to last for a maximum period measured by the lives of a reasonable number of living people plus 21 years.

This is an ancient rule, known as the Rule Against Perpetuities. It was developed centuries ago by the courts to prevent assets – particularly land – from being "tied up" by the present owners who wished to discourage or prohibit sale or other transfer by their heirs.

Federal law. Federal law provides the basic rules for handling the taxation of trust income. "Simple trusts" are required to distribute all of their income currently and may deduct the amount of income which the trustee is under a duty to distribute. The beneficiaries pay the income tax. "Complex trusts" include all others and likewise may deduct amounts of income for the taxable year which are required to be distributed. Thus, beneficiaries, as well as the trust itself, may be taxpayers. Income tax treatment of accumulations of income by a trust is subject to an intricate set of rules designed to prevent the accumulation of trust income by a complex trust over a period of years with a distribution to a beneficiary only in low income years.

The income tax rate schedule applicable to trusts (and estates) imposes a 15 percent tax on the first $1,600 of taxable income, 28 percent on taxable income between $1,600 and $3,800, 31 percent on taxable income between $3,800 and $5,800, 36 percent on taxable income between $5,800 and $7,900 and 39.6 percent on taxable income exceeding $7,900. These are the brackets for 1996 and are adjusted for inflation each year.

All trusts (both existing and newly created) other than tax-exempt and charitable trusts and grantor trusts are required to adopt the calendar year as the taxable year. Trusts and estates are required to pay estimated tax in the same manner as individuals but with an exemption for an estate's first two years.

The trust instrument generally contains a complete set of guidelines for trust operation. Except for limitations imposed by state law, the person setting up a trust can make his or her own rules about how the trust will operate. The trust instrument typically sets out the powers of the trustee in managing the property, specific rules establishing latitude for making investments, directions for paying out trust income, instructions for the timing of distributions of corpus from the trust and the identity of the beneficiaries.

The trust instrument is, basically, the charter for trust operation. It is drawn with care to fit precisely the objectives of the one establishing the trust.

The trustee may be a bank or trust company or an adult individual or individuals. Some use the services of the trust department of a bank in order to take advantage of investment, accounting or management services available. Others prefer the intimacy of having a member of the family serve as trustee. If an individual serves as trustee and is also a beneficiary, the trust powers must be drafted with care to avoid undesirable tax results.

With the possible exception of family members, a trustee usually receives a fee for managing the trust. This fee varies from area to area. A typical fee for managing a trust investing in corporate stock is one-half of 1 percent of the corpus annually. For farms, trustees often charge a farm manager's fee.

The trust instrument generally specifies who will be entitled to receive income from the trust during its operation. The income beneficiaries may be the same as those designated eventually to receive the corpus. Or, they may be different individuals. Even unborn persons or persons to be identified in the future may be named as beneficiaries of a trust.

A trust instrument might give the trustee discretion to distribute the income among children or grandchildren. This would be a "discretionary spray trust." The trustee might be given the power to distribute income or to retain it in the trust and add it to principal – to that extent it would be an "accumulation trust." A "spendthrift trust" is set up to prevent transfer of trust income or principal ahead of scheduled distributions by act of a beneficiary or a beneficiary's creditors. This does not, of course, prevent creditors from bringing an action to take the property after a beneficiary has received a distribution of principal or income.

An important point: The one setting up the trust (called a grantor or settlor) should know exactly what the trust instrument will accomplish and what it provides. Otherwise, his or her objectives may not be met. If the trust is amendable, that person will likely be unaware of when changes should be made unless he or she has a basic acquaintance with the contents of the trust instrument.

How trusts are used

One of the big uses of the trust is to manage property of minors who are not competent to sell, mortgage or manage their property. A minor's property may be placed in trust with the responsibilities of management handled by the trustee. Similarly, the trust may be useful for holding and managing the property of elderly persons and others not competent to make decisions.

Another major use of trusts is to manage property of people who are legally competent but who prefer not to manage their property. This group may include surviving spouses, those professional persons with insufficient time to manage their investments, and those who simply prefer to "buy" management from a trustee.

A trust is also useful where it is desired to leave someone only a limited interest in property. Thus, a husband may wish to leave his wife a life estate in certain property. Particularly for personal property, a life estate in trust is much more convenient to handle than a legal life estate created in the property itself. More on legal life estates in Chapter 2.

For example, what is a life estate in a cow? Or, a tractor? Problems of who can sell, mortgage or manage the property are solved by giving these powers – and others – to a trustee. A trustee can buy and sell livestock and trade farm equipment, reinvesting the proceeds in other assets, with a minimum of red tape.

Types of Trusts

Most trusts fall into two basic types: living or "inter vivos" trusts and testamentary trusts.

LIVING TRUSTS. Living trusts are set up during the grantor's life with property transferred to the trust. Living trusts may, and often do, continue on after death. A living trust may be revocable when established with the grantor retaining the power or right to amend, revoke or alter the trust. Or, it may be made irrevocable with the property transfer constituting a completed gift.

Living trusts offer the advantage of privacy. A living trust is a personal agreement between the grantor and the trustee. It may not become a matter of public record as does a will which becomes public when filed after death. However, part or all of trust agreements involving the holding of real property may have to be recorded eventually in order to assure good title to a subsequent purchaser from the trust.

REVOCABLE LIVING TRUSTS. Because of the retained right to revoke, alter or amend, revocable living trusts do not save death taxes. The value of the property in the trust would generally be included in the grantor's estate for death tax purposes. In some cases, revocable living trusts may save estate settlement costs since the estate settlement task is simplified.

Simplifying estate settlement. Estates are probated for three basic reasons: (1) to assure that the creditors of the decedent are paid off (proof of this may be necessary to get good title to the property), (2) to establish rights of heirs or others to the property of the decedent, and (3) to pay the necessary income and death taxes. Taxes must, of course, be paid even where a trust is used. But the first two reasons for probate may be met with a trust owning the property at death and providing rules for ultimate distribution of the property.

Management of property. One attractive application of the revocable living trust is in providing a management vehicle for the property of older members of the family as they advance in age. As older individuals pass into the stage of being unable or unwilling to manage their property, it can be helpful to have a revocable living trust already established. Then in the last few years of life, as competency to manage property may become an issue, the trust can function flexibly to provide the needed property management.

It might work this way – at age 65 or 70, the revocable living trust is set up with property transferred to it. The property owner could be the initial trustee, but with a trusted successor trustee designated. In most cases, income would be paid to the individual (or individuals) establishing the trust. Then as the initial trustee approached incompetency or simply desired to be less heavily burdened with property management, the trusteeship would shift to the designated successor trustee. The successor trustee could then function to manage the property, liquidating it as necessary to create funds for the care and support of the beneficiaries in their later years. Frequently, their income needs are high as they may be residing in a hospital, nursing home or extended care facility.

This approach to planning for property management late in life may sidestep the problems of alleging and proving incompetency which may be necessary in order for a guardian of the property or conservator to be appointed.

Funding living trusts. An essential step in setting up an effective living trust is to transfer assets to the trust. It is necessary to transfer the land, investments, bank and savings accounts and other assets to the trust.

Before transferring property to a revocable living trust, several points should be checked –

• Transferring the principal residence to a revocable living trust does not make the residence ineligible for a tax-free sale and reinvestment and does not preclude eligibility for excluding up to $125,000 of gain from income on sale of the residence after reaching age 55.

• Depreciation deductions are apportioned between trustee and income beneficiaries as trust income is allocated. Expense method depreciation cannot be claimed by most kinds of trust. However, a living trust that is treated as owned by the one who

206

set it up (a grantor trust) may not be subject to that limitation.

• Transfer of closely held business assets could terminate installment payment of federal estate tax unless it is a mere change in organizational form.

• Recapture of special use valuation benefits could occur unless all beneficiaries are qualified heirs and consent to personal liability for recapture tax.

• Series E bonds may be transferred without causing taxability of accrued interest.

• Conveyance of joint tenancy property to a revocable living trust apparently results in a severance of the joint tenancy. Any gift would be covered by the 100 percent federal gift marital deduction if to a spouse.

• In general, installment obligations may be transferred without recognition of gain. But special care is needed where the obligor under the contract is the trust beneficiary.

• Stock in an S corporation can be held by a "qualified Subchapter S trust" and a grantor trust (up to the grantor's death and for 60 days thereafter) and for up to two years after death if the entire amount of trust property is included in the grantor's estate. Ownership of S corporation stock by other types of trusts terminates the S corporation election and the C corporation rules apply.

• The ordinary loss deduction on sale, liquidation or worthlessness of stock of a corporation ("Section 1244 stock") does not apply to stock dispositions by a trust, regardless of how the stock was acquired. Again, there's a question whether this applies to a living trust that is a "grantor" trust.

• For encumbered land, check carefully to see whether a transfer to trust would constitute a disposition to accelerate the indebtedness.

• Relative to the range of recapture possibilities, such as soil and water conservation expense, recapture should not normally occur.

• Property interests are apparently not made ineligible for installment payment of federal estate tax if held in a revocable

207

living trust at death.

• Care should be exercised in including retirement accounts in a living trust because of possible adverse income tax consequences. In a 1991 ruling, a decedent's account balance in a profit sharing plan was included in a living trust with the plan balance distributed to a marital trust. The spouse as the income beneficiary also had a limited right to withdraw principal. However, IRS ruled that withdrawal of the maximum amount by the spouse followed by a rollover of the amount into an IRA was includible in the spouse's income.

A revocable living trust is generally treated as a "grantor trust" with all trust income taxable to the grantor. If the grantor is not the trustee, a Form 1041 is required to be filed with a separate statement attached showing income, deductions and credits attributable to the grantor from the trust.

If an individual is both grantor and trustee and all items of income, deduction and credit are treated as owned by the grantor, it is not necessary for the individual to file a Form 1041. The information is reported on the grantor's individual return.

In general, trusts are to obtain a taxpayer identification number. However, for trusts in which the same individual is both grantor and trustee and is treated as the owner of all assets held by trust, the requirement of obtaining an identification number has been eliminated.

Joint or separate trusts. The popularity of revocable living trusts has convinced many couples that it's a good idea. But planners have had differing views on whether a husband and wife should have one joint living trust or each should have their own.

• The arguments for separate trusts generally point out that, if each has their own, a spouse can revoke his or her own trust even though the other spouse dies or becomes incapacitated. And each can revoke their own trust if they simply cannot agree on what to do.

These are persuasive arguments for dividing the property and creating two trusts, usually with mirror-image provisions at death. Creating balanced estates represents sound planning – any time the combined family wealth exceeds $600,000 – if one of the objectives is to minimize the death taxes over both deaths. Or if the objective is to pass a maximum amount of wealth from the estate of the survivor.

• Those urging a single joint trust for the spouses usually have another objective in mind – obtaining a new income tax basis for all of the property at both deaths.

With separate trusts, at the death of the first spouse to die, the property in that spouse's trust is subject to federal estate tax – and gets a new income tax basis. The result is that potential gain on the property is wiped out. And because of the 100 percent federal estate tax marital deduction, there's no federal estate tax due if the property passes to the survivor outright.

By using a joint trust, and giving each spouse a general power of appointment over the entire trust, the entire value of the property is included in the estate of the first to die and it is typically hoped that the entire amount of property would receive a new income tax basis at that person's death. A general power of appointment means that the power could be exercised to benefit the person holding the power.

One problem with that approach has been that it may run up the tax bill at the survivor's death to leave all of the family wealth to the survivor outright. For those with estates over $600,000, some federal estate tax would be due at the second death if everything is left to the survivor.

Now the Internal Revenue Service has added a second reason to be cautious about joint revocable living trusts. IRS ruled in 1992 that only one-half of the property received a new income tax basis at the death of the first to die, not all of it as planned. In the facts of that ruling, the net income from the joint trust was to be distributed to the spouses. The trustee had discretion to distribute principal from the trust. During their joint lives, either spouse acting alone could revoke the trust. In that event, an undivided one-half interest in the property of the trust would be distributed to each spouse. Each of them had a general power of appointment over all of the property exercisable at death. If the power was not exercised, the entire amount of trust property passed to the surviving spouse at the first death.

The wife died about a month after the trust was created with the power left unexercised. The trust property passed to the husband. The entire amount of property was subject to federal estate tax. But only one half received a new income tax basis.

Although the ruling has been criticized, it dampens the enthusiasm for joint living trusts for spouses.

Separate trusts have the advantage of maintaining a clear cut outcome if one of the spouses decides to revoke the trust. That could happen if the other spouse dies or becomes incompetent or the couple can no longer agree on major decisions.

IRREVOCABLE LIVING TRUSTS. Irrevocable living trusts may save death taxes. If neither decision making power nor the right to receive income is retained by the grantor, the trust property would normally not be taxable in the decedent's estate.

Irrevocable trusts may also save estate settlement costs, since completed transfers during life would normally not be subject to probate at the death of the transferor.

For many people, irrevocable trusts are not particularly attractive estate planning tools. The grantor can keep little, if any, control over the trust or the trust property and would be unable to retain the right to income from the property if tax saving were important.

Medicaid qualifying trusts. In recent years, interest has grown in arrangements that would qualify individuals for Title XIX Medicaid benefits for health care. To qualify, three tests must be met: (1) the Medicaid applicant must be in a category of persons eligible to participate in the program (the "circumstances" test); (2) the applicant's assets must be within specified levels (the "assets" test); and (3) the applicant's available income must be less than a prescribed amount to avoid having any of the income used to pay medical expenses (the "income" test).

The assets test is generally the most difficult to meet. The rules as to the amount of assets that can be retained are complex and contain numerous exceptions. But a key provision disregards gifts made within 36 months of the application for benefits unless a satisfactory showing is made that the applicant intended to dispose of the assets at fair market value or the assets were transferred exclusively for a purpose other than to qualify for Medicaid assistance.

Before 1986, discretionary trusts (where the trustee had discretion to pay income or principal to a beneficiary receiving Medicaid benefits) could be used to isolate property from beneficiaries and to assure Medicaid eligibility. But under the 1986 amendments, amounts included in a discretionary trust were considered "available" to the maximum extent possible in the beneficiary's favor. However, that limitation applied only to trusts between an individual and that person's spouse and did not prohibit other kinds of trusts.

For transfers after August 10, 1993, assets of trusts created or funded by a Medicaid applicant or spouse are considered available to the applicant to the extent the applicant derives any benefit.

A major concern for many are the ethical aspects of deliberately transferring away assets to qualify for Medicaid benefits even where that can be done legally.

Grantor retained interest trusts. The enactment of the latest limits on estate freezes has focused attention on the use of various planning techniques whereby property is placed in trust with an interest retained by the grantor. The major approaches are the grantor retained income trust (GRIT), the grantor retained annuity trust (GRAT) and the grantor retained unitrust (GRUT).

The objective is to reduce the gift to children or other remainder holders by retaining an interest for a period of years and hopefully to live beyond the period of the retained interest, with the property passing to children or others under favorable tax circumstances.

General approach. In a typical situation, property is transferred in trust with an interest retained by the grantor for a specified number of years. A major concern with trusts involving interests retained by the grantor is how to value the retained interest. Under the 1990 legislation, retained interests in trust or term interests in property generally are valued at zero for federal gift tax purposes unless in the form of an annuity or unitrust interest. Thus, if a transfer is made in trust by the transferor to or for the benefit of a member of the family, and the transferor or family member retains an interest in the trust, the amount of the gift is the value of the transferred property less the value of any interest retained by the transferor or family member. Unless the retained interest is a "qualified interest," the retained interest is valued at zero. A qualified interest is a right to receive at least annually a fixed amount (or a fixed percentage of the initial value of the trust), a right to receive at least annually a fixed percentage of the value of the trust property valued annually, or a non-contingent remainder interest if all other interests in the property are qualified interests.

GRATS. A Granter Retained Annuity Trust (GRAT) requires that the interest be an irrevocable right to receive a fixed amount payable to (or for the benefit of) the annuitant for each taxable year of the term.

By adjusting the annuity payment amount or percentage and the term of the retained interest, it is mathematically possible to "zero out" the value of the remainder interest. However, in one case where payments equalled 99.171 percent of the amount transferred to the trust upon creation, IRS took the position that a taxable gift had taken place nonetheless because of the possibility the grantor might die during the term.

GRUTS. A Grantor Retained Unitrust amount (GRUT) requires that the transferor or applicable family member have an irrevocable right to receive payment at least annually of a fixed percentage of the net fair market value of the trust assets, determined annually.

Residence GRIT. Under a Grantor Retained Income Trust

(GRIT) involving the residence, the transferor uses the residence for a period of years, then the residence is distributed outright to the beneficiaries of the trust, usually the transferor's children, or held in trust for other beneficiaries. The amount of the gift by the transferor is calculated by subtracting the value of the transferor's retained rights from the value of the residence.

Example: X, a taxpayer age 65, transfers a residence valued at $100,000 to a trust and retains the right to use the residence for five years. The retained right is valued, under the actuarial tables, at approximately 36 percent of the value of the residence or $36,000. The gift would be approximately $64,000 which would come out of the unified credit. The federal gift tax annual exclusion would not be available inasmuch as the gift is a future interest.

If the transferor dies after the end of the period of retained use of the residence, the amount of the gift ($64,000) would be added back into the estate, not the value of the residence at death (probably $100,000 or more). This is the desired outcome.

If the taxpayer dies before the end of the period of retained use of the residence, the value of the residence itself is included in the transferor's estate at its date of death value (or as of the alternate valuation date). This is not the desired result, but the transferor is left no worse off than had ownership of the residence been retained.

A taxpayer may create only two personal residence trusts. A personal residence trust is prohibited from holding any asset other than one residence to be used as a personal residence of the holder of the term interest. The trust may hold proceeds payable as a result of damage, destruction or involuntary conversion of the residence. The proceeds must be reinvested within two years in a personal residence. The residence must not be occupied by anyone other than the taxpayer, a spouse or dependent and must be available to the taxpayer as a personal residence. Expenses of the residence may be paid directly by the taxpayer as term holder. A trust will not qualify as a personal residence trust if sold or otherwise transferred or used as something other than a personal

213

residence.

A personal residence may include adjacent land not in excess of that which is reasonably appropriate for residential purposes.

Example: M conveys 160 acres of farmland including a residence and business outbuildings and 155 acres of cropland to a trust, retaining a term interest in the trust. The trust is not a personal residence trust because it includes assets in excess of what is reasonably appropriate for residential purposes.

QPRT. A "qualified personal residence trust" provides additional flexibility. A qualified personal residence trust (QPRT) is similar to personal residence trusts with the same definition as to personal residence. A QPRT is permitted to hold assets other than the personal residence for certain time periods. Cash can be held in a separate account not exceeding what is required for payment of trust expenses, including mortgage payments, incurred or reasonably expected to be paid within six months from the date the cash is contributed to the trust, improvements to be paid within six months from the date of contribution to the trust, purchase of an initial residence within three months of the date of the contribution if the trustee has previously entered into a contract for the purchase, and purchase of a replacement residence within three months from the date of the contribution provided the trustee has previously entered into a contract for the purchase.

Using property after the term interest. If the grantor desires to continue using the property after the expiration of the term interest (which could well be the case for a farm or residence) the grantor could enter into a lease arrangement with the holder or holders of the remainder interest, after the end of the term interest for fair and customary rental or, the person who set up the trust arrangement could give the spouse a life estate to follow the grantor's retained interest. Another strategy suggested by some is for the one who set up the trust arrangement to repurchase the property (such as the residence) from the trust for fair market value. Apparently, no negative income tax consequences would occur and would enable cash or other property to pass to those holding the remainder interest (usually the children). Regulations have been proposed effectively preventing sale of the residence back to the grantor.

To avoid inclusion of the property in the grantor's gross estate, the grantor should avoid remaining an income beneficiary of the trust, or retaining control over the distribution policies of the trust including the power to sprinkle income, the power to accumulate income (especially if the income would pass to a third person), the power to invade principal, the power to alter or amend the trust instrument, and the power to terminate the trust.

TESTAMENTARY TRUSTS. Testamentary trusts are often set up as a part of individuals' wills and become effective at death. The property owner retains complete right to the property until death. Following estate settlement the property is transferred to the trust which then begins to function.

As might be expected, testamentary trusts save neither death taxes nor estate settlement costs. Their purpose is to provide for management of property after death.

Testamentary trusts for minors are often used to hold and manage the property of minor children if parents should die before the children reach legal age. The trust may provide for discretionary powers in the trustee to pay out income as needed for the care, support, maintenance and education of the children. Income not needed currently is accumulated and added to the corpus. When the children reach a specified age, they may receive their share of the accumulated income and corpus.

Often, the most difficult problems faced by the trustee of a testamentary trust for minors involve educational support. In which school may the minor enroll … the most expensive in the country? For how many years may the minor anticipate educational support … four years, or ten? Given a particular school, at what level should the minor be supported … tuition and fees only, or tuition, fees, books, fraternity or sorority costs, $400 per month spending money plus a new automobile every year? It makes a great deal of difference to the minor. And may make a great deal of difference to the other beneficiaries.

If desired, a will containing a testamentary trust for minors can spell out guidelines for educational support. Establishing fixed annual payments may not be wise because of the unknown effects of inflation. But a parent could, for example, define educational support in terms of the costs for tuition, fees and residence hall living at a specified educational institution at the time the question of educational support must be answered. Such a definition would create a fund of money for use by the beneficiary at a college or university of his or her choice.

Another problem in drafting testamentary trusts relates to the question of when the trust funds are carved up into shares for the respective children – or children of deceased children. Is this to be done when the trust comes into existence with each share thereafter maintained as a separate trust fund? Should the division of funds wait until the oldest child has reached the age of distribution? Or until the youngest child has reached that age?

In making this decision, one should keep in mind the possible built-in advantage for the older beneficiaries if the division is made when the trust is created. The older children may have obtained part or all of their education before the division was made while the younger ones' educations may be paid out of their own shares. Some use an "education equalization clause" as an equalizer with shares of younger children receiving an added amount representing educational support not yet received.

Another common use of the testamentary trust is the so-called "marital deduction" trust for the surviving spouse. As discussed in Chapter 4, a testamentary trust could be used to hold and administer the life estate portion of a Model II or Modified Model II plan. And a trust could be used to hold and administer the package B (life estate) part of a Model I plan or to hold both packages A and B in a Model I plan. A will including the latter is commonly known as a "two-trust marital deduction will."

SHORT-TERM TRUSTS. Short-term or "Clifford type" trusts

have been used in the past principally to save income tax. With such trusts, income producing property was transferred to the trust initially and was returned to the grantor at the termination of the trust. While the trust was in existence, income was paid to the designated income beneficiaries. If the trust was set up to last for more than 10 years, the income could be taxed to the income beneficiaries provided certain requirements were met.

However, authority for short-term or Clifford trusts has been repealed effective for transfers in trust made after March 1, 1986.

LIFE INSURANCE TRUSTS. Typically, as a planning strategy, the ownership of life insurance policies is transferred to another person – often the other spouse or an adult child. If the transfer occurs more than three years before death, the proceeds should not be included in the gross estate if made payable to a named beneficiary.

There are, however, several potential problems with individual ownership of life insurance policies. (1) The policy owner may die before the insured, with the chance that policy ownership may be held by the insured at death. (2) There is no assurance that policy proceeds would be available to the insured's estate to augment liquidity. (3) The management of policy proceeds may pose a problem, particularly if relatively large amounts are involved. (4) The insured may be reluctant to turn over control of the policies to the new owner, especially if the owner is the other spouse and a dissolution of marriage is a possibility. (5) Income from the policy proceeds after the insured's death would generally be taxed to the beneficiary. A life insurance trust can be used to solve all five of the problems with the life insurance policies held by the trust rather than by an individual owner. Life insurance trusts may be revocable or irrevocable, and can be funded or unfunded. Unfunded irrevocable life insurance trusts are relatively common in non-farm estate planning.

With irrevocable trusts, the transfer of life insurance policies – and the subsequent payment of premiums – are likely to involve gifts of future interests. Thus, the federal gift tax annual exclusion would not be available to offset the amount of the transfer. However, through the use of "Crummey-type" withdrawal powers, what would otherwise be a future interest can be transformed into a present interest eligible for the federal gift tax annual exclusion. Such withdrawal powers typically give beneficiaries the right to withdraw a limited amount – often up to $5,000 or 5 percent of the trust principal annually. Beneficiaries should have knowledge of the power's existence and a reasonable opportunity to exercise the power.

The grantor is usually taxed on trust income to the extent the income could have been used to pay premiums on policies on the life of the grantor or the grantor's spouse. Some trusts deliberately give the trustee the power to pay premiums on the life of the grantor or grantor's spouse with the objective of assuring that all income, deductions and credits are taxed back to the grantor. One reason is that interest deductions on policy loans are then available to the grantor. Such trusts have come to be known as "super trusts." IRS has indicated that advance rulings would no longer be issued on income and gift tax consequences of such trusts.

Another income tax problem can arise if policies subject to a loan are transferred to an irrevocable life insurance trust and the indebtedness exceeds the grantor's income tax basis in the policies. One possible outcome is that policy proceeds may become subject to income tax at death.

Life insurance trusts do not completely resolve the problem of making policy proceeds available to the insured's estate to augment liquidity. Of the four major alternative arrangements, none is completely trouble free.

• If the trustee of the life insurance trust is *required* to pay the insured's death taxes and estate settlement costs, the policy proceeds are subject to federal estate tax liability. This is usually not a desirable outcome if the insured's estate is large enough to incur federal estate tax liability.

• The trustee could be authorized to purchase assets from the insured's estate. Special problems arise if the estate has elected installment payment of federal estate tax. Any purchase would count as a disposition for purposes of the rule limiting dispositions or withdrawals to less than 50 percent of the business interest.

A life insurance trust with family members as beneficiaries would probably be an eligible purchaser of land under special use valuation. Purchase of land from the estate would trigger little – if any – recognition of gain at that time. However, massive income tax liability could result from resale by the trust. The income tax basis of special use value land to the trust as purchaser would be the special use value plus the excess of fair market value of the land on purchase over the fair market value at death. More on this in Chapter 3.

• If the life insurance trust makes loans to the estate, repayment of the loan would often involve the sale of assets with the usual income tax implications. If loans are not repaid, the estate of the insured runs the risk of realizing income on the discharge of indebtedness owed.

• In the event the trustee of the life insurance trust is empowered to make voluntary distributions of funds to the estate, gift tax challenges may be encountered unless the trust beneficiaries are identical to estate beneficiaries and the shares are the same. Also, generation skipping problems may arise upon distribution of proceeds from the trust unless carefully planned.

GENERATION SKIPPING TRUSTS. Generation skipping trusts are used to provide income to a generation or two of heirs with the property eventually passing to individuals two or three generations down the line. For example, an individual might leave property to a child for life, then to the grandchildren for life and then to the great grandchildren outright. In the past, if accomplished by will, federal estate tax was imposed at the death of the individual establishing the arrangement. But no further federal estate tax would be due until the deaths of the great grandchildren owning the property. Yet the intervening generations would receive the major economic benefit from the property – its income – without the property being subject to federal estate tax in their estates.

The Tax Reform Act of 1976 tightened the rules several notches on such generation skipping arrangements.

However, the Tax Reform Act of 1986 repealed the 1976 legislation and imposed a flat rate tax on generation-skipping transfers equal to the maximum federal estate and gift tax rate. An exemption of $1 million per transferor is provided in lieu of the credit and grandchild exclusion under the 1976 law. The 1986 provision is effective for death-time transfers after October 22, 1986, and to transfers during life after September 25, 1985.

The generation skipping transfer tax is discussed in greater detail in Chapter 3.

FAMILY-ESTATE TRUSTS. "Family estate" trusts, "pure" trusts "constitutional" trusts, "common-law" trusts or "Massachusetts business trusts" that promise to solve all of an individual's estate planning problems should be approached with caution. The firms selling the family estate-type trust do so almost on a door-to-door basis. Typically, they move into an area, solicit the help of some local individuals who know relatively little about trusts, perhaps hold a meeting or two and then begin a one-to-one campaign with local individuals owning a substantial amount of property. Farmers are generally a primary target. So are medical doctors, veterinarians and others with significant property holdings.

The essential message is that well-to-do people have made use of the trust for years – the Rockefellers, the Mellons, the Kennedys, and others. The promoters point out that you can take advantage of the trust as well. In fact, some promotional efforts stress your constitutional right to use such trusts. A strong element of patriotism is mixed with the explanation in some situations.

Basically, the trust they're promoting purports to be an irrevocable living trust. And such trusts have been used by well-to-do families for years. What they don't tell you is that such trusts haven't been used by such families in the ways they suggest.

In general, individuals are told they can create such a trust, transfer their lifetime services to the trust, charge family living expenses to the trust and avoid the usual income tax and death tax liability that comes with ownership of property or receipt of income. For an individual in a high income tax bracket who would face substantial tax liability at death, that is a welcome message.

The Internal Revenue Service, in 1975, staked out its position rather clearly. It wouldn't work. And IRS has been unusually successful in court in defending its position.

Assignment of income. A major attraction of family estate-type trusts is the representation that individuals can avoid paying income tax on their incomes. By assigning their lifetime services to the trust, so the explanation goes, they can avoid income tax as individuals. And the trust has all sorts of deductions that can be claimed, they argue.

In one case, a Nebraska radiologist had established such a trust, assigned his lifetime services to the trust and transferred the family real and personal property (including the family residence) to the trust also. Among the items of property transferred were "a popcorn popper, ice skates, drinking glasses, an aquarium and a bathroom scale." Initially, the radiologist's wife and son were the trustees. He also became a trustee at a later date.

After it was established, the trust then proceeded to provide its "manager" (the radiologist) with housing, transportation, health care expenses, and educational allowances. The trust agreed to foot the bill for the cost of recreation for the manager's family and all miscellaneous expenses except for food and clothing. All expenses for the personal residence were paid from the trust as were the expenses for all automobiles driven by the family.

As might be expected, IRS challenged the arrangement and the Tax Court agreed with the IRS. The radiologist got a bill for $73,994.18 in back income taxes and interest plus a 5 percent penalty for "negligence or intentional disregard of the rules and regulations of the Internal Revenue Code." The Tax Court referred to the arrangement as "a flagrant tax avoidance scheme."

That case isn't alone. It simply was more colorful than most.

More than 115 other cases have reached the Tax Court, all decided in favor of IRS. Most of the cases have held that the arrangement was so far off base that the expenses incurred in creating the trust were not deductible for income tax purposes.

The cases have made it clear that assignment of lifetime services to a trust isn't effective to shift income tax liability to the trust. The income is still taxed to whomever earned it.

Death Tax Liability. Promoters also typically represent that the "units of beneficial ownership" – received when property is transferred to the trust – aren't subject to federal estate or state death tax when the holder dies. IRS disagreed, in a 1975 ruling. And the IRS seems to be on firm ground. Any time property is transferred away but the right to income is retained or controls or powers are retained over the property, the value of the property is included in the individual's estate at death.

Gift Tax Liability. The promoters assure interested individuals that there's no federal gift tax liability on formation of the trust. And IRS agrees with that. The amount of control over the trust and over the trust property means that it's not a completed transfer for federal gift tax purposes. This is about the only point on which IRS and the promoters agree.

How the Trust is Taxed. In general, a trust is a separate entity for income tax purposes and computes its income tax liability using the separate estate and trust income tax rate schedule. With some exceptions, the determination of gross income of a trust is handled in essentially the same manner as for an individual.

IRS points out, however, that trusts of the family estate type have more corporate than non-corporate characteristics and may end up being taxed as a *corporation* rather than as a trust. That doesn't sound so bad on the surface, with corporations now being taxed at a graduated rate starting at 15 percent on the first $50,000 of corporate taxable income. The big question is whether corporate tax treatment would mean such a trust would be subjected to corporate tax rules on liquidation. Many of the trusts are liquidated when it is discovered how limited their usefulness is to the family. Liquidation under corporation rules could produce painful income tax results.

Title Problems. As indicated, most of the trusts purport to be irrevocable, at least for a stated period. If it is desired to terminate the trust prematurely and return the property to the individual creating the trust, difficult land title problems could arise. Again, the usual move is to try to terminate the trust once it is discovered that the trust cannot deliver on the representations made about it.

Expense Involved. By usual estate planning standards, family estate type trusts are expensive to create. Most promoters seem to charge in relationship to size of estate. Costs of $2,500 to $10,000 are not at all unusual. Some have paid $25,000 or more.

Part of the justification for the high cost is that the charge represents years of service from the promoter and that the trust will save on legal and accounting fees. In fact, some report that they are urged not to discuss the creation of such a trust with their attorney or accountant "because they'll only try to talk you out of it." As a result, some individuals may have such a trust for months – or even years – before getting up enough courage to discuss it with their professional advisors.

Off-shore trusts. The latest wrinkle in the family estate trust area is the multiple foreign or off-shore trust. Such trusts typically involve one or more domestic trusts (often as many as three) and one or more foreign trusts located in a low-profile foreign country. Belize in Central America and the Turks and Caicos Islands have been favorites.

The usual approach is for transactions among the domestic trusts and between the domestic and foreign trusts to produce a loss which is reported in a manner to offset other U.S. income. The foreign trusts end up with a gain which is typically not reported.

All such trusts are controlled, directly or indirectly, by the grantor. Any time the grantor wishes, the trusts can be made to collapse with any property returned to the grantor. Although appearing to be more sophisticated than run-of-the-mill family estate trusts, IRS has challenged successfully the use of such trusts. The foreign-type trust seems no more likely to succeed than the domestic version. Indeed, promoters have been convicted of criminal violations under federal law in several cases over the past few years.

IN CONCLUSION. As a flexible estate planning device the trust is worth considering in many situations. Property management may be turned over to a trustee who is empowered to make decisions in light of circumstances existing at the time decisions must be made. And income tax and death tax savings are possible. But be especially watchful of "family estate" type trusts. They are nothing but trouble.

12
Life insurance in estate planning

Life insurance deserves consideration during estate planning. All too often, the insurance part of the estate plan is not reviewed in the estate planning process and hence does not dovetail with the overall plan developed to accomplish the objectives identified to guide the estate planning effort. Even a modest life insurance program should be part of the general evaluation carried on as part of estate planning. It is especially important for beneficiary designations to be consistent with the rest of the plan for disposition of assets and for policy ownership to be consistent with tax saving objectives.

Role of life insurance

Acquiring life insurance involves making an investment. And, like all rational investments, it's well to consider (1) the need, (2) the alternatives to meeting the need, and (3) the most economical way to meet the need.

There are many uses for life insurance – to provide funds for the off-farm heirs (so on-farm heirs may receive farm assets); to assure retirement income for the parents, possibly through an annuity; to provide funds to pay off debt obligations at death; to generate liquidity for payment of death taxes and estate settlement costs; to create an estate where none might otherwise exist; and to protect those dependent upon an income stream. Fewer alternatives exist for the latter. It's typically the priority reason for including life insurance in an estate building program. The other uses mentioned – except for creation of an estate and payment of debt – tend to surface more as a matter of estate planning after the estate is built.

Economic dependency

Unanticipated death of someone on whom others are economically dependent can create serious problems. Death of a young parent with several children typifies the problem situation. Ironically, the greatest need for economic protection arises when the young family is least able to afford it. When the children are grown and the estate has increased from investments – in the farm business or otherwise – the need for economic protection may be far less.

Figure 6. Survivors' income needs.

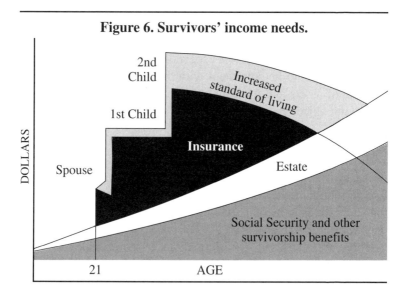

Actually, as shown in Figure 6, the greatest need for protection from interruption of income arises at the birth of the last child (unless, possibly, the ages of the children are spaced such that some are grown when the last one is born). The birth of each successive child pushes the need for income protection to new highs. For each day following the birth of the last child, each child is one day closer to being self-supporting and a dependent spouse is one day closer to death. Thus, the peak need for protec-

226

tion from interruption of the income stream on which the family is dependent typically occurs at the birth of the last child.

Eventually, social security and other survivorship benefits plus the income-creating capacity of accumulated assets may be sufficient for support of those dependent upon the insured's income stream. But in those crucial early years, when support needs are high and income for the survivors would otherwise be low, life insurance may play a crucial role in planning for financial security. With the support needs declining with time, it may be helpful to give some consideration to term insurance – particularly decreasing term insurance.

As portrayed in Figure 6, the effects of inflation plus gradually rising expectations with respect to standard of living may boost the income needs for the survivors over time; that is to say, an assessment of expected income needs by a young couple at age 25 with no children may indicate modest income needs for the expected survivors. But after acquiring a more expensive life style, the survivors might view the planned income amount as less than adequate. This suggests a need for periodic assessment of income needs for the survivors.

Use of life insurance to supplement survivorship benefits suggests a couple of rules of thumb:

1. Be sure the insurance protection is concentrated on the income generator. Insuring lives of children may be defensible on grounds of (a) guarding against the problem of non-insurability if illness or a disabling accident should strike, or (b) providing for last illness, death and burial expenses. But the overriding need is for adequate coverage of the person responsible for economic support.

2. Review available types of insurance, especially term insurance, with an eye to obtaining adequate coverage at a cost that can be afforded at that stage in life.

Realistic assessment of other forms of income or economic support should be part of the insurance portion of the estate building plan as noted in Figure 6. Survivorship benefits from social security coverage should be calculated. It takes "currently insured" status to be eligible for limited survivorship benefits. That generally means qualification for at least 6 of the last 13 quarters. After 40 quarters of coverage, a person is "permanently insured" which carries survivorship benefits. For older individuals, less than 40 quarters is required for permanently insured status.

Inventory items – stored grain, livestock and feed, machinery, land and other investments – figure into the picture, as well.

Insurance tends to be the variable investment that fills in to bring income protection up to the minimum level desired to assure a particular standard of living.

Liquidity for costs and taxes

Within a period of a little more than a year after death, estate settlement costs and taxes are due as discussed in more detail in Chapter 5. While the due date for state inheritance tax varies by state, the federal estate tax is due nine months after death. And the estate settlement costs are due on or before the closing of the estate which typically occurs 12 to 18 months after death. Debts of the decedent also may involve cash payment shortly after death.

Where it's hoped the farm business can continue to function after death of the parents or other major shareholders, loss of capital from the firm to pay estate settlement costs and taxes may either create a debt burden, possibly substantial, or lead to reduction in size of the business as assets are sold to create liquidity. Hence, the problems of illiquidity are generally more severe if it's planned for the business to continue or if for other reasons it's desired that the assets not be sold or mortgaged. Otherwise, liquidity can be created by sale or mortgage of inventory property or other assets.

As noted in Chapter 5, insurance provides one means for enhancing the liquidity position of the estate. This can be done by making insurance proceeds payable to the estate (which typically subjects the proceeds to death taxes and estate settlement costs), by making the proceeds payable to a trustee empowered to purchase assets from the estate (which may trigger substantial income tax liability and which may result in a debt obligation from the estate to the trust), by authorizing the trustee of a life insurance trust to loan funds to the estate or by arranging for the trustee to make voluntary distributions to the estate. These alternatives are discussed in Chapter 11.

There are other possibilities for solving the liquidity problems. Installment payment of federal estate tax, extension of time for payment of federal estate tax, corporate stock redemption after death and use of "flower bonds" (redeemed after death at par) to pay federal estate tax are discussed in Chapter 5.

Liquidity augmenting alternatives thus fall into two basic groups – (1) those such as life insurance and savings that involve accumulation of capital *before* death and (2) those such as installment payment of federal estate tax or post-death borrowing that involve payment of death tax and estate settlement cost obligations *after* death. Careful calculations are required to determine the most economically optimal alternative or set of alternatives for handling the liquidity problem.

Capital for inherited shares

Again, if business continuation becomes a key objective for the farm business, loss of equity or ownership capital to pay off-farm heirs their inherited shares may create serious problems for business continuation. Erosion of capital to meet these demands may dwarf the problems of paying estate settlement costs and taxes.

For a family of four children, three of whom live off the farm, the rights to 75 percent of the family wealth might flow out of the firm at death of the parents. Unless the parents have planned in anticipation of the problem, off-farm heirs as tenants in common with the on-farm heirs can usually demand partition and sale A frequent outcome is: (1) a heavy burden for the firm, (2) reduction in size of firm as assets are sold to create liquidity or (3) termination of the farm business.

A solution to this problem is discussed in Chapter 19 and Chapter 23 with the corporation reducing the leverage of off-farm heirs to demand partition and sale. Life insurance represents another possible solution as insurance proceeds are available for the off-farm heirs with the on-farm heirs acquiring the tangible farm property at death. Important economic questions are involved in the choice of means for solving the problem.

Retirement funds of parents

Typically, the retiring parents plan for income in the form of: (1) land rent and social security benefits if the farm business itself is phased out at retirement, or (2) a share of business income (possible salary, interest on debentures and stock dividends if a corporation is involved or a distributive share from a partnership), plus social security benefits if the farm business is to continue. The installment sale as discussed in Chapters 8 and 9, the private annuity in Chapter 10 and the self-canceling installment note, also in Chapter 10, afford additional alternatives.

Types of life insurance

Life insurance comes in a bewildering array of types and forms. The most widely sold and best known is whole life or ordinary life. Numerous variations exist: 20-payment life, 20-year endowment, life paid up at 65, and countless others. Then there is term insurance. And it comes in various types.

TERM INSURANCE. Because life insurance pays off at death, and the probability of death for an individual increases with each passing year, the "cost" of the insurance protection rises with age. For term insurance, with no cash value or savings account feature, that rising cost leads to rising premiums as age increases. Or, it leads to decreasing death benefits with an unchanging premium.

Term insurance, therefore, involves the purchase of pure protection. In effect, the policy holder's payment relates directly to the probability of death.

There's level non-renewable term with a fixed death benefit and a fixed premium (over say a five-year period).

Then there's decreasing term with a fixed annual premium and a diminishing death benefit as the insured grows older. Some find decreasing term particularly attractive since the decreasing coverage should be accompanied by decreasing financial responsibilities and a growing estate with the result that the needs of survivors could be met despite the decline in death benefits from insurance. See Figure 6.

Some term policies carry the right to convert to whole life or ordinary life without medical examination. This permits a young individual with limited means and heavy responsibilities to acquire substantial amounts of coverage at relatively low cost and then, if desired, to convert part or all of the coverage to whole life at a later time.

WHOLE LIFE INSURANCE. Whole life or ordinary life insurance is also known as cash value insurance protection. It combines a savings element with pure insurance protection. The premium amount remains constant over the life of the insurance contract. Payments in the early years exceed the cost of "pure protection" and build up a cash value.

The savings element of whole life insurance may be compared with alternative saving opportunities in terms of return on investment and accessibility. The cash value may be borrowed at a rate of interest specified in the policy or obtained if the policy is canceled.

Many whole life policies can be converted to an annuity paying a fixed monthly income for life. Likewise, the holder of a whole life policy can elect to take a reduced amount of paid-up insurance and terminate premium payment. Otherwise, premium payments continue as required by the policy.

Policy ownership & beneficiary designation

For estate planning purposes, policy ownership and beneficiary designations take on great significance. Both are important in determining whether policy proceeds are subject to the federal estate tax as discussed in Chapter 3. And one or both may be factors in state inheritance taxation as well. In several states, only policies payable to the estate as beneficiary are subject to the state inheritance tax and estate settlement costs (attorney's and executor's fees).

Beneficiary designations are also important for estate planning purposes in dovetailing with the overall plan for property disposition. Thus, if both parents die and the policies specify payment to the children equally, a carefully drawn testamentary trust for the children may sit unused as efforts must be made to deal with possibly large amounts of funds in the hands of minors who lack legal competence to deal with the funds. More on this in Chapter 25.

As beneficiary designations are considered, it's well to keep in mind that, in some instances, insurance proceeds are not subject to the claims of creditors. This feature of insurance treatment may influence the pattern of beneficiary designations established.

Other insurance aspects of estate planning

At some point, decisions must be made on what type of "settlement option" is desired. The policy owner may make these decisions during the life of the insured. Or the beneficiary or beneficiaries may be permitted to make the necessary elections after the death of the insured. Options typically include a lump sum payment, payments in installments over a period of years or over a life, or insurance company retention of funds with payment of interest.

For added flexibility, an insurance trust is sometimes used with the trust instrument providing the rules for distribution of income and principal derived from insurance policies.

13
Charitable giving

Within rather broad limits, you can dispose of your property during life – or after death – about as you like. Most don't feel tightly constrained by the limitations. You may not be able to completely disinherit a spouse, unless you had entered into an antenuptial agreement. You generally can't dissipate your wealth foolishly or dispose of it in a manner lacking in economic or social value – like scattering it over the ocean in $5 bills. One individual tried that, unsuccessfully, several years ago. And in some states, limits are placed on property passing to charitable organizations – the so-called Mortmain or death statutes as discussed in Chapter 25.

But otherwise, there's an enormous amount of latitude in the transfer of accumulated wealth.

Governing objectives

The process of property disposition is properly guided by our objectives. And to a considerable degree, we tend to favor those choices that give us the most satisfaction.

For nearly everyone, there's peace of mind in knowing that one's spouse and any dependent children will be adequately provided for. And satisfaction is often derived from planning for property disposition to adult children – and other family members. These are fundamental components of the guiding set of objectives for most individuals.

Especially as accumulated wealth grows to the point that family needs are met and the amount of family wealth permits consideration of a wider range of possibilities, development of a plan for charitable giving may offer satisfaction. In agriculture, even with the declines in land values in recent years, many families possess accumulated wealth sufficient to give serious attention to disposition of substantial amounts of property outside the immediate family.

There are several reasons why a great deal of satisfaction can be gained from the charitable giving part of the overall estate plan.

• First, many dream dreams of the things they would have *liked* to have done – given slightly different circumstances. They might have liked to be a talented musician, a skilled medical researcher or a fine artist. With their means, they may be able to help others do the things they could not do directly. It's a way to extend yourself – during life, and at death.

• Charitable giving can convey a powerful message to children. At a time when there are signs that individuals may be turning inward – to concern more about self than about others less privileged – charitable giving can convey an important legacy to family members of generosity and humanitarian concern for others. And that legacy may be of greater developmental value than the extra funds would have been had they been given directly to members of the family.

For the first time in history, a significant segment of farm families possesses the means to endow the next generation with sufficient wealth to view employment as not absolutely essential for survival. Some worry about the impact of this fact on motivation and incentive in succeeding generations.

• An argument can be made that charitable giving represents an efficient use of resources. Typically, there's little overhead involved – much of the work is handled by volunteers. That is especially true in churches, for example.

And some possibilities for charitable giving permit continual benefits to be enjoyed over a long period of time or even perpetually. Funds left for scholarships, as one illustration, represent a turn-over of funds that benefits society for years to come.

• Charitable giving lets you select the areas in which you are most interested in assisting. It could be medical research, educational opportunities for youth, creative and meaningful experiences for the elderly, generating a sense of universal concern about soil conservation or making possible a well equipped community center for groups to enjoy for generations. The choice is yours alone.

• Finally, there's a keen sense of felt responsibility in what we do with our resources. After all, "we can't take it with us."

Perhaps what this adds up to is that charitable giving should be viewed less as a "cost," reducing the amounts passing to family members, and more as a potential source of additional satisfaction.

Because charitable giving has likewise been viewed in a favorable light by the Congress, there are various tax breaks to encourage giving property to charitable organizations during life and at death. The tax advantages depend upon *when* the property is given, *how* the property is given, *how much* property is involved altogether, and *to whom* it is given.

The latter point is crucial from a tax deductibility standpoint. Not all groups that appear to be charitable can assure a tax deduction for gifts. Churches and subdivisions of government are viewed as charitable. Beyond that, the organization must have been approved by the Internal Revenue Service – and have an "exemption letter" to prove it. Such a letter makes gifts deductible for federal income, gift and estate tax purposes. A point to watch for – there are a dozen or so categories of organizations that can claim to be exempt from federal tax. But only a "Section 501(c)(3)" organization can assure a tax deduction for contributions.

Outright transfers

The simplest way to benefit charitable organizations is to make an outright transfer during life. Gifts can be in cash, stored grain, securities, land, insurance policies or about anything of value.

For a gift of cash, you can claim a federal gift tax deduction of 100 percent of the gift, of course. And, as a general rule, you can claim a federal income tax deduction up to 30 percent of your adjusted gross income and up to 50 percent for "public type" charities under certain circumstances. Excess contributions (with some exceptions) can be carried over for five years.

If it's a gift of appreciated property, like land, it's possible to make a gift of the fair market value, obtain an income tax and gift tax deduction for that value and not pay income tax on the gain. In general, deductions for charitable contributions of long-term capital gain property are subject to a 30 percent limitation except for property passing to a private foundation or used for a purpose unrelated to the exempt status. Contributions of long-term capital gain property to private non-operating foundations (30 percent organizations) are limited to the lesser of 20 percent of adjusted gross income or the excess of 30 percent of adjusted gross income over the long-term capital gains contributions to 50 percent organizations.

EXAMPLE: Assume a gift of 80 acres of land valued at $100,000 to a "50 percent" organization. The federal gift tax deduction for gifts to a qualified charity would be $100,000, enough to cover the gift. In general, an income tax deduction could be claimed on the $100,000 for transfer to a qualified charity. That deduction could be applied up to the limit of a percentage of adjusted gross income with a five-year carryover.

A major feature of gifts of appreciated property is that you escape paying income tax on the gain.

If the gift is of inventory property – like stored grain – the income tax deduction is generally limited to the owner's income tax basis in the property. For a farmer on the cash method of accounting, that basis is generally zero for raised assets. That means no income tax deduction for the gift. Under the IRS regulations, however, deductions for the costs of producing the gift item of inventory property such as grain can be deducted as a business expense.

Corporate charitable contributions are limited to 10 percent of corporate taxable income.

Transfers with retained interests

One especially attractive approach is to transfer property to a favorite charitable organization but with a life interest held by the surviving spouse. For a farm or personal residence, it can be done very simply with a transfer by deed during life or a simple will provision at death.

The surviving spouse has the income and the right to possession so long as the individual lives. And at the death of the surviving spouse, the property passes to the charitable organization. It's a form of deferred giving – the gift takes place but not until death of the surviving spouse does the charitable organization gain complete control over the property.

What about tax deductions? The value of the remainder interest would be deductible for federal income, estate and gift tax purposes if to a qualified charity. The amount of the gift would be the fair market value of the property less the value of the life interest held by the surviving spouse – and that depends, in turn, upon the age of the surviving spouse.

A couple of points to watch: first, specifying that the property be sold and the proceeds pass to the charity (rather than the property itself) could jeopardize the charitable deduction. Second, placing the farm or residence in a trust could disqualify the arrangement for this special treatment. Finally, it's necessary to reduce any charitable income tax deduction by the amount of straight line depreciation on depreciable assets.

For property *other than* a farm or personal residence, such as corporate stock, the same result can be reached. But it requires attention to the requirements for one of three techniques – a charitable remainder annuity trust, a charitable remainder unitrust or a pooled income fund.

• A charitable remainder annuity trust involves payment at least annually to the named income beneficiary or beneficiaries – such as a surviving spouse – of at least 5 percent of the initial fair market value of the property transferred. At the death of the income beneficiary (or beneficiaries) the trust terminates and the assets go to the charitable organization. There's no capital gains tax on transfer to the trust even if the trust is funded initially with appreciated property.

EXAMPLE: Robert and Mary Smith, age 75 and 74, respectively, transfer $100,000 to a charitable remainder annuity trust paying 5 percent to Robert so long as he lives, then 5 percent to Mary for the rest of her life. The value of the remainder interest, deductible for federal income tax purposes, would be $58,531.05. The 5 percent annual payment would total $5,000 per year.

• A charitable remainder unitrust involves payment, at least annually, to the named beneficiary or beneficiaries of varying amounts each year. That amount is figured as a fixed percentage (not less than 5 percent) of the fair market value of the trust assets refigured each year. Again, there's no capital gains tax on transfer to the trust even if the trust is funded with appreciated assets. A late 1993 private letter ruling approved the transfer of assets from a ranch operation – including the livestock, machinery and feed inventory – to such a trust.

EXAMPLE: Ellen Jones, age 70, transfers $100,000 in assets to a charitable remainder unitrust with a payment to her of seven percent of the asset value each year. The value of the deductible remainder interest would be $46,773.00. The 7 percent annual payment would total $7,000 the first year. If the fair market value of the assets rose to $110,000 the second year, she would receive $7,700 for that year.

Again, there may be a five-year carryover for any excess contributions above the allowable limit based on the type of charity involved.

Pooled income funds work similarly but are less widely used.

Another variation – the "lead" trust

Another approach to leaving something to a charitable organization involves a charitable "lead" trust. With this technique, property is left to create income for the charity for a specified number of years – perhaps under a guaranteed annuity arrangement – with the property then passing to family members. The family members have the remainder interest. And because the value of the remainder interest is reduced by the amount of the income interest passing to the charitable organization, it reduces the death tax liability.

The charitable lead trust may be useful in a closely held business where death taxes loom large, there's a strong desire to benefit a charitable organization for a few years, the business has a good, dependable cash flow and it's desired for the family ultimately to own the business.

Federal estate tax savings

In general, the larger the estate the higher the tax bracket and the greater the federal estate tax saving from a charitable gift. Thus, the larger the estate the smaller the "net cost" of making the gift.

But even with modest estates, federal estate tax savings can be significant.

EXAMPLE: Alice Page, a widow, died in 1996 with a $750,000 estate, with no charitable giving. The federal estate tax bill would be $55,500. If she had left $10,000 to her favorite charitable organization, the federal estate tax bill would be only $51,800. In effect, the net cost of the $10,000 gift would be only $6,300.

EXAMPLE: Fred Thomas, a widower, died in 1996 leaving a $1,000,000 estate. With no charitable giving, the federal estate tax would be $153,000. If a $50,000 gift had been made to a qualified charity the tax would be reduced to $133,500 or a savings of $19,500. The net cost of the $50,000 gift would be $30,500.

In most states, a deduction for state death tax would also be available and would boost the overall tax savings for a gift to a qualified charity.

IN CONCLUSION: The favored treatment of gifts to a qualified charity during life saves income tax and exempts the property from gift tax. For property retained until death and passed to a charity, there's a federal estate tax deduction and it's possible to leave an income interest – for example, to a surviving spouse – and still deduct the remainder interest for federal estate tax purposes.

But the fundamental motivation for leaving property to a charitable organization lies in your personal assessment of where the greatest satisfaction lies. Tax savings are "icing on the cake."

14
Retirement and estate planning

The retirement years are important ones for estate planning purposes. As retirement approaches, objectives may change or be viewed in a different light, thus suggesting that the estate plan be reviewed, and, possibly, amended.

Security of income

A key estate planning objective of most individuals is to assure adequate amounts of income regardless of how long the person lives. This feature typically takes priority over gifts to children during life, sales of property under installment contract or transfers under a private annuity, and other estate planning possibilities.

Social security benefits are the keystone to many retirement plans. Both men and women may receive social security benefits at age 62 or 65. Early claims for benefits qualify for reduced benefits to offset the longer period of expected payments.

The normal retirement age has been age 65 and will continue until rules enacted in 1983 phase-in after the turn of the century as noted below. Early retirement benefits are available at age 62. Unreduced retirement benefits are available to workers, spouses and widows and widowers at age 65. Reduced benefits are available at age 62 for workers and spouses and at age 60 for widows and widowers.

For those reaching age 62 after 1978, and who postpone retirement benefits, there is an increase in benefits of three percent for each year they continue to work after age 65 and before age 72. And widow's and widower's benefits may be increased by delayed retirement, also.

To be "fully insured" has required one quarter of coverage for each year between 1950 (or the year a person became 22, whichever was later) and the year a person became 62. A minimum of six quarters has been needed to be fully insured. (A recent change allows some benefits for those covered for shorter periods.) Coverage for forty quarters has insured a person for life.

For those reaching age 62 or who became disabled or died before January 1, 1979, social security benefits continue to be figured under the automatic cost-of-living increase provisions. But for those who become eligible for retirement benefits, die or become disabled after 1978, a new system for figuring benefits has been adopted. It's based on a system of "indexing" to express prior year's earnings in terms of their current dollar value.

Indexing creates an earnings history which reflects more accurately the value of an individual's earnings in comparison to the national average wage level at the time of eligibility. The indexing year is the second year before the year of eligibility.

EXAMPLE: For an individual who reached age 62 in 1981, his or her earnings record is indexed based on the indexing year 1979.

Earnings after the indexing year are counted at their actual dollar value.

Under the new rules, social security benefits will rise with the cost of living but no higher. The new computational methods are designed eventually to stabilize social security benefits at a level about equal to 43 percent of the average worker's pre-retirement pay. The old law tended to overcompensate for inflation.

For a worker who became eligible for benefits in 1983, the formula for calculating benefits is based on the average indexed monthly earnings (AIME). The figures are indexed each year to reflect changes in average wages in the economy.

Social security rules also limit the amount of earned income that can be received after retirement without reduction or loss of social security benefits. From retirement to age 70, social security benefits are reduced if a person receives more than the maximum allowable for personal services. That figure was increased to $12,500 for 1996, $13,500 in 1997, $14,500 in 1998, $15,500 in 1999, $17,000 in 2000, $25,000 in 2001 and $30,000 in 2002.

The Social Security Amendments of 1983 made several important changes in social security law.

• The rules raise the normal retirement age from 65 to 67 in two steps. The retirement age was increased to 66 by increasing the age for full benefits by two months per year for six years with the provision fully effective beginning with those reaching age 62 in 2005 (66 in 2009). The retirement age was increased from 66 to 67 by increasing the age for full benefits by two months per year for six years with the provision fully effective beginning with those reaching age 62 in 2022 (67 in 2027).

• Age 62 benefits would be maintained at an ultimate rate of 70 percent of full benefits (after the age for full retirement is changed to 67).

• The 1983 law made no change in the earnings test except that, beginning in 1990, the reduction for earnings is reduced to one dollar for every three dollars earned over the exempt amount (it was formerly a reduction of one dollar for every two dollars earned over the annual exempt amount).

• Cost-of-living adjustments are made in December (January checks) based on the Consumer Price Index (CPI) increase from the third quarter of the last year in which a cost-of-living adjustment was provided to the third quarter of the current year.

• Several categories of individuals are covered by social security for the first time including federal employees hired after 1983 and mandatory coverage of employees of non-profit organizations.

• Social security benefits (and some railroad retirement benefits) are subject to income tax if the benefits exceed a base amount. The amount to be included in income for 1993 and earlier years was the lesser of – (1) 50 percent of the benefits received during the year or (2) 50 percent of the amount obtained by sub-

243

tracting a base amount from the sum of an individual's modified adjusted gross income and 50 percent of the benefits received. The *base amount* for a single person is $25,000. For married persons filing a joint return the base amount is $32,000. For a married person not filing a joint return and who has not lived apart from the spouse at all times during the year, the base amount is zero.

The term *modified adjusted gross income* is adjusted gross income (figured without including any social security benefits) plus any tax-exempt interest, the deduction for a two-earner married couple, any exclusion claimed for foreign income and any exclusions from United States' possessions.

EXAMPLE: Earl and Irene Smith received a total of $13,800 in social security benefits during 1993. Their adjusted gross income (not counting social security benefits) was $28,200 ($20,200 in rental income and $8,000 in interest). The Smiths filed a joint return for 1993 so their base amount was $32,000. Their modified adjusted gross income was $28,200. The Smiths would figure their income subject to tax as follows –

Calculation 1 – 50 percent of the total social security benefits received or $6,900, or

Calculation 2 – modified adjusted gross income ($28,000) plus 50 percent of social security benefits received ($6,900) which equals $35,100 less the base amount of $32,000 or $3,100. One-half of $3,100 is $1,550. The lesser of the two calculations is $1,550 so that amount must be included in their income. Therefore, the Smith's adjusted gross income would be $28,200 plus $1,550 or $29,750.

After 1993, the maximum percentage of social security subject to income tax is increased from 50 percent to 85 percent. This creates a "second tier" of inclusion of social security benefits in gross income. The rules applicable before 1994 (at the 50 percent level) apply to those with "provisional income" below $34,000 for single taxpayers and $44,000 for married taxpayers filing joint returns. Above those levels, the 85 percent rule applies.

No benefits are taxed if provisional income does not exceed $32,000 for joint filers or $25,000 for others except married taxpayers filing separately.

"Provisional income" is the individual's modified adjusted gross income plus one-half of social security and Railroad Retirement Benefits.

The question of what earnings reduce social security benefits depends upon the relationship of the individual to the source of income. Dividends, interest, annuities, pensions, royalties and income from the sale of property not in the regular course of business are investment income and normally do not affect benefits.

For a retired farmer who rents land to a tenant, the question is whether the landlord "participates materially" in the production of income under the lease. Material participation converts rent into income from personal services and may reduce benefits accordingly. For a landlord not participating materially, rentals received may be treated as investment income. And, social security benefits are not reduced.

The Social Security Administration took the position in a 1982 letter that material participation is not possible where the tenant is a corporation, except possibly for a "family or close corporation [that] involves the landowner."

A 1995 Tax Court decision held that a farmer renting land to a family partnership (in which he had a 25 percent interest) was materially participating under the lease because of his role as a partner in the partnership.

The general rule has been that income from participation in government acreage diversion programs is treated like other income from the farm in terms of whether the income is subject to social security tax and reduces social security benefits. Thus, such income is self-employment income, subject to social security tax, for a landlord who materially participates under the lease. A 1983 IRS announcement that "a farmer who receives cash or payment in kind from the Department of Agriculture for participation in a land diversion program is liable for self-employment tax on the cash or payment in kind received" is misleading. A 1988 private letter ruling indicated that Conservation Reserve Program payments received by a retired farmer were not subject to self-employment tax. CRP payments are apparently treated as other farm income before retirement with the result that the payments are subject to self-employment tax. For those who retire after bidding land into the CRP program, the outcome is not completely clear. Some authority focuses on the status of the recipient at the time of the contract. This approach would suggest the payments continue to be subject to self-employment tax. Other authority emphasizes the status of the recipient when payments are received. This interpretation would suggest that payments received after retirement would not be subject to self-employment tax. A ruling is anticipated on that point in the future.

For a farmer maintaining a working relationship with a farm business – for example, as a partner in a farm partnership – the question is whether the individual renders "substantial services." If he or she does, the amounts received are treated as earnings and may reduce social security benefits. If less than 45 hours per month are devoted to the farm business, the services rendered are generally not considered to be substantial unless considerable skill or management is used or it involves a large business. In those instances, a special 15-hour rule may apply. A retired partner's share of partnership earnings may be excluded from social security tax if the partner is fully retired and renders no services with respect to the partnership. If a "retired" partner continues to perform some services with respect to the partnership, the special exclusion may be lost with social security tax imposed on the retired partner's share of partnership earnings as self-employment income.

A person retiring as an employee, however, need be concerned only with compensation received as salary and bonus for personal services rendered. Therefore, after retirement an employee of a farm corporation could be paid a part-time salary of the maximum amount allowable for personal services, without reduction of benefits. Additional income received in the form of dividends does not reduce social security benefits.

Watch part-time salaries, though. If an employee who also happens to be a major shareholder is underpaid as an employee, a part of the dividend income received as a shareholder may be treated as income from personal services. The salary must be reasonably related to the labor and management provided by the part-timer.

The substantial flexibility in setting salaries and paying additional income in the form of dividends encourages use of the corporation. The corporation can convert self-employed owners or partners into employees. Employee status accompanying incorporation may thus:

1. Enable the retiring individual to receive maximum social security benefits to which entitled.

2. Permit payment of additional amounts in a form that does not reduce social security benefits.

3. Make it possible for the retired employee to maintain a close association with the farm firm. This may be more difficult under "material participation" leases or where efforts are made to meet the "substantial services" test.

Domicile

Retirement often involves a change of permanent residence and, hence, a change of domicile. This can have important estate planning implications.

The state of domicile provides the rules for (1) settlement of the decedent's estate, (2) interpreting the will at death (a will valid where executed should be valid everywhere but interpretation may be left to the state of domicile at death) and (3) disposing of the decedent's property if there was no will.

If the decedent left real property in a state or states other than the state of domicile at death, estate settlement may be complicated still further. Real property or land can pass only under the law of that state at death; hence, ancillary probate is normally required in each state where land is located in addition to the regular probate or estate settlement proceeding in the state of domicile. Thus, careful attention should be given to how land is owned in states other than the state of domicile.

Insurance coverage

As time for retirement approaches, it's well to check life insurance coverage, especially term insurance.Typically, the face amount of term insurance under either individual policies or group plans begins to decline before a person reaches age 65. Thus, advancing age may uncover inadequacies in an insurance plan that was previously quite satisfactory. Other arrangements for liquid capital to pay estate settlement costs and taxes may be necessary as insurance amounts decline.

On the other hand, gradual increases in value of other relatively liquid assets in the estate may offset the drop in estate liquidity caused by declining term coverage.

IN CONCLUSION. Even though estate plans may be developed long before retirement, the retirement years represent an important period for and provide a keen test of an estate plan. Perhaps the most crucial test of an estate plan is that it assures not only an adequate amount of income and capital during retirement, but also an assurance that the income and capital are sufficiently secure to meet the objectives of the person involved.

15

Organizing the farm business: parent-child arrangements

In estate planning involving a farm business, decisions must be made as to its legal organization. This is important not only for estate planning, but also for business management and income tax purposes.

The decision of whether to incorporate, form a partnership, create a limited liability company or continue as a sole proprietorship has *business planning* as well as *estate planning* implications. The best choice of organizational form from an estate planning standpoint may not be the best so far as the business is concerned. And, vice versa.

Because estate planning and business planning decisions are inextricably intertwined, it's well to solve both problems at the same time. Otherwise, the resulting plans may be in conflict.

Business continuity

Traditionally, the farm business has been closely tied to the life cycle of the family. Farm businesses have been "born" and have also "died" within the lifetime of the sole proprietor as shown in Figure 7. This has often resulted in inefficiencies in the early life of the farm business as well as in the later years. An individual beginning farming is often short on equity capital and, for that reason, credit sources aren't too eager to lend large amounts of debt capital. The young farmer may also be short on management although he or she may have an excess of labor. Thus, the farm business is operated at a level of lower efficiency than is typically the case later in the family farm cycle.

As equity capital is accumulated and more debt capital is made available, the farm business normally expands in step with growing management ability. Usually, peak efficiency is reached mid-way through the life cycle.

Figure 7. Family farm cycle.

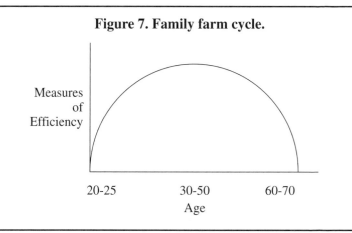

But then, several things begin to happen. The children leave home to go to college or enter other employment. The farmer becomes less willing to devote the long hours and driving force of earlier years and often becomes increasingly conservative in decision making. The farmer comes to realize that he or she may not be around to enjoy the benefits of long-term investments whether in soil fertility or expanded livestock facilities.

As a consequence, the efficiency level of the farm business drops off until at retirement or death the farm business is terminated. The cycle then begins all over again with another sole proprietor assuming ownership of the assets involved.

If the higher efficiency of mid-cycle could be preserved over time, important benefits might accrue to the individuals and families involved. Efforts to preserve that higher efficiency have caused many farmers to focus on the corporation and partnership as devices to permit a farm business, once built up to an efficient operating level, to continue to function into the next and succeeding generations.

The corporation, especially, may make possible a planned and orderly transfer of the farm business as an economic unit over time as owners and managers and their capital move into and out of the farm business in keeping with their own personal life cycle. Yet that movement of people in and out of the farm business need not necessarily cause the farm business itself to go through a convulsive cycle at the same time as seen in Figure 8.

Figure 8. Family farm cycle with planned ownership and management transfer.

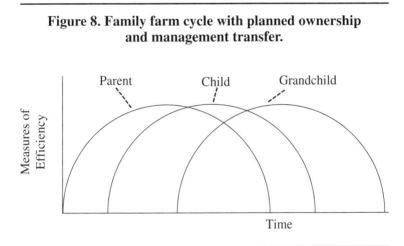

Three types of arrangements

Most relationships involving parents and children in a family operation fall into three distinct types. The basic outlines of the arrangement may appear to be a bit fuzzy. And the individuals involved may not have parallel expectations for the future. But existing agreements fall rather neatly into three groups.

THE "SPIN-OFF" MODEL. This approach functions under the general assumption that the relationship won't last forever. In fact, it's usually thought the arrangement may last five, possibly seven years, certainly no more than ten. During that time the parents are willing to work out preferential arrangements with a child or spouse of a child.

Typically starting out with a straight employer-employee relationship, it soon escalates into a wage plus bonus or wage plus bonus plus incentive arrangement of some type. The child begins to accumulate a line of equipment. The parents put in a good word with landlords in the neighborhood and agree to co-sign loans. Throughout, the child's labor is traded for use of the parents' machinery and equipment.

As soon as possible, the child spins off into his or her own orbit. And the parents' operation starts a long, slow decline toward economic oblivion.

A key point – throughout the relationship, the parents' operation remains fundamentally unchanged. In most instances it's a sole proprietorship. It's all handled as a matter of contract – possibly written but usually oral – with the child.

THE "SUPER FIRM." With this one, the parties proceed under quite different assumptions. The idea is that the family operation will expand enough for the additional family. And the son or son-in-law, daughter or daughter-in-law, becomes a permanent fixture in the family business. It's not a temporary proposition.

The super firm poses quite different problems. Typically, the organizational structure is changed to accommodate the multiple ownership of resources and multiple participation in management The partnership and closely held corporation are obvious choices.

LANDLORD-TENANT RELATIONSHIP. Finally, the landlord-tenant possibility exists for those willing to accept its features. Frequently starting off with a livestock share lease, the parents often function as financiers in helping the child acquire an interest in the machinery, livestock and feed inventory. The arrangement typically shifts to a crop-share lease as the child is able to swing the total machinery and livestock investment.

Problems? Basically two. The parents may not be willing to

252

accept the income pattern consistent with a landlord's role. And they may not be quite ready to play the landlord's role in providing management. The result may be a degree of over-management by the parents for awhile, somewhat to the chagrin of the tenant.

There's one problem with a great potential for destroying the relationship – especially spin-off and super firm types. And that's the situation where the parties are not in agreement on the type of relationship – but they don't know it. If the parents have long assumed that the child had a spin-off objective, but the child had a mind set on developing the parents' operation into a super firm, serious problems can arise. Full and frank communication is crucial. And from the earliest possible time – *before* expectations have hardened into immovable positions.

In one actual example surfacing recently in a Great Plains state, a son had always assumed parental agreement existed for a super firm. But he was perplexed as to the reluctance of the parents to permit him to buy in. Finally, after 13 years of non-committal responses to the son's query about investing in the operation, the parents responded forthrightly. There would be no chance to buy into the parents' operation. And the parents laid out their frustrations in seeing "spin-off" chances go by, with the son preferring to stay with the family operation.

It was obvious that the parents' expectations were quite different from those of the son. And it led to break up of the operation – with enough bitterness to last for years.

Problems common to all three

Regardless of how the arrangement is set up and operated, three problem areas seem to account for a large share of the difficulties – except for the fundamental communication problem already mentioned. These are the chief culprits responsible for a high percentage of failures in parent-child relationships.

INCOME SHARING. The inability to develop – and keep in

adjustment – the formula for dividing annual income from the operation ranks at the head of the list of problems. Even an economically perfect income sharing arrangement soon gets out of adjustment.

Why does this happen? Typically, the parent – after the child's return to the farm – starts working shorter hours. More time in Florida. Knocks off a little earlier in the afternoon. To the parent, that's defensible. After all, the parent's hit the ball for 20 or 30 years. And it's about time the parent slowed down.

But the work is there, generally increased from the expansion efforts to support another family. And the child is working longer and longer hours. Eventually, grandchildren add to the labor supply. The child's management ability is sharpened with experience.

If all of this isn't reflected in the income sharing plan, there's going to be trouble. It's even more severe as a problem if it involves persons other than parent-child. For example, in one case that arose in a midwestern state recently, two brothers had been farming together for more than 20 years. The son of one brother returned to the farm. Predictably, the son felt even less charitable toward his uncle who was easing back in the traces and attempting, at the same time, to maintain the former income sharing arrangement. Result: the operation blew apart after two years.

INVESTMENT OPPORTUNITIES. The second problem area relates to the opportunity for the younger generation to buy into the operation or otherwise gain control over assets. If that opportunity isn't available, enormous uncertainty tends to build up for the on-farm heir. And it tends to be corrosive. Years go by and there's no progress toward "buying in" to the operation. A suspicion begins to emerge that there'll be no chance. At least, not until the death of one – or both – of the parents.

About this time, numerous two-generation arrangements come to an end.

INVOLVEMENT IN MANAGEMENT. The third and final problem area involves management – involvement of the child or child's spouse in decision making.

In the successful two or three generation farm businesses, there's usually deft handling of the issue – on both sides. The power is in the idea advanced – not in who advances it. The parent realizes full well that control generally goes along with capital – the person providing the most capital generally has the whip hand of control. But it's seldom used. The younger individual is considered a full participant in decision making.

Most parents understand – at least on an abstract level – the importance of transfers of ownership to the continued good health of the farm business. What is perhaps less well understood is that gradual management transfer can be just as vital.

Strategies for shifting ownership

If the parents are interested in shifting ownership and control of the operation to the next generation – and that would be consistent with a "super firm" objective, two basic strategies are open to them. Of course, combinations of the two strategies are possible including a part gift-part purchase plan that could be used with either of the basic alternatives.

MAXIMUM RISK FOR ON-FARM HEIR. With this alternative, the on-farm heir purchases as much property as possible (perhaps 50 percent of the total) prior to formation of the partnership or corporation. Financing may come from the parents or from outside creditors. One significant disadvantage to this approach would be gain to the parents as well as recapture of depreciation (gain as ordinary income to the extent it represents depreciation previously claimed).

This strategy would be less attractive in a deflationary period than in a time of inflation. It involves heavy "leveraging" that pays off if prices keep rising.

MINIMUM RISK FOR ON-FARM HEIR. Typically, with this strategy, the on-farm heir commences the business relationship providing only labor and management for a salary or salary plus bonus or salary plus bonus (based on net income) plus an incentive arrangement (based on production). As funds become available, the on-farm heir acquires a greater interest.

If corporate stock or a partnership share is purchased from the parents, that means income tax consequences for the parents. Acquiring a greater interest directly from the partnership or corporation would side-step that problem and could be the most acceptable route unless the parents were counting on gradual sale of their interest to supplement retirement income.

A minimum risk strategy would be less attractive in an inflationary period than in a time of deflation.

Put it in writing

There's merit in putting the basic parent-child agreement in writing. If they go the corporate route, at least the basic corporate documents tend to reflect the understandings reached. Even there, it's well to have all of the details of the arrangement in writing.

If the decision is to go the partnership route or to form a contractual parent-child agreement, it's wise to memorialize the details in writing. Unfortunately, most are oral – perhaps only a small percentage involve anything resembling a written contract.

But the written word has two fundamental advantages – (1) preparing the written agreement tends to encourage discussion of points that would otherwise have been omitted, and (2) a written agreement is the best defense against the "selective recall" syndrome – people tend to remember best those past agreements that support their current point of view and to remember less well or not at all those past agreements at variance with current positions.

16
Structuring the farm business

The choice of organizational structure for the farm business has always been important. There are the traditional options – partnership, corporation and sole proprietorship. And there's been the additional wrinkle of using one type of structure for the operating side of the business – and another for the land.

But developments in recent years, especially in the tax area, have raised important questions about how the farm business is organized – especially plans calling for multiple entities. There are compelling reasons to use multiple entities – one to hold the land and another to carry on the farming operation – but care should be exercised in setting up an organizational structure that involves separating the land from the operating side of the business.

The problems are much the same where the land and the production assets have the same owners – but are in different entities – as where the land is held in one entity and is rented to an unrelated tenant. In both situations, the land is typically rented under a cash, crop-share or livestock share lease. As noted in the following sections, the nature of the lease can have a great deal to do with how some of the major tax considerations are handled.

Reasons for multiple entities

From a point of view of flexibility in planning, a great deal can be said for multiple entities. In general, that means one entity for the land – individual ownership, trust, general or limited partnership, limited liability company or corporation – and another entity for the production assets other than land with the same range of organizational choices that are open to the land owning entity.

• First, it may be easier to meet the retirement objectives of the parents if the land is retained in individual ownership. Rental income from the land is assured. And it doesn't affect social security benefits in retirement. However, a 1995 Tax Court case held that the payments received by the father as a 25 percent partner in the family farm partnership for rental of 731 acres of land to the partnership were subject to self employment (social security) tax.

• Keeping the land separate from the rest of the farm business assets creates additional options for meeting an objective of fairness to the off-farm heirs without their involvement in the farm business. By planning for division of land ownership ultimately among all the children – on-farm and off-farm heirs, it's easier to assure a fair allocation of wealth among all the children. And that can be accomplished without the off-farm heirs acquiring an interest in the production entity and becoming involved in day-to-day decision making for the farm business.

• Using two entities reduces the investment needed by the on-farm heirs to gain control of the operating side of the business. And that's a typical objective of on-farm heirs. Status as a minority owner may not be a matter of great concern to the on-farm heirs so long as one or both of the parents are alive and maintain a substantial ownership interest. But at the death of the surviving parent, the on-farm heirs typically want to be assured of control for fear that otherwise the off-farm heirs might act in concert to dissolve and liquidate the operation.

• For those who find the corporation attractive for the production entity, holding the land in a non-corporate entity sidesteps the often severe income tax problem of corporate liquidations.

Despite these solid reasons for creating multiple entities, some factors point the other way.

Personal holding company problems

If land is transferred to a new corporation – and then rented to another entity carrying on actual farming operations – it's important to be on the lookout for personal holding company tax problems. That's a 39.6 percent tax on personal holding company income and obviously not something to be taken lightly.

If more than 50 percent of the corporate stock is owned by five or fewer individuals (during the last half of the taxable year) and if 60 percent or more of its adjusted ordinary gross income is "personal holding company income," the 39.6 percent tax is imposed.

Basically, as discussed in Chapter 20, personal holding company income is passive investment income – including rents, royalties, dividends, and interest. But rents aren't counted if they're at least 50 percent of adjusted ordinary gross income and any other personal holding company income that exceeds 10 percent is paid out in dividends. So it's the mixture of rent and other passive investment income that's hazardous.

And a mixture of interest and rent is not unusual for land owning corporations. Typically, once mortgages and land contracts are paid off, cash balances begin to build up in the land owning corporation. Opportunities for removal of earnings from the corporation in tax-deductible form are few – salaries are the major item, and it's difficult to justify large salaries in a land owning corporation where management needs are limited. Therefore, rather than pay out earnings as dividends, cash begins to pile up in the corporation. The usual response is to loan funds to the operating entity or to place the funds in a savings account or certificate of deposit. In either case, interest is earned. The combination of interest and rent may trigger the personal holding company tax.

For corporations owning farm land rented to others, a major question relates to whether the income is "rent." In one leading case, income from crop share leases wasn't "rent" for personal holding company purposes where the land was managed by a professional farm management firm. The emphasis was on the amount of involvement in decision making under the lease. Here, the relationship of the agent (such as a farm manager) to the property owner is governed by the general rule as explained in Chapter 1. That means the activities of the agent count the same as activities or involvement by the property owner.

A cash rent lease is likely to produce "rent" for personal holding company purposes. Livestock share and crop share leases generally tilt the other way if there is material participation in the operation.

Thus, if it's desired to avoid personal holding company status – (1) the lease should be drafted with care to require substantial involvement in decision making under the lease by a representative of the corporation as landlord and (2) the corporate representative should keep a good daily, diary-type record of activity on behalf of the corporation.

S corporation as landlord

The personal holding company tax doesn't apply to corporations taxed under Subchapter S of the Internal Revenue Code – the so-called "tax option" corporations. But Subchapter S has had its own rule on passive investment income. The Subchapter S rules on passive investment income were changed in 1982 as explained in detail in Chapter 20.

Through 1982, Subchapter S status was lost if more than 20 percent of the corporation's gross receipts came from rents, royalties, dividends, interest, annuities and sales or exchanges of stock or securities. But income wasn't "rent" if corporate officers or agents participated materially in production through physical work, management decisions or both. That was from a 1961 revenue ruling. And a 1974 Tax Court case agreed.

To avoid loss of the Subchapter S election, if land was kept out of the corporation, it was important for the lease (cash rent leases could not make the grade) to be drawn with care to involve a representative of the corporation in decision making. Again, it was wise to keep a detailed record of what was done on a day-to-day basis. And it was important to keep a separate set of books for the corporation, of course, apart from the tenant's operation.

Effective in 1982, the limit on passive investment income has been eliminated *for S corporations which do not have accumulated earnings and profits from years the corporation was regularly taxed.* For S corporations with accumulated earnings and profits from years in which the corporation was regularly taxed, a tax is imposed at the highest rate for corporate income (now 35 percent) on passive investment income in excess of 25 percent of gross receipts. A Subchapter S election terminates if a corporation has earnings and profits at the close of each of three consecutive taxable years and more than 25 percent of gross receipts from each of the three taxable years comes from passive investment income. Thus, newly formed S corporations and existing S corporations that have no earnings and profits need not worry about the passive income limitation in structuring the farm or ranch corporation. The older authority on involvement by corporate officers or agents under a share lease to avoid the rental income problem continues to be applicable. A 1989 private letter ruling confirms that view. A late 1994 private ruling stated that income under a cash rent lease wasn't passive income for this purpose where representatives of the corporate landowner were substantially involved in farm operations.

Installment payment of federal estate tax

The way the farm business is structured can influence whether federal estate tax at the death of an owner can be paid in installments. That's become especially important since the 15-year installment payment provision became effective in 1977. See Chapter 5. Under that rule, interest at 4 percent is due on the unpaid balance for roughly the first million dollars of taxable estate attributable to a business (less the unified credit) if the 15-year installment provision is elected.

Two major questions: (1) what it takes to be a business and (2) how to treat multiple entities in meeting the requirement that closely held business assets must exceed 35 percent of the gross estate (less estate settlement deductions) to be eligible for 15-year installment payment of federal estate tax.

Let's take the second question first. More than one closely held business entity may be counted toward the 35 percent requirement if 20 percent or more of the total value of each is included in the deceased's estate. This suggests attention to how ownership patterns are established and to disposition of interests by gift or sale.

As to the first question, that it must be a business to qualify, there's not much of a problem if it's a sole proprietorship, partnership or corporation. For the latter two, 20 percent or more of the partnership capital interest or corporate voting stock must be included in the deceased's estate or the entity must have 15 or fewer partners or shareholders, as the case may be.

The more difficult question relates to property – particularly land – that's rented to a tenant. Revenue rulings indicate that a cash rent lease won't make the grade. A crop share lease may make the property eligible to be treated as a business if there's substantial involvement in decision making under the lease by the landowner or by an employee or agent of the landowner. It's the same old story – constructing a lease that tilts toward active involvement. And then keep good records of what's actually done under the lease.

One final point – interest in "residential buildings and related improvements" that are occupied on a regular basis *by the owner of a farm or the tenant or employee* can be counted toward the 35 percent requirement.

What it adds up to is that, if 15-year installment payment of federal estate tax is to be available, it takes careful attention to detail in planning the organizational structure of the business and continuing attention to maintain eligibility.

"Section 303" stock redemptions

In general, stock redemptions in closely held corporations run the risk of being treated as a dividend. This is especially true of redemptions of only part of a shareholder's stock.

But there's one provision that permits stock redemption after death to pay death taxes, estate administration expenses and funeral costs with the gain on the redeemed stock taxed at capital gain rates. One particularly attractive feature – redemption can take place over the 15-year period of installment payment of federal estate tax if the estate takes that route for paying the federal estate tax.

It takes careful planning for stock to be eligible for "section 303" stock redemption after death. The stock interest of a shareholder whose stock is redeemed must have been reduced, directly or through a binding obligation to contribute, by payment of the taxes and costs. And the value of the stock included in the deceased's estate must exceed 35 percent of the gross estate less estate settlement deductions. Thus, careful planning is called for in structuring the farm business and in making stock transfers, if a corporation is involved, as well as in drafting the deceased's will (to impose liability for death taxes and costs on those whose stock is to be redeemed).

If two corporations are involved, for example one owning the land and one the other production assets, both may be counted toward the 35 percent requirement if 20 percent or more of the stock of each corporation is included in the deceased's estate. Thus, careful attention is warranted in structuring the farm business and in planning stock disposition during life by gift or sale.

Special use valuation of land

The rules on special use valuation of land create two additional methods for valuing farmland as discussed in detail in Chapter 3. One, open only to farmland, uses rental information over the last five years before death The other, open to farmland and other land in a closely held business, makes use of a five factor formula. For those who can meet the requirements, the rent formula, especially, appears to be a tax saver.

It's not completely clear how land owned by a partnership, corporation or trust is to be handled. But it is clear that, for partnerships and corporations, at least 20 percent of the capital interest (or voting stock) must be included in the estate or the entity have 15 or fewer partners (or shareholders). A person apparently must hold a present interest in a trust to be eligible.

The eligibility rules include requirements for "material participation" by the deceased or member of the deceased's family for five or more of the last eight years before retirement, disability or death. And material participation must continue after death. Absence of material participation for more than three years during any eight-year period after death triggers recapture of tax benefits. This means that particular care should be exercised if the land is rented under a lease.

It's doubtful that material participation can be achieved through a cash rent lease. Material participation through crop share or livestock share leases should be possible if there's substantial involvement by the landowner or a member of the landowner's family. Because of a 1974 change in the law, it does not appear that material participation can be achieved through an agent who is not a member of the family. This is the "Section 1402" rule discussed in Chapter 1 governing whether involvement by an employee or agent counts for purposes of the property owner's need to meet a test of involvement in business operations.

Keep in mind that material participation can be gained through a member of the family – such as where a member of the family is the farm tenant. More on this point in Chapter 3 along with a discussion of "active management" as a substitute for material participation in some pre-death and post-death situations.

Eligibility for special use valuation also requires that the decedent or member of the decedent's family must have met the "qualified use" test at the time of death and for five or more of the last eight years before death. The qualified use test requires that an eligible individual have an "equity interest" in the farm operation. In general, cash rent leases – except to a family member as farm tenant in the pre-death period – do not meet the test. To avoid recapture of special use valuation benefits, each qualified heir must have an equity interest in the farm operation for the recapture period after death (except for the two-year grace period immediately after death and cash rent leases by surviving spouses who inherit special use valued land to a member of the surviving spouse's family). Otherwise, cash rent leasing is not permissible in the recapture period after death – even to a family member as farm tenant – if recapture of the federal estate tax benefit is to be avoided.

To sum up, care in structuring the farm or ranch business is needed if special use valuation eligibility is to be maintained and recapture is to be avoided.

Why is the farm business being restructured?

Aside from the numerous tax considerations, decisions on structuring the farm business should be shaped and molded by the reasons for changing the organizational structure of the farm business. If it's to provide an opportunity for a son or daughter to obtain a substantial interest in – or control of – the production side of the operation, leaving the land out of the production entity reduces the investment necessary to gain control by the time of the parents' deaths as noted above. And the on-farm heirs typically want to hold control following the death of the surviving parent. Otherwise, the off-farm heirs might initiate action to dissolve and liquidate the operation.

But if the reason for changing the organization of the farm business is to solve the parents' estate planning problems, leaving the land out means that the asset of perhaps the greatest value will not come within the part of the plan dealing specifically with the estate planning problem. That would leave the land to be handled through a separate entity or held in individual ownership and transferred at death under a separate set of rules.

Government program limitations

In recent years, factors influencing eligibility for the $40,000 payment limitation ($50,000 before 1996) have emerged as major considerations in structuring farm businesses. Each "person" is limited to one payment limitation.

A person receiving farm program payments may not hold, directly or indirectly, a "substantial beneficial interest" in more than two entities engaged in farm operations that also receive payments as separate persons. The limit is raised to three interests if the person does not receive farm program payments as a separate person.

Each individual is treated as one "person" for payment limitation purposes. Moreover, the rule has been that husband-wife situations are automatically considered to be one person even though both spouses owned the assets and were both involved in providing labor and management for the operation.

If the spouses were separately engaged in unrelated farming operations before marriage, each spouse is treated as a separate person with respect to the farming operation brought into the marriage by that spouse *so long as the operations remain separate.*

Legislation enacted in 1990 added another exception to the rule that a husband and wife as a married couple are ordinarily considered as one person. For a married couple consisting of spouses who do not hold, directly or indirectly, a substantial beneficial interest in more than one entity (including the spouses themselves) engaged in farm operations that also receive farm program payments as separate persons, the spouses may be considered separate persons if each spouse meets the other requirements necessary to be considered a separate person.

A person must be "actively engaged" in farming in order to receive farm program payments. To be actively engaged in farming, three conditions must be met –

1. The individual's share of the proceeds from the operation must be commensurate with the individual's contribution to the operation.

2. The individual's contributions must be "at risk"

3. An individual must make a significant contribution of – (a) land, capital or equipment and (b) active personal management or labor.

A corporation or other entity is considered actively engaged in farming if –

• The entity separately makes a significant contribution of capital, equipment or land,

• The shareholders or members, as the case may be, collectively make a significant contribution of personal labor or active personal management to the operation,

• The shares of profit and loss are commensurate with each individual's contributions to the operation, and

• Each individual's contributions are "at risk."

Special rules apply to tenant-operated farms and family-owned operations with multiple owners. In several situations, a person meeting specified requirements is considered to be actively engaged in farming in any event –

• A crop-share or livestock-share landlord who provides capital, equipment or land and personal labor or active personal management meets the test.

• For a farming operation conducted by persons, a majority of whom are family members, the rules are eased slightly. An adult family member may meet the "actively engaged" requirement by making a significant contribution of active personal management or personal labor if the shares of profit and loss are commensurate with contributions and contributions are at risk. Note that some adult must be providing *active personal management or personal labor* to meet the test.

• Neither a cash rent landlord nor a crop share landlord is actively engaged in farming if the rent amount is guaranteed as with a "bushel" lease. Some leases, for example, assure a landowner a designated number of bushels of crop as rent (such as 40 bushels of corn or 13 bushels of soybeans). Such leases involve a risk of price change in the crop for the landowner but no sharing in the risks of production.

• A cash rent tenant is generally considered the same person as the landlord for payment limitation purposes.

To be a separate person, a tenant renting for cash who contributes active personal management (but not personal labor) must contribute equipment to be eligible to receive payments separately from the landlord.

• A "sharecropper" who makes a significant contribution of personal labor to the operation meets the test if the shares of profit and loss are commensurate with contributions and the contributions are "at risk."

• A person using custom farming services is considered to be actively engaged in farming if the general rules on contributions, sharing of profits and losses and "at risk" requirements are met.

In general, a limited partnership or corporation is considered to be a person separate from an individual owner-partner or shareholder. However, a limited partnership or corporation in which more than 50 percent of the interest is owned by an individual (including the interest owned by the individual's spouse, minor children and trusts for the benefit of minor children) or by an entity is not considered a separate person. In the event two or more individuals, limited partnerships, corporations or other entities own more than 50 percent of the interest in each of two or more limited partnerships or corporations engaged in farming, all the limited partnerships or corporations are considered to be one person.

An individual in a joint farming operation is not considered to be a separate person unless the individual is actively engaged in the farming operations. The joint operation itself is not a separate person. The term "joint operation" includes general partnerships, joint ventures and similar kinds of entities.

In general, an irrevocable trust is considered to be a person separate from the individual beneficiaries of the trust. However, an irrevocable trust which has a sole income beneficiary is not considered to be a separate person from the income beneficiary. If two or more irrevocable trusts have common income beneficiaries (including a spouse and minor children) with more than 50 percent interest, all of the trusts are considered to be one person. The 1990 amendments added new rules for irrevocable trusts. To be considered a separate person under the payment limitations rules, an irrevocable trust may not –

• allow for modification or termination of the trust by the grantor (other than for a trust set up before January 1, 1987);

• allow the grantor to have any future, contingent or remainder interest in the trust; or

• provide for the transfer of trust property to the remainder beneficiary in less than 20 years after the trust is established except when the transfer is contingent on the beneficiary reaching at least the age of majority or on the death of the grantor or the income beneficiary.

For revocable trusts, the grantor of the trust and the trust itself are considered to be one person.

In the event a deceased individual would have been considered one person with an heir, the estate is considered to be one person with the heir. Presumably, the estate and an heir are separate persons otherwise. For two years after the year of death, an estate is considered to be actively engaged in farming if the estate makes a significant contribution of capital, equipment or land or a combination and the personal representative of the estate (executor or administrator) or heirs of the estate make a significant contribution of active personal labor, or active personal management, or a combination. After two program years following the year of death, the estate is no longer considered to be actively engaged in farming unless, on a case by case basis, it is determined that the estate has not been settled primarily for purposes of obtaining program payments.

In general, a minor (including a minor who is the beneficiary of a trust or who is the heir of an estate) and the parent or any court-appointed guardian or conservator responsible for the minor are considered one person. A minor is considered to be a separate person if the minor is a producer on a farm in which the parent or court-appointed guardian or conservator responsible for the minor owns no interest in the farm or in any production from the farm and the minor (1) has established and maintains a separate household from the minor's parents or any court-appointed guardian or conservator responsible for the minor and the minor personally carries out the farming activities with respect to a farming operation for which there exists a separate accounting or (2) the minor does not live in the same household as the minor's parent. In the latter case, the minor must be represented by a court-appointed guardian or conservator who is responsible for the minor and the minor must own the farm. A person is considered to be a minor until reaching age 18. Court proceedings conferring majority status on a person under age 18 do not change that person's minority status.

A person who is not a U.S. citizen or an alien admitted to the U.S. for permanent residence is ineligible to receive payments unless specified conditions are met. To be eligible, an individual must provide land, capital and a *substantial amount of personal labor* in the production of crops on the farm.

The same provision makes a corporation or other entity ineligible for benefits if more than 10 percent of the beneficial ownership of the entity is owned by persons who are not U.S. citizens or aliens admitted to the U.S. for permanent residence, again unless the persons provide a substantial amount of personal labor in the production of crops on the farm. If an entity becomes ineligible under those rules, USDA has the authority to make proportionate payments to owners who are U.S. citizens or aliens admitted for permanent residence.

Passive losses

Rules limiting the deductibility of losses from passive business activities may also influence the way the farm or ranch business is structured.

Material participation test. If the material participation test is met, losses from business activities may be deducted against other income. However, this is not the usual material participation test. For passive loss purposes, the material participation test is met only if the person "is involved in the operations of the activity on a basis which is regular, continuous, and substantial."

Temporary regulations issued in 1988 laid out seven tests for material participation, none of which is easily met.

• Under the first test, an individual is considered to be materially participating if the individual participates in the activity for more than 500 hours during the year. IRS believes the involvement of more than 500 hours during the year means that it is not a passive activity. Moreover, the big target is tax shelters and IRS believes that few tax shelter investors put that kind of time into investments.

• The second test is for situations requiring less than 500 hours of involvement – or less than 500 hours by any one individual – during the year. If an individual's participation in the activity constitutes "substantially all of the participation" in the activity by all individuals during the year, it is considered material participation.

• Under the third test, an individual is considered to be materially participating if the individual puts more than 500 hours per year into the activity and the individual's participation is not less than that of any other individual. This rule would not apply if a tenant were involved who put 500 hours per year into the activity and the owner put 300 hours per year into the venture, for example.

• The fourth test introduces a new term – "significant participation." An individual is treated as materially participating in significant participation activities if the individual's *aggregate*

271

participation in significant participation activities for the year exceeds 500 hours. A "significant participation activity" is a trade or business activity in which the individual participates for more than 100 hours for the taxable year.

This rule is intended to reach those individuals who devote more than 500 hours per year in total spread over several activities in which the individual devotes more than 100 hours to each of the activities. The idea is to treat an individual with several activities as favorably as someone who devotes an equivalent amount of time to a single activity.

• Under the fifth test, an individual is treated as materially participating if the individual materially participated in the activity for any five of the 10 preceding years. The idea behind this rule is that substantial involvement over a lengthy period indicates that it was probably the individual's principal livelihood. But if the individual had not been active within the past 10 years, it is more appropriately viewed as a passive activity.

• The sixth test is for those involved in personal service activities. An individual is treated as materially participating in a personal service activity in a particular year if the taxpayer materially participated in the activity for any three years preceding the year in question. Personal service activities are those involving the fields of health, law, engineering, architecture, accounting, actuarial science, performing arts, consulting or any other trade or business in which capital is not a material income-producing factor.

• The seventh and final test specifies that an individual may be treated as materially participating in an activity based on all the facts and circumstances. Several factors are identified as relevant to the facts and circumstances test – (1) an individual who does not participate for more than 100 hours in an activity cannot meet the facts and circumstances test, (2) the fact that an individual is materially participating for purposes of social security or special use valuation of land is not taken into account for purposes of the passive loss rules and (3) an individual's own participation in management of an activity is not taken into account in applying the facts and circumstances test *if a paid manager participates in the activity.* Thus, the presence of a paid farm manager precludes the owner from meeting the material participation test. This is the "passive loss" rule discussed in Chapter 1 governing the relationship of property owner to agent or employee.

Two additional rules are highly relevant for farm taxpayers. (1) The material participation test can be met by surviving spouses who inherit qualified real property from a deceased spouse if the surviving spouse engages in "active management." Active management requires considerably less than material participation. (2) Farm taxpayers are permitted to qualify as materially participating if they materially participated for five or more years in the eight year period before retirement or disability.

Active participation test. Under a special rule, individuals may deduct annually up to $25,000 of passive activity losses attributable to rental real estate activities in which the individual actively participates. The $25,000 allowance phases out as adjusted gross income increases from $100,000 to $150,000. The $25,000 allowance is not available to corporations.

A key term is "rental real estate activity." IRS has taken the position in regulations that a crop share lease (and, presumably, a livestock share lease) is *not* a rental real estate activity. Such leases are viewed as joint ventures. A letter in late 1990 from the U.S. Department of the Treasury confirmed that the regulations deny the $25,000 deduction for losses arising under most share leases. Therefore, individuals who attempt unsuccessfully to meet the material participation test with a crop share or livestock share lease apparently must shift to a cash rent lease in order to be in the running for the active participation test.

Other considerations

Separating the land from the rest of the assets used in production may create problems of a practical nature. The land often represents an important part of the collateral for production credit. Its absence may lead to a request for a personal guarantee of production loans by the land owners. Moreover, the production side of the farm business is usually a voracious user of capital. And payment of a reasonable rental to the owners of the land may lead to a build-up of capital in that entity and a shortage in the production side of the business.

This problem is generally most severe if the land is held by a corporation. Removal of capital through the dividend route may be too painful, tax-wise, and the amount that can be removed each year through salaries is constrained because of the limited effort needed to manage land that's under lease to a tenant.

There's also an element of added complexity in managing the financial, tax and accounting details for two entities rather than one. If the entities aren't kept separate, there's a good chance they won't be respected for tax purposes.

One final note – members of a controlled group of corporations are limited to one set of graduated rate brackets. Thus, the 15 percent rate on the first $50,000 of corporate taxable income as well as the rates on successive blocks of income can't be assured for both entities under common ownership if the land is held in one corporation and the other production assets are in another. More on the income tax treatment of a controlled group of corporations in Chapter 20.

IN CONCLUSION. It's always been important to give careful consideration to structuring the farm business. Recent federal tax legislation added several more points to think about when decisions are made as to whether land should be included in a new partnership, limited liability company or corporation. The safest bet – and probably the simplest solution – is to end up with a single entity. If solid business or estate planning reasons point toward multiple entities, there's a list of considerations that should be taken into account before the final decision is made.

In recent years, the multiple entity approach has become substantially more popular as some of the negatives associated with multiple entities have become less important.

17
Partnerships and estate planning

Most farms have been operated as sole proprietorships with the land either owned or rented from a landlord. Increasingly, farmers are turning to the partnership, corporation, or limited liability company, particularly if two or more persons are to be involved in ownership or management. The limited liability company is a relatively recent development and is discussed in Chapter 25.

A key factor in selecting a form of organization is whether it is anticipated that the farm business will continue beyond the lives of the parents. If the decision has been made that the farm business will terminate on or before the deaths of the parents, the sole proprietorship may be the best device. But if it is expected that the business will continue into the next generation, the partnership, corporation or limited liability company may be a better choice.

Partnership – what it is

A partnership is generally defined as an association of two or more persons to carry on, as co-owners, a business for profit. For partnerships based upon oral or written agreements, there's not much question about how the business is organized. But what about a livestock share lease? Or a parent-child operating agreement? Are these partnerships?

Tests for determining what is and what is not a partnership have been developed in each state. Most states require a sharing of profits for a partnership. Some require a sharing of losses. Crop share leases typically involve a sharing of the crop on a gross receipts basis with the landlord and tenant each bearing unique expenses. The same is generally true of a livestock share lease. However, after a number of years' operation, a maturing parent-child arrangement or a livestock share lease between related parties often moves toward sharing of more and more expenses before the income is divided. Ultimately, some parent-child arrangements (and livestock share leases) move to the point of sharing of net income. At that point the risk may be substantial that a court would consider the arrangement to be a partnership.

States generally give some weight to how the parties believe they are organized. That's why it's wise not to use the term "partnership" in commercial transactions, on bank accounts or in discussion or correspondence unless partnership status is desired or anticipated.

The safest route is to develop a written agreement and state clearly that a partnership is or is not intended. If a partnership is not intended in a livestock share lease or parent-child agreement, it is wise to say so.

Unless otherwise specified in the partnership agreement, partners have an equal voice in managing the business and a majority vote governs.

UNLIMITED LIABILITY. Probably the best known characteristic of partnerships is the unlimited liability of partners for obligations of the partnership. If a partnership drifts toward insolvency, the partnership creditors have first crack against partnership assets. The creditors of individual partners are first in line to grab the other property (that not in partnership) of the individual.

Then, if there's anything left, partnership creditors can go against assets of the individual partners. Also, creditors of the individual partners can go against any remaining partnership assets up to the amount of the individual's interest in the partnership.

Thus, each partner is fully liable, personally, for the obligations of the partnership. This feature of the partnership discourages some people from using it.

The concept of unlimited liability applies to both contract liability (such as from borrowing money) and tort liability (such as arises from accidents). Some deal with the tort liability part of the problem by carrying adequate liability insurance. Contract liability can be curbed by limiting who can commit the partnership to liability and by exercising prudence in entering into contractual obligations. Thus, many believe the risks of unlimited liability are manageable.

PARTNERSHIP TERMINATION. A partnership may not have as much stability as the parties would like. As with the sole proprietorship, the partnership is vulnerable to premature liquidation in the absence of prior planning. If the partnership agreement is in writing, the term of existence can be stated. But typically, partnership agreements provide that the partnership exists at the will of the partners.

Even though a term of existence is specified, courts do not generally force partnership continuation against the desire of a partner to withdraw. Dissolution of a partnership normally occurs whenever a partner ceases to be associated with the business. But *dissolution* need not necessarily cause a *winding up* of the business. Dissolving partners have three choices: (1) liquidate, (2) form a new partnership, or (3) shift to a sole proprietorship, corporation or limited liability company.

On death of a partner, the surviving partners are generally under a duty to wind up the business and make a distribution to the deceased partner's estate. But courts have recognized the right of partners to bind the survivors to continue the business after the death of a partner. When continuation is desired, steps should be taken to: (1) include a provision requiring continuation in the partnership agreement, and (2) give the administrator or executor of each partner power to act as a partner.

For federal income tax purposes, a partnership does not terminate on death of a partner unless the partnership ceases to operate or there is a change of 50 percent or more in partnership capital and profits within a 12-month period. Upon death of a partner, even in a two-person partnership, the partnership is not considered as terminated if the estate or other successor continues to share in profits and losses.

INCOME TAX TREATMENT. A partnership is not a taxpayer for income tax purposes. It simply files an information return – Form 1065 – each year. The partners pay income tax on their share of the partnership income as spelled out in the partnership agreement. Partners are taxable in their individual capacities on their distributive shares of partnership taxable income whether distributed to them or not. This includes ordinary income, capital gains or losses, operating losses and credits. The partnership also passes to the partners, tax privileged income and deduction items – charitable contributions, dividends, tax exempt interest and soil and water conservation expenses. The partnership as a new tax-payer makes several elections – the method of accounting, use of the installment sale provision and methods of cost recovery (depreciation), to mention the major ones.

Income tax return. A partnership income tax return is required even though the partnership has no taxable income for the year. There's a penalty imposed on partnerships of $50 per partner per month for failure to file a timely or complete Form 1065. The penalty reaches a maximum after five months. This penalty is in addition to the criminal penalties for willful failure to file a return or supply information. But the $50 per partner per month penalty is not imposed if failure to file was due to "reasonable cause." According to a Congressional Committee report, partner-ships with 10 or fewer partners should not be subject to the penalty if each partner files a detailed statement of income and deductions. But that exception isn't in the law itself. IRS now agrees with the Congressional Committee report, if the partner-ship is of a type that has not historically filed a partnership return and it is a domestic partnership composed entirely of non-corpo-rate general partners.

Family farm partnerships need not complete balance sheets and reconciliation of partners' capital accounts if the partnership has 10 or fewer partners; the partnership is a domestic partnership composed entirely of non-corporate general partners; the partnership is not a partner in another partnership; each partner's interest in partnership capital is the same as the interest in partnership profits; all of the income, deductions and credits are allocated to each partner in proportion to that partner's pro rata interest; and K-1 schedules (showing distributions to partners) are filed as required.

Partners are to treat items on their own income tax returns in a manner consistent with the way the items are treated on the partnership return unless the partner discloses the inconsistency to the IRS. The tax treatment of partnership income, losses, deductions and credits is generally determined at the partnership level in a unified proceeding rather than in separate proceedings with individual partners as has generally been the case in the past. Moreover, any partner with an interest in proceedings with IRS is treated as a party to the action. Partners failing to participate are bound by any settlement with IRS or any court decision relative to partnership items. These rules do not apply, however, to "small partnerships." Those are partnerships in which – (1) there are no more than 10 partners (with a husband and wife and their estates counted as one partner), (2) the partners are all individuals or estates and (3) each partner's distributive share applies equally to every partnership item.

The federal partnership income tax return is due on or before the 15th date of the fourth month after the close of the taxable year. That's April 15 for those on a calendar year – as most are. If a partnership is dissolved, the federal income tax return is due for the short taxable year.

Property can be expensed off for income tax purposes under the expense method depreciation provision. For a partnership, the annual dollar limitation ($17,500) applies at the level of the partnership and for each partner.

Method of accounting. In general, farm partnerships can be on the cash or accrual methods of accounting. The cash method of accounting is limited for farm partnerships in which a corporation is a partner if the corporation would be required to be on accrual accounting. That would be necessary if the corporation has gross receipts of more than $1 million per year unless it is an S corporation, members of a family own at least 50 percent of the stock, members of two families own at least 65 percent of the stock or three families own at least 50 percent of the stock and substantially all of the rest of the stock is owned by employees, their families or a retirement trust. The Revenue Act of 1987 requires certain closely held and family-owned farm corporations that have been allowed to use the cash method of accounting to change to the accrual method if the corporation has gross receipts in excess of $25 million in any year.

Taxable year. With respect to taxable year, under the 1986 legislation a partnership could not have a taxable year other than the taxable year of one or more of its partners who have an aggregate interest in partnership profits and capital of greater than 50 percent. If the partners owning a majority of partnership profits and capital did not have the same taxable year, the partnership had to adopt the same taxable year as its principal partners. In the event the principal partners did not have the same taxable year and no majority of its partners have the same taxable year, the partnership had to adopt a calendar year or other year as specified in regulations.

The Revenue Act of 1987 allows partnerships to keep their pre-1987 tax year if the entity pays additional tax. The additional tax imposed at the entity level is calculated based on a formula that estimates the amount of tax that would have been paid if the required change had been made.

Formation of partnership. Upon formation, no gain or loss is ordinarily recognized on the transfer to the partnership. The partnership adopts the partners' basis for property transferred and the partners' shares adopt the basis of the transferred property. In general, the partnership takes over the depreciation schedule for the transferred property. For property depreciated under ACRS or MACRS, the partnership must use the same recovery period and method used by the transferor (including use of any optional recovery period or method) for the transferred property.

The so-called "fast" methods of depreciation – double declining balance and sum-of-the-years-digits – claimed on non-ACRS property (property not depreciated under the Accelerated Cost Recovery System) cannot be used on property transferred upon formation of the partnership. So those items on fast depreciation must be moved to straight line or an acceptable non-accelerated method of depreciation. That's because the fast methods of depreciation can be used only on new property. And the transferred property isn't "new" to the partnership.

See Chapter 16 for discussion of the points to consider in structuring the farm business.

Organizational costs for forming a partnership can be deducted over the first 60 months of partnership life.

Family members as partners. For a family partnership, it may be desirable to make some or all of the children partners and reduce the income tax bill. But partnership arrangements may be disregarded for income tax purposes unless substantial amounts of capital, labor or management are provided by each partner. A family partnership may arise by gift to some partners if the transfer is complete and in good faith and adequate allowance is made for the services provided by the one making the gift.

Minors as partners

Estate planning for partners in a family partnership often involves transfer of partnership interests to minors. The idea may be to reduce the family income tax bill, to cut down on death taxes, or simply to involve older children in the business. But, minors as partners may create problems.

Minors are not legally competent to manage their property until they are of age. It is not clear in some states that one of the most useful devices for holding interests of minors – the Uniform Gifts to Minors Acts – may be used to hold partnership interests.

The Uniform Acts set up an easy-to-use custodianship under state law but in some states it can be used only for gifts of securities or money. In other states, the act has been broadened to a Uniform Transfers to Minors Act and about any property can be custodial property.

For federal income tax purposes, a minor is not recognized as a partner unless control is exercised by another person for the benefit of the minor or the minor is competent to manage his or her own property and participate in partnership activities equally with adults.

In most states, a minor can disaffirm some kinds of contracts made as a minor. As a partner, a minor can generally disaffirm the partnership agreement to the extent that he or she will not be personally liable to creditors. This might upset some creditors. However, a contract made by a partnership with an "outsider" acting in good faith generally may not be avoided simply because one partner is a minor.

Limited partnerships

In most states, a partnership may be organized with one or more limited partners if it has at least one general partner.

Limited partners are liable for partnership obligations only up to the amount of their investment in the partnership and may not be held personally liable. But the price of limited partner status is that a limited partner may not participate in management. The limited partner who does participate in management may become liable as a general partner.

A limited partnership may be useful if one of the partners – such as a parent – wishes to withdraw from active participation in the business. It permits the parent to leave capital invested in the business without the fear of unlimited liability. A limited partnership may also be used with non-farm heirs as limited partners. If a limited partnership is used to hold the land only, careful attention should be given to the potential problems with multiple entities as discussed in Chapter 16.

Unlike a general partnership, which need file no documents publicly about the partnership, a limited partnership is required to disclose specified information. States require limited partnerships to reveal the existence of limited partners and some information about the limited partnership. This is done by filing a document in a county office, often that of the recorder of deeds, and, in some states, in an office at the state level.

In recent years, a major use of the limited partnership has been in conjunction with tax sheltered investment activity such as livestock feed yards and residential real estate complexes. Losses early in the life of the project pass through to the partners to offset high tax bracket income from other sources with gains coming in a later year. The limited partnership has become the investment vehicle of preference for off-farm investors interested in tax shelters.

Special rules apply to "farming syndicates". The rules are mainly aimed at partnerships, particularly limited partnerships. A "farming syndicate" is a partnership or other enterprise (other than a regularly taxed corporation engaged in farming) if – (1) interests in the firm have been offered for sale – in any offering required to be registered with a state or federal regulatory agency, or (2) more than 35 percent of the losses during any period are allocable to limited partners or "limited entrepreneurs." The key point: in general, deductions cannot be claimed by a farming syndicate for seed, feed, fertilizer or other farm supplies until they're actually used or consumed.

Another rule affects limited partnerships used for tax shelter purposes. Partners in limited partnerships – such as those in the cattle feeding business – may not deduct losses in excess of their investment plus loans for which the partner was personally liable. These are the "at risk" rules and limit losses by investors to the amount of their tax investment in the venture. In general, the amount "at risk" is the cash and the income tax basis of property contributed to the investment activity plus amounts borrowed and contributed to the activity to the extent the taxpayer is personally liable for the loan.

Passive loss rules, added in 1986, have become the dominant income tax challenge to tax-shelter activity involving the offsetting of investment losses against wage or other active income. The passive loss provisions are discussed in detail in Chapter 16. In general, deductions from passive trade or business activities (exclusive of portfolio income) may not be deducted against other income. Losses from passive trade or business activities may only be used to offset passive income. Likewise, credits from passive activities are limited to the tax attributable to the passive activities. Losses and credits not allowed are carried forward to the following year and treated as deductions and credits from passive trade or business activities in that year. Upon disposal of the taxpayer's entire interest in the activity, suspended losses may be deducted for income tax purposes.

An activity is considered to be passive if it involves the conduct of a trade or business and the taxpayer does not materially participate in the activity on a "regular, continuous and substantial" basis. Up to $25,000 of losses may be allowed for "active" participation in a rental real estate activity for taxpayers other than corporations.

Even though an organization is formed as a limited partnership under state law, it may be treated for income tax purposes as a corporation. Under corporate taxation, losses cannot be passed through to shareholders (except for the S corporation option). A limited partnership will not be taxed as a corporation unless it has more corporate characteristics than non-corporate features. Those include – (1) continuity of life (most limited partnerships lack this feature), (2) centralized management (limited partnerships generally do not possess this characteristic unless the limited partners hold "substantially all" partnership interests), (3) free transferability of partnership interests (this one depends on state law and the limited partnership agreement), and (4) limited liability (this feature exists if the general partner or partners have no substantial non-partnership assets reachable by creditors).

Limited partnerships, especially those formed with tax shelter objectives in mind, should review these four characteristics with care and construct the limited partnership agreement accordingly if partnership status for income tax purposes is desired.

Partners as employees

The long standing rule has been that partners are self-employed for purposes of participating in employee benefits such as retirement plans and for social security and income tax purposes. Even guaranteed wages or salary are treated as self-employment income. A few cases have permitted a partner to be considered an employee for limited purposes.

A partnership may establish retirement or deferred compensation plans. The distinctions between employee plans of corporations and plans established for self-employed individuals including partners have been generally eliminated. Rules governing employee plans are discussed in Chapter 21.

In general, a limited partner's distributive share of partnership income is not self-employment income for social security purposes. There's an exception for guaranteed payments as remuneration for services.

IN CONCLUSION: A partnership, with proper planning, can be a highly useful estate planning device. It generally costs less to form than a corporation and is a little less formal to operate. The big disadvantages are (1) unlimited liability of partners, (2) dissolution on death or withdrawal of a partner, (3) problems with minors as partners, and (4) historic ineligibility of partners to participate in employee fringe benefits.

18
Farm corporations and estate planning

In nearly every state, farm corporations have increased in number during the past four decades. And research in several states points to estate planning advantages as a major reason why farmers incorporate.

Nearly all of the farm corporations formed in recent years have been of the small, closely held variety. The stock is typically owned by people related by blood or marriage. Some farm corporations – mostly "incorporated landlords" – are owned by unrelated shareholders yet they are also small and closely held. Few operating farm corporations are large enough to make public stock ownership practical.

Nature of the corporation

A corporation is a distinct entity, separate from the individuals who own it, manage it or work for it. With separate entity status, a corporation can sue and be sued, enter into contracts and own real and personal property. A corporation has most of the rights of an individual.

However, since a corporation is a creature of state law, it does not have the right to "do business" in other states without qualifying to do business there as a foreign corporation. For this purpose, doing business generally requires a sustained pattern of economic activity beyond an occasional transaction outside the state of incorporation.

One notable feature of separate entity status of the corporation is limited liability for the shareholders. Corporate obligations arising either from tortious activities (such as negligence) or contractual commitments may be satisfied only out of corporate assets. Thus, assets owned by the shareholders individually (other than their stock investment in the corporation) are shielded from corporate liability.

Shareholders may lose limited liability in three ways –

• By participating personally in a tort giving rise to corporate liability. For example, a shareholder who is also a corporate employee might become involved in an accident while driving a corporate vehicle.

• By signing personally on corporate contractual obligations. A signature of the form –

ABC Farm, Inc.

By A, President

generally binds only the corporation and not A personally. However, if A signs the instrument without indicating that he or she is acting on behalf of the corporation, that would normally bind A personally.

• If the corporation fails to meet the requirements for limited liability on a continuing basis including the requirements that (1) the corporation be validly organized; (2) corporate formalities such as meetings, minutes of meetings and separate bookkeeping and accounting be maintained; and (3) a reasonably adequate amount or cushion of equity capital be committed to the corporation by the shareholders to absorb corporate obligations that might arise.

Obviously, if the shareholders commit all or substantially all of their non-exempt property (not exempt from execution by creditors) to the corporation, limited liability has less meaning than if substantial investments are retained outside the corporation. One possible advantage, even where few assets are kept outside the corporation, involves the possibility of a judgment in excess of assets. Such a deficiency judgment against an individual may be good for years (10 to 20 years depending on state law) unless discharged in a bankruptcy proceeding. A deficiency judgment against an empty corporate shell is of less consequence.

In an effort to "manufacture" limited liability protection, some

288

individuals leave substantial assets (such as land) outside the corporation at the time it is formed. This may have adverse effects on credit availability to the firm and lead to requests by creditors for personal signatures of shareholders on corporate loans.

Corporate management

Theoretically, decision making in a corporation is divided among three clearly defined groups: the shareholders, board of directors and officers.

SHAREHOLDERS. As the basic decision making group, the shareholders approve changes in the corporate charter, the articles of incorporation, and also elect the board of directors. In exercising their decision-making power, each shareholder has one vote for each share of voting stock. Most states permit non-voting stock.

Typically, a majority vote governs and the holder or holders of 51 percent or more of the stock have control over corporate decisions directly at the shareholder level. Indirectly, shareholders control decision making at the other levels by virtue of their power to select the board of directors. Minority shareholders have little, if any, decision-making authority unless permitted by the majority.

To soften this sometimes harsh rule, a number of legal devices may be used to grant greater participation in decision making by minority shareholders (often the children in a family corporation).

• In most states, the vote required for shareholder action may be increased from a simple majority to some higher level, even to unanimity. While giving protection to minority shareholders, it sometimes leads to "the minority tail wagging the majority dog" as the veto power of minority shareholders may lead to deadlock.

• Cumulative voting, available either as an optional provision or on a mandatory basis in most states, permits shareholders to multiply their votes by the number of directors to be elected and cast the entire number for one director. This gives greater assurance that minority shareholders would be at least represented on the board of directors.

• Pooling agreements, voting trusts and shareholder agreements are ways whereby certain key decisions likely to affect minority shareholders may be "pre-decided" or left to be decided by third parties pursuant to a set of instructions. Such issues as employment of specified individuals, salary levels and dividend levels could be resolved with such agreements.

• Pre-emptive rights, where available, give minority shareholders the right to acquire their proportionate part of new stock issues. This right gives some protection against relative loss of power through issuance of stock only to favored shareholders.

BOARD OF DIRECTORS. As the policy making body of the corporation, the board of directors is charged with developing corporate policy and handling long-range management. Typically, directors receive fees for their services but are not salaried. The selection of officers is an important responsibility of the board of directors.

OFFICERS. The day-to-day decision makers of the corporation, the officers, often function as full or part-time employees and receive salaries. Officers are charged with executing policy developed by the board of directors, hence the term "executives." Authority to hire other employees, sign negotiable instruments, make contracts or borrow money may be granted to designated officers by the board of directors.

In most farm corporations, the same individuals hold membership in the three decision making groups. Despite possible commonality in membership, it is necessary to see that some decisions are made by the proper group. For example, salaries and bonuses should be set by the board of directors.

State limits on farm incorporation

The trend toward more family farm corporations has encountered a stiff crosswind in a few jurisdictions. Sentiment in some farm states in opposition to large scale farming, investments by non-farm interests, tax shelter activity and concern about vertical control of the food production, processing and distribution processes by non-farmers, has led to restrictive legislation that limits the formation of farm corporations.

NORTH DAKOTA: A North Dakota law, passed in the 1930s, prohibiting corporations from engaging in farming in that state was modified in 1967 to permit closely held farm corporations. But the modification was referred to a referendum in early November 1968 and was defeated, thus returning North Dakota to the statutory prohibition against farm corporations. A similar proposal was defeated at the polls in 1974. The North Dakota statute was amended, however, effective July 1, 1981, to allow family held farm and ranch operations with 15 or fewer shareholders to incorporate. To take advantage of the new provision –

• Each shareholder must be related to every other shareholder as parent, child, grandparent, grandchild, brother, sister, uncle, aunt, nephew, niece, great grandparent, great grandchild or first cousin or be a spouse of a person so related.

• Each shareholder must be an individual except that most family trusts and estates can be shareholders.

• The officers and directors must be shareholders actively engaged in operating the farm or ranch and at least one of the shareholders must reside on or operate the farm or ranch.

• At least 65 percent of the corporation's gross income over the previous five years (or for its term of existence if less than five years) must be derived from farming or ranching and no more than 20 percent of the corporation's gross receipts can come from rents, royalties, dividends, interest and annuities.

The North Dakota law was originally passed because it was feared that insurance companies and other financial institutions foreclosing on farm mortgages would become dominant land owners in the state.

KANSAS: A restrictive Kansas law, also passed in the 1930s,

was relaxed in 1965 to permit farm corporations having 10 or fewer shareholders with no more than 5,000 acres of land to operate in that state. All incorporators (but not necessarily all shareholders) had to be natural persons residing in Kansas. And none of the shareholders could own stock in another corporation authorized to engage in the prohibited purposes. Those purposes included "producing, planting, raising, harvesting or gathering of wheat, corn, grain sorghums, barley, oats, rye or potatoes or the milking of cows for dairy purposes." Other types of agricultural operations weren't affected by the Kansas law.

Effective July 1, 1981, the Kansas statute was amended substantially to eliminate many of the specific limitations in the Kansas law. With several specified exceptions, Kansas law prohibits corporations, trusts, "limited corporate partnerships" and "corporate partnerships" from owning, acquiring or leasing agricultural land except for –

• Family farm corporations which are founded for the purpose of farming and the ownership of agricultural land, a majority of the stock of which is held by related individuals and a majority of the shareholders are related, all shareholders are natural persons or persons acting in a fiduciary capacity for the benefit of natural persons, and at least one of the shareholders resides on the farm or is actively engaged in the farming operation,

• Authorized farm corporations formed for the purpose of farming and the ownership of agricultural land if all incorporators are Kansas residents, the shareholders do not exceed 15, the shareholders are all natural persons or persons acting in a fiduciary capacity for natural persons or non-profit corporations and at least 30 percent of the shareholders reside on the farm or are actively engaged in the farming operation,

• Family farm trusts where a majority of the equitable interest is held by and a majority of the beneficiaries are related, the beneficiaries are all natural persons or persons acting in a fiduciary capacity other than as trustee for a trust or non-profit corporation,

• Authorized farm trusts where the beneficiaries do not exceed

15, the beneficiaries are all natural persons, persons acting in a fiduciary capacity or non-profit corporations, and

• Testamentary trusts.

In 1991, the Kansas law was amended to allow a corporation or limited liability company to own land used as a feedlot, poultry confinement facility or rabbit confinement facility. In 1994, the Kansas legislature added a provision authorizing the county commissioners by resolution to permit swine production facilities in the county. A petition can, however, cause the matter to be referred to a county vote.

MINNESOTA: Minnesota, in 1973, repealed a 5,000 acre limitation on land that could be "acquired" by a farm corporation and enacted a detailed statute requiring farm corporations to file a special annual report and limiting corporate farming operations.

Farming operations are permitted by "family farm corporations" in Minnesota if a majority of stock is held by related shareholders, a majority of the shareholders are related, at least one related shareholder resides on or actively operates the farm, and no other corporation owns stock in the firm. Farming operations may also be carried on by an "authorized farm corporation" defined as a corporation with (1) five or fewer shareholders, (2) only individuals or estates as shareholders, (3) no more than one class of stock, (4) no more than 20 percent of gross receipts from rents, royalties, dividends, interest and annuities, and (5) a majority of the shareholders are residing on the farm or are actively engaged in farming. Authorized corporations may not, directly or indirectly, own an interest in more than 1,500 acres of real estate used in farming.

Other corporations owning or leasing agricultural land as of the date of the act may continue to engage in farming but cannot expand at a rate greater than 20 percent in acres in any five-year period except for expansion made necessary by pollution control regulations. The law also excludes research farms; firms producing breeding stock for resale to farmers, seed, wild rice, nursery plants and sod; large asparagus growing operations; and, with some restrictions, corporations acquiring land for development.

In 1994, the Minnesota law was amended to relax the rules on who could form and operate an authorized corporation. Authorized corporations may be formed if 75 percent or more of the "control and financial investment" is held by "farmers residing in Minnesota" and at least 51 percent of the required percentage of farmers are actively engaged in livestock production. Authorized corporations, for the 1994 limits to apply, must be formed for the production of livestock other than dairy cattle.

SOUTH DAKOTA AND MISSOURI: In 1974, South Dakota enacted a statute similar to the one then in force in Minnesota and Missouri followed suit in 1975. The Missouri legislation adopts a less restrictive definition of "authorized farm corporation." The Missouri law defines such a corporation as one in which all shareholders, other than an estate or revocable or irrevocable trust, are individuals and the corporation receives two-thirds or more of its net income from farming. The Missouri definition of family farm corporation is similar to that in Minnesota.

And the Missouri law, like Minnesota, limits other existing corporations (those not meeting the definition of "family farm" or "authorized" farm corporations) to expansion at a rate not to exceed 20 percent in acres in any five-year period plus that needed to meet pollution control regulations. The Missouri statute requires an initial and annual report by farm corporations.

The Missouri statute was amended in 1991 to make the restrictions inapplicable to north central Missouri (Mercer, Putnam and Sullivan counties) "for the production of swine or swine products."

WISCONSIN: Although it has numerous exemptions, a Wisconsin law passed in 1974 affects some farm corporations with more than 15 shareholders and limits growth to 20 percent in acres in any five-year period by holders. Moreover, the Wisconsin limitation applies only to production of dairy products (but not processing); cattle, hogs and sheep; and to wheat, field corn, barley, oats, rye, hay, pasture, soybeans, millet and sorghum.

OKLAHOMA: In 1971, Oklahoma adopted a statute providing for several limitations on farm corporations including a 35 percent limit on corporate gross receipts from sources other than farming, ranching or mineral rights; a restriction to not more than 10 shareholders (unless related by marriage or as lineal descendants); and a requirement that shareholders be individuals or estates or certain types of trusts or corporations.

In 1991, Oklahoma amended its limitation to allow "research and/or feeding arrangements or operations concerned with the feeding of livestock or poultry" and operations directly related to the production of livestock or poultry for sale or use as breeding stock and/or swine and other livestock operations. In 1993, limitations were added for trusts, general and limited partnerships and limited liability companies.

IOWA: Legislation passed in Iowa in 1975 calls for detailed annual reporting by corporations and limited partnerships owning or leasing agricultural land or engaged in farming. The law also requires reporting by non-resident aliens owning or leasing agricultural land or engaged in farming. Fiduciaries (such as trusts) with corporations, limited partnerships or non-resident aliens holding agricultural land as beneficiaries are required to report each year. The act also prohibits processors with more than $10 million in sales at wholesale from owning, controlling or operating feedlots in Iowa in which cattle or hogs are fed for slaughter. The legislation imposed a moratorium on corporations (other than family farm corporations and authorized farm corporations) from acquiring "agricultural land." The moratorium was made permanent in 1979.

Under the Iowa rules, authorized farm corporations include those with 25 or fewer shareholders and shareholders who are all natural persons or persons acting in a fiduciary capacity for the benefit of natural persons or non-profit corporations. To be a family farm corporation, the corporation must be founded for the purpose of farming and the ownership of agricultural land, a majority of the voting stock and a majority of the shareholders

295

must be related (spouse, parent, grandparent, or lineal ascendant or descendant of grandparents), the shareholders must be natural persons or persons acting in a fiduciary capacity for the benefit of natural persons and 60 percent of the gross revenues of the corporation over the last three-year period must come from farming.

In 1977, Iowa adopted limitations on ownership of land by trusts other than authorized farm trusts, family farm trusts and testamentary trusts. The trust limitations parallel those for corporate ownership of farmland.

In 1987, a maximum limit of 1,500 acres of land was imposed on authorized farm corporations in terms of land acquisition.

Effective July 1, 1988, a person may not become a shareholder of an authorized farm corporation, the beneficiary of an authorized trust or a limited partner in a limited partnership that owns or leases agricultural land if the person is already a shareholder of an authorized farm corporation, a beneficiary of an authorized trust or a limited partner in a limited partnership that owns or leases agricultural land (except for limited partners in a family farm limited partnership).

NEBRASKA: A Nebraska bill, enacted in 1975, requires more limited reporting than the Iowa legislation by corporations that have "acquired title to agricultural land" or obtained "any leasehold interest" or any other interest less than outright ownership. The law requires reporting of acreage and location of land and information about the shareholders, directors and officers.

In 1982, Nebraska voters approved a referendum measure for their state constitution barring corporations or syndicates from acquiring real estate in the state *except for* family farm or ranch corporations; non-profit corporations; Indian tribal corporations; land used for research or experimental purposes; land used for raising poultry; land leased by alfalfa processors; land used for growing seed, nursery plants or sod; mineral rights; land used for immediate or future non-farm use; land acquired by debt collection or forfeiture; bona fide security interests in land; custom spraying, fertilizing or harvesting; and livestock futures contracts, livestock purchased for slaughter or livestock purchased and resold within two weeks. The Nebraska limitation also does not apply to agricultural land ownership on the effective date of the provision.

Under the 1982 Nebraska law, a "family farm or ranch corporation" is defined as a corporation engaged in farming or ranching or the ownership of agricultural land, in which the majority of the voting stock is held by members of a family, or a trust created for the benefit of a member of that family, related to one another within the fourth degree of kindred or their spouses, and at least one of whom is a person residing on or actively engaged in the day-to-day labor and management of the farm or ranch. None of the shareholders can be a resident alien and none of the shareholders can be a corporation or partnership unless all of the shareholders or partners are persons related within the fourth degree of kindred to the majority of shareholders in the family farm corporation. Thus, the Nebraska Constitutional provision is lengthy and complex.

SOUTH CAROLINA: In South Carolina, land held by corporations that are not "closely held" is taxed at 6 percent of fair market value rather than the 4 percent rate applicable to other land owners. To be closely held, a corporation must have 10 or fewer shareholders, only individuals or estates as shareholders, no non-resident aliens as shareholders and not more than one class of stock.

OTHER STATES: Other states have minor restrictions on farm corporations. Texas law prohibits a corporation from engaging in both cattle raising and meat packing but owning and operating feedlots is not "cattle raising." West Virginia levies a special tax of 5 cents per acre on corporate land holdings over 10,000 acres.

Future of large scale farming

It appears that resistance to farm corporations has often been resistance to large scale agriculture carried on by employees and financed with capital from outside the agricultural sector. Since many large scale operations make use of the corporation, and since corporations are creatures of state law, unhappiness over structural changes occurring in agriculture has been channeled into pressure for laws barring or limiting the use of corporations in farming.

Whether large, publicly held farming operations would make significant inroads in agriculture in the absence of restrictive legislation is not known. The outcome would depend heavily upon the answers to three major questions:

1. What is presently the most efficient size of farm unit and what will be the most efficient size 10 years from now? For example, does the cost of producing a bushel of corn decline for acreages up to 2,000 acres? Or 4,000 acres? Or 10,000 acres? If corn is produced most cheaply at 2,000 acres, for example, pressures will build for farms to increase to that size.

Internal production efficiency isn't the only consideration. Possible economies in large scale purchasing of inputs and a price edge for large scale marketing of products may also influence the size of unit.

2. Compared to other investments, how profitable is farming and land ownership now and how profitable is it likely to be in the future? Outside investors are out to make money, especially in the long run. If there's no money in farming, outside investors aren't likely to be interested. Ironically, high profit levels in farming attract the attention of investors far and near.

3. What are likely to be the limiting factors for efficient operation of farm units? If it's capital, farm businesses tapping outside capital sources may have an advantage. And capital may be even more crucial in the future than in the past. A big problem facing family farms is how to protect the farm business from capital erosion to pay off farm heirs their inherited shares and to pay estate settlement costs each generation.

If labor is limiting, large scale operations may have difficulty in obtaining an adequate labor supply. However, the supply of farm labor is, at least in part, related to wage levels. At a price, large scale farm businesses may be able to attract sufficient labor.

If it's management that's limiting – and management has often been a limiting factor – the question becomes one of whether capable, qualified managers are likely to move to smaller operations with greater independence and flexibility or work for larger operations owned by others. For those with capital backing, the smaller, independent operations may look more attractive if their profitability is comparable.

Economic pressures for incorporating family farms

As family farms become larger, with more assets managed, and as ownership and management come to be provided by more than one person, economic reasons may develop within the farm business for shifting to the corporate form of business organization. Some of these reasons are subtle and may go unnoticed for some time. Others are fairly obvious.

BUSINESS PLANNING. Every person in business takes a long, hard look down the road ahead before making an investment. The distance viewed may be crucial in terms of whether a particular investment is made.

For a specific investment, a decision maker planning five years ahead demands a payoff greater than cost over the five-year period. One looking 10 years ahead focuses on the benefits expected over a period twice as long. Persons with short "planning horizons" often pass up what would otherwise be good investments.

It has been argued, although not conclusively, that the corporation encourages longer planning horizons. The relative ease of planning management and ownership succession, the minimal effect – with planning – of death of a shareholder on a perpetually organized corporation, and the effects of shareholder limited liability may encourage corporate decision makers to make some investments that might have been passed up by a sole proprietor who sees the end of the road approaching at an alarming clip.

DIVIDING UP FARM INCOME. Internal accounting may become incredibly complex in a farm business where assets are owned and furnished by more than one individual. This is often a problem in parent-child operations.

Aside from keeping abreast of property ownership for purposes of figuring depreciation and recapture of depreciation, conflicts may develop over how much of the annual farm income should go to compensate someone providing a tractor, one-third of a beef cow herd, or half a silo.

After a few years' operations, asset ownership in many farm businesses with multiple owners becomes quite complicated. And, chances of unhappiness over real or imagined unfairness may multiply as farm income is divided each year among more assets. Unhappiness may be kept to manageable proportions in high income years. But a year or two of below average net income brings out all the concerns about fairness in dividing up the annual income.

Problems of internal accounting are generally simplified if a corporation owns the land, livestock, machinery and equipment. Then it's not necessary, each year, to reach agreement on the amount of income earned by each asset. Decisions must, of course, be made with respect to salaries and bonuses as compensation to labor and management; to rent paid for land leased by the corporation; and to interest paid for funds loaned to the corporation. But once those decisions are made, the rest of the after-tax income is available for distribution to shareholders on the basis of a uniform amount per share of stock.

The holder of a share of stock, representing prior ownership of a specific item of property, receives compensation precisely equal to that of the holder of another share of stock. The amounts available for distribution to shareholders may either be distribut-

300

ed as dividends or retained by the corporation for expansion with the stock increasing in value. Shareholders, especially minority shareholders, may not be indifferent as to the choice between dividends paid or demonstrated increases in stock value. The latter may be of little practical value to a minority shareholder unable to compel corporate liquidation or purchase of stock so that increased stock value could be enjoyed.

Tax reasons may discourage dividend declarations in some instances since dividends by a regularly taxed corporation are taxed twice – once to the corporation when earned and again when received by the shareholder.

The valuation of property at the time the corporation is formed is crucial for it has a vital influence on the way shareholders benefit from corporate earnings, either as dividends or as increases in stock value. Unless all assets are valued at fair market value or some uniform percentage of fair market value, a scheme of stock ownership may be created that misallocates corporate income for all time.

19
The farm corporation and business continuation

Sound estate planning is possible regardless of how a farm business is organized. Whether a farmer functions as a sole proprietor, as a partner in a partnership, as a member in a limited liability company or as an employee-shareholder in a corporation, there's sufficient flexibility in estate planning techniques for a satisfactory plan.

However, certain characteristics of the corporation may make possible more complete accomplishment of the farmer's objectives and the objectives of the family. The objectives held by decision makers within the farm business are paramount in the selection of an estate plan and a form of business organization.

Each generation of farmers must face the choice of (1) whether efforts should be made for the farm business to continue as an economic unit beyond the death of the parents as majority or sole owners, or (2) whether it should be assumed that the farm business is destined to terminate with the assets of the farm business recombined with those of other firms at retirement or death.

Fewer of the latter group are likely to look to the corporation (except for possible income tax advantages), but the corporation may be quite useful for farms aiming for continuation.

Transfer of stock

Plans for continuation of the farm business should give attention to transfers of ownership and management from generation to generation. Without adequate planning in these respects, continuation of the farm business may be placed in jeopardy at retirement or death and the business may come to a halt.

Certain attributes of the corporation may encourage, simplify and facilitate transfers of stock within and between generations. For instance:

• Majority owners can make gifts or sales of stock without loss of control over decision making.

• Restrictions can be placed on the retransfer of stock by individuals receiving stock by gift or sale.

• Asset ownership can be divided into easily transferred shares of stock so that transfer of a share of stock transfers a portion of the entire business.

• Corporate stock can be used to channel farm income to low tax bracket taxpayers to minimize over-all income tax liability.

Parents who are sole owners or co-owners of property may – for reasons of personal income security – be reluctant to make gifts of land, livestock, machinery or equipment to children in order to achieve death tax savings or business continuation. Their reluctance may be compounded by the fact that once the gifts are made, the children are free to retransfer the property to others. Restrictions on transfer of such property are often unenforceable. In a corporation, reasonable restrictions may be imposed on stock transfer. The most popular type of restriction, the first option, gives the remaining shareholders, the corporation or both the option to buy the stock to prevent sale. A buy-sell agreement requires purchase of the stock held by a shareholder triggering the agreement. Both first option and buy-sell agreements are typically activated by death of a shareholder, departure from employment and in some instances, merely by a notice of desire to sell the stock. Consent restrictions, which are not upheld in some states, require the consent of the shareholders or the board of directors before stock can be sold or transferred otherwise. Absolute restrictions on stock transfer are not valid.

Stock transfer restrictions should be accompanied by a provision for determining stock value. Some use appraisal of corporate assets but appraisal is costly and may produce results unacceptable to the individuals involved. Book value, based on cost with adjustments for depreciation claimed, often understates the value of the stock.

A periodically renegotiated fixed price requires the shareholders or the board of directors to set the value after the books are closed for the year. If done carefully each year, the periodically renegotiated fixed price generally produces the most acceptable results.

IRS does not have to accept any values but is more likely to go along with valuations if done carefully and consistently each year. Even if gifts are otherwise acceptable, small gifts of some types of property, such as land, are not easily made. The transfer of corporate stock, however, can be accomplished in small (or large) amounts without these disadvantages. So long as the parents retain voting control (normally 51 percent of the voting stock) they can be assured of continued employment as officers of the corporation and of control over corporate dividend policy. This eases the income security problem.

In a corporation with one class of stock and with simple majority rule, up to 49 percent of the stock may be given away for purposes of death tax and estate settlement cost saving without loss of corporate control. Even more could be given away if part of the stock were non-voting. However, retention of control over the stock given away may subject the value of the gift stock to death taxes. Competent legal counsel is a necessity in this area.

Transfers to minors

It may be desirable to transfer interests in the farm business to minors to reduce the family income tax burden, to decrease the amount of death taxes paid on death of the parents, or to encourage the minors to develop a greater interest in the farm business.

Since minors are not considered legally competent to manage their property, transfers of property to minors have long created problems. The possibilities for gifts of business property interests to minors may be greater if the transfer is by shares of corporate stock.

Stock in a farm corporation is eligible for transfer to minors under the Uniform Gifts to Minors Act which is now available in every state. These acts provide basically for a simple trust or custodianship by which a bank or an adult holds and manages the property for a minor (see Chapter 6).

Only gifts of stock, securities or money are eligible for transfer under the model act. Gifts of land, livestock, machinery and equipment do not qualify in those states but other states have broadened the Act to a "Uniform Transfers to Minors Act" and about any property can be custodial property.

Commencing in 1987, unearned income of a child under age 14 who has at least one living parent may be taxed at the parents' income tax rates if the child's investment income is more than $1,000 for the year. This rule may lessen the advantage of making transfers to younger children.

Estate settlement simplified

At the death of shareholders, the estate settlement process may be simplified for the fundamental reason that the farm assets are owned by an entity that does not terminate when a shareholder dies. On death of an individual farmer, all of his or her property – real or personal – is normally subject to probate (estate settlement). This process is relatively complex as land, livestock, machinery, equipment and other assets are administered by the estate representative.

Upon death of a shareholder in a farm corporation, however, only the corporate stock owned by the decedent is subject to probate – not the underlying assets. The stock must, of course, be valued for federal estate and state inheritance tax purposes. But the operation of the farm business may continue without interruption if ownership and management succession have been planned. As an interim holder of stock, the estate representative has a shareholder's rights in the farm business.

Because titles to land and other farm property are not affected by death of a shareholder, it may be possible to take advantage of procedures under state law for "short-form" or simplified probate. A major reason for probating an estate is to assure clear title to assets, particularly land, held by the decedent. If title to these assets is held by the corporation, that reason for probate may be eliminated.

If an individual owns real property in two or more states, a probate proceeding is normally required in each state. A probate court of one state cannot pass title to land in another state. Thus, the original probate proceeding is held in the state of residence, and ancillary probate proceedings are held in the other states. In the event real property is owned in two or more states by a corporation, ancillary proceedings may be avoided because corporate stock as personal property generally passes under the law of the state of permanent residence at death.

Loss of capital by inheritance

Frequently, upon death of the parents, continuation of the farm business may be placed in jeopardy if off-farm heirs inherit an interest in farm property. Each heir generally has the right to have his or her portion of the assets set aside, or to have the assets sold and a portion of the proceeds set aside. In either case, the farm business may be liquidated or reduced in size, or the on-farm heir or heirs are faced with a heavy debt obligation as off-farm heirs are paid off to avoid sale of the assets.

The right of "partition and sale," which may generally be used by joint tenants or tenants in common to terminate co-ownership arrangements, is not available to individual shareholders, however. While the off-farm shareholders may have sufficient votes (generally requiring a majority or higher) to dissolve the corporation, the option of receiving their portions through division or forced sale is not open to off-farm shareholders.

This feature of the corporation may slow down or halt temporarily the out-flow of equity capital at death. But it may also generate disputes among the shareholders as "locked-in" minority shareholders find themselves holding an unproductive investment. Dividends are rarely declared on stock of closely held farm corporations, restrictions are often placed on stock transfer and minority shareholders have relatively few management rights.

To avoid problems of unhappy minority shareholders, it may be advisable for on-farm heirs gradually to purchase the stock held by other heirs. A buy-sell or first option agreement is often used to require the corporation or the remaining shareholders to buy the stock, or give the corporation and the remaining shareholders an option to purchase the stock of the off-farm heirs. These agreements may specify that the purchase price could be paid in cash or paid in installments over a period of several months or years with interest.

As an alternative, stock could be permitted to pass to off-farm heirs with specific rights granted to minority shareholders with respect to management, a minimum dividend level, and a ready market for their stock in the event that a sale might be desired. In this way, corporate stability is balanced against the rights of minority shareholders.

Use could also be made of debt securities to be passed to off-farm heirs at the death of the surviving parent rather than stock. As discussed in Chapter 24, debt securities carry no vote, specify a fixed annual interest rate, are issued for a specified term (often 10 to 15 years) and do not fluctuate in principal value as does stock. High income tax bracket off-farm heirs may prefer a shareholder's risk with compensation coming in the form of increases in stock value rather than ordinary income each year from debt securities.

Minority interests may also be protected through incorporation for a specific term rather than perpetually.

20
Income tax implications of farm incorporation

A farm corporation is a "farmer" for most income tax purposes. Special income tax elections available to an individual farmer, partner or farm partnership with respect to deducting such items as soil and water conservation expenditures, fertilizer and lime costs and land clearing expenses are available to a farm corporation. And a farm corporation as a new taxpayer has the usual choice in treatment of commodity credit loans – as income when the crop is sold or (by election) as income when funds are received as a loan.

But some aspects of corporate income taxation differ from the rules for individual farmers or partners.

Depreciation or Cost Recovery

Depreciation and salvage value are handled in essentially the same way after incorporation as before, with a few exceptions.

Expense method depreciation permits taxpayers to expense off up to $17,500. All taxpayers, including corporations, are treated basically the same under the expense method depreciation rules with the limit imposed at the corporate level. Members of a group of controlled corporations divide the expensed amount. For partnerships, the limitation applies to both the partnership and each of the partners.

Effects of death of shareholder

A major feature of corporate operation is the difference in impact of death of a shareholder on the income tax basis of specific assets. This problem area is discussed in detail in Chapter 22.

Methods of income taxation

Two methods of federal income tax payment are available to qualifying corporations – the regular method, and the tax-option method (Subchapter S). Most closely held farm corporations would be eligible for either method. The choice between the two alternatives may require considerable study.

REGULAR METHOD. If no election is made, it is assumed that a farm corporation will pay its tax under the regular method. A Form 1120 is filed on behalf of the corporation on or before two and one-half months after the close of the corporation's taxable year. That's by March 15 for corporations on a calendar year.

Federal corporate income tax rates were reduced in 1975, 1979, 1982, 1983 and 1986 and increased in 1993 as shown in Table 17. The attractiveness of the regularly taxed corporation is dependent upon the relationship of corporate income tax rates to the tax rates applicable to individuals.

Table 17. Federal corporate income tax rates (in percent).

Corporate Taxable Income	Before 1975	1975-78	1979-81	1982	1983-1987	1987-1992	1993-
0-$25,000	22	20	17	16	15	15	15
$25,000-50,000	48	22	20	19	18	15	15
$50,000-75,000	48	48	30	30	30	25	25
$75,000-100,000	48	48	40	40	40	34	34
$100,000-10,000,000	48	48	46	46	46	34	34
Over $10,000,000	48	48	46	46	46	34	35

Up to 1975, the first $25,000 of corporate taxable income had been taxed at 22 percent and all additional at 48 percent. *(These are federal rates. Many states levy corporate income taxes as well.)*

310

For 1975, the federal income tax rates for regularly taxed corporations were reduced to 20 percent on the first $25,000 of corporate taxable income, 22 percent on the next $25,000 and 48 percent on all above $50,000. The lower rates were continued through 1978. For corporations with $50,000 or more of taxable income, the new lower rates meant a reduction of up to $7,000 in income tax.

Commencing in 1979, the federal corporate income tax rate was reduced to 17 percent on the first $25,000 of corporate taxable income, 20 percent on the next $25,000, 30 percent on the third $25,000, 40 percent on the fourth $25,000 and 46 percent on all over $100,000 of corporate taxable income.

Legislation adopted in 1981 reduced the rates to 16 percent on the first $25,000 and 19 percent on the second $25,000 of corporate taxable income for 1982 with other brackets remaining unchanged. For 1983 through mid-1987, the bottom two brackets dropped to 15 percent and 18 percent, respectively.

Effective July 1, 1987, corporate income tax rates were restructured into three rates as shown in Table 17. The revised rates were effective for taxable years beginning July 1, 1987. An additional 5 percent tax (maximum amount of $11,750) is imposed on a corporation's taxable income above $100,000. This provision phases out the benefit of the 15 and 25 percent rates for corporations with taxable incomes of more than $335,000. Above $335,000, the rate is a flat 34 percent up to $10,000,000 of taxable income. A 35 percent marginal rate is imposed on corporate taxable income in excess of $10,000,000 effective for taxable years beginning on or after January 1, 1993. Few farm and ranch corporations need worry about the 35 percent rate.

In effect, a regularly taxed corporation represents the creation of a new taxpayer at the 15 percent rate (for the first $50,000 of corporate income). This may save on taxes (for those farmers paying at rates greater than 15 percent) for income left in the corporation for expansion.

Thus, a married farmer filing jointly with $60,000 of net

311

income would likely be paying income tax up to the 28 percent individual rate. Assuming four exemptions and assuming further that deductions are not itemized, the federal income tax bill would be about $7,635.

If the individual incorporates, pays a salary of $20,000 per year and leaves $40,000 in the corporation for expansion, the corporate rate would be 15 percent of the $40,000 for a total federal income tax bill of $6,000 at the corporation level. The federal income tax on the $20,000 salary, after claiming the deductions and exemptions, would be about $660.

Thus, the total federal income tax bill would be about $6,660 (with part of the income taxed to the corporation) compared to $7,635 (with all income taxed to the individual) for a saving of $975 per year. This saving is significant if it's possible to leave the income in the corporation for expansion. If it's ever desired to remove earnings from the corporation, an additional tax would be imposed (ordinary income if removed as dividends, possibly capital gains if removed on liquidation). In either case, the extra tax would cut into the original savings from the corporation.

A group of controlled corporations is limited to one set of graduated rate brackets. Thus, if there are three members of a controlled group of corporations and no plan for unequal apportionment is adopted, each member of the group is taxed at a rate of 15 percent on the first $16,666.66 of corporate taxable income, 25 percent on the next $8,333.33, 34 percent on taxable income in excess of $25,000 up to $3,333,333.33 and 35 percent above that level.

There are two types of controlled corporate groups. In general, a *brother-sister* controlled group exists if five or fewer individuals, estates or trusts own at least 80 percent of the stock of two or more corporations and the five or fewer persons own more than 50 percent of the stock.

A *parent-subsidiary* controlled group exists if one or more groups of corporations are connected through stock ownership with a common corporate parent, 80 percent or more of the stock

312

of each corporation in the group (other than the parent) is owned by one or more corporations in the group and the common parent owns at least 80 percent of the stock of one of the other corporations in the group.

All of this adds up to one basic message – it's not possible to create corporations with common ownership in order to take advantage of the reduced corporate tax rates on lower levels of corporate taxable income. For most farm operations, it means one set of graduated rate brackets below 35 percent if two corporations are established – one to own the land and another to carry on the farming operation as an *operating* corporation. That's if the requirements are met for either type of controlled group.

Before repeal of the long-term capital gains exclusion in 1986, regularly taxed corporations often paid a higher tax on long-term capital gains than did an individual farmer. If an individual farmer sold brood sows held for 12 months or more, the gain was 60 percent deductible and the other 40 percent was taxable as ordinary income. By contrast, a regularly taxed farm corporation paid a federal tax of 15 percent or 18 percent on long-term capital gains (depending on the income tax bracket) or a flat rate of 28 percent. The 60 percent deduction was not available to corporations. The special treatment for long-term capital gains was repealed in 1986. Beginning in 1991, net long-term capital gains are taxed at a maximum rate of 28 percent for individual taxpayers. But that maximum rate does not apply to corporations which can pay up to 35 percent on long-term capital gains. Also, the capital gains exclusion in effect before 1987 has not been restored.

Another difference in income taxation is in the minimum tax. For individuals, the alternative minimum tax rate on the first $175,000 of alternative minimum taxable income is 26 percent (after 1992) on preference income above $45,000 for married taxpayers filing jointly. Above that level, the rate is 28 percent. For corporations, an exemption of $40,000 is available with a 20 percent tax imposed.

313

The income tax treatment of dividends is a disadvantage of the regular method. Dividends are taxed twice – once when earned (at the corporate rate) and again when received by the shareholders (at their individual tax rate). Salaries, bonuses, interest and rent are deductible at the corporate level, however. So, an incentive exists in regularly taxed corporations to pay amounts in these forms rather than as dividends. This may tend to distort payments to labor and management on the upward side and to distort payments to shareholders (providing equity or risk capital) on the downward side.

A corporation taxed under the "regular" method of income taxation may encounter two "penalty" taxes. The accumulated earnings tax is designed to discourage build up of funds within the corporation in excess of reasonable business needs. A corporation can accumulate up to $250,000 of earnings and profits (earnings and profits in a technical accounting sense, not necessarily in terms of liquidity) without imposition of the tax. Beyond that level, the tax rate is 39.6 percent unless accumulations beyond $250,000 are justified as being retained for the reasonable needs of the business. For those farm corporations investing in more land, livestock and machinery, there should be no problem with the accumulated earnings tax above the $250,000 level. And a corporation may accumulate, in the year of the death of a shareholder or a later year, amounts reasonably needed for redemption to pay death taxes and estate settlement costs. In effect, the accumulated earnings tax provides a gentle nudge to declare dividends rather than build up large liquid balances within the corporation.

The personal holding company tax is intended to discourage use of the corporation as one's personal investor. The incentive to arrange for a corporation to make stock market investments, for example, is great. To limit that tax break, a 39.6 percent tax is imposed on "undistributed personal holding company income" of a "personal holding company."

The tests for "personal holding company" status have numerous exceptions and qualifications, but two basic rules are that a corporation is a personal holding company if (1) five or fewer people own more than half of the stock during the last half of the taxable year, and (2) 60 percent or more of "adjusted ordinary gross income" comes from passive investment income such as dividends, interest, royalties, annuities and rent (unless rent is 50 percent or more of adjusted ordinary gross income and dividends equal or exceed the amount by which non-rent personal holding company income exceeds 10 percent of ordinary gross income). A corporation engaged predominantly in rental activity may escape personal holding company status. But if its non-rental personal holding company income is substantial, it must make taxable dividend distributions. For a farm corporation owning land that is rented to tenants under a share lease, amounts received aren't rent if the corporation participates materially in the production of income under the lease.

TAX-OPTION METHOD. To remove some of the disadvantageous consequences of the regular method of income taxation for small businesses, including farmers, the tax-option concept was enacted in 1958 for figuring income tax. This method is sometimes referred to as the "Subchapter S" method. Legislation enacted in 1982 revised substantially the Subchapter S rules. The 1982 rules refer to "S" corporations (those taxed under Subchapter S of the Internal Revenue Code) and "C" corporations (those that are regularly taxed).

If a farm corporation elects to be taxed under the special tax option status, it is normally not a taxpayer although it is a corporation for every other purpose. An information return, Form 1120-S, is filed annually on behalf of the corporation.

How it works. An electing corporation hires employees and pays salaries and bonuses in the usual fashion and may declare dividends to shareholders. Then the electing corporation passes through to shareholders, for tax purposes, their pro rata share of capital gains, gains or losses from property used in the business (such as breeding stock, machinery and land), operating losses, capital losses, ordinary income, charitable contributions, depletion allowances, tax-exempt interest and other items affecting the calculation of a shareholder's income tax liability. Likewise, any credits are allocated to shareholders.

These amounts are reported by the shareholders on their individual income tax returns. Credit for federal excise tax on gasoline and lubricating oil may be claimed only by refund filed by the corporation, however.

Thus, items pass to the holders of the stock on a *daily* basis. So a shareholder holding a share of stock for one day during the year would be entitled to claim $\frac{1}{365}$ of the item attributable to that share of stock.

The distributions may be made in money or may be merely designations on paper to the shareholders. The amounts may be left in the corporation for expansion or paid out as dividends at a later time.

Distribute income each year? Normally, dividends paid out of income on which tax has previously been paid would not be subject to an additional income tax when received by shareholders. Thus, actual distributions from S corporations are normally not subject to further income tax in the hands of the shareholders. The rules on taxability of distributions are different if the corporation has accumulated earnings and profits. The following rules summarize the income treatment of S corporation distributions:

• In general, distributions from an S corporation without earnings and profits are tax-free to the extent of a shareholder's income tax basis in the stock. If a distribution exceeds a shareholder's income tax basis in the stock, the excess is treated as capital gain.

• Distributions to shareholders of S corporations with accumulated earnings and profits are income tax free to the extent of the corporation's "accumulated adjustment account." That's the gross income after 1982 less deductible expenses. Any excess distribution is treated as a dividend up to the amount of accumulated earnings and profits. Further distributions are treated as a

316

return of income tax basis in the stock until the basis is exhausted. Any distributions beyond that point are treated as a capital gain.

• If an S corporation distributes appreciated property to a shareholder, gain is recognized to the corporation as though the property had been sold to the shareholder at fair market value. The gain, however, is not taxed to the corporation. Rather, like all gain it passes through to the shareholders.

Changing stock basis. Distributions from the corporation affect the income tax basis of corporate stock. Undistributed taxable income on which tax is paid increases the basis of stock held by shareholders. Losses and tax-free distributions of previously taxed income reduce the basis. These features give rise to a constantly changing basis for stock in an S corporation. To avoid later confusion over stock basis, it's desirable for the basis of each shareholder's stock to be computed annually and made a matter of record. Appendix E illustrates how that can be done.

Sometimes, a succession of operating losses reduces stock basis to zero. Further operating loss deductions can be claimed if there are shareholder loans whose basis can be reduced. Before 1983, operating losses in excess of a shareholder's income tax basis in corporate stock and indebtedness to the corporation were not deductible. After 1982, excess losses may be carried forward to any later year in which the shareholder has an income tax basis in the stock or indebtedness.

Before 1983, a pass-through of income to shareholders after the income tax basis of indebtedness to the corporation had been reduced restored income tax basis only to the stock. Under pre-1983 law, repayment of loans whose basis had been reduced because of operating losses produced gain, often in large amounts.

After 1982, a pass-through of income first increases the shareholder's income tax basis in the loans to the corporation to the extent the income tax basis had been reduced previously by the pass-through of losses.

Appendix E provides a format for annual determinations of income tax basis for each shareholder's stock in an S corporation. This is a convenient way to check each year on whether particular shareholders run a significant risk of running out of income tax basis on their stock. Although the 1982 amendments reduce the risk of losing the tax benefits from operating losses where the losses exceed the income tax basis of stock and indebtedness, being able to claim loss deductions currently rather than later on a carry-over basis is more advantageous economically.

Employee benefits. The Subchapter S Revision Act of 1982 made major changes in the way employee fringe benefits are handled in S corporations. For any person owning more than 2 percent of the stock in an S corporation, fringe benefits are treated in the same manner as fringe benefits are treated for partners in a partnership. Essentially, such shareholders are treated as self-employed for purposes of employee benefits.

The changes affect – (1) the $5,000 death benefit exclusion from income, (2) the exclusion from income of amounts paid for or to an accident and health plan, (3) the exclusion from income for the cost of group term life insurance up to $50,000 of coverage on an employee's life and (4) the exclusion from income of meals and lodging furnished for the convenience of the employer.

Requirements for the election. Several requirements must be met initially and on a continuing basis for a corporation to be eligible for the Subchapter S election.

• The corporation can have no more than 35 shareholders. A point to note: Stock owned by a husband and wife regardless of how held – in sole ownership, as community property or in co-ownership – (tenancy in common, joint tenancy or tenancy by the entirety) – is considered held by only one shareholder for this purpose.

A surviving spouse and the estate of a deceased spouse are treated as a single shareholder.

• The general rule has been that the shareholders must be individuals – or the estates of individuals. That has meant no stock held by many types of trusts, or partnership or another corporation. The limitation on trust ownership of stock has been a major problem. It has meant that stock can't pass into a marital deduction trust for the spouse or a trust for minor children (if parents should die).

With the limits on trust ownership of stock, those with estates large enough to be concerned about death taxes may wish to consider a life estate arrangement. For example, if the husband owns all of the stock – and it's a major part of his estate – he might leave half of the stock to his wife outright with the other half left to his wife for life, remainder interest to the children. This procedure makes use of a *legal life estate* and not a life estate in trust. The authority for S corporation stock being held in a legal life estate (without loss of Subchapter S status) is based on a 1964 IRS ruling. However, *regulations have been proposed that would not permit Subchapter S corporation stock to be held in a legal life estate except where only one individual is involved in the life estate interest, the interest terminates at that person's death and the interest has not been transferred to another.* Those regulations bear careful watching.

Another point to watch: at the wife's death, the stock held by her for life would go immediately to those holding the remainder interest. That could make the number of shareholders rise beyond the permissible limit.

In recent years, the rules on trust ownership of Subchapter S stock have been eased somewhat. A grantor trust or a voting trust may hold stock and any trust receiving Subchapter S stock under a will may be an eligible shareholder for 60 days. And the 60-day period becomes two years if the entire amount of trust property is included in the deceased shareholder's estate.

The grantor rather than the grantor trust is considered to be the shareholder. The grantor must be a citizen or resident of the United States. This precludes an alien, partnership, another corporation or trust from being the grantor for a grantor trust and qualifying as a shareholder.

Stock can be held by a "qualified Subchapter S trust." That is defined as a trust which has as its sole income beneficiary a per-

319

son whose interest terminates at the death of the beneficiary or termination of the trust. The possibility of multiple beneficiaries after the death of the current income beneficiary does not disqualify the trust during the lifetime of the current income beneficiary. Also, a trust, all of which is treated as owned by someone other than the grantor, can hold stock in an S corporation. A major problem, however, is that trusts can own stock in an S corporation only for a limited period beyond the death of the beneficiary.

• A corporation cannot be under Subchapter S taxation if it has more than one class of stock outstanding. However, differences in voting rights are permissible and do not violate the requirement of a single class of stock. Preferred stock is not permitted.

The big argument in recent years has been over the Internal Revenue Service assertion that loans made by shareholders to the corporation may constitute a second class of stock. That point was heavily litigated between 1960 and 1973. The 1982 legislation addressed the question of whether debt securities should be treated as a second class of stock. The income tax regulations contain "safe harbors" for obligations issued by a corporation. Unwritten advances from a corporation not exceeding $10,000 in the aggregate at any one time, that are treated as debt by the parties and are expected to be repaid within a reasonable time, are not treated as a second class of stock even if considered to be equity under general principles of federal tax law. Also, proportionately held obligations are not treated as a second class of stock.

The failure of an obligation to meet the safe harbor test does not necessarily result in a second class of stock unless the obligation is equity and contravenes the rights of the holders of the stock or the limitation on eligible shareholders.

"Straight debt" is not treated as a second class of stock even if it would otherwise be treated as equity under general principles of federal tax law. Straight debt – (1) means a written, unconditional obligation, to pay a sum on demand or on a specified date; (2) does not provide for an interest rate or payment dates contin-

320

gent on profits, the borrower's discretion, the payment of dividends on common stock or similar factors; (3) is not convertible into stock; and (4) is held by an individual, an estate or a trust permitted to own stock in an S corporation.

• The shareholders must all consent to the election initially. A Subchapter S election may be revoked only if the holders of more than one-half of the corporate stock consent to the revocation.

• There can be no non-resident alien shareholders.

• As indicated earlier, the Subchapter S rules have contained a limitation on passive investment income. Until 1983, the election terminated if more than 20 percent of the corporation's gross receipts came from rents, royalties, dividends, interest, annuities and sale or exchange of stock or securities.

For a farm landlord interested in incorporating and electing tax-option status, income received under a lease arrangement was not "rent" if the corporation through its officers and agents participated materially in the production of income. Otherwise, the amounts received by the corporation were rent and Subchapter S election might terminate. If Subchapter S status was desired, a corporation owning land that was rented to tenants should have – (1) seen that the lease was drafted with care to require material participation by the corporation, (2) designated a specific individual or individuals to represent the corporation under the lease, (3) directed the corporate representative or representatives to keep a good, daily, diary-type record of "material participation" activities, and (4) required the corporate representative or representatives to report periodically to the corporate board of directors on material participation activities in order to build a further record of what was being done on behalf of the corporation.

Under the 1982 amendments to the Subchapter S rules, the limit on passive investment income was eliminated for corporations which did not have accumulated earnings and profits from years the corporation was regularly taxed. Thus, newly formed S corporations and existing Subchapter S corporations with no earnings and profits need not worry about the passive income limitation.

For corporations with accumulated earnings and profits from years in which the corporation was regularly taxed, an income tax is imposed at the 35 percent rate on passive investment income in excess of 25 percent of corporate gross receipts. If the 25 percent limit is exceeded for three consecutive taxable years, the Subchapter S election terminates.

The pre-1982 authority on rents continues to be applicable. Income under share leases with material participation is not considered passive income. In addition, a late 1994 private letter ruling noted that even income under a cash rent lease was not passive income where the representatives of the corporate landowner were substantially involved in farm operations.

• To be eligible to make the Subchapter S election, the corporation must be oriented toward making a profit. Hobby-loss ventures may be challenged. In a recent case, keeping cats on a grand scale wasn't enough.

• There are a couple of miscellaneous requirements. The corporation must be organized in the United States and it cannot be a member of an "affiliated group." An S corporation cannot, therefore, own 80 percent or more of the stock of another corporation. The affiliated group rule does not apply if the other corporation has not begun business and has no taxable income.

Once a corporation has elected to be taxed under Subchapter S and the election has been terminated either voluntarily or for failure to meet the requirements, the election generally cannot be made again for five years. In the meantime, income is taxed to the corporation under the regular method of taxation.

The corporation elects the Subchapter S method of taxation by filing Form 2553. An election may be made at any time during the preceding taxable year or on or before the 15th day of the third month of the taxable year in question. An election too late for one year may become effective the following year. The election, once made, continues and need not be renewed annually.

Shareholders enter their consent to the election on Form 2553 also.

Terminating the election. A corporation's election under Subchapter S can be terminated voluntarily – by unanimous vote of the shareholders – or involuntarily. The two are handled somewhat differently.

The traditional Subchapter S rule has been that a Subchapter S election could be revoked during the first month of a taxable year with the revocation effective for the entire year. Under the 1982 amendments, revocations filed on or before the 15th day of the third month of the taxable year are effective for the entire taxable year unless a prospective effective date is specified. Revocations after the 15th day of the third month of the taxable year are effective for the following taxable year, again unless a prospective effective date is specified in the revocation.

Several events can cause termination of a Subchapter S election. These include – (1) exceeding the maximum shareholder limit of 35, (2) transferring stock to an ineligible shareholder, (3) creating an ineligible class of stock, (4) acquiring an active subsidiary, or (5) violating the passive investment income rules.

Except for the rule causing termination of the election if the corporation has too much passive investment income, events causing loss of a Subchapter S election result in a termination of the election as of the day the event occurred. The corporation has a short taxable year as an S corporation, ending the day before the terminating event occurred, and a short taxable year as a C corporation. The corporation need not, however, close its books as of the termination date. Income or loss is simply prorated over the entire year. The last S corporation income tax return is due the same day as the return for the short taxable year as a regularly taxed or C corporation.

• If a corporation's Subchapter S election terminates because the passive investment income limit is exceeded, the election terminates for the entire taxable year.

Since enactment of the Subchapter S rules, a major problem

has been the inadvertent termination of the election. IRS is authorized to waive the effects of an inadvertent termination if the corporation acts in a timely fashion to correct the problem and if the corporation and the shareholders agree to be treated as though the election had been in effect for the period involved.

Investment tax credit problems. One of the more treacherous aspects of Subchapter S has been the possibility – or possibilities – of unintentional recapture of investment tax credit. With repeal of investment tax credit effective after 1985 except for transition property and farm finance property (through 1987), the concern about investment tax credit recapture is largely past. However, time continues to run on investment tax credit carried forward from an earlier year before the Subchapter S election. And investment tax credits carried forward from earlier years cannot be used while the corporation is under Subchapter S. The same fate is in store for operating losses carried over from an earlier year, also. Likewise, no carry forward or carry back of net operating losses or investment tax credit can arise *at the corporate level* for a taxable year a corporation is under Subchapter S.

Corporate elections

Methods of accounting. As a new taxpayer, a farm corporation may elect the cash or accrual method of accounting if the corporation books are so kept and the method clearly reflects income. The corporation is not necessarily bound by the method of accounting used prior to incorporation.

With four exceptions, a farm corporation with gross receipts of more than $1 million per year must use accrual accounting and capitalize pre-production period expenses. Exceptions are provided for –

• Subchapter S corporations,

• Family corporations if at least 50 percent of the stock is owned, directly or indirectly, by members of the same family,

• Corporations engaged in the business of farming as of October 4, 1976, if members of two families own, directly or indirectly, at least 65 percent of the stock, and

• Corporations engaged in the business of farming as of October 4, 1976, if three families own at least 50 percent of the stock and substantially all of the rest of the stock is owned by employees, their families or a retirement trust for employees.

If a corporation's gross receipts exceed the $1 million mark – and it doesn't fall within one of the exceptions – it must shift to accrual accounting. And it cannot shift back to cash accounting later merely because gross receipts fall below $1 million. Accounting adjustments caused by the shift in accounting method may be spread over 10 years. These rules do not apply to nursery operations or sod farms or to the raising or harvesting of trees other than fruit or nut trees.

Although relatively few farm corporations are affected, a 1987 amendment requires corporations coming within the above exceptions to change to the accrual method of accounting if the corporation has gross receipts in excess of $25 million in any year after 1985.

Taxable year. A farm corporation has been permitted to adopt a calendar or fiscal year for accounting and income tax purposes. Thus, a corporation and its shareholders could have different taxable years. For a tax-option corporation, this has permitted limited income tax deferral and provided flexibility in allocating income between shareholders' taxable years.

As an example of the flexibility involved, assume that an S corporation with a February 1-January 31 fiscal year declares a dividend in December 1995. That dividend would be includible in the 1995 income tax returns of the shareholders filed in early 1996. In the alternative, the corporation could wait and declare a dividend in January or await the constructive or on-paper distribution as of the end of the corporation's taxable year, January 31. In either event, the income involved would appear in the 1996 income tax returns filed in early 1997. Thus, by the simple expedient of declaring or not declaring a dividend, income could be channeled into the current year's return or held in abeyance for inclusion in the following year's return. This let corporate officers and boards of directors make management decisions with less concern about the income tax consequences. It's been an especially helpful alternative to the usual practice of holding livestock or grain off the market to avoid any more income in the current year.

A February 1-January 31 or March 1-February 28/29 year has worked fairly well. But a later year could run into problems. If the nature of the corporation's distributions (as ordinary income, capital gains or non-taxable return of capital) wasn't known when the shareholders filed their returns, problems could arise. And for a corporation on a July 1-June 30 fiscal year, for example, the nature of December dividend distributions wouldn't be known for sure when shareholders filed their returns – by April 15.

In fact, it wouldn't be known how the distribution would be taxed until after June 30 and the books were closed. And that could lead to amended returns in some years if they guessed wrong.

Effective in 1983, Subchapter S corporations were required to either be on a calendar year basis or another taxable year for which the corporation established a business purpose to the satisfaction of IRS. However, an S corporation in existence on December 31, 1982, could continue its existing taxable year *so long as at least 50 percent of the corporate stock was owned by the same persons who owned stock on December 31, 1982.* If stock ownership dropped below the 50 percent level, the corporation had to either use the calendar year or prove a business purpose for a different year. For this purpose, transfers of stock to family members by gift did not count nor did transfers by reason of a shareholder's death. Likewise, transfers to family members under a buy-sell agreement in effect on September 28, 1982, and at all times thereafter, were not considered changes in ownership for this purpose if the buy-sell agreement provided that on death of any party to the agreement, the stock held by the decedent had to be sold to the surviving parties to the agreement (who were parties to the agreement as of September 28, 1982).

The Tax Reform Act of 1986 tightened the rules for S corporations operating under pre-1983 provisions. Under the 1986 amendment, S corporations were required, effective in 1987, to adopt a "permitted year" regardless of when S corporation status was elected. A permitted year was defined as a year ending December 31 or any other year for which the corporation establishes a business purpose.

The Revenue Act of 1987 allows S corporations to retain their fiscal year, rather than shift to a permitted year, if the corporation pays additional tax. The additional tax is based on a formula that estimates the amount of tax that would have been paid had the required change been made.

IN SUMMARY. The tax-option or Subchapter S method of corporate income taxation is attractive to some operations.

Essentially, it means income would be handled similarly (but not identically) to the way it would be treated in a partnership. The Subchapter S Revision Act of 1982 moved the Subchapter S income tax option closer to the way partnerships are handled. The shareholders become the taxpayers for most purposes.

But Subchapter S is complex and has many well-laid traps for the unwary. Good tax advice and counsel are musts in any good-sized farming operation. And that holds true in spades for an S corporation.

For many farm corporations, the regular method of taxation may offer significant income tax savings, especially if substantial amounts of the earnings are to be left in the corporation for expansion.

21
Farm corporations – employee status of the farmer

Upon incorporation of a farm business, the self-employed farmer usually becomes an employee of the new corporation. Thus, a shift from sole proprietor or partner status to employee status often has important and far reaching implications. Typically, the transformation is accompanied by both advantages and disadvantages.

Social security tax

For employees under retirement age, in the past the social security tax has been higher for an employer-employee combined than for a self-employed farmer receiving the same amount of income. However, beginning in 1990 that difference has been eliminated. The social security tax on self-employment income is the same as if the amount were paid as a wage or salary and social security (FICA) tax were paid by the employer and the employee.

For 1996 a self-employed farmer pays social security tax at a rate of 15.3 percent on the first $62,700 of income from self-employment. The maximum tax, therefore, is $9,593.10. A portion of the self-employment tax is deductible. The calculation for the deduction is as follows –

(1) Net earnings from self-employment are first reduced by an amount equal to one-half of the total self-employment tax (7.65%). (2) One-half of the self-employment tax figured on the adjusted amount can be claimed as an income tax deduction.

EXAMPLE: a self-employed farmer has schedule F income

329

from the farm business of $40,000. The income tax deduction would be $2,826, calculated as follows –

Schedule F income	40,000
	x .9235
Self-employment income	36,940
	x .153
Self-employment tax	5,652
	÷ 2
	2,826

In 1993, a self-employed farmer paid the Medicare hospital insurance tax at a rate of 2.9 percent on up to $135,000 of self-employment income. After 1993, the $135,000 figure no longer applies and the 2.9 percent HI tax applies to all earned income. The OASDI portion of 12.4 percent applies up to the 1996 limit of $62,700.

A farm corporation employee, for 1996, pays 7.65 percent on the first $62,700 of wages or salary and the corporation as employer pays a like percentage for a total of 15.3 percent. This amounts to $9,593.10 per year if an employee's salary is $62,700. The corporation's share of the tax is deductible for income tax purposes. The corporation may pay the entire tax – both the employee's and the corporation's shares – and claim a deduction for the amount paid. But the employee's share then becomes additional income to the employee. For employees and employers, the HI tax (1.45 percent paid by employees and 1.45 percent paid by employers) applies regardless of the earnings level of the employee. The OASDI tax (of 6.2 percent) applies up to $62,700 for 1996.

The social security tax results thus are the same for self-employed status and for employer-employee status.

A continuing social security tax disadvantage involves wages paid to children working after school, on weekends or during the summer months. Wages earned by a child under 18 are not subject to social security tax if the child works for his or her parent.

But the wages are subject to the tax if paid by the parent's corporation. The same rule applies to a partnership unless the only partners are the parents of the child under 18 years of age who is employed by the partnership.

Possibly higher social security benefits

Incorporation may produce greater social security benefits for employees than would have been received as self-employed farmers. Even though the *average* annual income is the same over a period of years, the fixed salary of an employee may lead to higher benefits.

Self-employment income of farmers often fluctuates greatly, sometimes falling below the maximum covered amount ($62,700 for 1996). If earnings fall below that amount for more than the permissible drop-out period for computing social security benefits, the retirement benefits are reduced. And income above the maximum covered amount does not increase benefits.

But watch the requirement of reasonableness in amount of salary paid. High salaries paid simply to generate higher social security benefits may be challenged if the amount appears to be unreasonable in view of the assets and earning power of the business.

Lower social security taxes

Incorporation may result in lower social security taxes. Only salaries and bonuses are subject to social security tax in a corporation. For self-employed farmers, the entire amount of earned income (not merely that representing compensation for labor and management) is subject to self-employment (social security) tax. Of course, the outcome may be lower benefits in retirement for corporate employees than would have been the case under self-employed status.

The retirement years

An individual farmer operating as a sole proprietor faces difficulties in receiving social security benefits after retirement while retaining a close relationship with the farm business. Income for personal services above a certain level (set at $12,500 per year for 1996 for those 65 or older) reduces social security benefits.

If a self-employed farmer renders "substantial services," the entire amount of farm income may be considered as income from personal services. If a farm landlord "participates materially" in the production of income under a lease, the amount received as rent may be treated as income from personal services.

For purposes of social security benefit eligibility, an employee of a farm corporation in general need be concerned only with compensation received as salary and bonus for personal services rendered. After retirement a corporate employee could be paid a part-time salary of $12,500 per year, which is the maximum allowable for personal services without reduction of benefits after age 65 for 1996. The $12,500 figure (for those age 65-69) is scheduled to rise to $13,500 in 1997, $14,500 in 1998, $15,500 in 1999, $17,000 in 2000, $25,000 in 2001 and $30,000 in 2002.

Additional income could be received in the form of interest or dividends which are investment income and do not reduce social security benefits.

It's important that the part-time salary be reasonable in light of services actually performed by the semi-retired individual. In one case, a salary was challenged as being too low when the retired farm employee worked at the same pace after retirement as before. And social security benefits were reduced accordingly.

Withholding

Employee compensation. Until 1990, farm corporations were not required to withhold federal income tax on wages paid to agricultural labor although they could elect to do so. Some states have similar rules for state income tax withholding. For years, farm corporations have been required, of course, to remit social security taxes to the federal government on a periodic basis.

Beginning in 1990, withholding of income tax is required for cash remuneration paid to agricultural labor if the wages are subject to social security withholding. In general, agricultural employees are subject to social security (FICA) withholding if an employee earns at least $150 in annual cash remuneration or are covered because of the FICA withholding test. That test subjects employee wages to FICA withholding if the employer pays more than $2,500 during the year to all employees. Employees who are hand harvest laborers, are paid on a piece rate basis, commute daily to the farm from their permanent residence and were employed in agriculture less than 13 weeks during the prior year are exempt from application of the employer FICA withholding test.

What about quarterly payment of estimated tax after incorporating? If an individual's estimated gross income from farming is at least two-thirds of total estimated gross income, a return may be filed on or before March 1 in lieu of an estimate.

But is a farm corporation employee a "farmer"? That's a good question. In a 1965 ruling, the Internal Revenue Service said that a farm employee was not a farmer and, therefore, must make quarterly payments.

Wages paid in kind. Wages paid in kind to agricultural labor are not subject to FICA (social security) or FUTA (unemployment) tax. Likewise, as noted above, wages paid in kind are not subject to income tax withholding because wages not subject to FICA tax are not subject to income tax withholding. Moreover, payments in kind to agricultural labor are not considered wages for purposes of determining the amount of earnings in retirement. As the covered amount of wages and salaries for FICA purposes has risen, that rule has been examined closely by farm employers including farm corporations. In considering whether to pay wages in kind, however, attention should be given to the fact that employees receiving wages in kind do not build up retirement or disability credit under the social security system.

Payment of wages in kind in the form of grain, soybeans, cotton or other "passive" commodities poses relatively few problems. However, even with payment in those forms, the employee should be careful to assert dominion and control over the commodity. Decisions to sell the commodity should be made by the employee with sale preferably occurring on some date other than the date when the employer disposes of its inventory of the same commodity.

Payment in the form of livestock or the products of livestock poses additional problems although wages paid in the form of milk by a corporation carrying on a dairy operation have met the requirements of avoiding FICA tax in a situation where employees were compensated with a percentage of milk produced, a percentage of the calves and a percentage of grain production. With livestock, asserting dominion and control over the livestock after payment in that form is important with feed, labor and management preferably not provided by the employer. In a 1991 ruling, payment of wages to a spouse in the form of hogs that became the spouse's property after delivery to a market location was treated as a cash payment.

Payment of wages in a form readily converted to cash (such as commodity storage receipts) was treated as payment in cash and not as a payment in kind in a 1979 ruling. In the facts of that ruling, the value of the storage receipts was equal to the amount that the employees would otherwise receive and the employer immediately redeemed the employees' receipts for cash. In 1992, legislation was proposed (but not enacted) that would have repealed the special rule for payment of wages in kind to agricultural labor except for meals or lodging furnished on the premises, temporary lodging for seasonal workers and the threshold of $150 per worker and $2,500 for the employer.

In a 1993 ruling, payment to the husband in a family-owned farm corporation in the form of $6,000 in cash wages and $34,941 in hogs in one year and $11,000 in cash and $41,272 in hogs another year was all considered to be the equivalent to the payment of cash compensation.

In another 1993 ruling, payments of grain to a married couple who were employees of their wholly owned farm corporation were treated as the equivalent of cash. The grain was not removed to separate storage facilities nor was the couple charged for storage although the couple bore the risk of loss after payment and sold their grain. But in a 1994 ruling, payments of grain to a husband and wife as employees of their farm corporation were treated as the equivalent of cash even though the grain was removed to the employees' own storage facilities and held for periods of 5 to 60 days.

In response to the rising tide of negative rulings on the issue and the rising difficulty of taxpayers on audit with IRS, a Congressional group asked the Commissioner of Internal Revenue to examine the IRS position on paying wages in kind to agricultural labor. The Commissioner appointed a task force to recommend guidelines for the subject matter area. The task force was composed principally of IRS personnel but three non-IRS representatives, including this author, served on the task force. The resulting guidelines were issued by IRS on December 20, 1994.

The guidelines emphasize that the validity of a plan for paying wages in kind is dependent upon a facts and circumstances test. Here are the principal points to watch in paying wages in kind to agricultural labor –

• The commodity to be used should be identified in an employment agreement entered into before the beginning of the employment period. The strongest case is made if the wage to be paid is expressed in commodities, not in dollars to be fulfilled in commodities.

• The transfer of the commodity to the employee should be clearly documented, preferably in writing. The commodity should not have been acquired solely for the purpose of paying wages in kind.

• If the employer had given a lender a security interest in the commodity used to pay the employee, the security interest should be released formally.

• The commodity payment for wages should not be in the form of negotiable commodity storage receipts, generic commodity certificates or deferred payment contracts. These are likely to be considered the equivalent of cash compensation.

• The price risk and the risks of quality deterioration should be shifted to the employee. There should be no "hold harmless" or similar agreements shielding the employee from risks and assuring the employee a specified amount of compensation in dollar terms.

• The employee should bear the costs incident to ownership of the commodity. That includes the storage costs for grain and feed and management and veterinary expense for livestock, for example. The IRS view is that the costs incurred by the employee are employee business expenses and are only deductible to the extent such expenses exceed two percent of the employee's adjusted gross income for the year. Thus, a substantial part or all of the costs may be lost in terms of deductibility. That suggests, where possible, selecting commodities for wage payment that are likely to involve relatively little expense to the employee.

• There is no set minimum time period for the employee to hold the commodity before sale. But it should be long enough to assure that the employee has asserted dominion and control over the commodity.

• The employee should negotiate the subsequent sale of the item, preferably not at the same time the employer is selling the same or similar commodities. The commodity should not be sold back to the employer.

As for how wage payments in kind are handled, the employer must report any gain on the in-kind wage payment into income with an offsetting wage deduction. The wages are reported as "other income" on the Form W-2 without payment of FICA or FUTA tax or income tax withholding. The employee reports the fair market value of the payment for income tax (but not for FICA or FUTA) purposes. That gives the commodity an income tax basis. Any gain or loss on subsequent sale would ordinarily be reported as a capital asset transaction without self-employment, FICA or FUTA tax. If the employee is otherwise involved in the business of producing the particular commodity, the gain or loss would likely be reported as business income.

Dividends and interest. Legislation enacted in 1983 repealing mandatory withholding of income tax on dividends and interest provides for back-up withholding and imposes a "due diligence" requirement on payors of dividends and interest to obtain payee taxpayer identification numbers. The rules apply to payors subject to information reporting on interest and dividends.

Back-up withholding is to commence if – (1) the payee fails properly to report interest or dividend income, (2) the payee fails to give the payor the correct taxpayer identification number, (3) IRS notifies the payor that the taxpayer identification number is incorrect or (4) there has been a "payee certification failure." Payors may use Form W-9 to obtain certification of the taxpayer's identification number from the payee and certification that the payee is not subject to back-up withholding.

The taxable part of pension, profit-sharing, stock bonus and individual retirement act (IRA) payments are subject to income tax withholding. Periodic benefit payments are subject to withholding as if the payments were wages.

Workers' compensation

Traditionally, agricultural labor has been exempt from workers' compensation coverage. Most other employees came under the "no-fault" workers' compensation system more than a half century ago. Under workers' compensation, an employee suffering an injury or illness need only prove: (1) the injury or illness occurred, (2) the injury or illness was causally related to the employment and (3) the injury or illness occurred or was suffered while the employee was acting within the scope and course of employment. Fault of the employer is not a factor in recovery.

Over the past two decades, in part as a result of a national study focusing on the inadequacies of state workers' compensation systems, agricultural employees have been brought under workers' compensation coverage by several states. The employer's responsibility to pay benefits to injured or ill employees is typically discharged through special workers' compensation insurance. The premiums for such insurance are relatively expensive and often run 5 percent to 9 percent of payroll (although not all of the salary of highly paid employees is necessarily subject to the premium rate) because agriculture is rated as a relatively hazardous industry.

The added cost to cover employee-shareholders may be viewed as a peculiar cost of incorporating, especially in states covering all employees including the corporate officers, since self-employed farmers are not subject to workers' compensation coverage.

However, coverage of shareholder-employees may also be viewed as an additional employee fringe benefit, considered in light of insurance that might otherwise be carried to produce comparable benefits. Some states, including Iowa, Minnesota, Missouri and Ohio exclude officers of farm corporations from workers' compensation coverage.

Unemployment compensation

Some farm employers are subject to the Federal Unemployment Tax Act. In general, it's the larger operations that are subject to unemployment compensation tax. Again, employee status is the key.

Who's covered? That turns on the definition of "agricultural employer." That's someone who paid cash wages of $20,000 or more for agricultural labor during any calendar quarter in the current or preceding calendar year, *or* employed 10 or more individuals in agricultural labor for some part of the day on each of 20 days during the current or preceding calendar year with each day being in a different calendar week.

The federal tax is 6.2 percent of covered wages with a wage base of $7,000. However, employers qualify for a credit by reason of participation in an approved state program.

Employee benefits

Employee status may make individual employees eligible for employee or "fringe" benefits that are tax-privileged. The big question for many farm corporations is whether it's worthwhile to establish employee benefit plans for only a few employees. For some benefits it may not be feasible to set up a plan for one or two employees. For other benefits, the number of employees is less crucial.

Group term life insurance. Group term life insurance is often called a perfect fringe benefit. Costs are tax deductible to the corporation, the proceeds may not be subject to income tax, and the policies can usually be set up so that the proceeds are not subject to the death taxes. Qualified group term plans provide an opportunity for deducting life insurance premiums that are otherwise not tax deductible. For up to $50,000 of coverage, the employee is generally not taxed for premiums paid by the employer under a qualified group term plan.

Most states require a minimum of 10 employees for a group term life insurance plan although a few permit plans with as few as five. Some insurers offer "baby group" plans covering fewer employees. A plan covering fewer than the required number of employees may be an acceptable group plan if the amount of insurance for employees is computed either as a uniform percentage of salary or on the basis of coverage brackets under which no bracket exceeds 2½ times the next lower bracket and the lowest bracket is at least 10 percent of the highest bracket. However, if additional evidence of insurability beyond a medical questionnaire is involved, the plan still may not qualify.

In 1986, Congress imposed a comprehensive set of non-discrimination rules on several types of employee benefit plans, including group term life insurance and health and accident plans. The objective was to tax highly compensated employees on the value of employer-provided benefits under a discriminatory plan. However, the rules enacted in 1986 were repealed in 1989, returning the system to the anti-discrimination rules in effect before 1987.

Retirement plans. Deferred compensation plans – defined benefit (pension) and defined contribution (profit sharing) – afford considerable tax saving potential, particularly for high income employees. Pension plans involve a fixed annual payment and produce fairly predictable benefits at retirement. Contributions to profit sharing plans are based upon business profits with retirement benefits less certain. For profit sharing plans, up to 25 percent of an employee's compensation (maximum contribution of $30,000) can be contributed to a plan annually. The $30,000 figure remains fixed until the dollar limit on annual benefits under a defined benefit plan reaches $120,000. Above that level, the $30,000 on annual additions to defined contribution plans is adjusted to keep that limit at 25 percent of the defined benefit dollar limit.

The dollar limit for benefits under a pension plan is 100 percent of average compensation for the high three years or $90,000. The $90,000 figure is adjusted for inflation or deflation.

Contributions to qualified plans are tax deductible within allowable limits; benefits are taxed to the employee after retirement as received. A relatively new type of retirement plan – Employee Stock Ownership Plans or ESOPs – is attractive because plan benefits are funded with the corporation's own securities. In a typical approach to funding of an ESOP, the employer provides securities (usually common stock) that a lender takes as collateral for a loan to the ESOP. The ESOP uses the borrowed money to buy those securities. The employer subsequently makes cash contributions to the ESOP with which the ESOP repays the loan. The contributions are deductible by the employer, even to the extent of the portions used by the ESOP to repay the principal of the loan. The major drawback of ESOPs is that they tend to be relatively expensive to set up and maintain.

Health and accident plans. Health and accident plans may also be established by a corporation to cover its employees. These plans may offer greater tax benefits than plans maintained by individual employees.

In general, the costs of health and accident plans are deductible to the employer and the benefits are not taxable to the employees. This compares with 30 percent deductibility for health insurance costs for self-employed individuals. Legislation was pending in the Spring of 1996 to raise the 30 percent figure to 80 percent.

For insured plans, there is no nondiscrimination requirement. Plans for reimbursing medical expenses of employees are subject to nondiscrimination requirements. However, the plan may exclude –

• Those with less than three years' service.
• Those under age 25.
• Part-time and seasonal employees.
• Those covered by a labor union's medical plan.
• Nonresident alien employees.

"Cafeteria" plans. These are flexible benefit plans in which an employee may choose from an array of employee benefits provided by the employer. Some of the benefits may be taxable and some may not be taxable.

The term "cafeteria plan" means a written plan under which all participants are employees and the participants may choose among two or more benefits. Benefits may be cash, other taxable benefits or an array of non-taxable benefits such as medical and disability plans, group term life insurance (up to $50,000 coverage) and group legal services.

Death benefit. An employee's beneficiary may receive up to

$5,000 of death benefits paid by or on behalf of the employer by reason of the employee's death. For deaths after 1983, self-employed persons are considered to be eligible for the $5,000 death benefit exclusion as to lump sum distributions from qualified retirement plans.

The corporation's house

If the farm residence or residences are transferred to the corporation, occupancy by corporate employees or shareholders raises a question of how the matter should be handled for income tax purposes. Corporate ownership of the residence may be desirable because the corporation may then deduct depreciation, maintenance, repairs and other costs associated with the residence as a business asset. These items are personal expenses and would not be deductible by an unincorporated farmer. Most costs associated with the personal residence – other than property taxes and interest on a mortgage – are not deductible, although to a corporation these are business deductions.

But the rub comes when the corporation's tax-deductible house is occupied by a corporate employee or shareholder. The general rule is that the value of the personal use of a corporate residence may be taxed as additional compensation or as a dividend to the occupant unless a reasonable rental is paid.

However, the Internal Revenue Code provides that meals and lodging furnished to an employee for the convenience of the employer do not constitute taxable income to the recipient. To be excluded from income, the meals must be furnished on the business premises of the employer. For the value of the lodging to be excluded, the employee must be required to accept the lodging on the premises as a condition of employment.

Some farm corporations and their employees have argued that this rule applies to them because farm employees must be on the premises at all times to look after livestock, do the chores and keep an eye on security of the property. Farm taxpayers have won a few cases and lost a few on this issue.

The cases suggest that the taxpayer is more likely to be successful if actually expected to be on the premises at all hours and if his or her presence is reasonably required. Livestock farmers generally stand the best chance of succeeding, although a recent case involved a grain operation with drying and storage of grain. Another recent case involved swine raising and grain drying as the major reasons for being on the premises. The taxpayers won in both cases. For those intending to claim tax-free meals or lodging, it's important to have a board of director's resolution in force requiring employees to live on the premises and, if food is involved, eat their meals on the premises. Some courts have permitted groceries to be included in the definition of meals. Other courts have disagreed.

Lodging includes utilities necessary to make the lodging habitable if furnished by the employer. If the employee is required to pay for the utilities without reimbursement from the employer, the utilities are not considered furnished by the employer and are not excludible from income.

In recent years, S corporations have been able to deduct residential costs for shareholder-occupied residences *only to the extent of regular and exclusive business use.* Under the Subchapter S Revision Act of 1982, as discussed earlier, shareholders of S corporations owning more than 2 percent of the corporate stock are treated as partners in a partnership for purposes of participating in employee fringe benefits. The rules bar the exclusion from income of meals and lodging furnished for the convenience of the employer. The 1982 change was generally effective in 1983 but a special transitional rule delayed the limit until 1988 for most corporations that had elected S corporation status on or before September 28, 1982.

Another point to consider in deciding whether to transfer the farm residence or residences to the corporation: corporate-owned residences aren't eligible for the exclusion of up to $125,000 of gain for sale after age 55.

343

Using the corporation's auto

For most farmers, automobiles are individually owned and the business portion of automobile expenses is deducted on schedule F of Form 1040. After incorporation, the question arises whether automobiles should be owned by the corporation or by the individuals.

If the corporation owns the automobiles, all costs are business costs and are deductible by the corporation. And personal use of the corporate automobiles by employees and their families may be taxable income to the user. If the automobiles are individually owned and are used for both business and personal use, the corporation normally pays for business use on a per mile basis. If not, the employee may have a deduction for the portion of use attributable to the business.

But there's more to the decision of corporate versus individual ownership than the income tax aspects. If corporate-owned cars are used for personal driving, the corporation as the vehicle owner may be liable for damages caused by the automobile. This may be an unacceptable risk to the corporation. On the other hand, if a personally owned automobile is used for some business driving, the corporation may be liable anyway for damages caused if the driver is an employee of the corporation and is acting within the scope of employment at the time of the accident. Therefore, adequate insurance coverage is important in both situations.

Differences of opinion may also arise over the type of automobile to be purchased. Some employees may prefer to have access to higher horsepower models with luxury options. But the corporate board of directors may have other ideas if the corporation is footing the bill.

The rule of thumb often used is this: transfer the pick-ups and trucks to the corporation and leave automobile ownership in the hands of the employees. Each employee then submits a monthly account of business miles driven and is reimbursed accordingly on a per mile basis. Payments to employees equal to or less than the standard mileage rate for business driving (31 cents per mile for 1996) need not be reported in income. Payments in excess of the standard mileage allowance are reportable as income and are subject to withholding and, except for noncash amounts to agricultural labor, employment taxes.

Automobiles used heavily for personal driving are typically retained in individual ownership. Insurance coverage may then be adjusted to provide protection for the risks involved to the corporation.

22
Disadvantages of the corporation

Studies made in several states indicate that the number one reason farmers turn to the corporation is to accomplish estate planning objectives.

It's not that the corporation has a monopoly over sound estate planning. In fact, many estate plans do not involve a corporation. The key point is that the corporation offers a collection of attributes that makes the accomplishment of estate planning objectives somewhat easier.

But it's not a one-way street. The corporation carries with it estate planning disadvantages, as well. Some of these can be resolved with proper planning. Others are inherent in the corporation and can't be changed.

The disadvantages associated with employee status are discussed in Chapter 21. Other disadvantages are noted in the following paragraphs.

Tax-option corporations

Election by a corporation to be taxed under the Subchapter S or tax-option rules (shareholders, not the corporation, pay the income tax) creates estate planning problems as noted in Chapter 20.

To be eligible to elect tax-option status, a corporation can have no more than 35 shareholders. This could be insufficient to include the children and the grandchildren although relatively few farm or ranch operations would have more than 35 owners or potential owners. If the rule is violated, tax-option status is lost.

An S corporation's stock may not be held by a trust except for voting trusts, grantor trusts, "qualified Subchapter S trusts" and

347

certain other trusts – even though trusts are key estate planning devices. So, it isn't possible to set up a testamentary trust for the minors to hold stock of a tax-option corporation, for example, with the testamentary trust continuing for several years after the death of the surviving parent.

Stock in an S corporation may not be held by a marital deduction trust, either. This type of trust is often used to hold and manage the property left to the surviving spouse – particularly if the surviving spouse is left a life estate to save taxes at the second death.

Typically, under a marital deduction trust, each spouse leaves half of that spouse's property to the other spouse outright, or nearly so, and the other half to the other spouse for life – all in trust. An acceptable possibility, if the big asset is S corporation stock, is to leave half of the stock to the surviving spouse outright with the other half to the surviving spouse for life with a remainder in the children. *But not in trust.* The life tenant is considered to be the shareholder as long as he or she lives.

The surviving spouse's plight

An important estate planning objective of most couples is to assure an adequate amount of income for so long as they live. No matter how long they live, they want to be sure that their income doesn't expire before they do.

If a problem arises on this score, it will likely be after the death of the first parent to die. The surviving parent may be left with considerable property but perhaps little income.

Here's how the problem might develop.

The parents incorporate the farm business, transfer their land, livestock and machinery to the corporation and receive back shares of stock. The children on the farm gradually buy stock from the parents. And, the parents make periodic gifts of stock to the children. Then one parent dies. The other parent ends up with less than 51 percent of the stock.

Without control over decision making at the shareholder level, the surviving parent has no power at the board of director level to compel declaration of dividends on the stock. Moreover, the double taxation of dividends (in a regularly taxed corporation) and the desire by younger members of the family to accumulate capital for expansion may discourage dividend payment. Result: The surviving parent has control over considerable capital. But, it may generate little, if any, income.

One solution might be for the parents to hold debt securities (bonds, notes or debentures) as well as stock in the corporation. As noted in Chapter 24, debt securities issued since 1989 as part of a tax-free exchange have been treated as taxable boot. Therefore, debt securities – if used in the capitalization structure – are now likely to be created in a separate transaction, usually issued for cash well after incorporation of the farm or ranch business.

If debt securities are held by the parents, on death of the first parent to die, that parent might leave the debt securities to the surviving parent. That parent would be entitled to receive a fixed amount of interest each year on the debt security. For example, $100,000 in debentures issued at eight percent interest would assure payment of $8,000 annual income each year from the corporation. And, it's tax deductible to the corporation.

But there are drawbacks to the use of debt securities in addition to being treated as taxable boot if issued as part of a tax-free exchange on incorporation. As discussed in Chapter 24, problems of eligibility for special use valuation of farmland and installment payment of federal estate tax may arise if debt securities are used. The fixed interest obligation may be a serious economic burden for the corporation, particularly when added to the interest paid to the other creditors. Careful attention should be given to whether the projected cash flow would be sufficient for interest payments on debt securities. Consideration should also be given to repaying the principal amount at maturity.

There are other solutions to the problem of the surviving spouse's plight. A shareholders' agreement might ensure a minimum dividend each year. Or, the surviving spouse might be left enough stock to give control over elections to the board of directors and, therefore, over dividend policy.

Minority off-farm heirs

The position of a minority shareholder in a small, closely held corporation may not be a particularly happy one. A holder of a minority stock interest may have few, if any, management rights; may receive little, if any, income on his or her stock; may encounter restrictions on stock transfer if he or she wishes to sell the stock; and may find few buyers even if transfer restrictions pose no problems.

A minority, off-farm shareholder thus can easily become a dissatisfied, locked-in shareholder. In fact, such a shareholder becomes an involuntary contributor of capital for use by the corporation. Of course, the stock may be increasing in value. But that's little consolation if there is only a remote possibility of sale of the stock as a necessary step to enjoying the increased value. Declining stock value, which was the case for many farm and ranch corporations in the 1980s with decreasing land values, usually adds to the discontent of minority, off-farm shareholders.

With proper planning, well in advance of stock transfers to off-farm heirs, these problems may be solved. The possibilities involve assuring the off-farm heirs:

1. Some stake in management decision making at the director and shareholder levels,

2. A minimum dividend level on their stock, or

3. A market for their stock, at a fair value, if they desire to sell.

Another solution might be to give the off-farm heirs an opportunity to exchange their stock for debt securities with the accompanying assurance of continuing income. Remember, however, that assured income for the off-farm heir means a payment burden to the corporation.

Effects of shareholder death

One attribute of the corporation that may prove to be a disadvantage in some instances relates to the adjustment of basis of farm property at death of a farmer as shareholder of a farm corporation. Assets held until death receive a new income tax basis which is generally equal to the value used for federal estate tax purposes. This adjustment in basis cancels any unrecognized gain or loss on the property and the new basis provides values to be used for a new depreciation schedule for depreciable items and for figuring gain or loss on later sale.

Thus, typically, each generation of farmers has depreciated some of the same assets depreciated by preceding generations because an asset's useful life has often exceeded the useful life for income tax purposes.

When a shareholder dies, the shares of stock held at death receive a new income tax basis related to the value as determined for death tax purposes. But the underlying property – in the hands of the corporation – is not affected by death of a shareholder. And its basis remains unchanged.

Therefore, the sale of property by the corporation after the death of a shareholder creates the same amount of taxable gain or loss as if the property had been sold before the shareholder died. Even if the property is not sold, the fact of no adjustment in basis for corporate property at death of a shareholder means that property, once depreciated out by the corporation, may not be placed on the depreciation schedule with a new income tax basis after a shareholder dies.

To the extent that assets owned directly by a decedent continue to receive an increase in income tax basis at death, death of a shareholder will continue to be less of an advantage than death of the owner of individual items of property in terms of adjustment in income tax basis. Of course, if a step down in basis is in prospect death of a shareholder does not lead to a loss in basis of underlying assets as occurs on death of an individual owner of property. Upon conveyance of farm property to a corporation in a "tax-free" exchange (which is generally preferred over a "taxable" exchange as discussed in Chapter 24), the old income tax basis for each item of property carries over to the corporation. The basis of the property transferred also determines the basis of stock received by the shareholder in exchange.

This feature of the corporation may discourage incorporation by older farmers holding large amounts of property that have appreciated heavily in value.

Cost, red tape

As a more formal, more complex method of organization than a partnership or sole proprietorship, the corporation is more expensive to form and a bit more expensive to maintain. But, most of the initial costs are deductible over the first five years of corporate life. And the annual costs are typically deductible.

Costs of incorporating may run from $500 to $2,500 or more depending upon costs imposed by the state, the size and complexity of the farm business and the objectives to be satisfied. Most states levy an annual fee and require the filing of a relatively simple annual report.

Debtor relief

Farm incorporation raises several problems relative to corporate and individual liabilities. One aspect is bankruptcy.

An individual farmer may file a petition to be a voluntary bankrupt in an effort to obtain relief from debts. But an individual farmer, farm partner or partnership cannot be forced into bankruptcy involuntarily. This is in recognition of the price and yield uncertainty faced by farmers.

A farm corporation is likewise afforded the right to be a voluntary bankrupt. The difference comes in that a farm corporation, in the past, has also been subject to involuntary bankruptcy.

Under the federal bankruptcy law effective October 1, 1979, however, a corporation is treated as other business entities and all are exempt from involuntary bankruptcy if they are "farmers." To be a farmer, more than 80 percent of gross income in the preceding taxable year must come from a farming operation owned and operated by the "person" – individual, partnership or corporation.

The rules for instituting an involuntary bankruptcy proceeding have been changed under the federal bankruptcy law. Involuntary bankruptcy may be commenced by three or more creditors with claims totaling at least $5,000 unless there are fewer than 12 creditors, in which case one creditor holding a claim of at least $5,000 may file.

In most states, a debtor may hold specified property exempt from creditors. Midwestern and western states are particularly generous to farm debtors. Typically, the homestead, household goods, some livestock and a few items of equipment cannot be reached by creditors unless specifically encumbered. However, if exempt property is transferred to a corporation, the exemption is generally lost since the debtor must typically be an individual or head of a family to qualify for exemption of property from creditors' claims. And a corporate shareholder cannot claim the exemption out of the corporate stock received in exchange for the exempt assets.

Governmentally related loans

Restrictions are imposed on Farm Credit Bank loans to farm corporations. Such loans may be made to "bona fide farmers and ranchers" but most farm corporations should qualify.

A corporation may be a qualified borrower if it meets at least one of three criteria: (1) more than 50 percent of the stock is owned by individuals conducting the farming or livestock operation, (2) more than 50 percent of the value of its assets is related to production of agricultural products, or (3) more than 50 percent of corporate income originates from agricultural products. If the primary purpose of the operation is to conduct its business at a loss to absorb taxable income from non-agricultural sources, it's not eligible to borrow.

In the past, a farm corporation has not been eligible for Farm Service Agency (formerly Farmers Home Administration) real estate or operating loans. However, a corporation could borrow under the emergency loan and soil and water loan programs. "Family size" corporations, partnerships and cooperatives are now eligible borrowers from FSA.

The Small Business Administration (SBA) is authorized to make loans to farm businesses including farm corporations. Specifically, the SBA is permitted to aid and assist "small business concerns which are engaged in the production of food and fiber, ranching, and raising of livestock, agriculture, and all other farming and agricultural related industries." However, SBA loans may not be made unless the financial assistance applied for is not available from non-federal sources. A "small business concern" is one which is "independently owned and operated and which is not dominant in its field of operation."

Dissolution and liquidation

A corporation may usually be dissolved under state law either by written consent of all shareholders or by approval of the board of directors followed by majority or higher vote of the shareholders. The state-prescribed procedure for dissolution generally poses few problems. The greatest concerns are the income tax consequences of liquidation as assets are distributed to the shareholders in exchange for their stock.

A corporation can be formed without paying income tax on the gain in property transferred to the new corporation. Such a tax-free exchange is discussed in detail in Chapter 24.

Liquidating a corporation without adverse income tax consequences is more difficult to achieve, however. In the Tax Reform

Act of 1986, major changes were made in the liquidation of corporations including closely held farm corporations. Basically, liquidating corporations recognize gain or loss on the distribution of property in complete liquidation *as if the property were sold at its fair market value. And shareholders recognize gain or loss on their stock in liquidation.*

Requirements for liquidation before 1989. As noted, eligible closely held corporations were entitled to use the liquidation provisions repealed in 1986 for liquidations completed before January 1, 1989. This exception required that income tax be paid on distributions of ordinary income property and short-term capital gain property.

Tax on "built-in" gains. In an effort to thwart attempts by regularly taxed or C corporations to elect S corporation status to minimize the effects of the 1986 amendments, a corporate-level tax is imposed on the appreciation in value of assets (referred to as "built-in gain") prior to the S corporation election. The tax is imposed on appreciated assets which are disposed of within 10 years after the corporation has become an S corporation. The tax imposed is the maximum corporate rate tax for the year in which the disposition occurs applied to the lesser of – (1) the net built-in gains or (2) the amount of taxable income if the corporation were not an S corporation. The built-in gain is the fair market value of the assets of the S corporation as of the beginning of the first taxable year for which the S corporation election is in effect over the aggregate adjusted basis of the corporation's assets.

Gains on sale or asset distribution are presumed to be built-in gains except to the extent the taxpayer can establish that the appreciation occurred after the conversion. For that reason, it is advisable to obtain an appraisal of a C corporation's assets at the time it converts to S corporation status in order to establish the amount of the built-in gain potentially subject to the corporate level tax. It is important to note that the corporate-level tax applies to all assets including inventory property.

The tax on built-in gains does not apply if the S corporation election was made before 1987. A corporation that became an S corporation before January 1, 1989, could avoid the tax except as to built-in ordinary gains and short-term capital gains.

Liquidation after 1988. It's important to note that liquidations after 1988, even for closely held corporations, come under the tough, new liquidation provisions in the Tax Reform Act of 1986. For C corporations, gain or loss is recognized to a liquidating corporation on the distribution of property in complete liquidation as if the property had been sold. In addition, the shareholders face recognition of gain or loss, also.

Each shareholder's gain or loss is the difference between the amount of the distribution and the income tax basis of the stock. In S corporations, there is a single tax at the shareholder level. No gain is triggered at the corporate level unless the built-in gains tax applies. Income tax liability is due at the shareholder level as with C corporations.

Reorganizations

In some situations, the basic objective may be to split up the corporation and divide the assets so that one shareholder group can head off in one direction and another shareholder group can proceed down a different path. In those instances, a corporate reorganization may be less costly than a corporate liquidation. One of the most useful of the half dozen reorganization choices is the "type D" divisive reorganization.

Here's how it works in three major steps –

• A new corporation is formed, usually as a subsidiary to the old, parent corporation.

• Part of the parent corporation's assets are transferred to the new subsidiary.

• The stock in the subsidiary corporation (held by the parent) is distributed to some of the parent corporation's shareholders in exchange for their stock in the parent corporation.

The result is that one shareholder group owns the subsidiary corporation and its assets. Another shareholder group owns the parent corporation which is now diminished in size by the amount of assets in the subsidiary corporation. This is an especially useful procedure if the shareholders, for various reasons, simply prefer to take part of the assets and go their own way.

This type of reorganization can be carried out tax-free if several technical requirements are met. Because so much is at stake, it's a good idea to have first-class tax and accounting advice and counsel at your elbow before undertaking this – or any other – corporate reorganization.

One of the more touchy aspects of this type of reorganization is that both corporations must be engaged in the "active conduct of a trade or business." If one corporation ends up owning only land, which is cash rented to a tenant, there's a serious question whether that corporation meets the "active business" test. The courts are split over that issue. It helps if a land owning corporation enters into a crop share or livestock share lease with active involvement in management under the lease.

Another touchy point is that IRS is usually on the lookout to see if the whole reorganization process is a subterfuge for getting earnings and profits out of the parent corporation. If it is, that could lead to dividend treatment.

As for the range of "recapture" possibilities, most do not apply.

Other reorganization choices

There are five other reorganization choices that may be worth considering –

• A "type A" reorganization occurs when one corporation absorbs another and one disappears in the process. This is a typical merger.

• A "type B" reorganization involves an exchange of stock of one corporation for voting stock of the acquiring corporation.

• A "type C" reorganization is carried out with an exchange of property of the acquired corporation for voting stock of the acquiring corporation.

• A "type E" reorganization or "recapitalization" involves a modification of the capitalization structure of a corporation. It could be a stock-for-stock swap, a debt securities-for-stock exchange, a stock-for-debt securities transaction (usually the most hazardous, tax-wise) or a debt securities-for-debt securities exchange.

• A "type F' reorganization involves technical changes in the identity, form or place of organization of the corporation.

• A "type G" reorganization is for financially troubled corporations.

In conclusion ...

The choices for solving a basic problem of corporate disagreement or a desire to split up a corporate operation are many. The differences in income tax liability are typically enough to justify a great deal of planning attention before a particular plan is implemented.

For any dissolution and liquidation, competent tax advice is a must. To minimize the income tax burden, it's important that the right choice be made and then carried out by the rules. Because of the possibilities for income tax to be imposed on liquidation, the decision to incorporate should be made on the basis of a careful review of all alternatives.

23
Where does the corporation fit?

For a sound estate plan, it's fundamental that a careful evaluation be made of the organization of the business. In fact, *estate* planning and *business* planning ideally are carried out simultaneously.

If estate planning decisions are made without regard to how the business is organized legally and economically, later interest in changing the form of business organization may make it necessary to rewrite the entire estate plan. A comparable problem develops if business organization decisions are made without regard for the estate planning implications.

Why incorporate?

The major reason why most farmers incorporate relates to estate planning. In many instances, farmers incorporate to achieve a greater level of accomplishment of their estate planning objectives.

Let's examine two case situations in which the corporation proved to be helpful.

CASE I. In this actual situation, the father had been farming for nearly 25 years when the oldest son returned to the farm. Five years later, the second son completed military service and returned to the farm. After about five years of operating under an informal agreement, the father and both of the sons began to feel that the arrangement was unfair.

Property ownership had become enormously complex. The parents owned all of the land. Cattle were owned on a ⅗-⅕-⅕ basis. Part of the equipment was owned on a ⅓-⅓-⅓ basis. Of the rest of equipment, certain pieces were owned entirely by the father, others by one son (who was single and had more extra cash), others by the second son, and still other pieces of equipment were owned jointly by the two sons.

Figuring the annual income share for each individual was no small task. And disentangling machinery trades for purposes of figuring income tax basis, depreciation, recapture of depreciation, investment tax credit and recapture of investment tax credit had become a veritable nightmare.

After considering all organizational alternatives, the decision was made to determine the fair market value of the property, organize a corporation, and transfer the property to it in exchange for shares of stock. With the corporation as the owner of the property and as the "farmer," the details of income sharing and machinery trades were greatly simplified.

Each year, salaries and bonuses are used to compensate those contributing labor and management to the corporation. Borrowed capital is paid the going rate of interest. And rented land is paid whatever the local rental market suggests for that year. The remaining corporate income goes to compensate the equity or ownership capital. Dividends are rarely declared, so the effect is to increase the value of each share of stock outstanding.

Presently, the father and mother as *shareholders* own 1,590 shares of stock (originally issued at $100 per share). Until his recent death, the father alone owned 416 shares, one son owned 630 shares and the other son had 375 shares. These 3,011 shares of corporation stock represent prior ownership of $301,100 of property (now worth more than five times that).

The parents made annual gifts of stock to their children within the limits of the federal gift tax annual exclusion (see Chapter 6). It should be noted that recent cases have raised the question whether stock of small, closely held corporations with a history of no dividend declaration would be eligible for the gift tax annual exclusion on the grounds that transfer of such stock may involve transfer of a future interest, rather than a present interest. Only present interests are eligible for the federal gift tax annual exclusion. For that reason, it is always helpful for the corporation to have a history of some dividend payment even though modest. Returning to the case situation, a more ambitious gift making program, based on the old federal gift tax lifetime exemption (which has not been available since 1976) was implemented when the father reached age 60. After age 65, the father indicated that he was willing for the combined stock holdings of himself and his wife to drop below 51 percent.

The above describes the actions taken by one farm family to solve certain operational and business organization problems. So, how is it working after 30 years?

Quite well. Tension levels have been reduced. There's less suspicion over fairness in dividing the annual income. And, there's less uncertainty over the role of the sons in the operation and of their property ownership rights. The family has worked through the problems of a key shareholder's death. The business continues and is not in jeopardy.

Everyone tends to grumble about the greater formality required, as a corporation, in making and recording business decisions. But they concede that the extra records and minutes of meetings have been worthwhile and were badly needed.

CASE II. Now let's consider another case involving a slightly different family situation in which incorporation of the farm business served to help solve problems of both an economic and legal nature.

The father and mother (as farmers) have six children – five of whom are employed out of the state, and out of agriculture. The oldest son has farmed with the parents for nearly 30 years.

The problems – long anticipated by the farming son – were impressed upon the parents as they worked with their attorney in making wills, and as they considered the social security aspects of retirement at age 65.

Three major problems were identified in the process. First, although the farming son had some property in his own name, he had little to show for his contributions of effort and capital to the farm business over the past 30 years. Improvements in soil fertility and additions of farm buildings were the property of the parents. Value added by these improvements would likely be taxed in their estates at death and, unless other arrangements were made, would pass to *all* children after death. Yet the farming son felt (and the parents agreed) that he had provided much of the finances and effort for those improvements.

The second problem was the likelihood of a breakup of the farm business at death of the parents. Without prior planning, one of the off-farm heirs might request partition of the property after death of the parents. With the farming son holding only a one-sixth interest, this would probably be insufficient to forestall liquidation of the farm business.

The third problem is related to retirement of the father at age 65. He wanted to receive maximum social security benefits to which he was entitled. But he also wanted to continue meaningful contact with the farm business and to receive some income in addition to social security benefits. Neither the "material participation" rules (father as a landlord) nor the "substantial services" rules (father as a partner) appeared to permit the degree of involvement and income desired.

The solution ultimately agreed upon was to incorporate, with the farming son's *prior contributions* to the farm business (to the extent legally enforceable) recognized in the form of stock issued to him. The net value of the property transferred to the corporation in 1970 was $480,000 of which $100,000 of the parents' contribution was exchanged for 10-year, 7 percent debentures. The other $380,000 worth of property was exchanged for corporate stock. Of the 3,800 shares of stock issued (at $100 per share) the parents received 2,840 shares; the farming son, 960 shares.

The stock issue provided recognition of the son's property contribution. It was agreed that future capital contributions by the farming son would be recognized with payment of cash compensation or issuance of additional stock for labor and management contributions.

The articles of incorporation and bylaws included an elaborate provision granting a first option to the corporation and to surviving or remaining shareholders to purchase stock held by a deceased shareholder, a shareholder departing from corporate employment or a shareholder wishing to sell his or her stock. The provision also specified that the purchase price could be paid in up to 10 annual installments with interest on the unpaid balance.

This provision assured ultimate distribution of the family wealth to all of the children. The possibility existed for some to receive debentures and thus to be paid interest income each year. Those receiving stock, especially the off-farm heirs, might find the option to purchase exercised, with interest received on the unpaid balance until the purchase price was fully paid. Or, the stock might be permitted to pass to the first generation of off-farm heirs without the first option being exercised. It was generally believed in that operation that it would probably be unwise for stock to pass to succeeding generations of off-farm heirs. The chance of the farm business being placed in jeopardy at the death of the parents was thus sharply reduced.

The father's social security problem was handled by placing him on a part-time employment basis (one-fourth time) at a salary of the maximum allowable earned income then without reduction of social security benefits. This permitted him to receive the maximum social security benefits to which he was entitled. And, he could receive dividends and interest – as investment income – in unlimited amounts without reduction of his benefits from social security. The $100,000 in debentures produced an assured income of $7,000 in interest per year to the father so long as he lived and thereafter to the mother if she survived. Beyond that, the debentures could be redeemed or could pass to off-farm heirs preferring the certainty of income on debentures (but with no chance of increase in principal value) to the uncertainty of income on stock as dividends (but with a chance of increase in stock value).

The farming son, with 960 shares of stock in his own name, was well on his way to control of the corporation at the death of the parents. As the corporation was set up, 1,901 shares were needed to have control over shareholder voting. If debentures had not been used, 2,401 shares would have been needed to acquire control. The use of debentures thus influences the investment needed to gain control over corporate decision making.

The most serious problem encountered in this situation was the severe strain on the operation from the interest paid on the outstanding debentures. The operation survived the 1980s debt crisis but the experience convinced the family that a lighter debt burden would be prudent. As a consequence, the debentures were retired as the securities matured and were replaced with corporate stock.

There are, of course, other situations in which the corporation fits as an estate and business planning device. As a flexible tool in the estate and business planner's kit, the corporation merits consideration, particularly where the relevant objectives include business continuation beyond the life span of the majority owners of the business.

24
Steps in forming a farm corporation

It's easy to form a sole proprietorship. Even the partnership tends to be viewed as fairly simple, although preparing the written agreement can pose some difficult questions and partnership problems, particularly those relating to income tax, can be complex, indeed.

But the corporation is the ultimate in organizational and operational formality. This is due in large part to the fact that corporations of all sizes – from the smallest 160-acre farm corporation to the multi-million dollar giants – in most states are formed under the same state corporation laws and operate under basically the same tax laws. It takes a complex set of rules to handle the organizational intricacies and tax angles of the larger corporations. A few states have developed separate and less complex rules for closely held corporations.

Making the decision

The most important step in incorporating a farm business is the decision to go with the corporation. *This is not a decision to be made lightly.* A reversal of the decision after a year or two of operation may be quite costly in terms of wasted organizational expense and, possibly, added income tax paid upon the liquidation of the corporation. The decision should be made only after careful consideration, with the help of an attorney having knowledge of corporate and tax law.

Appendix C provides a handy check list of points to consider in forming a farm corporation.

Drafting articles of incorporation

Once the green light is flashed for incorporating, the key decisions on corporate structure must be made as the attorney drafts the articles of incorporation and bylaws.

Corporations are creatures of state law with the articles representing the compact between the corporation and the state. The articles are filed publicly, usually at both the state and county levels. The bylaws, which are not filed publicly, specify the internal governing rules under which the corporation will operate.

Determining the capitalization structure

STOCK. An important part of the articles is the capitalization structure which defines the classes of stock. Typically, farm corporations are created with one class of common stock authorized. But other classes may be defined in the articles with the classes differentiated on the basis of (1) voting rights, (2) rights to receive income annually, (3) preferences in receiving assets on liquidation, and (4) term of commitment as an investor.

Common stock, the risk bearing fund of the corporation, usually has voting rights (one vote per share), rights to annual income only as dividends are declared by the directors, no preference on liquidation and an indefinite term of commitment to ownership of the security. A class of preferred stock, by contrast, might have no voting rights, a specified annual dividend rate, priority on liquidation ahead of the common stockholders and an indefinite commitment to ownership.

Generally, about twice as much stock is authorized as is needed for immediate issuance. The rest is held by the corporation for possible later issue as assets are transferred to, or services performed for, the corporation.

DEBT SECURITIES. A corporation may also, generally by board of director action, create one or more classes of debt securities. These might include notes (short term, unsecured debt obligations), debentures (longer term, unsecured debt obligations) or bonds (longer term, secured obligations). The debt securities are typically defined with reference to the four characteristics noted above. Debt securities generally confer no voting right on the holder, pay income annually at a fixed rate of interest, give the holder priority on liquidation ahead of shareholders and involve a fixed term to maturity.

Debt securities may be used to:

1. Reduce the investment required for on-farm heirs to gain voting control over the corporation (since debt securities do not carry voting rights).

2. Assure substantial investment income (which does not affect social security benefits) to the parents so long as either of them live even if the surviving parent is a minority shareholder.

3. Create opportunities for withdrawal of capital from the corporation (such as for a new house in town) by later redemption of the debt securities without particularly adverse tax consequences, compared with redemption of stock which faces the distinct possibility of being treated as a dividend with taxation as ordinary income. However, debt securities issued at the time of incorporation (before October 3, 1989) in a tax-free exchange may very well have a basis considerably less than face value so gain would be recognized on redemption.

4. Provide an alternative for off-farm heirs who prefer certainty of income and principal of debt securities over the risks of stock ownership.

5. Provide an avenue for removal of some earnings from the corporation as tax deductible interest (dividends are not tax deductible at the corporate level).

6. Reduce the amount of investment needed for the on-farm heirs to gain control of the corporation at the death of the surviving parent. With debt securities not carrying voting rights, issuance of $200,000 of debentures in an $800,000 operation means the investment needed to gain control drops from just over $400,000 to just over $300,000.

7. Increase the incentive for shareholder-employees to perform by enlarging swings in stock value. An increase of $100,000 in corporate net worth translates into a 10 percent stock value increase in a $1,000,000 operation. But with $500,000 of debentures, the stock value increase would be 15 percent – if the debentures called for 5 percent annual interest. The $25,000 needed to pay interest on the debentures would leave a $75,000 increase in net worth for the $500,000 amount of stock. Fluctuations on a per share basis are thus magnified in classical leveraging form since the principal value of debentures does not change over time.

8. To the extent held by the parents, fixed principal debt securities tend to place a "cap" on further increases in estate value. This feature can also lead to problems for the parents if the principal amount is not sufficient to maintain an adequate level of income in the face of inflation and high costs for medical care.

Thus, debt securities such as debentures afford a degree of flexibility in the capitalization structure. As a general rule, issuance of more debt securities than stock in terms of total value should be done only after careful consideration of the tax rules limiting "thin capitalization." In general, it's believed that it's acceptable to use equal parts debt and equity in a closely held farm corporation. And it is possible to go beyond a one-to-one ratio of debt to equity but careful planning is required if tax challenges are to be avoided. Usually, estate and business planning objectives can be met well short of a one-to-one ratio of debt to equity.

For any use of debt securities in the capitalization structure of the corporation, the debt securities should be created with careful adherence to the characteristics of debt capital. That means any note, bond or debenture should carry a fixed rate of interest, have no voting rights, specify a fixed term to maturity and assure the holder priority to share in corporate assets on liquidation. Pure equity capital (common stock), by contrast, has no fixed right to annual income (it's discretionary with the board of directors), voting rights – one vote per share, an indefinite term of investor

368

commitment rather than a specified maturity and no priority on liquidation – shareholders are the "residual claimants" and, thus, are the risk takers in the venture.

There are several reasons *not* to use debt securities.

• Debt securities involve a fixed annual payment which can be a serious economic burden for a farm business with limited cash flow.

• Debt securities aren't an "interest in a closely held business" for purposes of installment payment of federal estate tax. This could jeopardize eligibility for 15-year installment payment of federal estate tax where the interest in a closely held business must exceed 35 percent of the estate less estate settlement deductions for federal estate tax to be deferred. See Chapter 5.

• Debt securities apparently aren't an "interest in a closely held business" for purposes of special use valuation of farmland. This could endanger eligibility for special use valuation. See Chapter 3.

Until a 1989 amendment became effective, debt securities could be and often were issued as part of a tax-free exchange. The debt securities ended up with an income tax basis comparable to the stock. In both instances, the basis was often substantially below fair market value. The available income tax basis from property transferred to the corporation (minus any indebtedness taken over by the corporation) was allocated between the stock and any debt securities issued in accordance with the respective fair market values of the stock and debt securities. Unless the stock was redeemed by the corporation or sold to another shareholder, the relatively low income tax basis per share of stock was of no great consequence. The same was true for debt securities – except the likelihood of redemption of debt securities was generally much higher. And redemption of low basis debt securities produced gain for income tax purposes.

For transfers of property to corporations after October 2, 1989, in taxable years ending after that date, debt securities issued in a tax-free exchange to a corporation are treated as "boot." That means the debt securities are generally treated as taxable income. This rule discourages the issuance of debt securities as part of a tax-free exchange.

For those wanting debt securities, one solution is to issue the debt securities for cash in a separate transaction well after the tax- free exchange of property to the corporation in exchange for stock. Those without the necessary cash to be transferred to the corporation in exchange for debt securities could generate the cash in a loan placed on the property before incorporation.

If debt securities are issued as part of a tax-free exchange and are treated as taxable boot, it appears the income tax basis from the transferred property which is available for allocation is allocated to the issued stock, up to its fair market value. Only then is the basis expected to be available to reduce the gain on the debt securities issued. Gain from the issuance of debt securities may, as a general rule, be eligible for installment reporting but several different provisions deny installment reporting for inventory and depreciable property.

Another solution to problems of gain on issuance of debt securities is to hold out some inventory property – such as stored grain – from the corporation. Upon subsequent sale of the grain, the cash could then – in a later transaction – be used to purchase debt securities from the corporation. The result from both solutions: debt securities with income tax basis equal to their face value. There should be no gain on later redemption of such debt securities.

Other components of articles of incorporation

The articles also typically contain a statement of purposes, specifications on corporate life (whether perpetual or for a term of years), the initial composition of the board of directors, a section on stock transfer restrictions, and any special rules on the vote required for decision making at the shareholder level if other than a majority.

370

Preparing the inventory

Upon acceptance of the articles of incorporation by the appropriate state office, the corporation gains legal status permitting it to own property, hire employees and otherwise carry on the business of farming. Before the organizational meeting of the board of directors – which is an important occasion – the individuals wishing to transfer property to the corporation should prepare an inventory.

The inventory normally lists (1) a description of each item of property to be transferred to the corporation, (2) its fair market value (typically determined by the board of directors), (3) the adjusted income tax basis for the property, (4) any indebtedness on the property to be taken over by the corporation, and (5) the method of depreciation being used.

For each individual transferring property to the corporation, the total fair market value figure minus indebtedness constitutes the net contribution to the corporation and determines the number of shares of stock to be received. Thus, transfer of $180,000 of property with a $40,000 mortgage would justify issuance of 1,400 shares of stock at $100 per share.

Issuance of stock based on fair market value of the property transferred to the corporation (less any indebtedness taken over by the corporation) is fundamental. If stock is issued for income tax basis of property transferred to the corporation, two major problems may arise.

• Unless each shareholder's basis for property contributed bears a uniform relationship to fair market value, massive gifts may occur from transferors with low income tax basis property to transferors with high income tax basis property.

EXAMPLE: In a mother-son operation, the decision was made to issue 1,000 shares of stock to the son in exchange for his machinery and equipment. His property had an aggregate income tax basis of $150,000 (on which stock was to be issued) with an aggregate fair market value of $160,000. The mother's land – her sole contribution – had an income tax basis of $150,000 so she was to receive 1,500 shares of stock also. The problem: her land had a fair market value of $1,240,000. If the corporation had been immediately dissolved, each would have been entitled to receive $700,000 of assets. The gift of $540,000 from mother to son can be seen in bold relief. Completion of the transfer as planned would have involved federal gift tax of about $140,000 on top of loss of the unified credit (which was $30,000 for that year, 1977).

Other situations may be less dramatic but just as illustrative of the principle involved. In all instances, the potential for inequities is present. If the transferors are related, the gift in the transfer would likely be subject to federal gift tax in the year of the transfer.

• Shareholders may be lulled into believing that a share of stock issued in exchange for $100 of income tax basis is really worth $100, when in fact the share of stock may be worth three or four times that amount. The implications for additional gift tax liability on transfers of such stock are obvious.

The last column in the inventory – method of depreciation – is important because fast methods of depreciation on non-ACRS or non-MACRS property (either because the property was placed in service before 1981 or 1987 or comes under one of several categories of property not eligible for ACRS or MACRS cost recovery) cannot be used by the corporation for *used* property. Before 1981, depreciable property received by the corporation at the time of incorporation was not eligible for the "fast" methods of depreciation. The "fast" methods include double declining balance and sum-of-the-years digits methods. The reason they could not be used after transfer of assets to the new corporation was that the "fast" depreciation methods could only be used on new property – technically, "the original use of the property must commence with the taxpayer." And for the new corporation, the assets acquired in the initial exchange are generally used property.

With this exception, the corporation, in effect, takes over the depreciation schedule of the transferors of property. For property depreciated under the Accelerated Cost Recovery System (ACRS) or Modified Accelerated Cost Recovery System (MACRS), the corporation must use the same recovery period and method used by the transferor (including use of any optional recovery period or method) for the transferred property. Property that was not ACRS property in the hands of the transferor does not become ACRS property upon transfer to the corporation. The same is true of MACRS property.

Tax-free or taxable exchange

The choice between paying and not paying income tax on the gain wrapped up in property transferred to the corporation (the difference between a taxable and tax-free incorporation) is not really an election. The choice is made in the way the transfer is handled.

For a tax-free exchange, two conditions must be met: (1) those transferring property to the corporation must end up with at least 80 percent of the stock (can't make massive gifts, therefore, at the time the corporation is formed), and (2) the property must be exchanged solely for "stock" in the corporation.

Until 1989, property could be issued for stock or securities in the corporation. The term "securities" had been defined to exclude short-term notes or other debt securities. Debt obligations issued by the corporation for shorter maturity than five years were definitely suspect. A maturity of 10 years or longer was recommended. For transfers after October 2, 1989, for a tax-free exchange, property can be transferred only for stock. Debt securities issued as part of a tax-free exchange are treated as taxable boot as noted earlier.

Because the stock received by the transferors of property may later be sold or given away, it is important to compute its income tax basis. For a tax-free exchange, with no gain recognized on incorporation (which is usually desired), the income tax basis for each transferor's stock is figured by subtracting the indebtedness taken over by the corporation from the tax basis of the property going into the corporation.

Thus, a transferor giving up property with a tax basis of $120,000 but with a $40,000 mortgage would end up with stock having an $80,000 income tax basis. Later sale of the stock for more than $80,000 would produce a gain.

A key point: If a transferor's liabilities that are taken over by the corporation exceed the income tax basis of assets transferred, *a taxable gain is incurred as to the excess.* This problem has arisen with some regularity in recent years as farmers have incorporated as part of a general refinancing effort because of heavy debt obligations.

Accounts payable have posed special problems as liabilities. However, for transfers to a corporation by a cash basis transferor for stock the accounts payable are not considered to be liabilities if the transferor would be entitled to a deduction if the accounts payable were paid.

If the amount of indebtedness to be taken over by the corporation exceeds substantially the income tax basis of property transferred to the new corporation, several solutions are possible – (1) review the loans carefully to see if some can be left with the individual transferor, perhaps some of the unsecured loans, with corporate stock pledged to secure the loans after incorporation; (2) consider whether more assets with a relatively high basis (perhaps more cash) can be transferred to the new corporation; or (3) pay the income tax on the difference.

Table 18 illustrates a tax-free exchange involving a father (A) and three sons (B, C and D). Appendix D contains another example of a tax-free exchange using equity capital only.

Note that the corporation's basis for the property – important in figuring depreciation and in calculating gain on later sale by the corporation – is obtained by taking over the basis of the property in the hands of the transferor.

A *taxable* exchange, perhaps handled as a sale, requires

374

income tax to be paid on the gain. And, the corporation receives a new basis for purposes of figuring depreciation and gain on later sale. For some assets, the gain may be treated as capital gain with later depreciation by the corporation deductible from ordinary income. A great move if capital gains are taxed more favorably than ordinary income (long term capital gains are eligible for a maximum rate of 28 percent for individuals beginning in 1991). But if the transferor, spouse or any estate, trust or partnership in which the transferor is a beneficiary or partner owns 80 percent or more of the stock, gain on depreciable property would not be capital gain. It would be ordinary income. And that takes much of the fun out of a taxable exchange even if capital gains are taxed more favorably.

On top of that, gain representing depreciation is subject to recapture as ordinary income; deductions taken on land held for less than 10 years for soil and water conservation and land clearing expense are recaptured as ordinary income; federal and state cost sharing payments excluded from income within the past 20 years are recaptured as ordinary income; losses on transfers to controlled corporations are not deductible; and production expenses and depreciation deductions are disallowed if an unharvested crop is involved in the tax-free exchange. It adds up to a great deal of complexity and often a substantial amount of ordinary income on the gain involved.

In general, formation of a farm or ranch corporation in the regular course of business with a tax-free exchange can be carried out completely tax free if the requirements for a tax-free exchange are met. That's the case even though the transfer may involve stored grain, growing crops or livestock being fed out. If the exchange involves clear tax avoidance motives, like running up a big operating loss for those transferring the property, IRS has four theories to use in challenging the tax-free nature of the transfer.

• IRS used the "assignment of income" doctrine to undercut a California farmer's plan to establish 14 separate corporations to receive crop sale proceeds.

Table 18. Tax-free incorporation process.

Assume four individuals, A, B, C and D, wish to form a farm corporation with the following property. Assuming a tax-free exchange, the incorporation process would produce the following results:

(1) Individual	(2) Property contributed	(3) Tax basis	(4) Fair market value	(5) Indebtedness	(6) Net contribution (4)-(5)	(7) Shares of stock received ($100 per share)	(8) Tax basis of stock received (3)-(5)	(9) Corporation's basis for property (from 3)	(10) Indebtedness assumed by corporation (from 5)
A	Land	$120,000	$180,000	$40,000	$140,000	1,400	$80,000	$120,000	$40,000
B	Machinery	36,000	40,000	10,000	30,000	300	26,000	36,000	10,000
C	Livestock	5,000	10,000	0	10,000	100	5,000	5,000	0
D	Cash	5,000	5,000	0	5,000	50	5,000	5,000	0
	Total	$166,000	$235,000	$50,000	$185,000	1,850	$116,000	$166,000	$50,000

Note that:

1. The amount of stock issued to each shareholder depends only on the shareholder's net contribution to the corporation (fair market value of property minus indebtedness). Tax basis does not affect stock issuance.

2. The corporation's basis for the property is the same as the basis in the hands of the shareholders.

3. A shareholder's basis for stock is the basis carried over from the property contributed minus any indebtedness assumed by the corporation.

• IRS has broad power to reallocate income, deductions and credits as necessary "in order to prevent the evasion of taxes or clearly to reflect … income." That power was used against an Oregon hop farmer who formed a corporation at mid-year and transferred the growing crop to the corporation. The result was a large operating loss for the hop farmer (because of production expenses incurred in planting and tending the crop) and a substantial amount of gain to the corporation (as the crop was harvested and sold). The IRS reallocated the production expenses to the newly formed corporation. Two 1983 cases did not require reallocation. In both cases, the transferors did not incur net operating losses. In recent years, it's been generally believed that if you avoid running up an operating loss in the period before corporate formation, you can probably sidestep the problem of distortion of income.

• The "tax benefit" challenge could be used (although it's been done only rarely) to require that purchased feed and other supplies on hand that had been previously deducted from income be brought back into income at the time of the transfer.

• Occasionally, tax-free exchanges have been challenged on the grounds of no business purpose for the transfer. That could possibly happen, for example, if only stored grain is transferred to a newly formed corporation.

However, as noted above, tax-free exchanges that are reasonably free of tax avoidance motives and that do not run up large operating losses for the transferor of property are not usually challenged. One possible exception to that rule is for landlords who incorporate and transfer growing or harvested crops to the newly formed corporation. Especially if the crops were produced under a non-material participation crop share lease, there is a possibility that transfer of the crops would be a taxable event.

Which assets to incorporate

For some, the decision to incorporate a going farm business

leads logically to the decision to include all assets previously involved in the operation. But for others, there may be compelling reasons to incorporate only part of the assets. Thus, it may be advantageous to (1) incorporate the operating side of the farm business – livestock, machinery and equipment – and leave the land in individual, trust or limited partnership ownership; (2) incorporate the land only and leave the operating side of the business in partnership or sole proprietorship form; or (3) form separate corporations for the operating assets and for the land. This problem is discussed in more detail in Chapter 16.

The following points summarize five of the major considerations in making the decision –

• Examine carefully the reasons for incorporating. If it's to help solve estate planning problems, leaving the land out may not accomplish the chief reason for forming the corporation. On the other hand, if a major reason for incorporating is to create a clear farming opportunity for a son or son-in-law, including only the operating assets may mean less investment is needed by the son or son-in-law to gain control over the operating unit. And that can be an important consideration.

• What would be the effect of incorporating only part of the assets on credit availability? A corporation holding only the operating assets – and no land – may not be as attractive a borrower as the unit was before incorporation divided the assets. This may lead to personal signature of individual land owners on corporate loans, for example.

Remember, the operating side of the business tends to be a big user of capital. And the land is usually important collateral and that may be crucial to lenders.

• Would capital flows tend to build up balances in a particular entity? Thus, if only the land is incorporated, will rents paid to the land-owning corporation tend to accumulate? With rental rates subject to a test of reasonableness, a build-up of funds may occur in the land-owning entity unless expansion of land ownership continues or dividends are declared. Income tax deductible salaries are generally modest in a corporation owning land rented to tenants because labor and management needed to handle corporate operations are generally limited.

• Would retention of some assets in individual ownership with those assets leased to the corporation create problems of eligibility for installment payment of federal estate tax, special use valuation of farmland at death or corporate stock redemption after death to pay death taxes and estate settlement costs?

Again, a careful review of the various points raised in Chapter 16 – including the five above – is strongly recommended.

The final decision on assets to include in a newly formed corporation depends on several key factors. There's no "best" way to handle it. Much depends upon the objectives of the individuals involved – what they're trying to accomplish.

First board of directors' meeting

The corporation really gets underway at the first meeting of the board of directors. At that time, the officers are elected, salaries are set and a bonus policy may be adopted.

PROPERTY TRANSFER. The board accepts the property transferred to the corporation and issues stock. Later, perhaps, debt securities (notes, bonds or debentures) can be issued for cash. It is usually unwise, from an income tax perspective, to issue debt securities as part of a tax-free exchange.

OTHER DETAILS. At its first meeting the board also adopts the bylaws and approves a resolution to the depository bank specifying the borrowing and check writing authority conferred on certain officers. And, if desired, the board takes action to elect taxation under Subchapter S (by which the shareholders, not the corporation, pay income tax on corporate income). The consent of each shareholder must be obtained along with the corporation's election on Form 2553.

The board may also consider employment contracts for the employees with special emphasis on sick leave, time off, annual vacation leave, employee benefits (such as group term life insurance, health and accident insurance coverage and retirement benefits), and workers' compensation coverage (providing specified benefits to insured employees). The corporation must apply for an employer's identification number for tax and social security purposes.

The first meeting of the directors may also be a good time to review all insurance coverage for the corporation. Special attention should be given to assuring that newly acquired vehicles and buildings are adequately insured. And, liability insurance coverage should be checked as well. In some instances, the corporation may wish to continue coverage in effect before incorporation; in other cases, changes may be desired.

Assets under special registration – such as motor vehicles and purebred livestock – should be reviewed and appropriate action taken to effect the necessary transfers.

But should all motor vehicles be transferred to the corporation? That depends on many factors – some tax and some non-tax. These considerations are discussed in Chapter 21. A policy on handling automobile expense should be adopted by the board at its first meeting.

The decision of whether to transfer the residence or residences to the corporation is similar to the automobile problem and is also discussed in Chapter 21. For residences individually owned, expenses (other than interest and taxes) are not deductible and depreciation is not allowable. Corporate residences (other than S corporation residences occupied by shareholders) are business assets and are handled as other business assets with repairs, maintenance and depreciation being tax deductible. For more details, see Chapter 21.

Individuals occupying corporate residences have three choices: (1) pay a reasonable rental to the corporation for the right to occupy the residence, (2) report as additional income the value of the right to occupy the residence, or (3) rely upon Section 119 of the Internal Revenue Code which provides that meals and lodging furnished to an employee for the convenience of the employer do not constitute taxable income to the recipient. S corporations face special limitations as to the third option as discussed in Chapter 21.

Again, the board of directors should decide, as a matter of corporate policy, how occupancy of corporate residences is to be handled in the event residences are transferred to the corporation. In some states, corporate residences are not eligible for such property tax preferences as a homestead tax exemption or credit although a few states have eased that rule. In Iowa, for example, a farm corporation is eligible for the homestead tax credit against property tax if the person occupying the homestead is a shareholder of the farm corporation that owns the property.

Update estate plans

Formation of a corporation should trigger review of wills and estate plans of each shareholder. Corporate stock is personal property and would pass as such at death. So wills set up to pass real property to one set of beneficiaries and personal property to another set may be outdated by incorporation.

If taxation under Subchapter S rules is elected, provision should be made in shareholders' wills to assure that the stock does not pass into a testamentary trust. If it does, after 60 days the election will likely be lost and the corporation will revert to the regular method of taxation with the corporation paying its own income tax. See Chapter 20 for the "two year" rule for ownership of S corporation stock by a testamentary trust.

25
Limited liability companies

For centuries, the basic choices of how a business could be organized have remained largely unchanged. Except for the emergence over the past 75 years of the closely held corporation as a unique organizational possibility for small businesses, the sole proprietorship, partnership and corporation have continued to be the basic ways to organize a business.

But over the past half-dozen years, a new possibility has emerged – the limited liability company or LLC. Nearly all of the states have enacted legislation authorizing LLCs. The first statute was enacted in Wyoming in 1977 but with most of the enactments since 1988. Although the statutes bear certain similarities, there has yet to be developed a uniform or model limited liability company act.

Basic nature

A limited liability company is a type of organizational hybrid. It is set up to have the limited liability of a corporation and yet it's taxed as a partnership for income tax purposes.

Partnerships, at least general partnerships, have unlimited liability. The obligations of the business can be satisfied out of the assets of the business, of course. And if that's not enough, the partners' individually owned assets can be reached as well. In a limited liability company, the obligations of the business can be satisfied only out of the business assets. If the LLC is set up properly, has a reasonable amount of equity capital and is respected as a limited liability company by the owners, the individually owned assets of the owners generally cannot be reached to satisfy business obligations.

For income tax purposes, an LLC is treated like a partnership. That means the income, capital gains, losses and credits of the

383

entity pass through to the owners. The LLC is ordinarily not a taxpayer.

But isn't this about the same as an S corporation? An S corporation also affords its owners limited liability. And there's a pass through of income, loss and credit items to the shareholders for federal income tax purposes. LLCs, however, are subject to fewer limitations than S corporations. For example, S corporations can have no more than 35 shareholders and other corporations and partnerships can't own stock in an S corporation. Those limitations don't apply to LLCs.

Limitations on activity

In general, LLCs may carry on any type of business except for those expressly prohibited in the state LLC legislation (such as banking, insurance and professional services). The Kansas and Utah acts specifically authorize an LLC to function in any capacity open to a professional corporation.

Most of the states limiting corporations in terms of ownership of farmland or carrying on of farming operations also limit LLCs in the same or similar manner.

Organization

An LLC is formed by filing brief articles of organization with a state agency, usually the Secretary of State. In some states, the maximum term of organization is limited.

One important feature, which distinguishes LLCs from S corporations, is no limit is imposed on the number of members in an LLC. Moreover, any kind of entity can be a member.

Management

One of the advantages of LLCs is the flexibility in how the business can be managed.

The legislation authorizing LLCs permits the owners, referred to as members, to define how the LLC is to be operated and the rights of the members. Unless the articles of organization or an operating agreement provides for management by a manager or managers, the management of an LLC is vested in its members.

The members of an LLC may enter into an operating agreement to establish or regulate the affairs of the LLC. The operating agreement may contain any provisions not inconsistent with the enabling legislation or the articles of organization. In the absence of a clear specification in the governing documents, several "default" provisions apply. Unless otherwise provided –

• A unanimous vote is required for major decisions such as dissolution, sale of assets or merger.

• Profits and losses are allocated on the basis of the respective capital contributions.

• Distributions are made on the basis of the members' respective contributions.

Tax status

In most instances, a major reason for forming limited liability companies (LLCs) is to obtain the income tax treatment of a partnership. Although the IRS rulings issued to date generally support that outcome, careful attention is needed in structuring an LLC to assure taxation as a partnership.

An LLC is treated as a corporation if it has more corporate than non-corporate characteristics. The four characteristics that distinguish a corporation from a partnership are –

• Continuity of life (which LLCs generally do not possess). The focus of the regulations is on whether any member has the power to dissolve the entity under local law upon voluntary or involuntary withdrawal. The Utah act, for example, provides for continuation of the LLC on the consent of members holding a majority of the profits' interest. This could cause problems of classification of the entity as a partnership for federal income tax purposes. On the other hand, if a state statute authorizes less than unanimous consent but the entity has not opted for such a provision, continuity of life may be lacking.

• Centralized management (which LLCs typically do not possess). IRS ruled, in one instance, that where the articles of organization of the LLC provided that management was reserved to the members (who were entitled to vote in proportion to their interests in the LLC), and the members of the LLC individually had the power to incur debts and liabilities on behalf of the LLC under that state's LLC act, if management was reserved to the members, centralized management was lacking on the grounds that those powers were similar to the powers of a general partner to bind all partners.

IRS has indicated that it will refuse to rule that centralized management does not exist if limited partners own more than 80 percent of the total interests in partnership. The ruling does not state, however, that a favorable ruling will be issued if the general partners own 20 percent or more of the total interest in the partnership. It is not clear what relationship these authorities on limited partnership classification bear to classification of LLCs.

• Free transferability of interests (which LLCs typically do not possess). A member of an LLC generally can assign or transfer that member's interest to another person who is not a member of the organization. However, the assignee or transferee typically does not become a substitute member and does not acquire all of the attributes of the member's interest in the LLC unless all of the remaining members approve the assignment or transfer.

Therefore, LLCs usually lack the corporate characteristic of free transferability of interests. This is essential for partnership tax status.

In the event the remaining members fail to approve the assignment or transfer, the assignee or transferee has no right to participate in the management or become a member of the limited liability company. However, the assignee or transferee is entitled to receive the share of profits or other compensation and the return of contributions to which the transferring member would otherwise be entitled.

• Limited liability (which LLCs possess). LLCs are conceded to have associates and the objective of carrying on a business and dividing the gains from the business. Of the remaining four characteristics, LLCs generally possess only limited liability. Thus, LLCs should generally be classified as a partnership for federal income tax purposes. Note, however, that even though classified as a partnership for federal income tax purposes an LLC may be subject to state corporate income tax in some states.

In 1995, the Internal Revenue Service announced that it was considering a proposal to allow entities to classify themselves for income tax purposes on an elective basis. This check-the-box approach is expected to be adopted in 1996.

Doing business in other states

It is generally believed that states with legislation authorizing LLCs would respect the concept for LLCs organized in other states. The greater concern is the treatment of LLCs by states that have not enacted legislation providing for LLCs. In that event, the foreign state may treat the LLC as a general partnership with unlimited liability.

Dissolution

State law of the states authorizing LLCs generally provides that an LLC is dissolved upon the occurrence of the earliest of several events –

• The end of the fixed duration set in the articles of organization for the entity.

• The unanimous consent of all of the members.

• The death, withdrawal, expulsion, bankruptcy or dissolution of a member unless the business is continued by unanimous consent of all of the remaining members, or

• The entry of a decree of judicial dissolution.

Cash accounting

For farm operations, which historically have been permitted to use the cash method of accounting even though inventories are a material income determining factor, a major concern with limited liability companies is whether the cash method of accounting is available to such entities. At the moment, a substantial question exists about eligibility for cash accounting, particularly if LLC members are viewed as limited partners in the event the LLC is classified as a partnership for federal income tax purposes.

Farming syndicate. If an LLC is classified as a "farming syndicate," some of the features of the cash method of accounting are likely not available. A farming syndicate is prevented from deducting feed, seed, fertilizer and other farm supplies until used or consumed.

A farming syndicate is defined as a partnership or other enterprise (other than a regularly taxed corporation) engaged in farming if ownership interests have been offered for sale –

• In an offering required to be registered with state or federal securities agencies, or

• Any other enterprise (other than a regularly taxed corporation) engaged in farming if more than 35 percent of the losses are allocable to limited partners or limited entrepreneurs.

The first test is not likely to be met but the second test poses a potential threat to classic cash accounting for some LLCs.

Proposed regulations take the position that a farming syndicate may include a general or limited partnership, a sole proprietorship involving an agency relationship created by a management contract, a trust, a common trust fund or an S corporation. The term "limited entrepreneur," which is a key term in the farming syndicate statute, is defined in the regulations as –

"... a person who has an interest in an enterprise other than as a limited partner and who does not actively participate in the management of such enterprise. The determination of whether a person actively participates in management or operation of a farming enterprise depends on the facts and circumstances of each case. Factors which tend to indicate active participation include participating in the decisions involving the operation or management of the farm, actually working on the farm, living on the farm, or hiring and discharging employees (as compared to only the farm manager). Factors which tend to indicate a lack of active participation include lack of control for the management and operation of the farm, having authority only to discharge the farm manager, having a farm manager who is an independent contractor rather than an employee, and having limited liability for farm losses … lack of fee ownership of the farm land shall not be a factor indicating a lack of active participation."

Farming syndicate rules not applicable. The rules limiting deductibility for the cost of inputs do not apply to – (1) amounts on hand at the end of the year because of fire, storm, flood or other casualty or because of disease or drought or (2) amounts charged to capital account. Moreover, several categories of individuals are not considered to be limited partners or limited entrepreneurs for this purpose –

• Individuals who have participated for not less than five years in the management of the business or farming,

• Individuals residing on the farm,

• Individuals actively participating in the farming business or in the further processing of livestock raised in the business,

• Individuals whose principal business activity involves active participation in the business of farming (even though it is not the business in question), and

• Any interest held by a member of the family (or a spouse) or a grandparent of an individual described above who is actively participating in the business.

The key question is whether members of an LLC with limited liability are considered to be limited partners (inasmuch as an LLC is presumably taxed as a partnership), limited entrepreneurs or some other category of owner. If LLC members are deemed to be limited partners or limited entrepreneurs, the question is whether a sufficient number are residing on the farm or are actively participating (or have actively participated) in a farm business or whether close relatives are so involved.

It appears that eligibility for full cash accounting necessarily requires a case by case review of whether the operation is a farming syndicate.

Self-employment tax

In general, an LLC member's net earnings from self-employment include the member's share of income or loss from the business carried on by the LLC. However, a member of an LLC is treated as a limited partner that can exclude distributions from self-employment income (and not pay social security tax) if –

• The member has not been designated as a manager, and

• The entity could have been formed as a limited partnership in that state and the member could have qualified as a limited partner in that limited partnership.

If an LLC has no designated managers, all members are treated as managers and thus pay social security tax even though some of the members have greater management authority than others under state law or the governing document.

Government farm programs

To date, neither the Congress nor the U.S. Department of Agriculture has recognized the limited liability company for payment limitation purposes under the federal farm programs. Therefore, it is uncertain how a limited liability company would be treated for that purpose.

Conclusion

LLCs are viewed by some as a promising new choice for organizing small, closely held businesses. Unfortunately, thus far the concept has generated more questions than answers. Additional guidance is needed in several areas before the concept can be viewed as genuinely useful.

26
The estate planning process: how to go about it

Estate planning is often a lengthy process. Expansion of the estate planning concept to include more than just the making of a simple one-page will stretches the time – and effort – required to develop a complete plan.

In addition to the making of wills, which may run considerably beyond a single page, estate planning also involves a look at property ownership or co-ownership. And, it includes a review of the life insurance program. Adequacy of insurance, ownership of the policies and beneficiary designations are all important points to check.

Establishing objectives

The first and most important step in the estate planning process is to decide what is to be accomplished.

What are the key objectives?

What ideas on property disposition at death are to be considered?

How important is death tax and estate settlement cost saving?

Is there a family business involved and should steps be taken to assure its continuation by others after death?

There's enormous flexibility in the rules on estate planning. Although some far-out objectives (such as disinheriting the surviving spouse) may be difficult – if not impossible – to accomplish, the latitude available assures accomplishment of most objectives.

It is awfully easy to spend an insufficient amount of time on objectives and start "cutting metal" too soon. Like deciding if one wants a marital deduction trust. Or, an arrangement to split property between husband and wife during life. These are crucial decisions. But they can – and should – wait until the basic objectives are well in mind.

The attorney, lender, extension specialist, accountant, insurance representative and others coming in contact with an individual motivated to do something about his or her estate planning situation are basically "educators" in the early stages of the process. They're idea persons. They can help to shape objectives. In fact, individuals often don't have their own objectives in mind until some of the possibilities and alternatives are opened to them. Emphasis in this first stage is on the unrelenting search for objectives.

It is well to get an attorney on the estate planning team early. If the attorney is not brought into discussions during the search for objectives, he or she should at least be involved before the inventory is developed. The attorney will have several ideas to contribute on what information needs to be brought together for the plan.

Preparing an inventory

In general, it's safe to conclude that the inventory should include all of a couple's – or a single individual's – property. The inventory should be exhaustive. Some assets that might appear insignificant in value compared to the total estate – like a small vacation cabin in another state – may loom large after death.

In conducting the inventory, several excellent forms are available. Several state universities publish a form or booklet for that purpose as do some banks and insurance companies.

A form is most helpful. It may call points to mind that might otherwise be missed. And it's handy to keep. But one can do a good job with a pencil and pad of ruled paper. Just make a list describing every item of property and giving location, value, indebtedness (if any), and the tax investment (income tax basis) in the property.

Here are the key points to look for on every asset:

DESCRIPTION. Each asset should be fully described – legal description for land, serial number for bonds, certificate number for corporate stock. Quantity should be clear – bushels of stored grain, numbers of corporate shares, or head of cattle.

Attaching a copy of the latest depreciation schedule may be the simplest way to handle machinery and equipment. Otherwise, items could be lumped together.

OWNERSHIP. A clear determination of ownership of each asset is crucial. Is ownership in the husband's name? Or, the wife's name? Or, are the assets held in co-ownership – tenancy in common or joint tenancy? Are any assets held as community property?

It's a must to check back to the actual documents of title. Don't trust one's memory. Look for the deeds, signature cards at the bank, certificates of deposit and government bonds. And copy off the names of the owners exactly as they appear.

LOCATION. The inventory should give the location of the asset as well as the permanent storage place for the document of title. This helps the survivors spot the property after death. Sometimes this saves days of searching.

INDEBTEDNESS. Is the property encumbered? Or, is it owned free of debt? If it's encumbered, where is the encumbrance filed or recorded? If it's encumbered by property owned in joint tenancy or tenancy by the entirety, will only one-half of the indebtness be deductible at death?

VALUE. It's also necessary to place a current value on each asset or group of assets. For some, it's easy. Just check the daily market quotations. But for many assets, it's a matter of judgment.

After the assets have all been valued using current figures, a couple of additional adjustments should be made before the figures are used to build an estate plan.

What will be the value of the estate in five years? Or, in 10 years? Very few expect to die shortly after their plan is developed.

Expected values five or 10 years hence may be more important than current values figured to the penny.

If the individual will be accumulating assets during the next five to 10 years, the estate may grow, perhaps at a 6 to 10 percent annual rate. But if the individual is nearing retirement and faces a period of dis-saving, the estate might shrink in value.

The latter may be unlikely for many individuals. Some live on social security and adjust their consumption accordingly. The key point is that expected future values are probably much more important than current ones.

A second consideration relates to expected inheritances. It may seem a bit presumptuous – or even improper – but a careful estate planner keeps an eye out for reasonably anticipated inheritances.

Deciding on basic alternatives

With the inventory complete and the objectives well in mind, the individual or couple is in a position to examine the basic alternatives. Perhaps the most basic relate to ownership of property during life between husband and wife and the implications for passing property at death.

For example, there are two fundamentally different ways to save death taxes (beyond making gifts during life and leaving the property to a qualified charity at death). These are discussed in Chapter 4.

If gifts are to be made during life, decisions should be made on whether to set up a revocable trust. Or, an irrevocable trust. Or, whether to use the Gifts-to-Minors Act or Transfers-to Minors Act under state law. Or, whether to simply make an outright gift.

If objectives can best be met by sale of the property during life, consider the potential income tax liability, effects of inflation (or deflation) and the management needed of the funds from the sale. Review the possibility of a sale with installment reporting of gain in contrast with a sale for cash. A private annuity or self-cancelling installment note may be worth considering, also.

Whether to "freeze" asset values

During the 1970s, when inflation persisted and eventually reached double-digit levels, efforts were made to accommodate inflation. One of those efforts was to "freeze" asset values by dividing property ownership into a fixed value segment (usually retained by the asset owner) and a variable value segment (usually transferred to a family member). Asset freezes or estate freezes were accomplished in various ways including the use of debt securities or preferred stock in a corporation, "tiered" ownership interests in a partnership or sale of assets under installment contract.

While estate freezes had a certain surface attraction, the experience of the 1980s has confirmed that capping or freezing asset values can be extremely hazardous to financial health in an era of economic uncertainty.

• If inflation occurs, fixed principal assets and fixed incomes are reduced in real value. In 10 years, at 8 percent inflation, the real value of $15,000 in annual income drops to $6,514.

• If deflation occurs, a larger estate may result than would have been the case had the property owner's assets remained free to fluctuate in value.

EXAMPLE: T owned 640 acres of farmland. In 1981, when the land was valued at $3,000 per acre, T formed a corporation with a primary objective of freezing estate values with preferred stock. At that time, T had cash assets of $80,000 in addition to land valued at $1,920,000 for a total estate of $2,000,000. The corporation was formed with $1,000,000 of corporate common stock and $1,000,000 in fixed principal preferred stock. Fifteen years later, at T's death, after giving away 25 percent of the common stock to children, the farmland had declined in value to

$1,500 per acre for a value of $960,000. Adding $80,000 in other assets, corporate net worth would be $1,040,000. T's preferred stock would still be valued at $1,000,000. The value of the common stock would have dropped to $40,000. T's estate would be valued at $1,030,000. Had the corporation been established with only corporate common stock, and T had given away 12½ percent of the stock (the same relative amount as above), T's estate would have totalled $910,000. Thus, capping or freezing the estate led to a larger estate by $120,000.

• With deflation, fixed payments sufficiently large to support the fixed principal obligation could become an onerous burden. The relatively low rate of return to agricultural assets, particularly land, makes fixed payments tied to market interest rates burdensome in any era. In a deflationary period, the burden can be fatal to the payer. The cash flow in many farm and ranch operations simply does not permit such payments to be made out of income.

• Implementation of an asset or estate freeze may lead to gift tax consequences unless the assured payments and rights created are adequately and fairly valued.

• Farmland represented by fixed principal obligations may be ineligible for special use valuation for federal estate tax purposes.

• If an estate freeze is accomplished by the issuance of debt securities by a corporation, installment payment of federal estate tax could be jeopardized. Debt securities are not an "interest in a closely held business" which is required for an estate to be eligible.

• Eligibility of corporate stock for Section 303 stock redemption after death may be endangered by heavy issuance of debt securities in a freeze. Only corporate stock counts toward the requirement that stock must exceed 35 percent of the gross estate less allowable deductions.

As a rule of thumb, asset or estate freezes seem prudent only if the amount of property is sufficiently large (probably more than $2 million) so that no event or series of events could cause serious economic problems for the property owner. For those with fewer assets, the risks from freezes simply seem to be too great.

Implementing the plan

With the basic decisions made on alternatives open in estate planning, the next step is implementation of the plan. This may involve sale of assets, transfer of assets by gift, preparation and execution of wills, making changes in life insurance policy ownership and beneficiary designations, creation of living trusts or making changes in the method of business organization.

Wills

The making of wills is a key feature in the implementation of the estate plan. Typically, any person of full age and sound mind who's not under another's undue influence may make a will. The will may include not only provisions for property disposition but also (1) nomination of guardians for minor children to function if both parents should die, (2) a testamentary trust to manage the property of minor heirs, and (3) designation of an executor (often to serve without bond) to manage the estate during estate settlement.

The wills for the husband and wife (normally each should have a separate will) usually specify rules for the disposition of property (1) if one spouse should die, (2) if both spouses die, and (3) if the entire immediate family should die.

Various restrictions are imposed by states on property disposition by will. Typically, spouses cannot be completely disinherited unless the surviving spouse is willing to be disinherited or the spouses, while still prospective spouses, had signed an antenuptial agreement. Such agreements are valid in some states and limit the right of the surviving spouse to inherit. Without an antenuptial agreement, the surviving spouse is usually entitled to a share, often one-third or more, of the deceased spouse's property.

Some states limit the amount of property that may pass to charitable organizations in an effort to cool off zealous charities in their drive for funds in the decedent's last days. In some states, a maximum percentage (such as 25 percent) is allowed to pass to charities if certain closely related persons survive and object. In others, wills made within a certain number of days prior to death (often 30 days but up to six months in a few) cannot pass property to charity.

And in nearly every state, it's required that bequests under a will not be frivolous or wasteful, but have redeeming social or economic features.

Even with all these limitations, there's a great deal of latitude in will making.

After the will is prepared, it is signed and witnessed by two or three disinherited witnesses (as required by state law).

Normally, only one copy of the will is executed. In some states, there's a presumption of revocation if all executed copies can't be produced after death.

The executed copy is then stored in a secure place. The attorney drafting the will may offer to store the will or it may be left in one's own safe, in a safe deposit box, or left with a county office (usually clerk of court or recorder) for safekeeping.

A checklist of the major considerations in settling an estate appears as Appendix G.

Changes in insurance

With the will executed, complementary changes should be made in insurance policy ownership and beneficiary designations.

The instructions to the insurance company on payment of proceeds in the event of death should be in agreement with the estate plan. For example, to keep insurance proceeds out of the estate and save as much taxes and estate settlement costs as possible, a typical beneficiary designation might include payment of proceeds to the wife if she survives, then to the testamentary trust for minors if she does not, then to the children equally if the trust does not come into existence (signifying that the youngest child is over the age of distribution set for the trust), and then to the estate if there are no children or descendants of deceased children surviving.

If insurance proceeds are paid to the estate, the provisions of the will take over and provide the rules for distribution.

Occasionally, the necessary changes in insurance policies are overlooked in the implementation phase. If this happens, the insurance plan may not be coordinated with the overall estate plan.

In one case where the bulk of the estate was insurance, upon death of both parents the proceeds went directly to the minor children, bypassing a carefully drawn testamentary trust for the minors included in the parents' wills.

Gifts

If the plan includes transfer of assets by gift, a document of gift conveying title to the new owner should be prepared and delivered to the donee. Gifts that are incomplete because of non-delivery to the recipient are generally ineffective to save death taxes and estate settlement costs. Again, attention should be given to filing gift tax returns, if required. See Chapter 6.

For all gifts, information on income tax basis should be given to the recipient since the donor's basis carries over to the donee. Depreciation schedules on depreciable property should likewise be provided to the recipient.

Keeping the plan up-to-date

Once the estate plan is fully implemented, care should be taken to keep the plan up-to-date. The wealth position may change.

Even the law might change. Thus, the plan should be monitored and reviewed every two to five years, perhaps more often if the need for change is clear.

It's also a good idea to keep the estate inventory up-to-date. That information is invaluable to the survivors who have the responsibility of collecting up the assets after death. We're all guilty of keeping too much information stored solely between our left ear and our right. And, when we expire, that information goes with us, much to the distress of the survivors.

APPENDIX A
Federal unified estate and gift tax rate schedule

Amount on which tentative tax is computed	*Tentative tax*
Not over $10,000	18% of such amount
Over $10,000 but not over $20,000	$1,800 plus 20% of the excess of such amount over $10,000
Over $20,000 but not over $40,000	$3,800 plus 22% of the excess of such amount over $20,000
Over $40,000 but not over $60,000	$8,200 plus 24% of the excess of such amount over $40,000
Over $60,000 but not over $80,000	$13,000 plus 26% of the excess of such amount over $60,000
Over $80,000 but not over $100,000	$18,200 plus 28% of the excess of such amount over $80,000
Over $100,000 but not over $150,000	$23,800 plus 30% of the excess of such amount over $100,000
Over $150,000 but not over $250,000	$38,800 plus 32% of the excess of such amount over $150,000
Over $250,000 but not over $500,000	$70,800 plus 34% of the excess of such amount over $250,000

Over $500,000 but not over $750,000	$155,800 plus 37% of the excess of such amount over $500,000
Over $750,000 but not over $1,000,000	$248,300 plus 39% of the excess of such amount over $750,000
Over $1,000,000 but not over $1,250,000	$345,800 plus 41% of the excess of such amount over $1,000,000
Over $1,250,000 but not over $1,500,000	$448,300 plus 43% of the excess of such amount over $1,250,000
Over $1,500,000 but not over $2,000,000	$555,800 plus 45% of the excess of such amount over $1,500,000
Over $2,000,000 but not over $2,500,000	$780,800 plus 49% of the excess of such amount over $2,000,000
Over $2,500,000 but not over $3,000,000	$1,025,800 plus 53% of the excess of such amount over $2,500,000
Over $3,000,000	$1,290,800 plus 55% of the excess of such amount over $3,000,000

APPENDIX B
Credit for state death taxes paid

Adjusted taxable estate*	Maximum tax credit
Not over $90,000	8/10ths of 1% of the amount by which the adjusted taxable estate exceeds $40,000
Over $90,000 but not over $140,000	$400 plus 1.6% of the excess over $90,000
Over $140,000 but not over $240,000	$1,200 plus 2.4% of the excess over $140,000
Over $240,000 but not over $440,000	$3,600 plus 3.2% of the excess over $240,000
Over $440,000 but not over $640,000	$10,000 plus 4.8% of the excess over $440,000
Over $640,000 but not over $840,000	$18,000 plus 4% of the excess over $640,000
Over $840,000 but not over $1,040,000	$27,600 plus 5.6% of the excess over $840,000
Over $1,040,000 but not over $1,540,000	$38,000 plus 6.4% of the excess over $1,040,000
Over $1,540,000 but not over $2,040,000	$70,800 plus 7.2% of the excess over $1,540,000
Over $2,040,000 but not over $2,540,000	$106,800 plus 8% of the excess over $2,040,000
Over $2,540,000 but not over $3,040,000	$146,800 plus 8.8% of the excess over $2,540,000

*Taxable estate minus $60,000

Over $3,040,000 but not over $3,540,000	$190,800 plus 9.6% of the excess over $3,040,000
Over $3,540,000 but not over $4,040,000	$238,800 plus 10.4% of the excess over $3,540,000
Over $4,040,000 but not over $5,040,000	$290,800 plus 11.2% of the excess over $4,040,000
Over $5,040,000 but not over $6,040,000	$402,800 plus 12% of the excess over $5,040,000
Over $6,040,000 but not over $7,040,000	$522,800 plus 12.8% of the excess over $6,040,000
Over $7,040,000 but not over $8,040,000	$650,800 plus 13.6% of the excess over $7,040,000
Over $8,040,000 but not over $9,040,000	$786,800 plus 14.4% of the excess over $8,040,000
Over $9,040,000 but not over $10,040,000	$930,800 plus 15.2% of the excess over $9,040,000
Over $10,040,000	$1,082,800 plus 16% of the excess over $10,040,000

APPENDIX C
Checklist for farm incorporation

1. **NAME.** What is to be the corporate name? Consider application to reserve corporate name.

2. **DURATION.** Is the corporation to be organized to exist perpetually? Or for a term of years?

3. **PURPOSE.** What are to be the purposes of the corporation? Narrowly defined or broadly stated?

4. **STOCK AND DEBT CAPITAL STRUCTURE.**
   a. How many classes of stock to be authorized? How many shares of stock to be issued? What are characteristics of each as to:
   (1) Voting rights – voting stock, non-voting stock, proxy voting, cumulative rights.
   (2) Dividend rights.
   (3) Preference on liquidation.
   (4) Conversion rights, if any.
   (5) Par value – consider low par value to minimize annual fee on stated capital (possible in some states).
   (6) Fair market value on issuance.
   (7) Pre-emptive rights.

   b. Is debt capital to be used? (Watch tax-free incorporation limitations (with debt securities treated as boot) and debt equity ratio).
   (1) Type of debt security (note, bond, debenture) and amount.
   (2) Time of maturity.
   (3) Conversion to stock.
   (4) Interest rate.
   (5) Priority on liquidation.

c. Is the corporation likely to be subject to the "freeze" rules enacted in 1990? If so, check the federal gift tax consequences of entering into property value freezes.

5. **STOCK TRANSFER RESTRICTION.** What type of restriction to be used (consent, first option, buy-sell agreement)? Method of stock valuation (book value, appraised value, periodically renegotiated fixed value)? Arrangements for payment by purchasers?

6. **SHAREHOLDERS.** Names and addresses? Date of annual meeting? Place of annual meeting? Voting requirements? Quorum requirements? Pooling agreements? Voting trusts? Shareholders' agreements? For minor shareholders, consider using Uniform Gifts to Minors Act or Uniform Transfer to Minors Act custodianship. Custodian should be someone other than donor.

7. **BOARD OF DIRECTORS.** Number of directors on board? Names of first directors? Voting requirements? Quorum requirements? Arrangements for meetings? Director fees? Is pre-incorporation agreement desirable?

8. **OFFICERS.** What offices are to be authorized? Who is expected to be elected to each office? What salary is to be authorized for each officer? Is corporation to pay entire social security tax or only one-half? Is a bonus policy to be authorized? What authority are officers to have in terms of signing other documents? Explain proper format for signatures on corporate documents.

9. **OTHER EMPLOYEES.** What individuals are to be employed by the corporation in addition to the officers? What are terms of employment? Is an employment contract to be drafted? Arrangements for compensation? Is corporation to pay entire social security tax or only one-half?

10. **ASSETS TO BE OWNED BY CORPORATION.** What property is to be transferred to the corporation?

a. Prepare inventory for each transferor and list each item by name of owner, description of asset, income tax basis, fair market value, indebtedness and holding period. Preserve copies to be submitted with income tax returns and for the permanent file.

Watch gifts between and among transferors of property, especially upon conveyance of property held in co-ownership. Any gift (to the other spouse) on conveyance to a corporation of property co-owned by a husband and wife is covered by the 100 percent federal gift tax marital deduction. See Chapter 6. Note insurance carried on assets and assets under special registration.

b. Is transfer to be tax-free or taxable? Check eligibility requirements for one desired.

c. Who is to value assets?

d. Have property taxes been paid by transferor to date of incorporation?

e. Are documentary stamp taxes required on land transferred?

f. Abstracts of title?

g. Prepare deeds and bills of sale.

11. **ASSETS TO BE LEASED BY CORPORATION.** What property is to be leased to the corporation? List each item by name of lessor, description of property and rental to be charged. Prepare leases.

12. **BANK.** What bank is to be the depository bank? Resolution of officer authority to borrow money and sign negotiable instruments to be prepared and sent to bank.

13. **INCOME TAXATION.** What method of income taxation to be followed?

a. Regular. File Form 1120 annually.

b. Subchapter S – review eligibility requirements for election; prepare Form 2553 with consents by each shareholder; if corporation has operated previously as regular corpora tion, check operating loss carry-over, and investment tax credit carry-over and whether there are accumulated earnings and profits. File Form 1120-S annually.

14. **IDENTIFICATION NUMBER.** Prepare and submit Form SS4, "Employer's Application for ID Number."

15. **REGISTERED OFFICE.** What is the address of the registered office of the corporation?

16. **REGISTERED AGENT.** Who is to be the registered agent of the corporation?

17. **NOTICE OF INCORPORATION.** If required by state law, prepare notice of incorporation, forward to publisher of eligible newspaper and, where required, send affidavit of publication to secretary of state.

18. **INCORPORATION KIT.** Order corporate kit, specifying type of seal, if any; number and type of stock certificates (have stock transfer restriction printed thereon or type restriction on certificate when received); minute book.

19. **LOANS, MORTGAGES.** What loans or mortgages are to be assumed or taken subject to by corporation? Give special attention to Farm Credit Bank and Farm Service Agency (formerly Farmers Home Administration) loans. See Chapter 22.

20. **BASIS.** Determine corporation's income tax basis of assets for purposes of depreciation and sale. Calculate and make a record of each shareholder's basis for stock and securities received. Because of changes repeat every year for S corporations.

21. **FISCAL YEAR.** What is to be the corporation's fiscal year? If fiscal year other than calendar year is considered for S corporations, check restrictions on selecting fiscal year.

22. **METHOD OF ACCOUNTING.** Is the corporation to be on the cash or accrual basis? Is the corporation required to be on accrual accounting by virtue of gross receipts, method of taxation and stock ownership? See Chapter 20. How are inventories to be valued?

23. **SPECIAL ELECTIONS.** Check on elections for treatment of Commodity Credit Corporation loans, soil and water conservation expenses, and land clearing expenses.

24. **RESIDENCES.** Are houses to be transferred to corporation? Reasonable rental to be paid by occupants? Or occupants to report value of occupancy as additional income? Or rely on I.R.C. § 119? See Chapter 21.

25. **MOTOR VEHICLES.** What vehicles to be transferred to corporation? Insurance arrangements? Title transfer? What vehicles to be individually owned? Rate of compensation for business use? Insurance coverage for accidents involving employee-owned vehicles within scope of employment?

26. **RECAPTURE.** If the transfer of assets to the corporation is a taxable exchange, amounts may be recaptured. See Chapter 24.

27. **FRINGE BENEFITS.** What fringe benefits are to be provided? Check health and accident plan, group term life insurance (minimum number of employees required by state law – 10 or more in most states – or "baby group" plan), and deferred compensation for retirement.

28. **DOING BUSINESS IN OTHER STATES.** Will the corporation be doing business in another state? How much? Necessary to qualify to do business as foreign corporation?

29. **MINORITIES.** Is stock to be permitted to pass to off-farm shareholders? Consider assuring management rights, current income, and market for stock in planning for protection of minority shareholders.

30. **WILLS.** Do wills and estate plans of shareholders need to be updated by codicil or completely rewritten? Consider provisions to direct executor not to object to Subchapter S election and to comply with restrictions on stock transfer. For holders, or potential holders of S corporation stock, consider substitute provisions in lieu of trusts – for example, legal life

estate rather than marital deduction trust.

31. **MEMBERSHIPS.** What about memberships in cooperatives? Farm organizations? Breed associations?

32. **INSURANCE.** Check on casualty insurance, liability insurance, workers' compensation, and motor vehicle liability.

APPENDIX D
Tax-free incorporation of Willess Farm, Inc.

(1)	(2)	(3)	(4)	(5)	(6)
					Net
		Fair market	Income tax	Indebt-	contribution
Individual	Property	value	basis	edness	(3)-(5)
Jay A. Willess	Var.	$926,000	$473,200	$54,000	$872,000
John Willess	Cash	36,000	36,000	0	36,000
TOTAL		$962,000	$509,200	$54,000	$908,000

		(7)	(8)	(9)	(10)
		Shares of		Corporation's	Indebtedness
		stock	Tax basis	basis for	assumed by
		received	of stock	property	corporation
		($100/share)	received	from (4)	from (5)
		8,720	$419,200	$473,200	$54,000
		360	36,000	36,000	0
TOTAL		9,080	$455,200	$509,200	$54,000

APPENDIX E
Annual determination of basis of stock in S corporation

	Prior basis[1]	Distribution of income	Current income	Net operating loss	End of year basis	Basis per share
			($5.00/ Share)			
A. Jay A. Willess						
1. 6,630 shares[2]						
($48.07)	$318,708.70	0	+33,150.00	0	$351,858.70	$53.07
2. Debentures[3]						
($96,147)	$96,147.00	0	0	0	$96,147.00	–
B. John Willess						
1. 360 shares						
($100.00)	$36,000.00	0	+$1,800.00	0	$37,800.00	105.00
2. 30 shares						
($48.07)	$1,442.10	0	+$150.00	0	$1,592.10	53.07
C. May Willess						
1. 30 shares						
($48.07)	$1,442.10	0	+$150.00	0	$1,592.10	53.07
D. George Willess						
1. 30 shares						
($48.07)	$1,442.10	0	+$150.00	0	$1,592.10	53.07
TOTAL	$455,182.00	0	+$35,400.00	0	$490,582.00	

[1]Adjusted for transfers during the year.

[2]Gifts of 30 shares made during the year to each of the three children.

[3]Issued before October 3, 1989.

414

APPENDIX F
Deduction for income in respect of decedent

EXAMPLE: A non-materially participating farm landlord, a widower, on the cash method of accounting, died on January 2, 1996, holding corn produced under a crop share lease totaling $15,000, as income in respect of decedent. The decedent's gross estate was $660,000.

1. Calculate federal estate tax

Gross estate	$680,000
Deductions	20,000
Adjusted gross estate	660,000
Marital deduction	0
Taxable estate	660,000
Tentative federal estate tax	215,000
Unified credit	192,800
	22,200
Credit for state death tax paid	16,400
Federal estate tax due	5,800

2. Calculate net value of income in respect of decedent items

Value of income in respect of decedent items included in gross estate	$15,000
Deductions in computing gross estate for claims representing deductions described in I.R.C. § 691(b)	2,000
Net value	13,000

3. Calculate portion of federal estate tax attributable to net value of income in respect of decedent items

Federal estate tax	$5,800
Net value of income in respect of decedent items	13,000
Federal estate tax without income in respect of decedent items	-0-
Amount of deduction	5,800

APPENDIX G
General checklist for estate settlement
(major steps in the process)

1. Determine extent and nature of property owned by the decedent and ascertain whether special steps should be taken to – (a) secure the property or (b) prevent deterioration. Are some assets perishable? Do some warrant special protection? The decedent's death may have left some assets vulnerable to theft or vandalism.

If immediate action is needed, appointment of a special administrator may be in order. Arrange for management of property as needed.

2. For consumable or expendable items, for example feed and grain, note approximate supply levels. This may be especially important if the alternate valuation date is later used (valuation six months after death rather than as of the date of death) and, in some instances, for handling "income in respect of decedent."

3. Keep detailed records of *all* income and *all* expenditures for the estate. Start immediately to maintain a written record of all income and expense items and to keep all receipts.

4. Check the nature of all lease arrangements with the decedent as lessor (land owner). Was the decedent (or an agent or employee) achieving "material participation" under the lease? This could be important for purposes of installment payment of federal estate tax. Material participation by the decedent or member of the decedent's family is important for purposes of eligibility for special use valuation of land. In some instances, "active management" may substitute for material participation. See Chapter 3.

Consider whether "qualified use" test was met which requires that the decedent (or member of the decedent's family) have an

417

equity interest in the farm operation at the time of death and for five or more of the last eight years before death. A cash rent lease, other than to a family member as farm tenant, may make the land ineligible for special use valuation.

Examine the requirements to avoid recapture of special use value benefits during the recapture period after death. In general, material participation must be provided by each qualified heir or a member of the qualified heir's family. In some instances, "active management" may substitute for material participation.

Each qualified heir must have an "equity interest" in the farm operation to avoid recapture except for a two year grace period after death. This generally means no cash rent leases during the recapture period (except for the grace period and cash rent leases by a surviving spouse to a member of the surviving spouse's family).

A change of lease to meet the material participation or qualified use tests may require lease renegotiation. Has the time for giving notice for lease termination under state law passed for the next year?

5. Resolve to keep all beneficiaries well informed during estate settlement. Brief family members at periodic intervals and provide written summaries of financial transactions every three to six months, or as needed to keep family members informed. THIS MAY WELL BE THE MOST IMPORTANT STEP IN THE ENTIRE ESTATE SETTLEMENT PROCESS.

6. Ascertain whether the decedent had made arrangements for disposition of body organs or the entire body.

7. Complete funeral or memorial arrangements.

8. Ascertain whether the decedent left a will. Check the decedent's safe deposit box (requires the decedent's key and the institution's key). No more than the will generally may be removed before an inventory is taken of the contents. If not located in the safe deposit box, check with the attorney who drew the will to see if it was left with the attorney for safe keeping. The will might have been placed with a designated county office for safe keep-

ing or left in a secure place at home.

9. Except where it is clear that no significant estate settlement action is required or needed, consult an attorney to determine what type of estate settlement is appropriate under state law – (a) small estate, (b) short-form or (c) regular probate. The choice usually depends upon the way property was owned at death, the type of property and, in some instances, the amount of property. The attorney can provide helpful information on type of estate settlement to pursue and will assist in estate settlement.

10. Check ownership of checking account and automobile or automobiles and determine if in joint tenancy (for ease of access). Take necessary steps to assure access to checking account and automobile, where appropriate and necessary.

11. Social security –
    a. File for death benefit, if eligible.
    b. Return uncashed social security benefit checks for reissuance.
    c. File for survivors' benefits, if any.

12. If appropriate, file application for monetary allowance for surviving spouse and children and obtain court approval as required.

13. The attorney prepares a petition to the court to open the estate and files the will (if one was left by the decedent). The executor or administrator is appointed. A notice is given publicly that the estate is open, usually by newspaper publication. A bond is posted, unless waived or is not required under state law.

14. If the decedent left a will, consider whether the surviving spouse should elect to take against the will or should take by the provisions of the will.

15. Open an estate bank account, if regular probate procedure is to be followed; file for a federal tax identification number.

16. Review scope and adequacy of insurance coverage for all property –
    a. Motor vehicle liability, collision and other coverage.
    b. Home owner's or business policy – casualty loss and

liability.

17. Inventory safe deposit box contents. Normally, a representative of the institution maintaining the box must be present and may be charged with assuring that a copy of the inventory is transmitted to the state tax department or commission.

18. Inventory all other property of the decedent; review all leases and other contractual commitments for date of expiration and content.

19. File the property inventory with the court (usually within 60 days after death).

20. Arrange for the sale of assets not to be retained. For livestock, locate health records or check with attending veterinarian and meet all requirements for sale as to proof of vaccination or prescribed test.

a. Consider the income tax implications of sale of assets (especially income in respect of decedent items).

b. Check the implications of sale of assets for alternate valuation purposes for federal estate tax (sale within six months after death).

c. Watch estate sale of farmland or other farm property (or corporate stock or partnership shares), other than to qualified heirs, if special use valuation is to be elected. If *purchased* by the qualified heirs, the property is "acquired from or passed from the decedent" as required. But remember, the purchaser of land under special use valuation does not receive a new income tax basis. The special use value in the estate continues to be the basis. This could be a sizeable trap on resale by the purchaser.

d. Ascertain whether asset sale would jeopardize installment payment of federal estate tax or special use valuation of land because of possible acceleration or recapture, as the case may be, stemming from post-death disposition of assets.

e. Watch installment sale of farmland *by the estate* – distribution of the installment obligation to the heirs could trigger taxable gain in the contract (that could be a very substantial amount of gain, especially for land under special use valuation).

21. If statutory fee of executor, administrator or attorney is to be waived, file waiver as required to assure that the fee will not be "constructively received" and included in income anyway.

22. Determine whether "flower" bonds had been purchased before death –

a. Check circumstances of purchase to see if purchase should be ratified by the estate (any question of competency of decedent at time of purchase that could have affected validity of purchase).

b. Obtain forms for redemption.

c. If flower bonds exceed probable estate tax liability, retain enough to pay any likely deficiency on audit.

d. In community property states, check to see if bonds were purchased from community funds (only one-half redeemable at par to pay federal estate tax) or separate funds of the decedent (all redeemable).

23. Life insurance policies on decedent's life –

a. Locate the policies.

b. Determine the mode of settlement to be elected.

c. File the appropriate claim form with the company and request Form 712, Life Insurance Statement.

d. Check beneficiary designation and policy ownership to see if proceeds are subject to federal estate tax and state death tax.

24. Check on other death benefits – retirement plan, Veterans Administration, other – and file forms as required.

25. Prepare state and federal final income tax returns for the decedent (and spouse, if appropriate). Consider whether to include accrued but untaxed U.S. Government Series E bond interest in the final return of the decedent.

26. Determine where estate settlement costs should be deducted for maximum benefit – income tax return or death tax return.

27. If requirements are met, consider redemption of corporate stock to pay death taxes and estate settlement costs.

28. Elect a calendar or fiscal year for the estate and file the state and federal income tax returns for the estate. Watch for

availability of income tax deduction for portion of federal estate tax paid attributable to "income in respect of decedent" items such as Series E bond interest, payments under installment obligations entered into by the decedent, last paycheck of the decedent and share rents (grain or livestock) held by a farm landlord under a non-material participation farm lease.

29. Value the decedent's property –

a. Request valuation of land (and other assets not objectively valued) by court appointed appraisers (or request relief from appraisement).

b. For land to be valued under special use valuation using cash rent capitalization method, obtain gross cash rent on comparable land in the locality and adjust for property tax. If cash rents on comparable land do not exist, obtain "net share rentals" from crop share lease arrangements on comparable land.

(1) Check all pre-death eligibility requirements.

(2) Review with the heirs all post-death events that could trigger recapture of special use valuation benefit.

(3) Review with the heirs the expected effects of the federal estate tax lien on special use value property.

(4) Reach understanding on who is to pay any federal estate tax arising under the recapture rules.

30. Prepare the federal estate tax return (within nine months after death) –

a. Elect special use valuation and installment payment of federal estate tax, if desired.

b. File protective elections where permissible if special use valuation, alternate valuation date or installment payment of federal estate tax could later become advantageous and feasible.

c. If federal estate tax payment is deferred (installment payment or one year extensions of time) check whether interest to be paid on deferred tax should be deducted for federal estate tax purposes or for federal income tax purposes.

31. Prepare state inheritance or state estate tax return where required (check state law to see when due).

32. Obtain tax clearances, where appropriate, for filing in local probate file –

    a. State inheritance or state estate tax; any fiduciary clearance.

    b. Federal estate tax.

    c. Personal property tax.

33. Pay the lawful claims of creditors.

34. Prepare final state and federal income tax returns for the estate. If the estate continues more than two years after the decedent's death, arrange to pay estimated tax.

35. After audits have been completed, prepare the final report to the court with an accounting of receipts and expenditures (unless waived); seek discharge of executor or administrator; and obtain court approval for property distribution as required.

36. Distribute property to the beneficiaries with an explanation of income tax basis for their records.

APPENDIX H
Tax treatment of leased property

Tax Treatment of Leased Property

	Cash	Non-MP Share	Agent's MP Share	Activity Imputed
Income in respect of decedent	–	Yes	No	Yes
Passive activity losses deductible				
Active participation	Up to $25,000	No	No	No
Material participation	No	No	Yes	No
Deductibility of losses (§1231 or capital)	Capital	§ 1231	§ 1231	Yes
Personal holding company income	Yes	unc	No	Yes
Special use valuation				
Pre-death	Yes, if to family	Yes, if to family	Yes	No
Post-death	No, except spouse	Yes, if to family	Yes	No
Installment payment of estate tax	No	Yes	Yes	Yes
Rent as self-employment income	No	No	Yes	No

Index

–A–

Absence of material participation 53
ACRS 281
Accumulated adjustment account 316
Accumulated earnings tax 314
Active management 36, 44, 56
Active participation 284
Actively engaged in farming 266
Adjusted gross estate 80, 83
Adjusted ordinary gross income 315
Adjusted tax difference 58
Adjusted taxable gifts 87
Adjustment of titles 151, 152, 153
Advisors, role of 9, 394
AFR 178
Agent 10, 66, 272-273
Agricultural employer, definition 338
Alternate valuation 30
Alternative minimum tax 313
Annuity, estate tax aspects 196
Annuity, gift tax problems 194
Annuity, income tax treatment 197
Annuity, value of 195
Antenuptial agreements 27
Applicable federal rate (AFR) 178
Assets to incorporate, considerations 377
At risk, rules & provisions 283
Automobile, corporate 344

–B–

Bankruptcy...57, 136
Base person...37
Basis, income tax..47, 158
Bond acquisitions, joint ownership 151
Bushel lease...52
Business continuity...249
Business planning, horizons 299

–C–

Capital gains taxation, corporations 313
Capitalization rate, special use valuation 32, 33
Cash rent capitalization 31
Cash rent lease.....................33, 39, 51, 67, 131, 132, 136, 357
Changing co-ownership..19
Charitable deduction...84
Charitable giving, appreciated property 236
Charitable giving, reasons for.............................234
Charitable lead trust..238
Charitable pooled income funds 237
Charitable remainder annuity trust 237
Charitable remainder unitrust 237, 238
Closely held business, interest in.........................129
Common law state, property acquisition 26
Community property..26
Comparable land, special use valuation 34
Consideration furnished rule 21
Constructive receipt..181
Consumer Price Index, Social Security benefits 242
Contracts, uses...187
Co-ownership..17
Corporate dissolution and liquidation....................354

Corporation, special use valuation..............................60
Corporation, taxable year 325
Corporate group, brother-sister controlled 312
Corporate group, parent-subsidiary controlled............312
Corporate residences, choices...................................341
Corporate stock.......................61, 62, 63, 64, 130, 366
Corporation, income taxation 310
Corporation, management 289, 379
Corporation, nature of..287
Corporation, shareholder liability...................287, 288
Corporation, state limits 290
Credit for services rule 22
Credit shelter trusts..105
Crummey-type withdrawal powers 217

–D–

Death taxes, ways to save 29
Debt securities 61, 366, 369
Debt securities, reasons against.................................369
Debt securities, uses 367
Deductions allowable 78
Defined benefit 340
Defined contribution..340
Depreciation/depletion reducing basis......................160
Depreciation, fast methods 281
Depreciation schedule, obligor's, private annuity 198
Disclaimers..98
Disposition of installment obligations.......................183
Disposition of property..165
Dissolution and liquidation, corporations..................354
Dividends, due diligence requirement, withholding.....337

Dividends, income tax on 314
Doctrine of emblements..15
Domicile 247

–E–

E bond interest, strategies 164
ESOP retirement plans...340
Education equalization clause 216
Effective interest rates, special use valuation...............32
Election, special use valuation......................................70
Eligibility as business, installment payment of
  federal estate tax 129
Employee benefits 339
Equal property ownership..108
Equity interest, special use valuation 62
Escrow arrangements...181
Estate "freezes"..77
Estate probate, reasons 306
Estate tax marital deduction 80
Expense method depreciation..309
Extensions of time, paying federal estate tax 139

–F–

Fair market value, federal gift tax 145
Family business, landlord-tenant, problems.................252
Family business plans..4
Family business, reasons for written contracts............256
Family estate trusts 220
Family farm cycle..250
Farm business, continuity choices 252
Farm Real Estate Market Developments, special
  use valuation..33

Farming syndicate...283, 388, 389
Federal corporate income tax rates.................................310
Federal state tax calculations...86
Federal estate tax, rules of thumb...................................91
Fee simple...14
First option agreement..304
Fixed principal equity securities....................................366
Flower bonds...122
Foreclosure, special use valuation...................................58
Forfeiture by buyer, installment obligations....................190
Fractional share rule..22, 80
Freezing asset values..154, 397

–G–

Gain or loss at death, income tax...................................160
Generation skipping...94
Generation skipping transfer tax.....................................94
Gift property, income tax basis.....................................159
Gift-sale transactions, conditions..................................169
Gift tax annual exclusion...144
Gift tax calculation...145
Gift tax charitable deduction..145
Gift tax marital deduction..144
Gift tax return..147
Gifts, exceptions to tax..150
Gifts, farmland...148
Gifts, includible in estates...87
Gifts, joint tenancy, exceptions...............................151, 152
Gifts, life insurance..149
Gifts, minors...154, 155
Gifts, pros and cons..143
Gifts, purchase of real property.....................................153

Gifts, within three years of death 72

Government farm programs, limitations 266

Government farm programs, special use valuation 53

Gross profit, installment obligations 176

Gross profit percentage 176

Gross estate 29

–H–

Health and accident plans 341

–I–

Idled land, special use valuation 40

Incidents of ownership 74

Income in respect of decedent 163

Installment obligation, cancellation 183

Installment obligation, death of seller 185

Installment obligations, related party transactions 181

Installment obligation, transfer 181, 183

Installment payment, 15-year 124, 261

Installment payment, 10-year 139

Installment payment, benefits 127

Installment payment, dispositions 135

Installment sales, land 173, 175, 187

Interest in a closely held business 129

Interest rates, installment transactions 153

Interest rates, unpaid federal tax 125

Internal Revenue Code, Subchapter S 315

Intestate, dying 7

Inventory, what to include 371, 394

Involuntary conversion 49

–J–

Joint tenancy 75

–L–

Land contracts, drafting 188
Land, IRS definition, installment obligation interest 178
Lead trust 238
Lease, installment payment of federal estate tax 131
Levels of concern (in planning) 5
Lien, installment payment of federal estate tax 137
Lien, special use valuation..70
Liens against property, exceptions..137
Life estate 14
Life estate, granted 16
Life estate, legal..15
Life estate, retained...16
Life expectancy, estate tax planning 112
Life insurance 73, 225
Life insurance, alternative arrangements.................................232
Life insurance, economic dependency.....................................226
Life insurance, liquidity funding 228
Life insurance policy ownership...232
Life insurance, role of...225
Life insurance, survivorship benefits.......................................227
Life insurance, trusts...217
Life insurance, types...230
Life tenant..14
Limited entrepreneurs...283
Limited liability companies 383
Limited partnerships...282
Limited partnerships, corporate characteristics 284

Liquidation choices, corporations................................354
Liquidity augmentation...121
Liquidity augmentation, alternatives 117
Liquidity plan..119
Liquidity plan, components 120
Living trusts..205
Loans, governmentally related 353

–M–

Marital deduction...80
Material participation 53, 65, 271
Material participation, four tests..................43, 44, 65
Material participation, leases................................65
Maximum marital deduction, conditions...............80, 81
"Member of family" term, special use valuation......36
Minimum tax 313
Minority interest discounts 63
Minority ownership, corporation............................350
Minors as partners 281
Model I planning 102
Model II planning 108
Modified Model II planning 112
Mortgages...179
Multiple entities...257

–N–

Non-marketability discounts...................................63
Non-materially participating landlords, income
   in respect of decedent 163
Non-tax risk, private annuities.............................194

–O–

Objectives, role of...2, 233
Optimal marital deduction, variables...................................112
Organizing the farm business 249
Ownership, choices..13

–P–

Part gift-part sale 169
Partition and sale 307
Partnerships 275, 285
Partnership, dissolution, choices 277
Partnership, small, requirements 279
Partnership, special use valuation...60
Partnership, taxes..278
Partnership, termination..277
Passive activities...284
Passive assets..133
Passive losses..271
Payment-in-kind program...40, 53
Payments in year of sale 176
Penalty taxes, corporations 258
Person, government farm programs.....................................266
Personal holding company, basic rules...............................259
Personal holding company...258
Phantom tax 147
Post-death funding for liquidity..124
Powers of appointment 77
Powers of attorney, flower bond purchase..........................124
Pre-death funding 121
Present and future interest, gift tax annual exclusion..............144
Present interest test, special use valuation............................40

Private annuity 173, 193

Probate, simplified 25

Productivity indexes, special use valuation 34

Property passage, special use valuation choices 37, 38

Property transfer, retained power and control 75

Property values, income tax basis 158

Proportionate recapture 59

Protective election 71

Pure equity interest 62

–Q–

QTIP arrangements 81, 82

Qualified borrower, criteria for Farm Credit
  Bank loans 353

Qualified charities 84

Qualified exchange property 49

Qualified heir 37, 38

Qualified use test 39, 51

–R–

Reasonable cause, extension to pay federal estate tax 139

Recapture, special use valuation benefits 48

Regular method of income tax, corporation 310

Remainder interests and life estates 14

Reorganizations 356, 357

Reorganization, type D 356

Residence, special use valuation 43

Residence, transferring, gain 166, 167, 169

Retained powers 75, 237

Retention of property until death 160

Retirement planning 241

Revocable living trust 205

Right of survivorship 18

Rules taxing gain on resale under installment
   sale, exceptions..181

–S–

S corporations, income treatment, rules 315

Safe harbor rules, S corporation shareholder loans 320

Section 303 stock redemptions 139

Securities, tax-free exchange 373

Self-cancelling installment notes......................................173, 199

Selling price, installment obligations 176

Settlement options, insurance 228, 229

Shareholders, minority vote...350

Short-form probate 25

Small Business Administration, loans 354

Small business concern, definition 354

Social Security Amendments of 1983 243

Social Security, earned income limits..331

Social security, employee status 246

Social security, income tax 243

Social security, indexing...243

Social security, material participation..245

Social security, modified adjusted gross income.......................244

Social security, retirement benefits..242

Social Security tax 329

Sole ownership 13

Sole proprietorships, installment payment
   of federal estate tax...131

Special use valuation 30, 263

Special use valuation, five factor formula 31
State limits on corporations 290
Stock and partnership interests, installment payment 130
Stock, common 366
Stock, preferred 366
Stock redemption 139, 262
Stock transfer planning, off-farm heirs...................................307
Subchapter S 315, 316, 324, 347
Subchapter S, built-in gains..355
Subchapter S, election 318
Subchapter S, election termination 323
Subchapter S, Form 2553 322
Subchapter S trust, qualified...318, 319
Subchapter S, rent requirements..321
Subchapter S Revision Act of 1982...................................315, 327
Super priority obligations 138

–T–

Tax basis 158
Tax calculation (federal estate)..86
Taxable estate...86
Taxable incorporation 374
Tax-free incorporation 373, 376
Tax-option corporations...347
Tenancy by the entirety..17
Tenancy in common...17
Tenancy, joint...17
Tentative tax...88
Terminable interests...81
Test rate of interest...177
Tier I test, installment payment of tax 129
Tier II test, installment payment of tax....................................134

Tier I test, special use valuation..61
Tier II test, special use valuation 62
Tier III test, special use valuation...62
Timber, special use valuation 42
Total contract price 176
Transfer of property, rules of thumb..171
Trust instrument...203
Trustee 203
Trusts, accumulation..203
Trusts, Clifford-type (repealed) 216
Trusts, complex..202
Trusts, transfer of property 206
Trusts, income taxes 202, 222
Trusts, discretionary spray..203
Trusts, elements of...201
Trusts, family estate...220
Trusts, funding living trusts...206
Trusts, generation skipping...219
Trusts, grantor...207
Trusts, grantor retained interest 211
Trusts, GRATS 211, 212
Trusts, GRITS 211
Trusts, GRUTS 212
Trusts, how used 204
Trusts, irrevocable living 210
Trusts, installment payment of federal estate tax 131
Trusts, joint or separate..208
Trusts, life insurance..217
Trusts, living 204, 205
Trusts, medicaid qualifying 210
Trusts, nature of 201
Trusts, offshore 223

Trusts, pure 220

Trusts, revocable living 205

Trusts, simple..202

Trusts, special use valuation 60

Trusts, spendthrift...203

Trusts, super..218

Trusts, testamentary..215

Two-trust marital deduction will 103

–U–

Undue hardship, extension of time to pay tax 139

Unemployment compensation 338

Unified tax credit...87, 92

Uniform Gifts to Minors Acts 156

Uniform Transfers to Minors Act.......................................156

Units of beneficial ownership, family estate trust 222

–V–

Variable payment plans, installment sales 189

–W–

Wages paid in kind...333

Wills, if none..7

Wills, provisions 399

Withholding, back-up, conditions..337

Workers' compensation, requirements 337

–Z–

Zones, federal estate tax 102